RECEDING TIDE

Vicksburg AND *Gettysburg*
THE CAMPAIGNS THAT CHANGED THE CIVIL WAR

EDWIN C. BEARSS

with

J. PARKER HILLS

NATIONAL GEOGRAPHIC

WASHINGTON, D.C.

Published by the National Geographic Society
1145 17th Street N.W., Washington, D.C. 20036

Library of Congress Cataloging-in-Publication Data

Bearss, Edwin C.
Receding tide : Vicksburg and Gettysburg : the campaigns that changed the Civil War / Edwin Cole Bearss with Parker Hills.
 p. cm.
Includes index.
ISBN 978-1-4262-0510-1 (hardcover) -- ISBN 978-1-4262-0560-6 (e-book)
1. Vicksburg (Miss.)--History--Siege, 1863. 2. Gettysburg, Battle of, Gettysburg, Pa., 1863. I. Hills, Parker. II. Title.
E475.27.B424 2010
973.7'344--dc22

                                2009044647

The National Geographic Society is one of the world's largest nonprofit scientific and educational organizations. Founded in 1888 to "increase and diffuse geographic knowledge," the Society works to inspire people to care about the planet. It reaches more than 325 million people worldwide each month through its official journal, *National Geographic,* and other magazines; National Geographic Channel; television documentaries; music; radio; films; books; DVDs; maps; exhibitions; school publishing programs; interactive media; and merchandise. National Geographic has funded more than 9,000 scientific research, conservation and exploration projects and supports an education program combating geographic illiteracy.

For more information, please call 1-800-NGS LINE (647-5463) or write to the following address:

National Geographic Society
1145 17th Street N.W.
Washington, D.C. 20036-4688 U.S.A.

Visit us online at www.nationalgeographic.com

For information about special discounts for bulk purchases, please contact
National Geographic Books Special Sales: ngspecsales@ngs.org

For rights or permissions inquiries, please contact National Geographic Books
Subsidiary Rights: ngbookrights@ngs.org

Interior design: Cameron Zotter

Printed in the United States of America

10/WCPT-CML/1

CONTENTS

MAPS

Foreword

AN AMERICAN ICON

THE UTTERANCES OF THE MAN ARE MORE OF A GROWL THAN A VOICE, WITH *an occasional bark thrown in for good measure. As he growls, he paces. He sometimes snaps his words as he measures his steps, and after a short, rhythmic stride, he suddenly halts, about-faces, and thrusts his hand upward, often with his coupstick. Then, after a pause, his gravelly tones reach a crescendo, and the stick is lowered and aimed like a handgun at an oncoming foe. Thus, the older warrior regales the spellbound council members with stories about battle exploits with eyewitness accuracy, describing the heroism, humanity, and horror of battle.*

This scene, repeated countless times around the post-battle campfires of warriors throughout time, is actually a description of an Ed Bearss battlefield tour. The recounting of the events by Ed on a battlefield is an intense experience—an intensity that is enhanced by the vivid descriptions of the combatants and their deeds, seemingly accentuated with the smoke of black powder and the singing of bullets.

Edwin Cole Bearss is the epitome of an American. He was born in the midst of rugged countryside in Billings, Montana, on June 26, 1923. He grew up on his family's cattle ranch near Sarpy, Montana, during the Great Depression. His father, Omar Effinger Bearss, a World War I Marine, often regaled Ed and his brother with accounts of military history. Then, when Ed read Marine Capt. John W. Thomason's 1930 biography, JEB Stuart, *a lifelong passion was ignited in the impressionable youth. The oft-repeated tale of Ed's subsequent boyhood christening of the ranch's farm animals after Civil War generals and battles is true. His favorite milk cow was, indeed, named Antietam.*

Ed graduated from high school in 1941 and began his peripatetic lifestyle by embarking upon a hitchhiking adventure around the United States, visiting Civil War battlefields at every opportunity. Then, following in his father's footsteps, he enlisted in the Marine Corps on April 28, 1942. He was swiftly trained, and in just over two months he found himself on a troop transport in the Pacific. He served with the Third Marine Raider Battalion at Guadalcanal and the Russell Islands, and with the Seventh Regiment, First Marine Division, on New Britain (now part of Papua New Guinea). On January 2, 1944, Ed was severely wounded by Japanese machine-gun fire at Suicide Creek on Cape Gloucester, New Britain, and was evacuated to California, where he spent 26 months in recuperation. On March 15, 1946, Corporal Bearss was honorably discharged from the Marines and returned home to Montana.

After the war, Ed took advantage of the GI Bill and attended Georgetown University, graduating in 1949 with a B.S. degree in Foreign Service studies. He secured a position with the U.S. Navy Hydrographic Office in Maryland, working there for three years and taking advantage of his strategic location to tour eastern Civil War battlefields. He then attended Indiana University to earn his M.A. in history, selecting as the subject of his thesis Confederate Major General Patrick Ronayne Cleburne. Ed visited western theater battlefields as he conducted his research, and in 1954 he met park historian Charles E. "Pete" Shedd at Shiloh battlefield. Pete soon inspired Ed to become a battlefield historian after he earned his M.A. in 1955.

Ed found employment with the U.S. Army's Office of the Chief of Military History, but soon left the confines of an office to follow his passion by joining the National Park Service as a historian at Vicksburg National Military Park, in Mississippi. On November 12, 1956, with 13 months of service at Vicksburg and with pocket compass in hand, Ed ventured forth in a wooden fishing boat with Warren Grabau and Don Jacks to locate the Union ironclad, U.S.S. Cairo, sunk by a mine on December 12, 1862, in Yazoo River. The result is the magnificent and unique gunboat display in today's Vicksburg National Military Park. Aside from successfully locating the last of the Eads-built ironclads in the muddy waters of Yazoo River, Ed toiled and sweated through the kudzu vines and poison ivy of Claiborne County, Mississippi, to locate two forgotten forts at the abandoned town of Grand Gulf.

During his Vicksburg stay, Ed rumbled over the washboard gravel rills of the central Mississippi roads in a dilapidated delivery truck with a candy salesman, who Ed said would "rather talk than sell candy." Ed took advantage of the salesman's loquacious nature: At every delivery stop, he managed to find a seat around the cracker barrels of the weathered general stores, chatting with the locals to capture oral histories from the grandchildren of Civil War veterans—treasure troves of memories that were evaporating as generations passed.

In Vicksburg, Ed met fellow historian Margie Riddle. They were married on July 30, 1958. That same year, Ed was promoted to the position of Southeast Regional Research Historian, still working out of Vicksburg. Rather than entomb himself in a library, Ed continued his field research, walking the grounds of virtually every Civil War battlefield in the country. Because of his extensive knowledge of the grounds on which American soldiers fought, during the Civil War Centennial (1961–1965), Ed was much sought after to develop new battlefield parks, to include Pea Ridge, Arkansas, and Wilson's Creek, Missouri.

In 1966 Ed's work took him to Washington, D.C. On November 1, 1981, he became Chief Historian of the National Park Service, and he held that position until 1994, when he served as special assistant to the director of the National Park Service. When Ed retired in 1995, he was awarded the title of Chief Historian Emeritus.

Ed's legacy, in part, is his preservation of historic sites all over North America. He led efforts to preserve Fort Smith, Arkansas; Stones River, Tennessee; Fort Donelson, Tennessee; battlefields near Richmond, Virginia; Bighorn Canyon, Wyoming and Montana; the Eisenhower farm at Gettysburg, Pennsylvania; the gold miner's route over Chilkoot Pass, British Columbia; the LBJ Ranch, near Johnson City, Texas; Fort Moultrie, part of Fort Sumter National Monument; Fort Point in San Francisco, California; the William Howard Taft house in Cincinnati, Ohio; Fort Hancock at Sandy Hook, New Jersey; and the Herbert Hoover National Historic Site in West Branch, Iowa.

Despite his unparalleled record of historic preservation, perhaps the most remembered part of Ed's contribution is his field interpretation of battlefields and campaigns. Ed began his tours while stationed at Vicksburg in the 1950s, and he has never stopped, traveling as many as 200 days a year around the world to astound military and civilian personnel with his incredible knowledge, not only of the events, but also of the people involved.

Edwin C. Bearss has spent a lifetime preserving and interpreting. Perhaps he has the soul of an ancient Greek. He is part the historian Herodotus, who traveled widely and reported what he heard. He is part the Athenian Thucydides, in his remarkably disciplined approach to recording history based upon strict standards of evidence-gathering and analysis. Most important, he is part the Spartan Leonidas, with the experience and mentality of a warrior in his determined preservation of hallowed grounds and of the exploits of warriors past. But after all is said, Ed Bearss is an American who has dedicated his life to preserving his country's history.

As a part of the ongoing work to preserve the immense body of historical facts and unique insights accumulated by Ed Bearss, National Geographic's Fields of Honor *was published in 2006, featuring transcripts of Ed's tours of pivotal Civil War battles.*

This book is a follow-on to that one, using more-detailed Bearss tour transcripts to focus on a specific period in the Civil War—the end of the year 1862 and the first of the year 1863. At the commencement of this critical period in 1862, the Union war effort had descended to its nadir, while the Confederate hope for recognition as an independent nation had ascended to its zenith. By the conclusion of this period, the North, along with key world powers, realized that the Union could, and most probably would, win the war. By those first few days of July 1863, Southern hope for independence, like the smoke of the battlefields, had vanished.

While this book discusses the campaigns and battles in the color and detail that is signature Ed Bearss, it also places these events in the larger, strategic, context. How did the actions of one army affect not only the actions of the opposing army, but also the actions of other armies, both friendly and enemy? As the poet John Donne observed, "No man is an island, entire of itself; every man is a piece of the continent, a part of the main."

This work then is Ed's words in the field, admittedly without the growl, the bark, and the stick. My editorial introductions and comments are presented in italics and serve as transitional and explanatory material. The reader should be prepared—for to travel with Ed is to be bombarded beyond one's imagination with facts, color, humor, and pathos. These are Civil War "factual fables," as told by the master historian-warrior of our time.

Parker Hills
Clinton, Mississippi
December 28, 2009

Introduction
TRINITY AND TIDE

War is not only a veritable chameleon, because in each concrete case it changes somewhat its character, but it is also, when regarded as a whole, in relation to the tendencies predominating in it, a strange trinity. . . . The first of these three sides is more particularly the concern of the people, the second that of the commander and his army, the third that of the government.

—*Carl von Clausewitz*

ON A SWELTERING SUMMER DAY IN WASHINGTON, D.C., PRESIDENT ABRAHAM *Lincoln drew a piece of "executive mansion" letterhead from his desk drawer, dipped his pen, and scrawled a note to the general commanding the Union Army of the Tennessee: "July 13, 1863. I write this now as a grateful acknowledgment for the almost inestimable service you have done the country." He wrote as the Commander in Chief to a field general, and he revealed for the first time his differing thoughts as to how the military objective should have been achieved. Lincoln then paused, breathed a sigh of relief, and concluded with perhaps the most remarkable statement ever written by an American president to one of his generals: "I now wish to make the personal acknowledgment that you were right and I was wrong."*

The letter was sent to Gen. Ulysses S. Grant in Vicksburg, Mississippi. The "almost inestimable service" referred to was Grant's remarkable campaign that opened the Mississippi River for the Union. In the process, the Confederate Army of Vicksburg had been captured.

One day later, as an ironic testament to the volatile nature of the times, the President sighed again, but this time in despair rather than relief, and penned another letter to another general, this one to Gen. George Gordon Meade, commanding the Army of the Potomac near Williamsport, Maryland. Measuring every word, Lincoln wrote: "I do not believe you appreciate the magnitude of the misfortune involved in Lee's escape. He was within your easy grasp, and to have closed upon him would, in connection with our other late successes, have ended the war. As it is, the war will be prolonged indefinitely."

The President then wisely slid the never-to-be-sent missive back into his desk drawer. After all, Gen. Robert E. Lee had retreated from Gettysburg, Pennsylvania, and the cities of Washington and Baltimore were no longer threatened. At long last, not only the North, but the world, could see that Lee was not invincible.

The following day, Lincoln's mood improved. Now feeling profoundly grateful, he composed a "Proclamation for a Day of Thanksgiving, Praise, and Prayer," to be observed on August 6. He wrote, "It has pleased Almighty God to hearken to the supplications and prayers of an afflicted people and to vouchsafe to the Army and the Navy of the United States victories on land and on the sea so signal and so effective as to furnish reasonable grounds for augmented confidence that the Union of these States will be maintained, their Constitution preserved, and their peace and prosperity permanently restored."

The Confederate tide had receded. Its recession began at 11 p.m. on January 3, 1863, in a drenching rain in Murfreesboro, Tennessee, when Confederate Gen. Braxton Bragg took counsel of his fears after fighting a stalemated battle and began his retreat in the face of the army of Gen. William S. Rosecrans. Shrewdly, Lincoln proclaimed that battle a victory, and later wrote to Rosecrans that this victory had checked "the dangerous sentiment which was spreading in the North."

This "dangerous sentiment" was the specter of northern defeat that had been bolstered by a movement to recognize the Confederacy. It began to materialize in 1861 when the Federal armies failed to win what the northern populace had expected to be a short war. It became more viable as the war dragged on for more than a year, and northern anticipation of victory slowly turned to fear of defeat. It loomed over the North during the last months of 1862, as political and military disasters threatened to put an end to Lincoln's efforts to save the Union.

Lincoln's increasingly unpopular war, characterized by unthinkable casualties, had been financed by a Republican Congress, resulting in that political party experiencing nearly catastrophic midterm state elections in October and early November 1862. Five key Republican states that had supported Lincoln in the election of 1860—New York, Pennsylvania, Ohio, Indiana, and Illinois—sent Democratic majorities to Congress, with the Democrats gaining 28 seats and the Republicans losing 22. After the elections, the Republicans clung to an 18-vote edge in the House of Representatives, but many antiwar Republicans sided with the Democrats on war *issues. The Democrats had also won key gubernatorial races in New York and New Jersey, prompting the* New York Times *to call the election a "vote of want of confidence" in Abraham Lincoln.* The President was losing the support of the people.

What the Lincoln Administration desperately needed were military victories, and Union Army commanders were prodded to go on the offensive. In response to this, Ambrose E. Burnside, William S. Rosecrans, and Ulysses S. Grant embarked upon three December offensives over an 18-day period. Two were defeats, and one was a stalemate. The Federal armies suffered casualties on a scale that today seem incomprehensible. From December 11 to January 2, 1863, Union combat casualties totaled 27,678, with 3,222 killed in action. The South suffered too, but Confederate casualties for the same period were 60 percent of those of the North: 15,830 southern casualties with 1,959 of these killed in action. Thus, the normally festive periods of Christmas of 1862 and New Year of 1863 would forever be remembered in thousands of homes as a season of grief. The extent of these casualties further alienated already jaundiced northern-elected officials toward funding the war. The President was losing the support of the government.

With defeat and death on the Federal fronts in Virginia and Mississippi, as well as more than 13,000 casualties in Middle Tennessee, officers and soldiers were losing confidence in their generals. In Virginia, General Burnside was wantonly criticized by his officers and men, and on the Mississippi River, rumors of General Grant's insobriety and of Gen. William T. Sherman's insanity were revived. Soldiers began to curse those that appointed their generals, and the military situation for the North seemed grim. The President was losing the support of the armies.

Signaling this loss of confidence in "Mr. Lincoln's War," speculation in Washington persisted that the President would renege on his promise to sign the Emancipation Proclamation. But on January 1, 1863, the President signed the document, stating, "I never, in my life, felt more certain that I was doing right, than I do in signing this paper. If my name goes into history it will be for this act, and my whole soul is in it." Even friendly Republican papers soon espoused that the proclamation could cause "discord in the North" while strengthening the "spirit of the rebellion." Democratic, or "Copperhead," opposition to the war grew even stronger, as opposition to the proclamation gave weight to the demand for Lincoln to make peace with the South.

As late as January 3, Governor of Indiana Oliver P. Morton, a staunch Republican and supporter of President Abraham Lincoln, telegraphed Secretary of War Edwin M. Stanton with a warning: "I am advised that it is contemplated when the Legislature meets in this state to pass a joint resolution acknowledging the Southern Confederacy, and urging the states of the Northwest to dissolve all constitutional relations with the New England states." Morton also predicted that "the same thing is on foot in Illinois."

Lincoln's endeavor to save the Union appeared to be in grave danger when suddenly, almost miraculously, news arrived from Murfreesboro on January 5: General Bragg had retreated two nights earlier. Lincoln exuberantly wired General Rosecrans commanding in Tennessee, "Your dispatch announcing retreat of enemy has just reached here. God bless you, and all with you!" The rising Confederate tide had culminated and was now beginning to recede.

The tidal ebbing continued through the spring and into the summer of 1863, despite a pyrrhic Confederate victory at the hamlet of Chancellorsville, Virginia, in early May. The tide gave one last undertow tug at Gettysburg in the first days of July 1863, and then disappeared forever on Independence Day at Vicksburg.

Robert E. Lee had been beaten at Gettysburg, the Mississippi River had been opened, and a Confederate army had surrendered in Vicksburg. The sociological, political, and military gains were enormous. The northern people, the government, and the Army could now dare to believe that the Union would be preserved.

Chapter 1
RICHMOND AND THE RIVER

November 6, 1860–January 1, 1863
Abraham Lincoln, in his Inaugural Address on March 4, 1861,
emphatically stated that armed conflict would not be due to his
actions. He declared: "In your hands, my dissatisfied fellow
countrymen, and not in mine, is the momentous issue of civil war.
The Government will not assail you. You can have no conflict
without being yourselves the aggressors. You have no oath
registered in Heaven to destroy the Government, while I shall have
the most solemn one to 'preserve, protect, and defend' it."

WHEN CIVIL WAR BECAME A REALITY, A COLOSSAL BURDEN WAS EXERTED
upon Lincoln. His Republican Party had campaigned on a platform opposed to
the expansion of slavery; thus, it was Lincoln's November 6, 1860, election to the
Presidency that ignited the conflict. The election results had proved unacceptable
to the slave states, which were now in the minority in the House of Representatives and were facing a minority in the Senate and in the Electoral College. As
a result, even before Lincoln was inaugurated, seven of the eleven Confederate
states seceded from the Union, with South Carolina leading the way on December 20, 1860, seconded by Mississippi on January 9, 1861. Florida declared
secession a day later, and the following day Alabama left the Union. Georgia
seceded on January 19, Louisiana on January 26, and Texas on February 1.

Particularly troubling was the secession of the states of Mississippi and Louisiana along the Mississippi River—at least it was troubling to the states of the
Northwest Territory, also known as the Old Northwest. The Mississippi River,
for nearly 60 years, had served as an economic artery for the residents of the states
of Illinois, Ohio, Iowa, Indiana, Wisconsin, and other parts of the Northwest
Territory. Along the muddy waters, dubbed by William T. Sherman as "the spi-
nal column of America," the produce of these states moved downstream to the

second busiest port in America in 1860—New Orleans. True, the railroads had signaled the decline of river commerce, but the recognition of the transformation of commercial travel, so evident to an observer today, was not so apparent then.

When the southern river states seceded, the people of the Northwest were adamant that they would not accept the prospect of a closed river. With so many eyes focused on that river, amid the political firestorm of election and secession, rumors soon spread that northern forces were racing down the Father of Waters to occupy the river forts in Louisiana. On January 11, 1861, the militia in Vicksburg impetuously responded to the threat of an armed force from the North and fired on the unarmed steamer *A. O. Tyler* as it approached the city from upriver. The first shots had been fired, but because they were unsanctioned, there was no war.

Still, this unprovoked attack had its consequences. Governor Richard Yates of Illinois, in his inaugural address to the Illinois legislature on January 14, responded to the firing on the A. O. Tyler *with his own verbal cannonade. "Can it be for a moment supposed," he said, "that the people of the valley of the Mississippi will ever consent that the great river shall flow for hundreds of miles through a foreign jurisdiction, and they be compelled, if not to fight their way in the face of the forts frowning from its banks, to submit to the imposition and annoyance of arbitrary taxes and exorbitant duties to be levied upon their commerce?"*

He then declared, "I know I speak for Illinois, and I believe for the Northwest, when I declare them a unit, in the unalterable determination of her millions, occupying the great basin drained by the Mississippi, to permit no portion of that stream to be controlled by a foreign jurisdiction." So, despite assurances from Louisiana and Mississippi that the river would remain open, northern threats to float down and free the river were on record.

The situation continued to ratchet up. After South Carolina seceded, Union troops occupied and refused to abandon Fort Sumter in Charleston Harbor despite the protests of the South Carolina government. On March 29, to prevent the fort from running out of supplies, President Lincoln ordered a fleet of ships to steam to the relief of the garrison. The lead ship arrived off the Charleston bar just before midnight on April 11, 1861.

The Confederate troops at Charleston were commanded by Gen. P. G. T. Beauregard, who was agitated by the refusal of Maj. Robert Anderson at Fort Sumter to surrender. Knowing that aid to Fort Sumter's garrison was on the way,

Beauregard fired on the fort at 4:30 a.m. on April 12. This was one government firing upon another, and the Civil War officially began with the predawn muzzle flashes of those Confederate cannon. Abraham Lincoln had honored his Inaugural promise—he had cleverly maneuvered the South into firing those first shots.

After Sumter was fired upon, the Commonwealth of Virginia seceded on April 17, and two days later Lincoln issued a Proclamation of Blockade against Southern Ports. His plan was to prevent the export of southern cotton and other goods, as well as to stop the import of war materiel into the South.

On April 24, Governor Yates of Illinois sent Chicago militia to garrison Cairo, Illinois.

Cairo had been disparaged by famed English author Charles Dickens in 1843 as "a place without one single quality, in earth or air or water, to commend it." But Dickens was wrong, because Cairo had at least one quality— its strategic location at the confluence of the Mississippi and Ohio Rivers.

Two days after Cairo was garrisoned, the steamboat *C. E. Hillman*, which was passing downriver from St. Louis with a hundred tons of lead consigned to the Commonwealth of Tennessee, was detained and the lead was removed.

The Tennessee legislature immediately protested by saying, "The Mississippi River is declared to be free by the Constitution of Tennessee, and yet this vile usurper stations troops at Cairo to obstruct the navigation of this great highway and its tributaries."

In a twist of irony, while the Northwest placed the blame on the South for closing the Mississippi River, the closing was actually initiated by Union troops at Cairo.

On May 2 and 3, the governors of Illinois, Michigan, Indiana, New York, Ohio, and Pennsylvania met in Cleveland to discuss cooperation with the federal government. The result was a memorandum to President Lincoln that included a statement urging that the Mississippi and Ohio Rivers be the principal lines of operations against the South.

The governors also demanded that these rivers "must be kept at all times open to the legitimate commerce and business of the Northwest." But on May 8, Federal authorities in Louisville, Kentucky, blocked the shipping of weapons and materiel down the Ohio River to the South. The classification of war materiel could include virtually any commodity, since who could define "legitimate commerce and business"? The rivers were anything but open.

The Confederate government quickly responded to northern actions on the Ohio and Mississippi Rivers. On May 10, President Jefferson Davis and the Confederate Congress passed legislation to end all trade with the United States. The false hope of the South was that cotton would be the economic weapon that would bring the North to the bargaining table, but the bountiful 1860 cotton harvest had created huge surpluses, and when this surplus was gone, other ways to obtain the fiber would be found.

While the politicians passed their resolutions, in Washington 75-year-old General in Chief Winfield Scott, a veteran of both the War of 1812 and the Mexican War, politely turned down a strategic proposal from the commander of the Ohio militia, Gen. George McClellan in Columbus. Scott liked McClellan's idea of a strategic plan, but disliked his approach. The old general then proposed his own plan, which involved "a powerful move down the Mississippi to the ocean," coupled with "a complete blockade of the Atlantic and Gulf ports." When the Washington press heard of Scott's proposal, it was derisively dubbed the Anaconda Plan, in reference to the South American snake that squeezes its prey to death. This "constriction of the South" would have to be a gradual, time-consuming process, and the press believed the Rebels needed to be taught an immediate lesson.

Scott's Anaconda Plan did call for a shallow-draft navy to control the inland waters, and to his credit, General McClellan had recognized the need for such a navy. McClellan, however, differed with Scott over how to use this navy, as he recommended not a "powerful move" down the Mississippi River as Scott proposed, but an "active defense" of Cairo, Illinois. If McClellan had his way, the offensive action would be taken by a huge Federal Army.

While strategy was being debated in the North, the Confederacy was soon bolstered by the secession of the states of Arkansas on May 6, Tennessee on May 7, and finally North Carolina on May 20. This brought the total number of Confederate States to 11, and northern pressure to end the matter mounted. Something had to be done.

Though General Scott and General McClellan differed on how to use a riverine naval force, there was agreement on the need to build gunboats, and in June conversion of three riverboats into shallow-draft gunboats began in Cincinnati.

These boats, the *Lexington, Conestoga,* and ironically, the *A. O. Tyler,* which had been fired on at Vicksburg and renamed *Tyler* during its conversion, would carry heavy 32-pounder and eight-inch guns protected by five-inch-thick oak bulwarks. Thus, they became known as timberclads. After being converted, they completed the trip from Cincinnati down the Ohio River to the Cairo base on August 12.

On August 7, while the timberclads were being completed, a St. Louis civil engineer, James Buchanan Eads, was awarded a government contract to construct seven ironclad gunboats. Eads elected to construct four of these boats on the Mississippi River at Carondelet, Missouri, now in modern St. Louis, and three at Mound City, Illinois, five and one-half miles north of Cairo on the Ohio River. These heavily armed and iron-plated boats would form the nucleus of the Western Flotilla, an aquatic force which would later be dubbed the Brownwater Navy for operations on the rivers that led into the South. In addition, two additional riverboats belonging to Eads were being converted into ironclads. With 12 gunboats, either on the rivers or soon to be launched, President Lincoln was cementing his plans to wrest control of the lower Mississippi from the South.

In the South, President Jefferson Davis could not be sure if the North would invade. What he was certain of was that his oath required him to "protect and defend" the territory of the Confederacy. He made plans to do that.

In Washington there was an abundance of overconfidence about dealing the Rebels a whipping, and a quick strike by the Federal Army to Richmond to end the war was deemed the answer. Scott knew better, and he tried to avert a premature military venture. At a dinner party in late May, he warned administration officials, including cabinet members Salmon P. Chase, William Seward, and Simon Cameron, that the matter had become "a military question." "Such being the case," he said, "since, unfortunately, soldiers must settle it, you must allow the soldiers to do what they know they ought to do; and you must be careful not to force them to do what they know they ought not to do." Scott's plea fell on deaf ears. At a June 29 White House meeting of Cabinet officials and top military officials, the aging warrior again warned against waging "a little war by piecemeal." Scott was told, in no uncertain terms, that the public wanted and demanded immediate military action.

"On to Richmond" was now the cry in Washington. Horace Greeley's *New York Tribune* warned its readers that the Confederate Congress was scheduled to convene in Richmond on July 20, and that it must be stopped before it could meet. To that end, a Federal Army would march south from Washington into Virginia and whip the Confederate Army known to be in the vicinity of Manassas Junction. Since Scott was physically incapable of leading in the field, Union Gen. Irvin McDowell, an Ohio-born West Pointer, drew the short straw.

On July 16, an uneasy McDowell, concerned about the raw troops he commanded, was nevertheless ordered southwestward into Virginia to strike the blow that would somehow end the war. It was a northern disaster. On July 21, near Manassas Junction, Virginia, barely 25 miles from Washington, D.C., 35,000 raw Federal forces were routed by 32,500 equally green Confederates commanded on the field by General Beauregard and reinforced by Gen. Joseph E. Johnston. Adding to the bewilderment of the retreating Yanks were civilian onlookers, festooned in their finest garb and heavily laden with picnic lunches. These rubbernecks had followed the army from Washington to witness their Yankee soldiers spank the Rebel upstarts. But, when anticipated victory turned to unexpected defeat, civilian buggies and military wagons fled ingloriously back to the capital city in the precursor of a modern Washington traffic jam.

The Confederate victors failed to pursue their vanquished foe to Washington, despite the urgings of Jefferson Davis, who had arrived on the battlefield in time to see the Federal soldiers take flight. Pursuit after victory was a rare thing among Civil War generals, who, like the Byzantine general Belisarius, feared that a pursued foe might suddenly turn and, like a wounded and cornered beast, rip apart its antagonist. Still, the Federal attempt to take Richmond had failed.

On July 27, General McClellan was appointed commander of the Military Division of the Potomac. His responsibilities included the protection of Washington, D.C., and within a month McClellan had organized the Army of the Potomac, naming himself as its commanding general. McClellan soon convinced himself that the Confederates were planning to attack Washington, citing the paranoid figure of more than 100,000 Southerners across the Potomac, when there were actually around 35,000. On August 8, fearing this phantom enemy, McClellan called for a state of emergency in Washington. Meanwhile, he continued to build his Army of the Potomac and to work against his superior officer, General in Chief Scott, who was much more realistic about Confederate strength. The two generals strongly disagreed over the issue, and President Lincoln unsuccessfully attempted to mediate.

On August 12, the situation in the North seemed bleak. With his two senior generals fighting among themselves, a troubled Lincoln called for a day of national fasting. His proclamation read: "When our own beloved Country, once, by the blessing of God, united, prosperous and happy, is now afflicted with faction and civil war, it is peculiarly fit for us to recognize the hand of God in this terrible visitation, and in sorrowful remembrance of our own faults and crimes as a nation and as individuals, to humble ourselves before Him, and to pray for His mercy."

Even as the prayers emanated from Washington, politicians in the Northwest continued to demand action to open the Mississippi River. In September, former Illinois Congressman John Logan, who had resigned his congressional seat to become colonel of the 31st Illinois, warned, "Should the free navigation of the Mississippi River be obstructed by force, the men of the West will hew their way to the Gulf with their swords."

The rhetoric from the North and the rapid buildup of boats and men at Cairo, as well as the goading of Gen. Gideon J. Pillow, convinced Confederate Gen. Leonidas Polk, commanding in that department, that the northern troops would violate the Commonwealth of Kentucky's declared neutrality by crossing the Ohio River from Cairo and occupying Paducah. From Paducah, Polk believed, the enemy would move southward to occupy Columbus, Kentucky, a scant 17 miles south of Cairo on the Mississippi River. With this in mind and without seeking authority from President Davis, Polk sent troops to occupy Columbus on September 4, thus violating the declared neutrality of Kentucky. It was a huge political and military blunder.

An immediate Union response resulted from Polk's violation of Kentucky's neutrality, and it came from an obscure brigadier general, so newly appointed that he did not yet have a uniform. Ulysses S. Grant, who had arrived to assume command in Cairo the same day that Polk's men occupied Columbus, took the initiative.

On September 5, in one of the brilliant but largely unsung moves of the war, Grant learned that Polk was dispatching a force 35 miles northeast from Columbus to occupy Paducah, Kentucky.

Sensing the urgency of the situation, Grant sent a telegraph to his commanding officer, asking permission to seize the town before the Rebels could arrive. Receiving no reply, Grant acted without orders, saying to his staff, "Come on; I can wait no longer. I will go if it costs me my commission."

At 10:30 p.m. Grant took two regiments and a battery of artillery on steamboats 45 miles up the Ohio River from Cairo, Illinois, to Paducah, a town strategically located at the confluence of the Tennessee and Ohio Rivers. The steamboats of Grant's expedition were escorted by two of the timberclad gunboats, *Tyler* and *Conestoga*. The boats departed Cairo so quickly that Capt. Andrew Hull Foote, who had arrived to assume command of the Western Flotilla soon after Grant's departure, was forced to commandeer a steamer to join the expedition. Grant's men landed at 8:30 a.m. on September 6 and occupied Paducah without opposition.

At this time Ulysses S. Grant was a virtually unknown Union general. Grant was born on April 27, 1822, in Point Pleasant, Ohio, a hamlet located 19 miles southeast of Cincinnati on the Ohio River. Grant entered West Point at the age of 17, and was commissioned in the Fourth U.S. Infantry upon his graduation in 1843. A scant three years later, Lieutenant Grant served admirably in combat during the Mexican War under Gen. Zachary Taylor and Gen. Winfield Scott.

Grant's observations of his two commanding generals defined his own generalship. He recalled, "The contrast between the two was very marked. General Taylor never wore uniform, but dressed himself entirely for comfort. . . . Scott was the reverse. . . . He always wore all the uniform prescribed or allowed by law when he inspected his lines." Grant was later known for the simplicity of his uniform.

Grant noted that, Taylor "moved about the field in which he was operating to see through his own eyes the situation," whereas "Scott saw more through the eyes of his staff officers than through his own." Years after the war, in 1879, Grant confided to a reporter, "The only eyes a general can trust are his own."

Grant remembered, that General Scott "was precise in language, cultivated in a style peculiarly his own; was proud of his rhetoric" and, he said, "not averse to speaking of himself, often in the third person." Taylor, however, "was not a conversationalist, but on paper he could put his meaning so plainly that there could be no mistaking it." Grant became renowned for his precise and clearly written orders.

Grant also made other critical observations that would serve him well with President Lincoln during the Civil War. "General Taylor was not an officer to trouble the administration much with his demands, but was inclined to

do the best he could with the means given him. . . . No soldier could face either
danger or responsibility more calmly than he." Lincoln would say of Grant,
"He doesn't worry and bother me."

In 1853, Captain Grant was stationed at Fort Vancouver, in the Oregon Territory, while his wife and two children remained in the East. Grant, lonely and despondent on the Columbia River, began drinking, and it was observed that Grant "had very poor brains for drinking." In the spring of 1853 several military parties came to Fort Vancouver to survey a northern route for a Pacific railway, and among them was the party of Capt. George B. McClellan, West Point class of 1846. Unfortunately, Grant was drinking at the time.

McClellan quartered with Grant at Fort Vancouver for three months and,
according to a lieutenant who was present, Grant "got on one of his little
[drinking] sprees, which annoyed and offended McClellan exceedingly, and
in my opinion he never quite forgave Grant for it."

Grant resigned from the army in 1854 to avoid harsh disciplinary action, amid rumors about his gambling and drinking. These rumors would haunt him the rest of his life.

In 1861, Grant was clerking in his father's general store in Galena, Illinois, when word arrived on April 15 that the Fort Sumter garrison had surrendered the previous day to the Confederates. The residents of Galena met in the courthouse at dusk on April 16, and Grant listened as the partisan politicians characteristically blamed the opposition party for the state of affairs.

Then John A. Rawlins, a man whom Grant knew and respected, addressed
the audience. Rawlins's fiery words changed the atmosphere of the room com-
pletely: "I have been a Democrat all my life; but this is no longer a question
of politics. It is simply a matter of country or no country. . . . We will stand by
the flag of our country, and appeal to the god of battles!"

Walking home from the meeting, Grant turned to his brother Orvil and said, "I think I ought to go into the service." Two days later Grant presided over a rally to recruit volunteers, and on April 25 he accompanied the Jo Daviess Guards to Springfield, Illinois. By April 29, he was serving as an aide to Governor Richard Yates.

On May 24, Grant wrote to Col. Lorenzo Thomas, Adjutant General of the Army, saying, "I have the honor, very respectfully, to tender my services, until the close of the war, in such capacity as may be offered."

By June 17, Ulysses Grant was colonel of the 21st Illinois Infantry, a regiment of insubordinate troops whose colonel had been relieved of duty.

Swiss-born John E. Smith, who would soon be the colonel of the 45th Illinois, recalled Grant's arrival at the regiment on June 18: "Grant was dressed in citizen's clothes, an old coat worn out at the elbows, and a badly damaged hat. His men, though ragged and barefooted themselves, had formed a high estimate of what a colonel should be, and when Grant walked in among them, they began making fun of him."

When told his men were an unruly lot, Grant simply said, "I think I can manage them." In a month he had them in trim.

Congressman Elihu Washburne, from the northwest corner of Illinois, ensured that Lincoln's Cabinet nominated one brigadier general from his district—Ulysses S. Grant. Grant was nominated by President Lincoln on July 31, and confirmed by the U.S. Senate on August 5. By September 2, he was on his way to assume command at Cairo, Illinois.

A few days after occupying Paducah, Grant sent troops to Smithland, Kentucky, a town strategically located at the confluence of the Cumberland and Ohio Rivers. Because of Grant's initiative, the North had jumping-off points for river movements southward along the Mississippi River to Memphis, along the Tennessee River to a point near the vital railroad crossing at Corinth, Mississippi, and via the Cumberland River to Nashville. These three rivers were like daggers of water that pointed directly to the vital organs of the Confederacy, and these daggers were now available for Federal thrusts southward as soon as the ironclad fleet was ready.

In Washington, Winfield Scott and George McClellan continued to feud until the elderly and bone-tired Scott retired on November 1. McClellan was appointed general in chief and continued to organize and train the Army of the Potomac, but he refused to share with either the President or Cabinet his thoughts on strategy.

Frustration over the lack of offensive movement, or even a timetable for a movement, prompted President Lincoln to sign General War Order Number 1 on January 27, 1862, requiring offensive operations on the part of all the Union armies and navies by February 22. If McClellan wouldn't move from Washington, Lincoln would boot him southward, but in the process the President decided to give a kick to all of his army generals and naval flag officers in both the eastern and western theaters.

McClellan largely ignored the President's order, but in the West, General Grant and newly promoted Flag Officer Foote decided to seize the initiative. By the end of January, the last of the new ironclads had been completed, and though there were not enough crews to man all 12 gunboats, both officers sensed that the time was right for a river-borne invasion. After twice asking his superior officer, Gen. Henry W. Halleck, Grant received permission to organize an army of 17,000 soldiers at Cairo and Paducah. The soldiers would move southward on the Tennessee River on river steamboats. They would be escorted by seven of Foote's shallow-draft gunboats.

On February 6, Foote's gunboats captured Confederate Fort Henry on the Tennessee River, and Grant's and Foote's combined forces captured Fort Donelson on the Cumberland River on February 16. These victories soon led to the capture of the first Confederate state capital, Nashville, 65 miles southeast of Fort Donelson on the Cumberland River, on February 24. Nashville was occupied by Gen. Don Carlos Buell's Army of the Ohio.

Grant correctly described Nashville as "a place of great military and political importance." Strategically located on the Cumberland River, Nashville was also a rail hub that was soon converted into a bustling supply depot for a Union invasion into the heart of the Confederacy. And it was just as important politically. Optimism for the defeat of the Confederacy reappeared in the northern papers, with the *New York Times* predicting, "The End at Hand."

That prophecy proved grossly premature. From Fort Henry, Grant's victorious army moved southward on the Tennessee River with the vital railroad crossing of Corinth, Mississippi, as its goal. At Pittsburg Landing, Tennessee, Grant's Army of the Tennessee came dangerously close to being annihilated on Sunday, April 6, 1862, by Gen. Albert S. Johnston's Confederate forces at the Battle of Shiloh. The bad fortune of Grant's army was reversed when Johnston was killed during the fighting early that afternoon, and when General Buell's Army of the Ohio, marching from Nashville, arrived that night and the next day to provide reinforcements. But the North suffered 13,000 casualties compared to the Confederate's 10,700, and Grant and his subordinate, Sherman, came under severe criticism from the press for being surprised by Johnston's attack.

Seventeen years later Grant would still deny being caught unawares, saying, "There was no surprise about it, except perhaps to the newspaper correspondents." Still, the aggressive Grant learned a hard-bought lesson about underestimating his foe.

A powerful Federal Army group commanded by General Halleck moved south from Shiloh, and on May 30 captured the key Confederate railroad crossover at Corinth, thus flanking Memphis on the Mississippi River.

On June 10, Confederate Gen. P. G. T. Beauregard made the dire prediction that the evacuation of Fort Pillow, located 35 miles north of Memphis on the Mississippi River, "was the natural consequence of the retreat from Corinth, as will be the loss of all the Mississippi Valley. . . . I regard [Vicksburg's] fate as sealed."

President Davis did not share in Beauregard's negativity and was not about to concede Vicksburg. He wrote to the commander in Vicksburg on June 14 that "Disasters above and below increase the value of your position."

Back in Washington, all eyes remained focused on the capture of Richmond. To that end, General McClellan had resorted to in-fighting with the President and his Cabinet over the strategy for invading Virginia. Ever the pessimist, and quick to believe fantastically exaggerated Confederate strength figures, "Little Mac" wanted more men—so many more that he was eventually relieved of the duties as general in chief on March 11.

Still, while McClellan lost the top job in Washington, he was retained as commander of the Army of the Potomac. Relegated now to field army command, on March 17 McClellan finally understood the message that he was expected to move on Richmond. He began the transport of a huge army of 121,500 men from Alexandria to Fort Monroe, Virginia, thus initiating his ill-fated Peninsula Campaign. After arriving at Fort Monroe, McClellan began his march northward on April 4 toward Richmond, 70 miles northwest, along the peninsula between the James and York Rivers.

During the Peninsula Campaign, which was doomed by McClellan's overly cautious movements, arguably the most significant event was the wounding of Confederate commander Gen. Joseph E. Johnston at the Battle of Seven Pines only seven miles east of Richmond on the last day of May. Johnston had repeatedly fallen back in the face of McClellan's forces, until he was finally compelled to fight at the gates of the capital city. When Johnston was wounded, Gen. Robert E. Lee, senior military adviser to President Davis, assumed command of the army defending Richmond. He would designate it the Army of Northern Virginia, and he would remain at its head until the end of the war.

Lee was 55 years old when he assumed command of Johnston's army, then called the Confederate Army of the Potomac. Lee, born on January 19, 1807, into a Virginia gentry class family at Stratford Hall in Westmoreland County, Virginia, was the son of Henry "Light Horse Harry" Lee III, the Revolutionary War cavalry officer and favorite of Gen. George Washington. Light Horse Harry Lee had managed to lose the family wealth and lands through bad investments, landing him in debtor's prison, and he eventually abandoned his wife and children. Lee's half brother, Henry (known as "Black Horse") Lee IV, the son of Light Horse Harry by a previous marriage, went so deeply in debt that he sold Stratford Hall, the ancestral home. Robert was raised by his mother, a deeply religious woman, in Alexandria, Virginia, and the influence of Lee's mother and his religious upbringing greatly affected his life.

Lee attended West Point in 1825 and graduated second in his class in 1829, having never received a demerit. He was commissioned as an engineer officer and served as an engineer for the next 17 years.

During the Mexican War, Lee served with distinction on the staff of Gen. Winfield Scott. In 1847 Lee personally reconnoitered a route through the treacherous Pedregal—a Mexican lava field near Mexico City that was considered impassable—a feat that Winfield Scott said was "the greatest feat of physical and moral courage performed by an individual" in the campaign. Lee was slightly wounded while storming the heights of Chapultepec, again winning Scott's praise for being "as distinguished for felicitous execution as for science and daring." He was brevetted—a temporary promotion without an increase in pay—three times during the war, the last brevet being to the rank of colonel.

Lee returned home in 1848 to work for four years on the defenses complementing Fort McHenry in Baltimore Harbor. In 1852 he was appointed the ninth superintendent of the United States Military Academy. During his three years at West Point, Lee made many improvements while spending time with his cadets. In 1854, Lee's eldest son, George Washington Custis Lee, graduated first in his class from West Point.

In 1855 Lee was promoted to the lieutenant colonelcy of the newly formed Second U.S. Cavalry Regiment, and was ordered to the newly admitted state of

Texas to protect settlers from attacks by Kiowa and Comanche Indians. When his wife became an invalid from chronic arthritis and his father-in-law died, Lee had no choice but to request an extended leave from his regiment to tend to family affairs at Arlington, Virginia.

While at Arlington, Lee received a note on October 17, 1859, delivered by Lt. James Ewell Brown "Jeb" Stuart, to report to the War Department across the river in Washington. Lee soon learned that the Federal armory and arsenal at Harpers Ferry, Virginia, had been seized by John Brown and a band of insurrectionists. He received orders to proceed to Harpers Ferry and put an end to the matter. On October 18, when Brown refused to surrender upon Lee's demand, a storming party composed of a lieutenant and a dozen U.S. Marines was ordered in. After three minutes, Brown and the rest of his party were captured or killed, and the hostages were freed unharmed.

On April 17, 1861, Virginia seceded from the Union, but that information had not yet reached Lee at Arlington when, the next day, in answer to two summoning notes, he rode across the Potomac River to Washington. He made two visits that fateful April 18. Lee answered the first note and visited Francis P. Blair, Sr., founder of the Republican Party and an unofficial adviser to President Lincoln. Blair offered, in the name of the President, command of the Union Army assembling in and around Washington and with the rank of major general. His mission would be to take this army into Virginia to enforce Federal law. The offer must have been difficult to resist.

That previous January, Lee had said, "If the Union is dissolved and the government disrupted, I shall return to my native state and share the miseries of my people and save in the defense will draw my sword on none." So on April 18, he declined Blair's offer, saying he "could take no part in the invasion of the Southern States." Then Lee answered the second note and visited Gen. Winfield Scott, advising him of his decision. Scott warned, "Lee, you have made the greatest mistake of your life; but I feared it would be so."

Lee did not learn of Virginia's secession until April 19, and on April 20 he submitted his resignation from the United States Army after 32 years of service. He sent a note to General Scott, thanking him for his friendship and mentoring.

On May 14, Lee was confirmed by the Confederate Congress as a brigadier general in the Confederate Army, and on June 8 he formally turned over command of Virginia's military and naval forces to the Confederate government—a government that had moved from Montgomery, Alabama, to Richmond, Virginia, on May 21.

Lee was well acquainted with Jefferson Davis, and during the first months of the war he was often called upon by the President for advice on military matters. On March 13, 1862, Lee was "assigned to duty at the seat of government . . . under the direction of the president." He was to be President Davis's military adviser. Lee wrote to his wife the following day: "It will give me great pleasure to do everything I can to relieve him and serve the country, but I do not see either advantage or pleasure in my duties."

On May 31, at the Battle of Seven Pines, everything changed. Lee and Davis were on the battlefield near Richmond when, at dusk, a litter carrying the wounded Joseph Johnston approached.

Davis recalled that "it was probably a shell loaded with musket balls, as there appeared to be a wound of a ball in his shoulder ranging down toward the lungs." He continued, "When riding from the field of battle with General Robert E. Lee, . . . I informed him that he would be assigned to the command of the army."

On June 1, 1862, when Lee took command of the Confederate Army on the outskirts of Richmond, he went on the offensive, and the cautious McClellan quickly struggled against the aggressive new Confederate commander. From June 26 to July 1, Lee drove McClellan hard in the Seven Days Battles, resulting in the withdrawal of Union forces 23 miles to the southeast and to the safe haven and friendly naval gunboats at Berkeley Plantation and Harrison's Landing on the James River. A second attempt to capture Richmond had failed.

On the Mississippi River, Memphis, Tennessee, cut off by the capture of Corinth and attacked by a Federal fleet, was captured on June 6. Like Nashville, Memphis soon became a secure northern logistics base. It would remain a base for northern operations for the rest of the war, supplying Grant's army during the Vicksburg Campaign. Progress was being made in the West, yet the Mississippi River remained closed.

In the East, President Lincoln and Secretary of War Stanton sought new leaders to put an end to the embarrassing situation in Virginia. McClellan's stalemated Army of the Potomac was still closeted at Harrison's Landing, and new leadership was needed. So two successful Western generals were brought to the East—Gen. John Pope and Gen. Henry W. Halleck. On June 26, Pope was given command of the newly constituted Army of Virginia, a force hurriedly patched together from independent commands. On July 11, Halleck was appointed general in chief with authority over all Federal Armies.

Only three days after assuming his new duties, General in Chief Halleck ordered General Pope, with his freshly organized Army of Virginia, southeastward toward Richmond from Front Royal, Virginia. Pope's orders were daunting. He was to protect Washington, to draw the Confederates away from McClellan, and then to advance on Richmond to cover Mac's withdrawal from the peninsula. On August 3, Halleck ordered McClellan to get into position to support Pope by moving north to Aquia Creek on the Potomac River.

> *The next day, General McClellan, still in his haven at Berkeley Plantation on the James River, protested Halleck's movement order. He gave his reasons as "the certain demoralization of this Army which would ensue, the terribly depressing effect upon the people of the North, and the strong probability that it would influence foreign Powers to recognize our adversaries." He then wrote that he felt it was his "imperative duty to urge in the strongest terms afforded by our language that this order may be rescinded." When Halleck refused to budge, McClellan petulantly delayed the beginning of his movement until August 14, leaving Pope out on a limb.*

When McClellan failed to move promptly to Pope's support, Pope was resoundingly defeated by Gen. Robert E. Lee's forces, commanded by Gen. James Longstreet and Gen. Thomas J. "Stonewall" Jackson, at the Battle of Second Manassas on August 28–30, 1862. Another thrashing had been dealt to Lincoln's army in the East. After three northern attempts, Richmond had not been taken.

After the dramatic southern victory at Second Manassas, Lincoln relieved John Pope and combined his Army of Virginia with the Army of the Potomac. Despite the protests of his Cabinet, Lincoln left George McClellan in command of this consolidated army.

> *Lincoln's response to the protest was, "We must use what tools we have." The pragmatic President knew that McClellan, despite being a poor fighter, was a good organizer, and he knew that the two armies were in bad need of integration and reorganization.*

With the Union armies in disarray, Robert E. Lee felt the time was ripe for a southern offensive. He advanced his Army of Northern Virginia across the Potomac River into Maryland beginning September 4, with the hope of recruiting Confederate support and affecting the upcoming Union state midterm elections. McClellan was sent in pursuit.

Lee's foray into Maryland was not successful. On September 17, the two armies clashed at the Battle of Antietam, producing a grisly harvest of 23,000 blue and gray casualties in a single day in the cornfields and woods near the town of Sharpsburg. While the battle was a tactical draw, Lee withdrew back across the Potomac River into Virginia to lick his wounds, and McClellan, much to Lincoln's chagrin, did not pursue. The Army of the Potomac remained immobile from September 17 to October 26, and McClellan's unwillingness to move resulted in his relief of command by President Lincoln on November 7. Gen. Ambrose E. Burnside assumed command of the Army of the Potomac.

In the West, President Davis had personnel problems of his own, starting with Gen. Earl Van Dorn commanding at Vicksburg. Van Dorn's military failures aside, Mississippians, and particularly the citizens of Vicksburg, viewed the general as a "seducer, drunkard, and libertine." His removal was demanded. Meanwhile, Beauregard had gone on sick leave without securing permission from the War Department and had been relieved as the commander of the Army of the Mississippi. Popular in South Carolina as the captor of Fort Sumter, he was designated to replace Maj. Gen. John Clifford Pemberton as commander of the Department of South Carolina and Georgia. This now gave Davis a spare general.

On October 14, Davis relieved Van Dorn and promoted the 48-year-old Pemberton to lieutenant general in command of the Department of Mississippi and East Louisiana.

Pemberton was born in Philadelphia on August 10, 1814, to an established Pennsylvania Quaker family. John's father dealt in real estate after the War of 1812, and during a trip to Tennessee had become a close personal friend of future President Andrew Jackson. As a result, in 1833 Pemberton received a presidential appointment to West Point from "Old Hickory." In 1837 Pemberton graduated and was commissioned in the artillery.

In the fall of 1837 Lieutenant Pemberton was sent to Florida with the Fourth U.S. Artillery, and in January 1838, he fought his first battle against the Seminole Indians at Loxahatchee. Thereafter he served in a variety of posts until, in 1842, he was assigned to Fort Monroe, Virginia. He served for the next three years alternately at Fort Monroe and at Carlisle Barracks, Pennsylvania.

While at Fort Monroe, Pemberton met his future wife, Martha "Pattie" Thompson from Norfolk, whose family owned and operated a number of ships that sailed from Charleston and Norfolk to British and French ports. Pattie was a diminutive but strong-willed southern woman from a good family. Pemberton's marriage to her, coupled with their mutual affinity for Virginia, would greatly influence Pemberton's subsequent decision to fight for the Confederacy.

Pemberton served with the Fourth U.S. Artillery during Gen. Zachary Taylor's Mexican War campaign, and on May 8, 1846, he fought as an artilleryman at Palo Alto. The following day he led an infantry detachment with gallantry at Resaca de la Palma. In August, he became aide-de-camp to brevet Gen. William J. Worth, and was brevetted captain for his actions at Monterrey on September 23.

While serving as Worth's aide, Pemberton met Capt. Ulysses "Sam" Grant, who described the Philadelphian as a "conscious, honorable man." Pemberton also became familiar with Robert E. Lee when Lee reported that an alternate route to Mexico City had to be found because of Mexican fortifications guarding the roads.

On September 8, Pemberton fought at Molino del Rey, where he was brevetted major for "gallant and meritorious conduct." In this same action, Ulysses Grant was brevetted first lieutenant for his gallantry in action when he cleared armed Mexican soldiers from the rooftop of the mill.

On September 13, when the Americans stormed Chapultepec citadel in Mexico City, Joseph E. Johnston led two battalions of volunteers. Grant, in the attack on the San Cosme gate of the citadel, supplied artillery support by placing a gun in a church belfry. General Worth, admiring the effect of Grant's gun from the steeple, had Pemberton bring Grant to him so that he could express his appreciation for the effectiveness of Grant's well-placed fire.

On November 29, 1861, Pemberton was a Confederate general working for Gen. Robert E. Lee, who commanded the South Carolina coastal defenses and had placed Pemberton in command of District No. 4 in and around Charleston. Pemberton was promoted to major general on January 14, 1862, but he soon ran afoul of Governor Francis Pickens of South Carolina over the defense of Charleston, a city that Pemberton felt should be abandoned, if necessary, to save his outnumbered troops. Despite Lee's warnings to Pemberton that the civilian leadership must be mollified, matters deteriorated, and Pemberton had to go.

The lesson Pemberton took with him from Charleston to Vicksburg was that, regardless of military considerations and the danger to his troops, politics had to be factored into the equation.

Shortly after Pemberton assumed command of the Department of Mississippi and East Louisiana, the October and November state midterm elections in the North proved to be a disaster for Lincoln. These elections were viewed by many as a referendum on the Republican Party, and it took the loyalty of the die-hard Republicans in the New England and the Border States for the Republicans in Congress to hold onto an 18-vote advantage.

> *The results prompted the lamentations of one of Lincoln's friends, Col. William W. Orme, who would soon serve at Vicksburg. He wrote, "The democracy has carried everything, and I think the country is ruined. The result of these elections will palsy the arm of the President."*

While Lincoln's political problems multiplied, Jefferson Davis's military ones were exacerbated by a lack of confidence in Gen. Braxton Bragg. The general, envisioning his own Confederate offensive, in August marched northward from Chattanooga, Tennessee, to initiate his disastrous Kentucky Campaign. The prize was to be the support and secession of Kentucky. The campaign, in which Bragg and his subordinates frittered away their tactical opportunities against General Buell's Army of the Ohio, culminated in the Battle of Perryville, Kentucky, on October 8. After achieving a tactical victory Bragg, in typical fashion, then lost confidence and began to withdraw from Kentucky on October 13. He finally established his headquarters in Murfreesboro, Tennessee, where he and his generals began to blame each other for the failure of the campaign. Complaints that Bragg was "either stark mad or utterly incompetent" soon reached Richmond. Still, Davis decided to leave Bragg in command.

Meanwhile, the states of the Northwest continued their clamor to open the Mississippi River. Even with the Federal capture of Memphis, a 240-mile-long expanse of the Mississippi River remained closed to commerce from the frowning fortifications of Vicksburg southward to the guns of Port Hudson.

On November 10, Gen. John A. McClernand, like John Logan an Illinois congressman turned general, wrote to Secretary Stanton, describing the economic and political problems resulting from a closed river.

> *McClernand wrote, "The blockade of the Mississippi River has left to the people of the Northwest but one outlet for their immense surplus of grains and livestock, and that by the lakes and railroads alone, to the East. These channels are closed for the greater portion of the most favorable season for moving*

these articles to market, leaving the producers and traders at the discretion of exclusive monopolists."

McClernand reinforced the message conveyed by the recent elections. "Already are there those who are beginning to look beyond the pale of Federal authority for new guarantees for the freedom of the Mississippi River. The late election, in some instances, affords unmistakable indications of this fact. Not a few of the candidates preferred to office are represented to be opposed to the war and the policy that would continue it."

McClernand then proffered a warning: "I am conscious that if something is not soon done to reopen that great highway that a new party will spring into existence, which will favor the recognition of the independence of the so-called Confederate States, with the view to eventual arrangements, either by treaty or union, for the purpose of effecting that object."

McClernand had narrowly missed being elected Speaker of the U.S. House of Representatives in the 36th Congress, and he, of all people, understood the public's wishes.

Jefferson Davis wanted to make John McClernand's dire prediction a reality. To do this in the West, he needed Bragg in Tennessee; Pemberton in Mississippi and East Louisiana; and Theophilus H. Holmes, in command of the Trans-Mississippi, the area west of the Mississippi River, to cooperate with one another on shifting troops to protect the Mississippi River. To Davis, the answer to the problem of cooperation was a commander who could supervise the Confederates in Tennessee, Mississippi, and East Louisiana, strangely leaving the Trans-Mississippi out of the equation.

Davis only had three field commanders who had the necessary rank for this proposed command. They were Robert E. Lee, who was needed in Virginia; Joe Johnston, who was still recuperating from his wounds; and P. G. T. Beauregard, who had already failed in the West at Shiloh and at Corinth but was now in command at Charleston.

The solution to Davis's problem seemed to fortuitously appear during the second week of November, when Gen. Joe Johnston recovered from his Seven Pines wounds and reported to Richmond for duty. Davis jumped at the opportunity, and on November 24, Johnston was given command of the new Department of the West.

The concept, according to Davis, was "to secure the fullest cooperation of the troops in those departments." However, he went on to say that the appointment was "to avoid delay by putting the commander of each department in direct correspondence with the War office." By allowing the commanders to communicate directly with Richmond, Johnston was cut out of the loop, thus, Davis deprived Johnston of unity of command. And Johnston, even though he requested it, was not given command over General Holmes's troops in the Trans-Mississippi. Johnston felt, properly so, that one commander should control troops on both sides of the river. That would never happen.

Johnston was born February 3, 1807, in Cherry Grove, Virginia. His mother was a niece of Patrick Henry, and his father had fought under Light Horse Harry Lee. Johnston entered West Point in 1825. While there, he became the good friend of a classmate, Robert E. Lee. Johnston graduated in 1829, and was commissioned in the Fourth U.S. Artillery.

In January 1836, Lieutenant Johnston was assigned duties as an aide-de-camp to Gen. Winfield Scott during the Second Seminole War. In 1847 Major Johnston served as a topographical engineer on the staff of Winfield Scott, along with Capt. Robert E. Lee, Lt. P. G. T. Beauregard, Lt. George B. McClellan, and Lt. George G. Meade. On April 12, while scouting the advance near Cerro Gordo, Johnston was severely wounded by cannon fire. For his service during the reconnaissance, Johnston was brevetted lieutenant colonel. When he recovered from his wounds in June, he was assigned as second in command of a regiment of newly arrived volunteers.

In mid-August, Scott's army, thanks to Robert E. Lee's reconnaissance, emerged from the Pedregal lava field, six miles south of Mexico City. Then, on September 8, Johnston fought at Molino del Rey, where both Pemberton and Grant were brevetted.

Mexico City was Scott's next objective, and on September 13, Johnston led two battalions of his regiment to the gate of the southern wall of the citadel of Chapultepec. P. G. T. Beauregard joined Johnston's men as a volunteer, recalling, "I never saw new troops behave so well." Johnston was brevetted colonel for his actions. He recalled, "There is no comfort like that of going into battle with the certainty of winning." Indeed, Johnston was said to have a morbid fear of failure, and a friend said that he hated "to be beaten, even in a game of billiards." He was described by another friend as an excellent marksman, but that on hunting expeditions he would not take a shot unless he was sure of a hit. After all, a miss could ruin Joe Johnston's reputation as an excellent marksman.

After the Mexican War, Johnston remained in the Army, and on June 28, 1860, became quartermaster general of the Army with a general's star. News of

Virginia's secession reached Washington on Friday, April 19, 1861, and Johnston presented his resignation to Lincoln's Secretary of War, Simon Cameron, on Monday, April 22.

Johnston told Cameron: "I must go with the South. I owe all that I am to the government of the United States. It has educated me and clothed me with honor. To leave the service is a hard necessity, but I must go."

As Jefferson Davis's new commander of the Department of the West, on November 24, 1862, Joe Johnston departed Richmond for Chattanooga, where he established his headquarters. After arriving in Chattanooga on December 4, Johnston did not find the military situation to his liking.

That day he wrote to a friend, "Nobody ever assumed a command under more unfavorable circumstances."

Johnston had learned that General Grant had initiated a move in late November against General Pemberton in north Mississippi, and was pushing south with 40,000 men down the Mississippi Central Railroad toward Jackson. Pemberton, after abandoning his defensive line along the Tallahatchie River, 30 miles south of the Tennessee-Mississippi state line, was now falling back another 50 miles with his force of 22,000 soldiers. Pemberton's plan was to establish a defensive line behind the Yalobusha River at Grenada, Mississippi, 110 miles north of Jackson. A bewildered Johnston knew that if Grant continued to be successful in his push he would soon be in Jackson. If Jackson were captured, Vicksburg would be flanked, as was Memphis when Corinth fell.

Johnston also learned that there was a new opponent in front of the 47,000 soldiers of General Bragg's Army of Tennessee at Murfreesboro. Gen. William S. Rosecrans had taken command of General Buell's Army of the Ohio, and much of this 60,000-man army was now in Nashville, a scant 30 miles in front of Bragg.

Buell had been relieved of command after Bragg retreated from Kentucky. Buell, whose bellicose language belied his tentative actions, simply ensconced his army at Bowling Green, Kentucky, with no plan for a pursuit of Bragg. And, through a series of unwise actions, he managed to alienate the civilian leadership of the Northwest.

On October 21, Governor Oliver Perry Morton, a friend of President Lincoln, complained to Lincoln; "Nothing but success, speedy and decided, will save our cause from utter destruction. In the Northwest distrust and despair are seizing upon the hearts of the people." The next day, Horace White, chairman of the Illinois Republican Party state central committee, wrote to Lincoln; "If we are beaten [in the mid-term elections] in this state two weeks hence, it will be because McClellan and Buell won't fight."

After their defeat in those midterm elections, the Republicans howled that "Buell's slows cost us the votes." The camel's back was broken when, on October 30, Governor David Tod of Ohio wrote to Secretary Stanton, "The army from Ohio demands the removal of General Buell." Buell, a Democrat and protégé of McClellan, was relieved of command of the Army of the Ohio by President Lincoln that same day. Command of Buell's army went to Rosecrans, who had fought with some success at Iuka, Mississippi, in September and at Corinth in October. Rosecrans, however, had developed a contentious relationship with his superior officer, Ulysses Grant.

On November 4, Rosecrans accompanied his new command, the former Army of the Ohio, which he would soon redesignate the Army of the Cumberland, from Bowling Green southwest to Nashville. Rosecrans was 30 miles northwest of Bragg, but then "Old Rosy" developed his own case of "the slows." This did not bode well in Washington, because after the disaster at the polls, a military victory was needed.

A month later the need for a northern victory was less than subtly expressed to Rosecrans on December 4, the same day that Johnston arrived in Chattanooga. General Halleck telegraphed Rosecrans: "The President is very impatient at your long stay in Nashville. The favorable season for your campaign will soon be over. . . . If you remain one more week at Nashville, I cannot prevent your removal. As I wrote you when you took the command, the Government demands action, and if you cannot respond to that demand some one else will be tried."

Rosecrans had to know that he had received his new task largely because of the election results. In fact, his date of rank had been backdated by Lincoln to give him the seniority for command. Rosecrans would have to go on the offensive soon.

But Rosecrans remained oblivious to political concerns. When he received the telegram from Halleck, in his long-tongued and short-tempered way, he defiantly sent his reply: "To threats of removal or the like I must be permitted to say that I am insensible."

While Rosecrans delayed, President Lincoln understood well the importance of the Mississippi River to the Northwest. On December 1, in his second annual message to Congress, he reiterated the prewar concerns of Illinois Governor Yates and the recent apprehensions of Illinois General McClernand.

First, the President acknowledged the importance of the Northwest, "the great interior region, bounded East by the Alleghenies, North by the British dominions, West by the Rocky Mountains, and South by the line along which the culture of corn and cotton meets." He acknowledged that "in the production of provisions, grains, grasses, and all which proceed from them, this great interior region is naturally one of the most important in the world."

Second, he noted the importance of free access to the Gulf. "And yet this region has no sea-coast, touches no ocean anywhere. As part of one nation, its people now find, and may forever find, their way to Europe by New York, to South America and Africa by New Orleans, and to Asia by San Francisco. But separate our common country into two nations, as designed by the present rebellion, and every man of this great interior region is thereby cut off from some one or more of these outlets, not, perhaps, by a physical barrier, but by embarrassing and onerous trade regulations."

Of course, Lincoln's words were read avidly in the South, and if Lincoln wanted control of the river, it stood to reason that Davis should deny him that control.

But things were also brewing in Virginia as the Army of the Potomac began to ramp up for an offensive, prompting Jefferson Davis to comment that "an idle winter is not anticipated for the Army of Northern Virginia." In view of this, Davis wanted to visit Lee's Army of Northern Virginia, which had now gone into defensive positions at Fredericksburg to oppose any offensive move by General Burnside and his Army of the Potomac.

Davis's desire to visit Lee's army would go unsatisfied, however. Despite his appointment of General Johnston to command the Department of the West, the situation in Mississippi and Tennessee still demanded the president's attention. Grant was on the offensive in Mississippi, and problems remained in Bragg's army in Tennessee. Davis would have to let Lee handle the situation in Virginia.

On December 10, the president boarded a train for Chattanooga, arriving there the next day. He and Johnston then left for Murfreesboro on December 12 and reviewed Bragg's army the next day.

Davis was impressed with the "fine spirits" of Bragg's army, and his discussions with Bragg reassured him. There is an old military axiom that "you can look too good," and such was the case with the Army of Tennessee. Bragg assured Davis that he had dispatched a cavalry force under Gen. Nathan B. Forrest that would "create a diversion in favor of Pemberton," and that it may well "force the enemy to retire from Mississippi." Because of the great disparity of numbers between Pemberton and Grant, Davis remained unconvinced, and since all was so well in Tennessee, he ordered troops to be sent by rail from Bragg's army to Pemberton's.

Johnston protested taking any troops from Bragg, because Bragg was already outnumbered by Rosecrans. He warned that what was left of Tennessee could well be lost if Rosecrans went on the offensive. Despite the protest, Davis usurped Johnston's command prerogative and ordered Bragg to send 9,000 men to Mississippi immediately. Davis told Bragg, "Fight if you can, and fall back beyond the Tennessee." To Davis, denying the Mississippi River to the North and preserving the connection with the Trans-Mississippi for the South was the overriding concern, even it if meant the loss of the rest of Tennessee.

Davis and Johnston departed Murfreesboro on December 14. Upon their arrival in Chattanooga, Davis received a telegram from Richmond advising him that Burnside's Army of the Potomac had attacked Lee's Army of Northern Virginia at Fredericksburg the previous day. The results of the battle were not in the message. Davis would have an excruciating wait of a day for that news.

Burnside, responding to Lincoln's and Halleck's prompting to go on the offensive, had marched south from Warrenton, Virginia, on November 15, 1862. His vanguard arrived just two days later at Falmouth, upstream from Fredericksburg. Burnside's progress was then hampered by slow-moving pontoon trains, which his army needed to cross the Rappahannock River. He hesitated, providing time for Lee to concentrate his scattered army and fortify on the high ground west of Fredericksburg. It was not until December 11 that Burnside's pontoons were positioned on the Rappahannock in front and below the city. The Union troops then crossed the river and deployed in town and downstream.

Over the next two days the Federals furiously looted the abandoned city, much to the anger of Lee's men who watched from Maryes Heights to the west of town. Finally, at 8:30 a.m. on December 13, Burnside's men formed their lines and marched forward to attack the Confederate positions. The hapless soldiers in blue were slaughtered as wave after wave charged into a hail of lead and iron fired from the Confederate small arms and cannon on the hills above and the high ground downstream. It was another Union defeat, and it could not have come at a worse time for Lincoln.

When Davis learned on December 14 of the successful outcome of Lee's defense at Fredericksburg, he and Johnston happily boarded a train to Mississippi to visit Pemberton's troops in that threatened department. When they reached Mississippi they were pleased to learn that Grant's offensive down the Mississippi Central Railroad had been turned back. Things seemed to be as they should be.

On December 8, Grant had decided to launch a two-pronged attack on Pemberton, with Grant holding Pemberton in place at Grenada by knocking on the front door, while Sherman stole his way into Vicksburg by the back door via an amphibious operation down the Mississippi River from Memphis. Grant's movement south, however, was turned on its head by the Forrest-led cavalry raid in west Tennessee that Bragg had promised Davis, and by another cavalry raid authorized by Pemberton and led by Van Dorn, who was first and last a cavalryman.

After losing his command at Vicksburg, Van Dorn was wisely given command of a provisional cavalry division by Pemberton on December 12, and this 3,500-man unit of Mississippians, Texans, Missourians, and Tennesseans managed to successfully circle around and behind Grant's lines and surprise the Federal garrison at the supply base at Holly Springs in the predawn hours of December 20.

Forrest had destroyed Grant's railroad supply line in west Tennessee, and now Van Dorn had incinerated Grant's forward supply depot in north Mississippi. There was nothing left for Grant to do but to bite hard on his cigar and turn back toward the supply base at Memphis.

On December 26, in Jackson, a very happy and relieved Davis addressed the Mississippi legislature. "There are now two prominent objects in the programme of the enemy," he warned. "One is to get possession of the Mississippi river and to open it to navigation in order to appease the clamors of the West and to utilize the capture of New Orleans, which has thus far rendered them no service."

Davis continued: "The other is to seize upon the capital of the Confederacy, and hold this out as a proof that the Confederacy has no existence. We have recently repulsed them at Fredericksburg, and I believe that under God and by the valor of our troops the capital of the Confederacy will stand safe behind its wall of living breasts."

Emphasizing the defense of the river, Davis said: "Vicksburg and Port Hudson have been strengthened, and now we can concentrate at either of them a force sufficient for their protection. I have confidence that Vicksburg will stand as before, and I hope that Johnston will find generals to support him if the enemy dare to land. Port Hudson is now strong, and Port Hudson will stand; but let every man that can be spared from the other vocations, hasten to defend them, and thus hold the Mississippi river, that great artery of the Confederacy, preserve our communications with the trans-Mississippi department, and thwart the enemy's scheme of forcing navigation through to New Orleans."

Davis had obviously read Lincoln's December 1 address to the U.S. Congress, for he then addressed Lincoln's economic concerns: "By holding that section of the river between Port Hudson and Vicksburg, we shall secure these results, and the people of the West, cut off from New Orleans, will be driven to the East to seek a market for their products, and will be compelled to pay so much in the way of freights that those products will be rendered almost valueless. Thus, I should not be surprised if the first daybreak of peace were to dawn upon us from that quarter."

More than pleased with the end-of-the-year military results, Jefferson Davis then left Johnston in Mississippi and departed for Richmond, arriving in the Confederate capital early in the New Year. But two belated Christmas presents awaited the president, and he would not learn about them until he reached Virginia.

The first was the Battle of Chickasaw Bayou. Davis knew something was afoot, because he had written a letter to General Holmes in the Trans-Mississippi on December 21, warning that "a large [Union] force is now ready to descend the Mississippi and cooperate with the army advancing from Memphis to make an attack upon Vicksburg." And while Davis spoke to the Mississippi legislature on the day after Christmas, the "large force" to which he referred was disembarking on the south bank of the Yazoo River near Chickasaw Bayou north of Vicksburg, led by General Sherman.

Sherman's soldiers, after spending several days of the Yule Season slogging through the frigid swamps, attacked the Confederates entrenched on the opposite bank of Chickasaw Bayou. But without the anticipated support from Grant, Sherman was soundly thrashed by the Confederates on December 29. The noise of the arriving trains in Vicksburg with reinforcements from Tennessee could be heard in the Union lines, and it was obvious to Sherman that the Confederate defenses had been bolstered. Deciding against another frontal assault, Sherman ordered his thoroughly wet and miserably cold men to reembark on the steamboats. Thomas Knox, a stowaway reporter for the *New York Herald*, was on the scene. He sent his disparaging dispatch northward with the first courier he could find, announcing, "Our failure has dashed the hopes of the nation."

The second present for Davis was from Tennessee. On December 26, Rosecrans was finally prodded out of Nashville by Washington. He advanced toward Murfreesboro on the same day that Sherman's men slogged ashore near Chickasaw Bayou. Rosecrans had hoped to surprise Bragg, but he was beaten to the punch in a predawn attack on December 31 by his adversary. However, Bragg, after repeated attacks, failed to break the last compacted Union line. The battered and bloody Union Army managed to survive the onslaught. Still, Rosecrans's soldiers paid a heavy price for being surprised while boiling their coffee on the last day of the year.

Things could not look better for the Confederacy. On the final day of 1862, on the heights above Fredericksburg, General Lee congratulated his Confederate troops upon their lopsided victory against the luckless Burnside two weeks earlier, telling them, "The eventful and glorious campaign of the year just closing gives assurance of hope that . . . the coming year will be no less fruitful of events that will insure the safety, peace, and happiness of our beloved country."

On the opening day of 1863, General Bragg in Murfreesboro telegraphed Richmond, saying, "God has granted us a Happy New Year." Rosecrans's advance had been halted and his army had been given a bloody nose.

While Bragg telegraphed Richmond, Johnston telegraphed Murfreesboro from Jackson. Elated over the blunting of Grant's and Sherman's thrusts, and very happy with the results of Bragg's fight with Rosecrans, Johnston wrote, "I congratulate you on your glorious termination of last year."

The Union thrusts on all three fronts had been stopped. Richmond was still secure, and the Mississippi River was still closed. The Confederate tide was at its peak.

Chapter 2
A SERIES OF EXPERIMENTS

January 2–March 30, 1863
A wave rolling up the smooth, wet sand of a beach eventually runs
out of energy and reaches a point of culmination, which is the precise
moment that the foaming water ceases its progress upward and begins
its backward motion. At that moment of culmination is an almost
imperceptible pause between progression and recession—a blink-of-
the-eye moment in which the water's motion is suspended. The almost
invisible interlude between the rising and ebbing of the Confederate
tide occurred on January 3, 1863. It was the period between the
arrival of a note suggesting a course of action to Gen. Braxton Bragg
in Murfreesboro, Tennessee, and his decision eight hours later.

WHILE THE CONFEDERATES WERE CONGRATULATING THEMSELVES ON
the first day of 1863 in Fredericksburg, Virginia; in Murfreesboro, Tennessee;
and in Jackson, Mississippi; there was soul-searching in Washington, D.C. New
Year's Day was the day that Abraham Lincoln had been planning to sign the
Emancipation Proclamation, a document that would provide the legal frame-
work for freeing nearly four million slaves—that is, if the Union Armies advanced
farther into the South. But with all of the recent Union setbacks, was this the
time for Lincoln to sign it?

Another issue faced the President on this momentous day. After the thrashing given to the Army of the Potomac at Fredericksburg in December, Gen.
Ambrose Burnside, understanding the political need for a victory, had planned
another offensive for his army, to begin on the last day of 1862. His ultra-
secret plan; however, was thwarted when two of his midlevel senior officers,
Gen. John Cochrane and Gen. John Newton, traveled to Washington at the
end of the year and complained to the President that the demoralized army
was in no condition to go on the offensive. If the Army of the Potomac was
defeated again, they asked the President, what would become of the country? A
very concerned Lincoln, heretofore unaware of Burnsides's plans, immediately

telegraphed Burnside and cancelled the offensive. Burnside, properly confused and concerned, traveled to Washington to meet with the President on the morning of New Year's Day. The general was shocked to learn that his own officers had thwarted his plans. He then angrily offered his resignation, which the President refused to accept. The general was told to come back later that afternoon to discuss the matter further, because the President had other business on his calendar.

That other business was the signing of the Emancipation Proclamation. Regardless of how bad the military and political situation had become, the President felt that his failure to sign the promised document would only add to the nation's woes. It was a calculated risk, and Lincoln, the riverboat gambler, was not going to fold his cards.

When Burnside returned to the White House later that day, he again offered his resignation, which the President again refused. He was, however, given permission to resume plans for his offensive.

The next day, January 2, Gen. Braxton Bragg at Murfreesboro, Tennessee, awaited news of the expected retreat of Gen. William S. Rosecrans's army back to Nashville. After all, Bragg had dealt Rosecrans a devastating blow on December 31—a blow which had nearly destroyed the Federal Army. Strangely, news of a retreat did not come. In fact, Bragg learned that Rosecrans had dared to advance a Union division across Stones River. That was all Bragg needed to hear, and he decided to attack at 4 p.m.

Bragg ordered Gen. John C. Breckinridge to attack with his reinforced division. After an hour and 20 minutes of ferocious combat, the Confederate attack was beaten back. The night of January 2, 1863, found both armies licking their wounds and manning their lodgments along Stones River at Murfreesboro. It seemed to be a stalemate. No one could know that the Confederate tide was about to culminate.

At 2 a.m. on January 3, Bragg's sleep was interrupted by a messenger who handed him a note from two of his commanders. The note advised Bragg to withdraw his army from Murfreesboro. Bragg adamantly replied, "We shall hold our position at every hazard." But then Braxton Bragg did what Stonewall Jackson once cautioned against; he took counsel of his fears. By 10 a.m., Bragg allowed himself to be convinced by an erroneous scouting report that Rosecrans's army had been strongly reinforced. He issued a withdrawal order for his army. Late that night, in a cold, driving rain the Confederate Army marched south out of Murfreesboro, slogging through the mud toward Tullahoma.

Cautiously, Rosecrans did not move into Murfreesboro until January 5. When he found Bragg's army gone, he telegraphed President Lincoln to advise him of the Confederate withdrawal. Realizing for the first time that his calculated risk of January 1 had paid off, Lincoln wired back, saying to Rosecrans, "God bless you, and all with you!" Without comprehending the meaning of his retreat from Murfreesboro, General Bragg had given Abraham Lincoln precisely what he needed.

The same day that Lincoln sent blessings to Rosecrans, Jefferson Davis spoke in Richmond. Davis was unaware of Bragg's withdrawal as he addressed his audience. "Recently, my friends, our cause had had the brightest sunshine to fall upon it, as well in the West as in the East. Our glorious Lee . . . has achieved a victory at Fredericksburg, and driven the enemy back from his last and greatest effort to get 'on to Richmond.' . . . In the West, too, at Murfreesboro you have gained a victory over hosts vastly superior to our own in number. . . . You have achieved a result . . . at Vicksburg, where they were struggling to get possession of the great artery, the control of the Mississippi River, to answer the demands of the Northwest."

Abraham Lincoln is a savvy politician, and he is quick to take advantage of the opportunity that Bragg's withdrawal has presented. What does he do? He takes the facts and he spins them, turning the stalemate between Rosecrans and Bragg at Stones River into a great Union victory.

Braxton Bragg has no idea what his withdrawal will mean to Abraham Lincoln and to the northern cause once Lincoln puts a new face on the situation. When Bragg retreats from Murfreesboro, he originally intends to retire 50 miles south to Elk River. But when he discovers that Rosecrans is not pursuing, he halts on Duck River, 30 miles south of Murfreesboro, and establishes his headquarters at Tullahoma, 18 miles farther south.

Rosecrans, with an extended and vulnerable line of communications, consolidates and goes no farther than Murfreesboro. He decides to rest on his laurels, reconstitute and reinforce his army, and amass huge supply depots. He will not move again for five and a half months, all the while demanding huge amounts of supplies and transportation, to include transport boats badly needed by Grant. No matter how hard President Lincoln, Secretary of War Stanton, who replaced Simon Cameron on January 15, 1862, and General in Chief Halleck push, Rosecrans refuses to see the political considerations—that is, that the time is right for action. But Rosecrans will not budge.

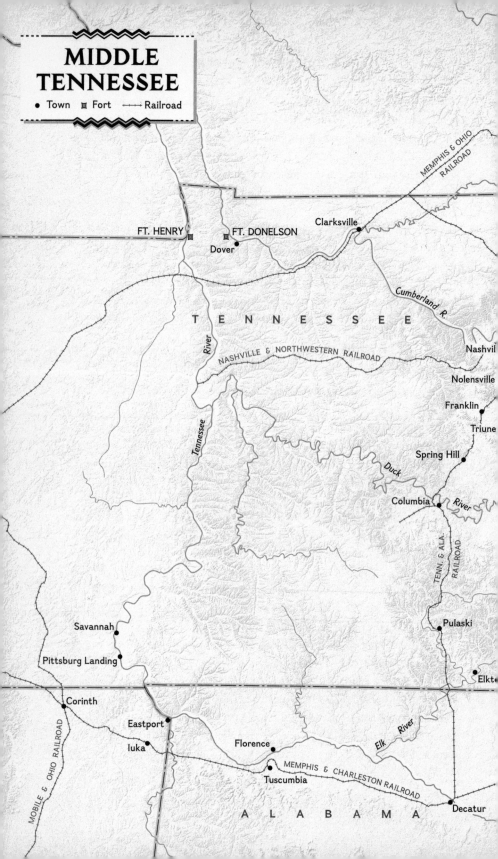

MIDDLE TENNESSEE

- ● Town
- ▥ Fort
- ⊢—⊣ Railroad

MEMPHIS & OHIO RAILROAD

FT. HENRY   FT. DONELSON   Clarksville

Dover

T E N N E S S E E

Cumberland R.

River

Nashvil

NASHVILLE & NORTHWESTERN RAILROAD

Nolensville

Franklin

Triune

Tennessee

Duck

Spring Hill

Columbia   River

TENN. & ALA. RAILROAD

Savannah

Pulaski

Pittsburg Landing

Elkt

Corinth

Eastport

Iuka

Florence   Elk River

MEMPHIS & CHARLESTON RAILROAD

Tuscumbia

MOBILE & OHIO RAILROAD

A L A B A M A   Decatur

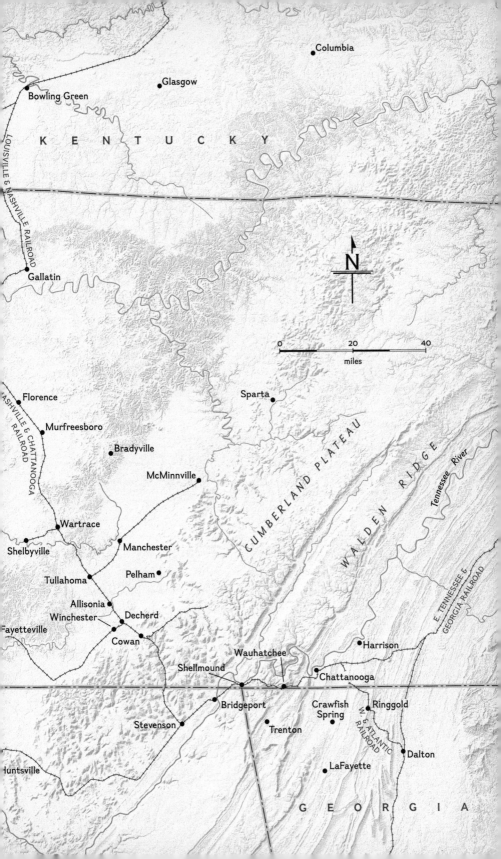

Gen. Ulysses Grant is different. After his withdrawal from Mississippi, Grant has made Memphis his headquarters in early January 1863. Grant is not in a good mood because he is facing the aftereffects of bad press due to his retrograde from Oxford and Holly Springs, as well as from Sherman's defeat at Chickasaw Bayou. Sherman's men had to withdraw from their Yazoo River beachhead under cover of darkness the night of January 1, and they arrived at Milliken's Bend, Louisiana, the next afternoon. So now much of Grant's army is downriver in Louisiana. All that those poor soldiers can look forward to is a cold winter in the wetlands along the Mississippi River.

While Grant is in Memphis, he thinks a great deal on how to capture Vicksburg and open the lower Mississippi. When he learns of Rosecrans's "victory" Grant sends no congratulatory message to his former subordinate, because Grant is no friend of Rosecrans. In 1865 Grant will say to Lincoln's Cabinet, "Murfreesboro was no victory, and had no important results." Grant, the soldier, was correct, militarily speaking, but even in 1865, he still did not recognize the psychological victory that Lincoln, the politician, was so quick to capitalize on in 1863.

Despite Lincoln's spin on Murfreesboro, the North needs a real victory. In early 1863 Grant knows he must do something, and he must do it soon.

In 1879, Grant recalled this period of the war, "The North needed a victory. . . . I felt that the Union depended upon the administration, and the administration upon victory."

On the afternoon of January 17, Grant steams downriver from Memphis to meet with Gen. John McClernand and Gen. William T. Sherman, and Adm. David D. Porter. McClernand had already arrived at Milliken's Bend on January 4, and, due to his seniority and a special arrangement made with President Lincoln and Secretary of War Stanton, he assumed command of Sherman's forces.

In the second week of January, McClernand, having replaced Sherman, headed back up the Mississippi River and ascended the Arkansas River to move against Arkansas Post. Supported by Porter's gunboats, McClernand's troops captured the post with more than 4,800 defenders on January 11.

Grant holds a series of meetings and sends a prophetic message to Memphis to be telegraphed to Halleck in Washington. "What may be necessary to reduce the place [Vicksburg] I do not yet know, but since the late rains [I] think our troops must get below the city to be used effectively," In this message, Grant displays his understanding of the geography and hydrology of the area.

Grant then returns to Memphis on the 19th and telegraphs Halleck that neither the army nor the navy has sufficient confidence in McClernand as a commander. As the ranking officer, Grant intends to go down to Milliken's Bend and take personal command.

While Grant's forces are encamped in Louisiana, in Virginia General Burnside has his Army of the Potomac opposite Fredericksburg at Falmouth, on the north side of the Rappahannock River. Per his New Year's Day discussion with the President, Burnside has plans for another offensive against Robert E. Lee's Army of Northern Virginia, which is dug in on the heights behind Fredericksburg on the south side of the Rappahannock River. Burnside is going to take another shot at Richmond. His offensive was originally scheduled for January 17, the same day that Grant steamed down the Mississippi River to meet with McClernand, Sherman, and Porter. But Burnside's offensive has been delayed due to intelligence reports that the Confederates might be shifting troops upstream toward the intended crossing locations. Still Burnside sets aside his fears that the Confederates have perceived his plan. He sets everything in motion on the morning of January 20. The weather is unseasonably warm, and after an easy one-half day's march, the army goes into encampment with all of Burnside's plans on schedule. Then, as though the gods themselves are plotting against the mutton-chopped general, around 7 p.m. the bottom falls out of the sky.

A huge two-day storm front moves into the area, and the Virginia countryside is soon converted into a sea of mud. Torrential rain is accompanied by rapidly dropping temperatures that turn raindrops to sleet, and punishing winds increase the misery of the drenched army. On January 21, the conditions worsen as wheels of vehicles, hooves of dray animals, and boots of soldiers churn the roads into knee-deep mud wallows. First the soldiers, and then the officers, begin to blame their commanding general for his army's being, according to one soldier, "bamboozled and gaining nothing." Burnside himself loses his confidence, and later reported that "the elements were against us." On the 22nd the movement is cancelled, and the bone-tired, drenched, and dispirited army returns to its camps.

After the failure of what soon becomes known as Burnside's "Mud March," President Lincoln and Secretary of War Edwin Stanton decide that Burnside must be replaced as commander of the Army of the Potomac. The Republican

Party radicals demand that Gen. Joseph Hooker be placed in the position, and Lincoln, needing to appease the radicals within his own party, gives Hooker the nod.

Joe Hooker was born in Hadley, Massachusetts, on November 13, 1814, and graduated from West Point in 1837. He served in the Second Seminole War and in the Mexican War on the staffs of Persifor F. Smith, William Orlando Butler, and Gideon J. Pillow. Hooker is well known for his fondness of alcohol, gambling, and women.

On January 26, Lincoln writes to Hooker to advise him that he is the new army commander. Then Lincoln tells Hooker that he is "not quite satisfied" with him. Hooker was instrumental in undermining the authority of Ambrose Burnside, and Lincoln warns Hooker that his disloyalty in criticizing Burnside did the country a great wrong. Worse, Lincoln believes that this disloyalty might come back to haunt Hooker.

Two days after Hooker assumes command in the East, Grant decides it's time for him to go downriver and assume personal command of his army in Louisiana. He leaves Memphis aboard the steamer *Magnolia* and arrives at Young's Point at 9 p.m. on January 28. The next day he begins to issue orders. On the 30th, he is challenged in writing by General McClernand, who has been signing letters and orders with the heading of "Headquarters, Army of the Mississippi." McClernand protests that Grant has been issuing orders directly to the corps commanders and not through him. He claims the title of army commander by order of the secretary of war and the President, saying that "two generals cannot command this army."

That's all that Grant can stand, and before the day is done he issues General Orders Number 13, announcing that he is taking active command of the entire army. McClernand testily informs Grant that he will obey the order, but that he will protest it to Washington. The protest will go all the way to President Lincoln, but Grant wins. The name Army of the Mississippi is junked, and instead of leading an independent army, McClernand is now commanding the XIII Corps in Grant's Army of the Tennessee.

While McClernand and his XIII Corps land and encamp at Milliken's Bend, 18 river miles upstream from Vicksburg, Sherman's XV Corps goes ashore 8 miles downriver at Young's Point.

William T. Sherman was born on February 8, 1820, in Lancaster, Ohio. He graduated from West Point, a member of the class of 1840, and was commissioned a second lieutenant in the Third U.S. Artillery. He and Henry Halleck, a member of the class of 1839, served in California during the Mexican War but saw no combat. Still, a friendship between Sherman and Halleck that began at West Point was reinforced on the long voyage around Cape Horn.

Both Sherman and Halleck resigned from the Army in the early 1850s to forge second careers in San Francisco—Sherman as a banker and Halleck as an attorney and businessman. After his bank failed, Sherman became a lawyer, but he soon missed the comradeship of his Army years. In 1859, he became superintendent of Louisiana State Seminary of Learning and Military Academy at Pineville. Sherman thought he had finally found a career he enjoyed, but when Louisiana seceded from the Union in early 1861, he resigned and went home.

On May 14, 1861, Sherman was commissioned colonel of the recently authorized 13th U.S. Infantry. He led a brigade at First Manassas, and committed his four regiments piecemeal in the afternoon's futile fight for Henry Hill. He received a star on August 7, and in early October he replaced Gen. Robert Anderson as commander of the vital area embraced in the Department of the Cumberland. He lasted one month in this assignment before being replaced by Gen. Don Carlos Buell. Sherman's irrational actions had raised serious concern regarding his mental health. His friend Halleck, now commanding the Department of the Missouri, came to his rescue, and on February 14, 1862, Sherman was reassigned to command the District of Cairo. He established his headquarters at Paducah, Kentucky, and during the campaign against Fort Donelson, he forwarded supplies, troops, and encouragement to Grant.

By mid-March Sherman was commanding a division in Grant's Army of the Tennessee, which was encamped at Pittsburg Landing, Tennessee. At dawn on Sunday, April 6, Confederate troops led by Gen. Albert S. Johnston stormed out of the woods, inaugurating the Battle of Shiloh. Although Sherman was surprised, he rallied his division, and the next day Grant, aided by Buell's Army of the Ohio, eked out a victory. For his performance at Shiloh, Sherman received his second star on May 1.

Halleck came south from St. Louis to take command of the Federals at Pittsburg Landing, and marched his army to Corinth. After the capture of Corinth on May 30, Grant, despondent over the uselessness of his role as second in command to Halleck, planned to resign. Sherman reminded Grant that just a few months earlier the newspapers had labeled Sherman as crazy, but that now the Battle of Shiloh had given him new life, and he was in "high feather."

Sherman then advised Grant that "if he went away events would go right along, and he would be left out; whereas, if he remained, some happy accident might restore him to favor and his true place."

Sherman's advice was taken, and Grant decided to stay in the game. In January, 1863, Sherman is again working for Grant in the wetlands of Louisiana.

While the XIII and the XV Corps of the Army of the Tennessee are downriver in Louisiana, the XVII Corps, commanded by Gen. James B. McPherson, remains behind in Memphis due to lack of transportation downriver. As soon as steamboats become available, McPherson's men clamber aboard, and the procession of boats makes its way downstream. The soldiers soon disembark and occupy the area near Lake Providence, Louisiana, a short distance south of the Arkansas line.

Like Grant and Sherman, McPherson was born in the Buckeye State, in Clyde, Ohio, on November 14, 1828. McPherson, too, was a West Pointer, graduating first in the class of 1853 and assigned to the Corps of Engineers. A bright, handsome, personable 33-year-old bachelor, McPherson became an aide-de-camp to Henry Halleck, commander of the Department of the Missouri. McPherson was soon promoted to lieutenant colonel, and in January 1862 was sent by Halleck to assist Grant as his engineer during the expedition to Fort Henry. But Halleck had another motive—McPherson was to report to Halleck on rumors of Grant's drinking.

Apparently, McPherson was the man for the job, because Sherman later said, "Whenever I had occasion to learn any thing that I wished to know, I invariably went to McPherson, who, while he attended to his own business, was very observing of every thing that interested the whole army."

Whether Grant was aware of McPherson's mission or not, the general took an immediate liking to the affable young lieutenant colonel. McPherson served on Grant's staff in the Fort Henry and Fort Donelson Campaign, and then went with Grant to Shiloh. On May 1, he received his colonel's eagles. Before the silver thread could even tarnish on the eagle shoulder straps, two weeks later McPherson was sporting a general's star. In mid-October, McPherson received his second star.

McPherson's meteoric advancement in rank is rivaled only by two captains and one first lieutenant in the Army of the Potomac—Farnsworth, Merritt, and Custer. As early as 14 months before, McPherson had been a first lieutenant of engineers. But, in the Vicksburg Campaign, he will prove that he is overly cautious and not a risk taker. Possibly, McPherson was a victim of the Peter Principle, which says that sooner or later people will be promoted to their level of incompetence. More likely, he was just promoted too fast, without the necessary experience needed to be a corps commander.

Grant has a fourth corps, the recently constituted XVI Corps, commanded by Gen. Stephen A. Hurlbut. During the Vicksburg Campaign, Hurlbut will be headquartered in Memphis, and his troops will be tasked with holding Memphis and Corinth and guarding key railroad lines in north Mississippi and west Tennessee. Expeditions sent out by Hurlbut into counties of west Tennessee, in accordance with orders from Grant and requests from Rosecrans, will harass the Confederate military and civilian infrastructures. On two occasions in April, Hurlbut and troops from his corps will play important roles in the Vicksburg Campaign through deep-interdiction raids on Confederate railroad lines of communication.

After Grant takes command at Young's Point on January 30, he establishes his first objective: "to secure a foothold upon dry ground on the east side of the river from which the troops could operate against Vicksburg."

Grant understands that a retreat from Louisiana to Memphis would be viewed as another major defeat—one which neither he nor Lincoln could survive. He writes in his memoirs that the proper military move was to get his troops out of their miserable conditions by going back to Memphis and then waiting for spring to move down the Mississippi Central Railroad line—a repeat move, along the same railroad, that he attempted in December. That is exactly what Sherman advises him to do. But Grant knows that a retrograde to Memphis is not an option because it will be reported by the press as another retreat, and news of another retreat at this critical time would be disastrous for the President.

In Personal Memoirs of U. S. Grant, *Grant wrote: "At this time the North had become very much discouraged. Many strong Union men believed that the war must prove a failure. The elections of 1862 had gone against the party which was for the prosecution of the war to save the Union if it took the last man and the last dollar. . . . It was my judgment at the time that to make a backward movement as long as that from Vicksburg to Memphis, would be interpreted, by many of those yet full of hope for the preservation of the Union, as a defeat, and that the draft would be resisted, desertions ensue and the power to capture and punish deserters lost. There was nothing left to be done but to go forward to a decisive victory. This was in my mind from the moment I took command in person at Young's Point."*

Meanwhile, Gen. Joe Johnston is unhappy with his new position as commander of the Department of the West, and writes to Davis in mid-January, saying that command of an army is his desire and that his new position makes him more of a staff officer than a commander.

Johnston writes, "I respectfully and earnestly beg some other position which may give me better opportunity to render such service as I may be capable of." Johnston knows he cannot go back to Virginia. Lee's successes have ended any chance of that. And he does not wish to take either Bragg's or Pemberton's army. Still, he writes, "I have already lost much time from service, and therefore can ill-afford to be inactive at any time during the remainder of the War."

Johnston is unhappy, but where could he expect Jefferson Davis to send him? Meanwhile Davis still has the nagging problem of Braxton Bragg.

On January 10, Braxton Bragg begins to realize the gravity of his withdrawal from Murfreesboro. He sends a letter to his generals saying that he has been "assailed in private and public by the press, in private circles by officers and citizens, for the movement from Murfreesborough." He then makes an incredible offer: "I shall retire without a regret if I find I have lost the good opinion of my generals, upon whom I have ever relied as upon a foundation of rock."

But Bragg has a sagging foundation, because after his withdrawal from Murfreesboro, many of Bragg's generals advise him that they have, indeed, lost confidence in him.

When President Davis learns of this strange episode, he writes to Johnston on January 22: "The events connected with the late battle at Murfreesboro, and retreat from that place, have led to criticisms upon the conduct of General Bragg. . . . You will, I trust, be able, by conversation with General Bragg and others of his command, to decide what the best interests of the service require, and to give me the advice which I need at this juncture. As that army is a part of your command, no order will be necessary to give you authority there, as, whether present or absent, you have a right to direct its operations and do whatever else belongs to the general commanding."

Joe Johnston now has the opportunity to grant his own wish. The command that he has solicited is his for the taking simply by assuming command of Bragg's army. Johnston turns down the opportunity.

Johnston writes to Davis on February 3 that his confidence in Bragg "is confirmed by his recent operations, which, in my opinion, evince great vigor and skill. It would be very unfortunate to remove him at this juncture, when he has just earned, if not won, the gratitude of the country."

The target—the command of an army—that Johnston wants is there, but it appears that Johnston, the expert marksman, does not want to risk the shot.

Jefferson Davis, confused and frustrated, writes to Johnston, "You limit the selection to a new man, and, in terms very embarrassing to me, object to being yourself the immediate commander."

Nothing changes. Bragg, despite having confirmation from many of his generals that they have no confidence in his leadership, remains in command. Just as detrimental to the cause, Johnston is still unhappy with his assignment.

Meanwhile, Ulysses Grant decides to remain in front of Vicksburg. He searches for ways to secure a foothold on dry ground on the east side of the river. To that end, he begins a "series of experiments" known as the bayou expeditions. These four "experiments," or expeditions, are Grant's Canal, the Lake Providence Expedition, the Yazoo Pass Expedition, and the Steele's Bayou Expedition.

In his memoirs, Grant writes that he wanted to "divert the attention" of the enemy, of his troops, and of the public, and that he "never felt great confidence that any of the experiments resorted to would prove successful." However, Grant was writing in the mid-1880s, with the advantage of hindsight. In the winter of 1862-63, he was optimistic that he would achieve success in at least three of these attempts, and he was fully prepared to take advantage of any opportunity.

GRANT'S CANAL

At Young's Point, Grant sees the remnants of a canal, actually more of a ditch, cut by Gen. Thomas Williams's men in the summer of 1862 during then Flag

Officer David G. Farragut's unsuccessful attempt to capture Vicksburg. Williams planned for this canal to be dug through the neck of De Soto Point, where the river makes a hairpin curve in front of Vicksburg. The idea was to divert the waters of the Mississippi River south of the city. If successful, the "Gibraltar of the Confederacy" would then be left high and dry.

While Grant doesn't think much of the canal idea, he has been forewarned by Halleck, "Direct your attention particularly to the canal proposed across the point. The president attaches much importance to this."

Grant decides to resume work on this project. If successful, he could take steamboats downriver to a landing point on the eastern bank without having to pass the Vicksburg batteries. When Sherman arrives with his XV Corps at Young's Point on January 23, he inherits the unfinished canal. Sherman says the canal they find is "no bigger than a plantation ditch." Nevertheless, he is ordered to convert the ditch into a canal 6 to 6½ feet deep, 60 feet wide, and 1½ miles long. These measurements are based on the width and depth requirements of the Eads ironclads. Though Sherman doubts the wisdom behind this project, Grant knows he has to humor the President, who championed the canal the previous summer. Lincoln has not lost interest, so work starts on January 24.

Grant's chief engineer is Capt. Frederick Prime, number one in his West Point class of 1850. Making some changes in the design of the canal, Prime concludes that the canal entrance does not take advantage of the washing of the river. He relocates the entry point to take advantage of the current.

The Federals are going to use black labor wherever possible, but Sherman is also going to employ many soldiers. These soldiers are working in miserable circumstances due to the rainy, cold weather. The sick lists grow and deaths multiply as the Mississippi River begins its seasonal upward surge, flooding the camps. As early as January 26, the levees breach, because they are only seven or eight feet high, having been built by the plantation owners.

The work starts with picks, shovels, and wheelbarrows, but the Yanks will soon go high tech. By February 19, they are using steam pumps to draw the water out. Then their prospects look better when the Mississippi River crests and the water starts to drop.

But in the last week of February heavy rains pelt the area for four of seven days, keeping the troops in camp. Even the steam pumps aren't working, so the answer is to import floating steam dredges from the Ohio River. The dredge

Sampson soon arrives and begins work on March 2. The weather gets better and the situation improves. A second steam dredge, *Hercules,* arrives on March 6, and Grant becomes optimistic. He advises the top brass in Washington that the "canal is near completion."

> On March 1, General in Chief Halleck is under political pressure to get the armies moving and procure the Federal victory so badly needed. President Lincoln has been able to milk the Murfreesboro "victory" just so much. Then, to provide the "carrot on a stick," Halleck sends identical telegrams to Rose-crans, Grant, and Hooker. He promises a "major generalcy in the Regular Army" to the general "who first wins an important and decisive victory." Rosecrans is indignant, and he unwisely telegraphs to Halleck that he feels "degraded to see such auctioneering of honor." Grant, digging away in the mud in Louisiana, is stoic and does not reply to Halleck. Neither does Hooker, who continues to reorganize the Army of the Potomac.

Grant, when he said the canal was almost finished, spoke too soon. A day later a massive crevasse occurs in the Young's Point area. Water pours through the levee out into the low-lying campgrounds, and Yankee soldiers have to rush for the safety of higher ground and perch themselves on the levee, looking like roosting chickens. The rush of the current enlarges the crevasse to 150 feet wide, and the bluecoats work for the next week trying to control the rising water.

The Mississippi's flood stage eventually begins falling, but what have the Confederates been doing all this time? They know about the canal, so they relocate several big guns south to the area opposite the canal's exit. These cannon command the canal for at least one-half its length. If the Federals ever finish the canal and put riverboats into the 60-foot-wide ditch, the boats will be like ducks sitting in a puddle. Realizing this, on March 27 Grant orders work on the canal stopped.

LAKE PROVIDENCE EXPEDITION

Grant is no fool, and he has not put all his eggs in one basket. While work is proceeding on the De Soto Point canal, Grant searches for other ways to bypass Vicksburg. He has his engineers investigate the possibility of opening a 200-mile-long route from the Mississippi River into the Red River near Port Hudson, Louisiana, 240 miles by river below Vicksburg. If this route can be opened, Grant can reinforce Gen. Nathaniel Banks in his campaign against Port Hudson. General McPherson at Lake Providence is tasked to figure out the details of the plan to navigate a series of riverlike bayous to get to the Red River.

Port Hudson, like Vicksburg, is a bastion on the Mississippi River. The two fortified positions deny the Federals complete control of the river between Vicksburg and Baton Rouge, as well as the mouth of the Red River and its tributaries. Of course, if either Vicksburg or Port Hudson falls, their advantage is lost.

The Lake Providence route could also lead Grant to the high ground south of Vicksburg without his having to run the Vicksburg batteries, which is the same concept of Grant's Canal but with a different execution. And that is Grant's objective—get to the dry ground on the east side of the river. So this route is worth exploring.

In early March, McPherson checks out Lake Providence and the area north of it along the Louisiana-Arkansas state line. Because the Mississippi River is eight feet higher than the flat land behind the levee at Ashton, Arkansas, McPherson says that the levee should be breached at Ashton so that the Mississippi will flood the area all the way to Bayou Macon, just over two miles west of Ashton. Bayou Macon flows south to the Tensas River, the Tensas flows into the Black River, the Black flows to the Red River, and finally the Red discharges into the Mississippi River.

On March 4, the levee is blown at Ashton. With the Mississippi River being near flood stage, the levee breaks and floods the lowlands beyond the natural levee. By mid-March the area is flooded all the way from Ashton south to Lake Providence and west to Bayou Macon, and small boats can navigate across the inundated landscape. Then McPherson breaches the levee at Lake Providence on March 17. By March 23 McPherson is brimming with the optimism of youth, bragging that the levels of the lake and the river are nearly the same. He writes that "any steamboat that runs on the river can be taken in."

The following week, however, McPherson writes to advise Grant of a problem. A cypress swamp lies west of Lake Providence along the last portion of Bayou Baxter, a waterway which flows out of Lake Providence into Bayou Macon. This swamp is 250 to 300 yards wide and is only 3½ feet deep at the shallowest point. McPherson says that he can dredge the area out in a short time, but first he must cut 12 to 15 virgin cypress trees, and the cut must be under the water line. To do this he needs an underwater sawing machine that should have already arrived from Memphis. After that, McPherson writes, the waterways can be navigated. Grant, however, pulls the plug on the Lake

Providence Expedition. He thinks he has found a better route at the Yazoo Pass, 320 river miles north of Vicksburg.

Although the Lake Providence water route through Louisiana will never be employed, the flooded area will serve Grant well in his future operations. It will provide a water barrier to protect the right flank of his long supply column, and it will also provide an obstacle to protect Union supply depots against attacks and raids by the Trans-Mississippi Confederates during critical days of the Vicksburg siege.

YAZOO PASS EXPEDITION

Grant abandons the Lake Providence route because he has turned his attention to another water route, the Yazoo Pass.

The pass, located six miles south of Helena, Arkansas, ran from the Mississippi River through nearby Moon Lake and then eastward to the Coldwater River. The Coldwater flows southeast to the Tallahatchie River, which flows south to Greenwood, Mississippi. There the Tallahatchie and Yalobusha meet to form the Yazoo River. From Greenwood the Yazoo runs southwest to the Mississippi River and past the high ground north of Vicksburg.

The Yazoo Pass was used for decades by small boats as the shortest and safest route to travel from Yazoo City to Memphis, but was closed when the Mississippi River levee was built in 1856. So the memory of the pass is a recent one, and everyone who knew the Mississippi was familiar with this route.

Grant sends Lt. Col. James H. "Harry" Wilson, his chief topographical engineer, to look into reopening the Yazoo Pass. Harry Wilson graduated from West Point in 1860, and he is no dummy, graduating sixth in a class of 41. Wilson lives to be almost 88, so he outlives almost every other Civil War officer, and like Joshua Chamberlain, Wilson writes prolifically after the war. Also like Chamberlain, every time Wilson writes, he gets a little bit bigger in the picture. He will later claim that it was his idea to run the Vicksburg batteries with the fleet, cross the river below Vicksburg, establish a base of operations at Grand Gulf, and move into the interior of Mississippi. Of course, Grant, Sherman, McClernand, McPherson, Rawlins, and just about everyone who was at Vicksburg is dead when Wilson publishes this tall tale in 1912, so who can argue? There are lots of reasons why you want to live a long time, and one of them is that you get to be the last one to tell the story.

On February 2, Wilson reaches the levee that blocks entry to the Yazoo Pass from the Mississippi. The next day his men place 50 pounds of black powder under the dike, ignite the powder, and breech the levee. Wilson reports to Grant that the operation is a success. Grant is so excited about the possibilities that he writes to General in Chief Halleck on February 6, saying he hopes to get Adm. David D. Porter's light-draft gunboats and 600 army riflemen into the Yazoo River via the pass and the long route southward.

Grant needs naval support for this Yazoo Pass scheme, so he sends a message to Porter the same day that he writes to Halleck, asking for his support.

No such entity as the Joint Chiefs of Staff exists during the Civil War. There is nothing like that until 1942. The Navy and the Army commanders don't have a joint command authority, and Porter does not have to cooperate with Grant if he doesn't want to. But Porter is a working-clothes officer who doesn't like a lot of show, so he supports Grant and Sherman, even though he generally doesn't like West Pointers. At the same time, he intensely dislikes political generals such as John A. McClernand, Benjamin F. Butler, and Nathaniel P. Banks. Porter also possesses an ego and ambition second to none.

To protect Grant's steamboats employed as transports during the expedition, Porter sends Lt. Cmdr. Watson Smith up the Mississippi with the tinclad gunboats *Rattler*, *Romeo*, and *Signal* to support the *Forest Rose*, which is already positioned at Yazoo Pass. The tinclads are sometimes called light drafts, because they draw from two to six feet of water. Most are about 150 feet long and displace about 200 tons. They are designed to protect troop transports, and they usually have light sheet metal armor one-half to one inch in thickness on the forward part of the casemate, around the engines and pilothouses. This means that the boat's personnel and machinery are only protected against small-arms fire, and the crews can't go toe to toe with shore guns, even though tinclads are frequently armed with eight-inch guns.

Watson Smith, who is sick from a fever he caught in the Yazoo swamps, writes to Porter that he "will go as far as possible" but that he "feels of very small worth." A commander with a faint heart and a lack of self-confidence is not a good person to lead an expedition.

Porter knows that if the tinclads run into any field artillery, they will be in deep trouble, so he orders the ironclad *Chillicothe*, captained by Lt. Cmdr. James Foster, to accompany the expedition. *Chillicothe* has two 11-inch Dahlgren smoothbores housed in a gun casemate with three inches of armor in the bow and two inches port and starboard. Like the other ironclads, she is designed to fight with her bow facing the enemy, because that's where the thickest armor is located, and that is where her most powerful guns are positioned. But the

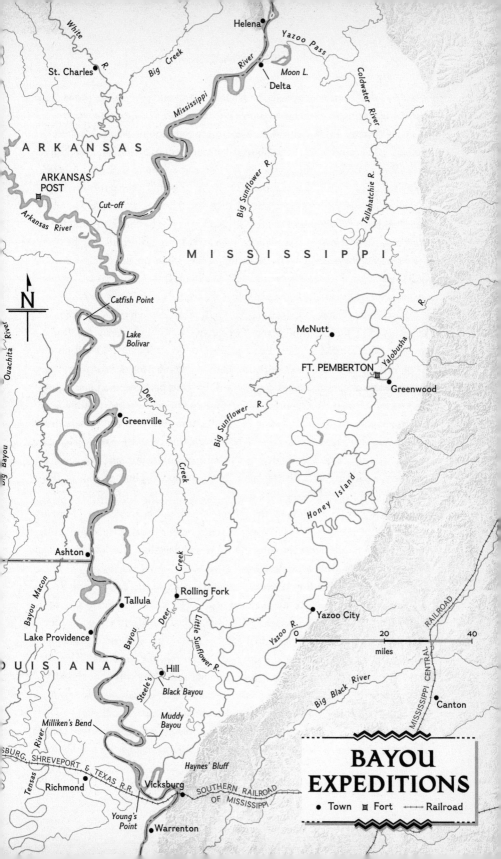

BAYOU
EXPEDITIONS

● Town   ▪ Fort   ┈ Railroad

Chillicothe has been poorly built in Cincinnati by contractor Joseph Brown and has only recently been fitted out, so her weaknesses are yet to be discovered.

On February 13, Porter sends orders to Lt. Cmdr. John Walker of *Baron de Kalb* at the fleet anchorage near Young's Point to steam upriver and join Smith's fleet. *Baron de Kalb,* formerly the *St. Louis,* is one of the "city series" ironclads built by Eads in 1861. She is a powerful ironclad with 13 big guns: two rifled 42-pounders, six 32-pounders, one 10-inch smoothbore, two 9-inch smooth-bores, and two 30-pounder Parrott rifled guns. Despite her firepower and heavy armor, she only draws six feet of water, even at 512 tons. The trouble is she's 175 feet in overall length and 51 feet 2 inches in breadth at the knuckle, where the bulkhead and deck meet to form an angle. She's a big boat for the Yazoo Pass, and she's a stern-wheeler, which gives her a wider turn radius.

Meanwhile, Harry Wilson has been sending favorable reports to Grant on the progress of the expedition, and on February 15 Grant orders a 4,000-man division, commanded by Gen. Leonard Ross, to go to Greenwood and up the Yalobusha River to destroy the railroad bridges at Grenada. Grant unsuccessfully tried to destroy these bridges with cavalry raids back in December during his first move against Vicksburg, because the two railroads over these bridges are important lines of communication for Pemberton. After the gunboats destroy the bridges, they are to go back down the Yalobusha River to the Yazoo River and then down the Yazoo to the high ground above Vicksburg at Yazoo City. So if all goes well, Vicksburg not only is flanked, but it also loses its lines of communication leading north.

On February 28, the head of the Federal fleet enters the Coldwater and waits for the rest of the fleet to exit the pass. Even though this takes three and a half days, Watson Smith wants the entire flotilla to stay together. The delay frustrates General Ross and Colonel Wilson.

On March 10, the flotilla ties up along the bank of the Tallahatchie River, 32 river miles from Greenwood, and the Federals get detailed information from local blacks about a Confederate fortification, called Fort Pemberton, 20 miles downstream. The Yanks are told that the fort has a battery of three guns—one rifled—a parapet of cotton and sand, and a ditch fronting the works. They are also told about a raft of gum logs that is prepositioned and ready to be swung into place to block the stream. For insurance, the steamer *Star of the West* is just below the raft, ready for scuttling to block the Tallahatchie if necessary.

On the morning of March 11, *Chillicothe* is boarded by Watson Smith, Leonard Ross, and Harry Wilson. Not only does *Chillicothe* have the big 11-inch guns, but she is a side-wheeler and handles better than the stern-wheeler *Baron de Kalb* in the narrow Tallahatchie. The plan is to reconnoiter to see what the Confederates have downriver. As soon as the officers are aboard, *Chillicothe* casts off, and at 10:15 a.m. they see Fort Pemberton dead ahead.

By the morning of March 11, thanks to the Union delays in approaching, the Confederates have had time to respond, and Fort Pemberton is in a reasonable state of defense. Confederate Gen. William W. Loring has received two heavy guns and positioned one on each flank of the dirt and cotton bale fort. The fort commands an 800-yard reach of the Tallahatchie, and the narrow width of the river will prevent more than two gunboats attacking at a time. The land side of the fort is protected by 600 yards of cleared ground and by Clayton's Bayou. The flanks of the fort are protected by the waters of the Yazoo and Tallahatchie Rivers.

At 10:15 a.m. the Confederate gunners spot the black, box-shaped bow of the *Chillicothe* with two 11-inch bow guns bearing down on them. The Confederates fire first with five guns and score two hits. A conical 68-pound bolt fired from a rifled and banded 32-pounder slams into the *Chillicothe*'s turret. The bolt fractures the armor plates and embeds abaft of the armor in the nine-inch pine wood backing. A solid 18-pound Whitworth bolt strikes the boat's port bow about 18 inches above the water line, but the armor holds. Captain Foster immediately backs upstream until all of his boat, except the bow, is hidden behind a slight river bend. The Confederates have drawn first blood by wounding one Federal, and they haven't suffered any casualties.

At 4:15 the Federals try again. As *Chillicothe* approaches Fort Pemberton, the Confederates open fire. *Chillicothe* sends four shells at the fort, yet she retires after a mere seven-minute fight, because four Rebel explosive shells have ripped into her, including a dreadful one from the rifled 32-pounder. This shell penetrates a three-inch-thick iron-plated gun port slide, weighing 1,600 pounds, which is covering the firing port of the 11-inch gun on the port side. Entering the casemate, or armored gun compartment, of the boat, the steel-tipped conical shell then slams into the tulip, or muzzle swell, of the 11-inch gun just as the crew is reloading. Both the incoming 32-pounder and the 11-inch shell in the barrel explode, and the concussion blows off both gun port slides. The pressure from this explosion is monstrous, because the two slides total 3,200 pounds, and one of them careens into the water. Part of the wooden turret backing is blown off, and the nuts on the bolts that hold the armor to the wood are simply wrenched away. On that day the buckets of sand on board are put to good use, because the deck is awash with blood. Captain Foster of *Chillicothe* reports that he has three men killed outright, one mortally wounded, ten seriously wounded, with five more sailors suffering from gunpowder in their eyes. It is doubtful that anyone in the gun turret has any intact eardrums after the explosion. Foster decides that his boat "is almost a failure and will remain so until alterations are made in the backing of the turret."

At 11 a.m. on March 13, *Chillicothe* and *Baron de Kalb* try again. They steam downriver and pull abreast, again about 800 yards in front of Fort Pemberton. Behind them is a scow with a 13-inch mortar. Watson Smith is worried about his ironclads, and he has lines strung from them back to the tinclads so that the big gunboats can be towed out of range if they are disabled. As soon as the ironclads pull aside one another, the Confederates open fire. The two bow guns of *Chillicothe* and three bow guns of *Baron de Kalb* return fire. This fight lasts two hours. *Chillicothe* fires 54 shells from her 11-inch guns before she withdraws from the fight. She has been hit another 38 times. Ten of the incoming rounds have banged into the port side of her turret; seven have gone through the wheelhouses; and the rest are scattered around the boat. The cotton bales on her decks are afire, but the fires are put out by a squad of black firemen. *Chillicothe*'s crew suffers six more wounded.

Baron de Kalb stays in position after *Chillicothe* withdraws, and systematically fires her guns at 15-minute intervals. The rifled 32-pounder in the fort has to stop firing late in the afternoon battle because of an ammunition shortage. But since there are no Union gunboats on the Yazoo River between the fortifications at Greenwood and at Snyder's Bluff above Vicksburg, that night a Confederate steamboat is able to complete its 97-mile journey up the Yazoo River from Yazoo City, bringing with it badly needed ammunition for the guns. *Baron de Kalb* doesn't withdraw until after dark, and she has been hit only six times. One solid bolt has penetrated the two-and-one-half-inch armor of her forward casemate and has lodged in the 24-inch laminated oak that backs the armor. Another bolt enters between two gun ports and cuts through at least six beams, spraying sharp splinters throughout the casemate. Three sailors are dead and three are wounded. During the fight the 13-inch mortar fired 49 shells, each one weighing 220 pounds, but no real damage was inflicted on the Rebels.

The attacks cease for the next two days, and this infuriates Wilson. He writes to Grant's chief of staff, John Rawlins, on March 15 that they are no nearer to Greenwood because the navy decided to honor the Sabbath. He tells Rawlins he has talked to all the naval officers and "tried to give them backbone," but he says that Watson Smith is not "the equal of Lord Nelson."

On Monday morning, March 16, the attack again gets under way. The two gunboats are low on shot and shell, so they plan to close rapidly on the fort and smother the Confederate gunners with grapeshot. Smith, still cautious, again attaches lines to the ironclads so that they can be towed out of harm's way if they are knocked out of action. If, on the other hand, the Confederate guns are silenced, General Ross has three infantry regiments on board three of the tinclads, ready to carry the fort by escalade.

Around 11:45 the two ironclads steam downriver for "close quarters and quick work," as the navy says. But as *Chillicothe* gets within 1,100 yards of the fort she is hit several times from the rifled 32-pounder and the newly emplaced 8-inch smoothbore gun. Within 15 minutes both of *Chillicothe's* gun port slides are bent so badly that they can't be operated, so her guns can't fire. Foster orders her to retire, and Commander Walker on *Baron de Kalb* decides discretion is the better part of valor, and follows suit. The attack is over.

On March 21, Ross is reinforced by the lead elements of Gen. Isaac Quinby's XVII Corps division. Quinby assumes command of the task force because Grant "has a great deal of confidence" in Quinby's judgment. But, on March 22, Grant writes McPherson to say that the tardiness of the expedition has given the Confederates time to fortify and that the only option open is for the expedition to withdraw. The withdrawal begins on the night of April 4, and by dawn of April 5, the expedition is heading upriver.

STEELE'S BAYOU EXPEDITION

While the Federal gunboats are attacking Fort Pemberton, Grant reads in a Vicksburg newspaper that the Confederates are fortifying Greenwood. He knows that General Ross's line of communication from Helena, through Yazoo Pass, and down the Coldwater and Tallahatchie Rivers to Greenwood is vulnerable. Grant later writes that he was "much exercised for the safety of Ross." He has a right to be concerned, for if the Confederates can sever the Federal supply line along one of the narrow waterways while attacking Ross's command with a powerful striking force, the entire Federal expeditionary command could be destroyed, including the gunboats and transports.

While Grant looks for ways to assist Ross, Admiral Porter works on another possible route. Porter has been studying his charts and obtaining local intelligence about the Mississippi Delta waterways, and after careful study, the admiral finds a local river pilot and heads up the Yazoo River on March 13. He wants to see if a Steele's Bayou route is feasible.

The Steele's Bayou route calls for entering the Yazoo River from its confluence with the Mississippi west of Vicksburg, and steaming to the mouth of Steele's Bayou at Johnson's plantation, well below the Confederate guns guarding the Yazoo. From there the route travels a winding course northward along Steele's Bayou for 30 miles by water to Black Bayou, then eastward for three miles along Black Bayou to its confluence with Deer Creek at Hill's plantation. From Hill's the tortuous course of Deer Creek is northward for 32 miles by water to its confluence with Rolling Fork Creek. The route then travels east, for a scant four miles, on Rolling Fork Creek to the Big Sunflower River. The Big Sunflower flows southeast to the Yazoo River, entering the Yazoo well above the Confederate cannon. After the boats are in the Yazoo, they can steam northeast to Fort Pemberton if necessary. If not, it is just ten miles by water up the Yazoo to the high ground at Satartia, Mississippi, where a good road leads south to Vicksburg.

Porter performs a personal reconnaissance up the Yazoo River and sees that the mouth of Steele's Bayou on the north side of the river is overgrown with overhanging trees and bushes. He boards a tug and his men chop away at the brush and trees with axes and cutlasses to clear a pass wide enough for three vessels abreast. He then steams up Steele's Bayou to the point where Black Bayou enters Steele's Bayou from the east. Porter romantically recalls the "discordant notes" of thousands of crows as his men disturb the silence of the forest. His men are taking soundings to measure water depth, singing out "quarter less three," and Porter becomes convinced that there is depth enough for his city-series ironclads, which were named for cities along the Ohio and upper Mississippi Rivers, to make the trip. He does see that Black Bayou is very narrow, but he figures that if the trees in the water are removed, his boats can be kedged—or pulled by lines attached to trees on the banks—around the sharp bends.

Admiral Porter advises Grant that he has found a route to get to Greenwood and behind Fort Pemberton, thus relieving Ross's expedition. Grant is intrigued by the idea. "Task Force Porter" steams ahead on the morning of March 14. The force consists of five of Eads's city-series ironclads—*Louisville, Cincinnati, Carondelet, Mound City,* and *Pittsburg*—as well as four tugs, each one towing a mortar scow with a 13-inch mortar.

On the morning of March 16, Grant orders Sherman to send a detachment of the XV Corps to support Porter's gunboats in the mission of maneuvering through the different waterways into the Yazoo River. Sherman, always skeptical, wants to see the Steele's Bayou route for himself, so as soon as he receives Grant's order to support Porter, he steams for the Yazoo River on the tug *Fern.* After

following the Steele's and Black Bayou routes, Sherman arrives at Hill's plantation, where he pulls alongside Porter's flagship, *General Price*, and invites Porter
to accompany him on his reconnaissance up Deer Creek. Porter gladly accepts,
and he and Sherman steam up Deer Creek aboard *Fern* for three miles before
returning. Late on the 16th, Sherman writes to Grant and says that he does not
believe the route is practical due to lack of dry ground for marching troops, and
because of the narrowness of Black Bayou and Deer Creek for transporting them
by water. Porter doesn't share Sherman's pessimism.

Porter casts off with his flotilla the next morning. He is optimistic because
Deer Creek is much wider than the narrow, tortuous Black Bayou, and the creek
is lined by natural levees with canebrakes and cultivated fields and gardens. It
looks like good water for the navy and favorable ground for the army. Porter figures that he has 32 miles of water to travel to Rolling Fork Creek, even though it
is only about 14 miles to the Rolling Fork as the crow flies.

By the next morning, though, Porter discovers that the channel of Deer Creek
is becoming much narrower and that it is choked with thousands of willows. The
willows get into the paddle wheels of the boats and the fleet can only move about
a mile an hour. Porter soon sees that the sky is black with burning cotton, as the
Confederates would rather burn the "white gold" than let the Federals confiscate
it. That means the presence of the fleet is now well known. Porter tries to push
harder, but the going gets even tougher as the willows get thicker and the creek
gets narrower. The fleet soon slows to a half mile an hour, traveling only about
ten miles that day. What's worse, during the night Porter learns that Confederates
are using impressed blacks to fell trees across Deer Creek to his front.

When the flotilla reaches a point within three miles of Rolling Fork on the
afternoon of March 19, Porter sees black coal smoke coming from the direction
of the confluence of Big Sunflower River and Little Sunflower River and receives
a report that Confederate troops are arriving by boat and are landing where Rolling Fork Creek meets the Big Sunflower River. Porter orders the skipper of the
lead ironclad *Carondelet,* Lt. John M. Murphy, to assemble 300 volunteers as
a landing party to race ahead and secure the confluence of Deer and Rolling
Fork Creeks until the fleet arrives. Murphy forges ahead with his men and two
12-pounder boat howitzers, and secures the confluence of the two creeks while
placing his guns on the largest of three Indian mounds that command the area.

Porter continues to inch his flotilla forward to Rolling Fork Creek. When
he gets to within one and a half miles of the confluence of the two creeks, he
writes a dispatch to Sherman, asking him to get his troops up fast. Porter says

he thinks a large Confederate force will be used to trap the fleet, and he needs land support.

Porter's instincts are correct. On March 17, Confederate Lt. Col. Sam Ferguson, from Charleston, South Carolina, a West Pointer from the class of '57 and a good soldier, was in camp with a squadron of cavalry and six guns 30 miles north of Rolling Fork on Deer Creek.

That night Ferguson gets word that five Yankee gunboats are on Deer Creek at Hill's plantation and are heading north to Rolling Fork. Ferguson reacts quickly and sends his cavalry south to Rolling Fork as fast as horseflesh can carry them. There they are to obstruct Deer Creek by felling timber. Ferguson then marches his infantry and artillery eastward for two miles to the Bogue Phalia River, where the task force boards the steamer *Sharp* and casts off for Rolling Fork.

Ferguson's men travel down the Bogue Phalia waterway for the 11-mile trip to the Big Sunflower River and steam south for 38 miles, where they arrive at the mouth of Rolling Fork Creek at 4 p.m. on March 19. The Confederates are now only 4½ miles southeast of Union Navy Lieutenant Murphy's new bastion on the Indian mound.

The next day Colonel Ferguson moves three 10-pounder Parrott rifles to within a mile of Deer Creek and opens fire. The primary target is Murphy's two boat howitzers on the Indian mound, and the 300-man Union work party is quickly driven back to the boats. Since his big boat guns are below the level of the creek bank, Porter uses his 13-inch mortars to successfully check the Confederate attacks, but the admiral has learned from Murphy's men that the Confederates are landing a large force of infantry at the mouth of Rolling Fork Creek. Things are going from bad to worse for Porter's sailors.

Ferguson now learns that Confederate Gen. Winfield Scott Featherston is close behind with reinforcements—two infantry regiments and two pieces of artillery. When Featherston arrives, Ferguson recommends an immediate attack, and Featherston concurs. Featherston rushes his Mississippians forward, and by 5 p.m. dispositions are made. The Confederate battle plan is simple. The artillery will open the fight and draw the fire of the gunboat gun crews while the two Mississippi regiments charge from the woods and, reminiscent of a pirate movie, board and capture the gunboats.

An hour later, eight Confederate cannon open fire at two locations—from north of Deer Creek and from the Widow Watson's plantation east of the creek. Murphy's men, who have returned to the Indian mound, are caught in a deadly crossfire and are compelled to again retreat to the gunboats. Porter returns fire and a spirited artillery duel lasts until dark, but, inexplicably, Featherston's two Mississippi infantry regiments don't attack. Featherston, unlike his subordinate Ferguson, doesn't have the stomach for fighting Union ironclads.

Porter, aboard *Carondelet,* knows that he is in an embarrassing situation. To make matters worse, during the night he receives three scraps of bad news. First, he learns that the Confederates are obstructing Deer Creek to his rear, trying to trap his flotilla. Second, he learns that the Confederates are planning to send 5,000 reinforcements. Third, he learns from Sherman that the army is having difficulties clearing Black Bayou and that movement is very slow, so Porter should not expect too much help from Sherman. This is all that Porter needs to make a decision. He decides it's time to beat a hasty retreat.

Knowing that he has Confederates between him and the Federal infantry, Porter scribbles a distress note to Sherman on tissue paper during the night of March 20, and rolls it up in a tobacco leaf. Porter asks Sherman to "Hurry up, for Heaven's sake." He then adds that he never knew how helpless an ironclad on a narrow creek could be without the army for support.

Porter gives the note to a black man to deliver to Sherman. The man describes himself to Porter as "the county telegraph," and he promises to take the note to Sherman if Porter will pay him fifty cents in advance. According to Porter, the man hides the note in his hair and disappears into the night.

Porter then prepares for the worst. The twin rudders on the gunboats are unshipped and the vessels are allowed to drift downstream, bouncing off the trees along the creek banks. Porter writes general orders during the night of March 20 providing instructions on how the crews will repel Rebel attempts to board the boats and on how the boats will be destroyed if they're successfully boarded. Clearly, the situation is desperate.

Without rudders Porter's gunboats drift southward past the Indian mounds near Rolling Fork on the night of March 20. They are traveling about two miles an hour with a four-knot current. Unfortunately, in the darkness the ironclad *Louisville,* formerly the trail gunboat and now the lead, accidentally rams and sinks a coal barge, effectively blocking the exodus of the flotilla at a point only two and three-quarters miles south of Rolling Fork.

While Porter withdraws in the darkness, the Confederates move forward and occupy the large Indian mound, placing several rifled cannon on it, and at 6 a.m. on March 21 they open fire. *Carondelet* and *Cincinnati,* the two lead gunboats, are the targets, but the Confederates have shell, not solid shot, and 10-pounder exploding shell is ineffective against 2½ inches of armor plate. The striking shells make a lot of noise but cause no real damage. Within a half hour the Confederate artillery fire ceases—the guns' ammunition is exhausted.

Ferguson's men then push forward their attack, expecting at any moment to hear the guns of Featherston's boarding parties. But, to Colonel Ferguson's dismay and disgust, after three hours of fighting he sees that General Featherston's men are farther upstream than they were the previous day, and are withdrawing from the creek bank, across the fields into the woods. Ever the fighter, Ferguson continues to scrap until dark, with or without Featherston's assistance.

Around 3 p.m. Porter's sailors happily learn from local blacks that Federal infantry is fast approaching. Porter's "tobacco leaf" message reached Sherman about 12 hours earlier, and he is on his way. Sherman has Col. Giles Smith in the lead, and at 4 p.m. the head of Smith's Federal column arrives, much to the relief of Porter's sailors.

Smith discovers the fleet in dire circumstances. It is blocked by the sunken coal barge to its rear and by felled trees to its front. The fleet is also surrounded by sharpshooters, ready to gun down any sailor who appears upon deck. Work parties trying to clear the obstructions are suffering from sniper fire, and work has come to a halt. Fortunately for the Federals, the big guns on the bows of the boats are keeping the Confederates from boarding.

A relieved Porter places Smith in charge of a 150-man landing party and the two boat howitzers, with orders to mop up the sharpshooters. Other soldiers of Smith's command head south on Deer Creek to prevent the placing of additional obstacles to the fleet.

To establish an outpost during the night of March 21, Smith sends three companies of the Sixth and Eighth Missouri on a five-mile march south. At modern Cary, Mississippi, they establish an observation post on an Indian mound at a sharp bend in Deer Creek so that they can guard the creek as well as the southern flank of the Federal forces.

By daylight on March 22, the Federals have finally cleared the sunken coal barge out of the way, and the fleet continues to drift downstream for about two miles to Egremont Plantation, located on a sharp bend of the creek. At Egremont, the fleet confronts a monstrous jackstraw log barricade across Deer Creek.

Soon gunfire is heard from the south, and Smith is fearful that his southern outpost on the Indian mound at Cary is being cut off and attacked. *Louisville* attempts to ram her way through the logjam to go to the assistance of the imperiled outpost, but cannot break though the log barricade. In desperation, Smith orders Maj. Dennis Kirby to take four companies of the Sixth Missouri Infantry and cut his way through two Confederate regiments to go to the aid of their fellow Missourians on the Indian mound.

As Kirby's men follow their orders, General Featherston's two Mississippi regiments on the east side of Deer Creek are astonished to see four companies of Union troops coming directly at them. While their attention is focused on this forlorn-hope attack, small-arms fire erupts to Featherston's rear, and his men are surprised to see Sherman's column approaching from the south. With the Federal fleet and Giles Smith's soldiers to their front, the Federal column to their rear, and Deer Creek to their left, the Mississippians skedaddle to their right, into the woods to the east of the fields bordering Deer Creek.

As Featherston's Confederates withdraw and Sherman's men march to the trapped gunboats, the Union sailors emerge from their iron turtle shells and "cheer most vociferously" as the general rides by. Sherman soon finds Porter on the deck of *Carondelet* with a shield of quarter-inch iron plate to protect him from small-arms fire. Porter is grateful for the relief, later saying that he did not know when he felt more pleased to see Sherman.

Sherman asked Porter what were his plans, and Porter said that it was time to give up on this expedition. The leading elements of Sherman's column reach Hill's plantation at 11 a.m. on March 24, and the last gunboat, *Carondelet,* arrives after dark the same day. Porter later wrote how happy he was to get out of that ditch.

Early on March 26 a dispatch boat from Grant heaves to at Hill's plantation and delivers to Sherman a message from Grant ordering him to return with the fleet to Young's Point. The bayou expeditions are over.

As winter gives way to spring, Grant has gone on the offensive and has been unsuccessful. Yet, he has remained on the move, trying to make something happen, and this has been noticed by President Lincoln, who, when once asked to get rid of Grant, said, "I can't spare this man; he fights."

Still, with Grant's failures comes the criticism of second-guessers, and on March 28 one of Grant's own generals, Gen. Cadwallader Washburn, brother of Elihu Washburne, Grant's sponsor in Congress, writes, "All Grant's schemes have failed. He is frittering away time and strength to no purpose. The truth must be told even if it hurts. You cannot make a silk purse out of a sow's ear."

While Grant and Porter are out in the rivers and bayous of the West, Joe Hooker is busy reorganizing the Army of the Potomac in the East. A priority is to restore the morale of the army by improving the diet and sanitary conditions of the soldiers, improving the quartermaster system and the hospitals, and by instituting an improved furlough system. Hooker reorganizes the army by doing away with Burnsides's grand divisions and reverts to the corps system. He combines the Federal cavalry into one corps, which is the first step in making the cavalry of the Army of the Potomac an effective fighting machine. This step will be very important during the Gettysburg Campaign.

Hooker establishes a new intelligence agency known as the Bureau of Military Information. His choice of Col. George H. Sharpe as its chief is inspired. Sharpe has a mind like a steel trap. He also has strong analytical skills, and he quickly collects intelligence from all sources. Soon he is providing Hooker with detailed and accurate information on General Lee's army. Sharpe expertly ferrets out the names of leaders and the number and size of units and other related information.

On March 21, Hooker also introduces a new wrinkle that is initially designed to identify stragglers and skulkers: new distinctive badges for each of the army corps. This way the offending soldier's unit can be identified. But soon the badges become popular with both officers and men. They create a sense of identity—an esprit de corps.

According to General Couch, who is second in command under Joe Hooker, because of the changes to the Army of the Potomac, the army had gone from the "lowest depression to that of a healthy fighting state" by the end of March.

Joe Hooker is now going to do something that some may think is blasphemous, especially if one happens to be the deeply religious Oliver O. Howard. Hooker knows that the condition of the Army of the Potomac has greatly improved, so he boasts, "I have the finest army on the planet. I have the finest army the sun ever shone on. If the enemy does not run, God help them. May God have mercy on General Lee, for I will have none."

Robert E. Lee has a fine army, too, quite possibly the finest on Earth, and he is not about to see that army run from the likes of Joe Hooker. He is also under no illusion that the war is almost over, even though he wrote his wife at Christmas with the prayer that "better thoughts may fill the hearts of our enemies and turn them to peace."

On January 16, 1863, Lee goes to Richmond, where he is told "gold had advanced to 200 in New York; that the war was over and peace would be announced in 60 days." Yet, Lee is a realist, and on February 6 he writes to Gen. John D. Imboden: "The enemy will make every effort to crush us between this and June, and it will require all our strength to resist him." On February 12, Lee writes to his son, Custis, who is Jefferson Davis's aide: "Our salvation will depend upon the next four months." His words are prophetic.

Robert E. Lee's Army of Northern Virginia is a formidable fighting machine. In the seven months since Lee has been in command he has changed the complexion of the war. His army has fought 11 battles in Virginia and Maryland and inflicted almost 71,000 enemy casualties while suffering just over 48,000. His army has captured nearly 75,000 small arms while losing only 6,000, and he now owns 155 Union cannon while losing only eight.

Lee has also purged his army of weak leaders and cumbersome division organizations. Fifteen of the brigadier generals that he inherited at the Battle of Seven Pines are now gone; a few were killed in action, but the incompetents and the politician-generals have been quietly sent to other assignments. Lee now has two well-commanded corps under Gen. Stonewall Jackson and Gen. James Longstreet, Lee's Old War Horse. Lee seems to have the perfect military combination in these two men.

Jackson, with his offensive mindset, is Lee's Judas Maccabeus—his hammer— whose philosophy is to "move swiftly, strike vigorously, and secure all fruits of victory." Longstreet, with his defensive mindset, is Lee's Jomini—his anvil— and believes in Napoleon's advice to Marmont, "Select your ground, and make the enemy attack you."

Lee knows for sure that some Federal mischief is in the making when, on February 14, a fleet of Federal transports, loaded with the Union IX Corps, steams down the Potomac, presumably to move south of the James River, and from there to Richmond. To counter this move, the next day Lee orders Gen. George Pickett's division of Longstreet's I Corps to Richmond. As Lee learns more, he orders Longstreet to send Gen. John Bell Hood's division to Richmond.

Finally, Lee orders Longstreet to Richmond to command Pickett's and Hood's divisions, and on February 19 Longstreet and his staff board a train south. This leaves two of Longstreet's divisions, those of Lafayette McLaws and Richard Anderson, to work alongside Jackson's four divisions on fortifying a 25-mile-long line south of the Rappahannock from Banks's Ford to Port Royal, Virginia.

While in Richmond, Longstreet meets with Secretary of War James Seddon for four days to discuss the disposition of his troops, and Seddon telegraphs Lee that "General Longstreet is here, and under his able guidance of such troops no one entertains a doubt as to the entire safety of the capital."

Longstreet establishes his headquarters 20 miles south of Richmond at Petersburg. On February 26, he is appointed commander of the Department of Virginia and North Carolina, an area from Richmond, Virginia, to Wilmington, North Carolina, giving him command of not only Pickett's and Hood's divisions, but also the troops of Gen. D. H. Hill, Gen. Samuel G. French, and Gen. Chase Whiting—43,000 troops total. Longstreet's instructions from Richmond are to protect the capital city and the approaches to the city from the south and east, so he posts his troops near the Blackwater River, 40 miles south and east of Petersburg to keep an eye on the Federals at Suffolk and Newport News.

The winter months in Fredericksburg are hard on Lee's army as rations, forage, and supplies are in short supply. So in March, Secretary Seddon puts Longstreet to work gathering grain and meat in the counties of southeastern Virginia and in northeastern North Carolina. But Longstreet is warned that he must be prepared to send Hood's and Pickett's divisions back to Fredericksburg if the Federals attempt to threaten Lee's army and Richmond from the north. This means that the two divisions cannot move far from the railroad, because they will be needed quickly.

On March 19, Longstreet, clearly enjoying his independent command, writes to Lee: "I know that it is the habit with individuals in all armies to represent their own positions as the most important ones, and it may be that this feeling is operating with me, but . . . it seems to me to be a matter of prime necessity with us to keep the enemy out of North Carolina in order that we may draw out all the supplies there, and if we give ground at all it would be better to do so from the Rappahannock."

On March 28, Lee learns that the Federal IX Corps has been withdrawn from the Norfolk area by boat and is traveling westward by rail to Ohio, chiefly to protect the Louisville and Nashville Railroad that is Rosecrans's line of communications to Murfreesboro. Because the arrival of the IX Corps at the Norfolk–Newport News area had been a trigger for sending Longstreet and his two divisions south, that begs the question: Where will Longstreet's two elite divisions be needed the most? It's a tough choice. Does Lee call them back to the Rappahannock, or does he allow Longstreet to continue his commissary campaign and gather the much needed provisions?

On March 30, Robert E. Lee, for the first time during the war—in fact, for the first time since 1849—falls ill with a serious throat infection and with pains in his chest, which might be the symptoms of an inflammation of the pericardium or possibly even angina. Uncharacteristically, Lee dodges the decision of the Rappahannock versus the commissary. He sends a message to Longstreet: "I leave the whole matter to your own good judgment."

WAR HAS RESPONSIBILITIES

March 31–April 30, 1863

"The great object of your line now is the opening of the Mississippi River, and everything else must tend to that purpose. The eyes and the hopes of the whole country are now directed toward your army. In my opinion, the opening of the Mississippi River will be to us of more advantage than the capture of forty Richmonds."

Henry W. Halleck to Gen. Ulysses S. Grant
March 20, 1863

GRANT, THOUGH DISAPPOINTED IN THE FAILURE OF HIS BAYOU EXPEDITIONS, is not about to throw in the towel. Spring is coming and the time is almost right for an offensive.

> *Grant later wrote, "I had had in contemplation the whole winter the movement by land to a point below Vicksburg from which to operate. . . . This could not be undertaken until the waters receded."*

All this time Grant has been looking hard at his enemy's railroad line of communications. He learned a valuable lesson when John Pemberton sent Earl Van Dorn to destroy the Union forward supply depot at Holly Springs in December, and it will soon be time for payback. As early as February 13, Grant sent a message to Gen. Stephen A. Hurlbut in Memphis, suggesting a raid on Pemberton's railroads. Hurlbut then began preparation for a cavalry raid to strike the Southern Railroad of Mississippi, Pemberton's line of communication with the East.

> *On March 9, Grant sends a reminder to Hurlbut, stating, "The date when the expedition should start will depend on movements here. You will be informed of the exact time for them to start."*

Grant is now looking south for a land movement. Below Milliken's Bend and west of Young's Point, the land in Louisiana is low, level, and scarred by a chain of meandering waterways—remnants of thousands of years of the Mississippi River's wandering. Grant has been waiting for spring, when the Mississippi's waters subside and the bayous begin to drain, so that he can march southward.

New Carthage, a village 17 miles south of Milliken's Bend on the west side of the Mississippi River, is Grant's choice for a point of embarkation. New Carthage is below the Warrenton casemate south of Vicksburg, and is also 32 miles by river above the guns of Grand Gulf. It seems to be the perfect place to stage an expeditionary force to cross the Mississippi; that is, if Porter's gunboats and the army transports can force a passage past the Vicksburg batteries. At New Carthage, Grant will have the option of moving by boat upriver to capture Warrenton or downriver to storm Grand Gulf.

On March 29, Grant orders Gen. John McClernand's XIII Corps to march from Milliken's Bend, Grant's major supply depot, to New Carthage, which will hopefully become the new forward supply depot. McPherson's XVII Corps will fall in behind McClernand's XIII Corps, and Sherman's XV Corps will bring up the rear. McClernand issues the necessary marching orders, and on March 31 his vanguard marches south.

On April 2, Halleck sends a message, advising Grant, in true Jominian fashion for which Halleck is famous, to concentrate his forces before he strikes any blow. "What is most desired is that your forces and those of General Banks should be brought into cooperation as soon as possible. If he cannot get up to cooperate with you on Vicksburg, cannot you get troops down to help him on Port Hudson, or at least, can you not destroy Grand Gulf before it becomes too strong?"

That same day, Grant advises Porter that he is "fully determined upon operating from New Carthage either by the way of Grand Gulf or Warrenton." This decision is controversial in Grant's headquarters. Adam Badeau, an early Grant biographer, wrote: "When the idea became known to those in [Grant's] intimacy, to his staff, and to his corps commanders, it seemed to them full of danger. . . . Those who have since acquired reputations of the most brilliant character strove to divert their chief from what they considered this fatal error. Sherman, McPherson, Logan, Wilson, all opposed— all of course within the proper limits of soldierly subordination, but with all energy."

Lt. Col. Harry Wilson, who has returned from the Yazoo Pass Expedition, is on Grant's staff. He remembered that Grant "was counseled to wait for the dry season, and in the meantime to send a part of his army to help Rosecrans overwhelm Bragg. Sherman advised him to return at once to northern Mississippi, and renew the overland campaign; McPherson and Steele rather favored the same plan."

Despite the doubts of his subordinates, Grant intends to stay the course. Though the march southward begins on March 31, on April 4, Grant, having received Halleck's message instructing him to concentrate his forces, sends a reassuring message to his very cautious boss: "This is the only move I now see as practicable, and hope it will meet with your approval. I will keep my army together and see to it that I am not cut off from my supplies or beat in any other way than a fair fight." Grant tells Halleck exactly what he knows a good disciple of Jomini—and Halleck taught Jomini at West Point—would want to hear. Grant assures Halleck that he will concentrate his forces and protect his line of communications.

When Grant marches his men south through Louisiana, he would like one to believe that his army walked through the swamps with the water up to their crotches, or up to their navels, or up to their necks. They don't. The Mississippi is an alluvial river, and through the eons of time the river has moved back and forth from east of the bluffs of Vicksburg to west and beyond Monroe, Louisiana, all the time building up natural levees along the old channels. The land along these natural levees is higher than the swamps, and it's heavily cultivated, containing some of the garden spots of Louisiana. Grant's men march along this elevated ground, albeit only about 12 feet in elevation, but not in the swamps.

Grant tells Sherman his plan in a small house near the levee at Young's Point. Behind a closed door Sherman says that he believes that Grant is putting himself in a position the enemy would be glad to maneuver a year to get him in. He tells Grant that he should take the army back to Memphis and use it as his base. From Memphis, Sherman says, they should move down the railroad to Grenada. But for Grant, going back to Memphis is not an option. If the army retreats, it will discourage the people of the North so much that a base won't be needed.

As Grant recalled in his memoirs: "The problem for us was to move forward to a decisive victory, or our cause was lost. No progress was being made in any other field, and we had to go on."

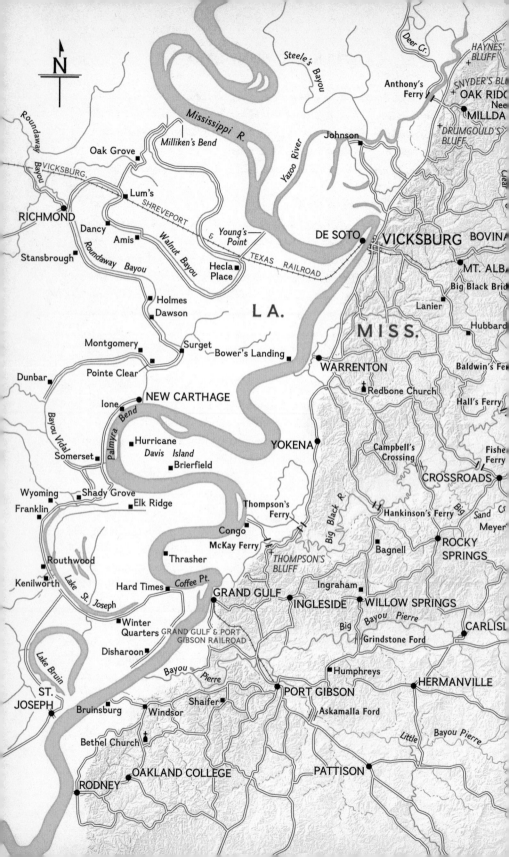

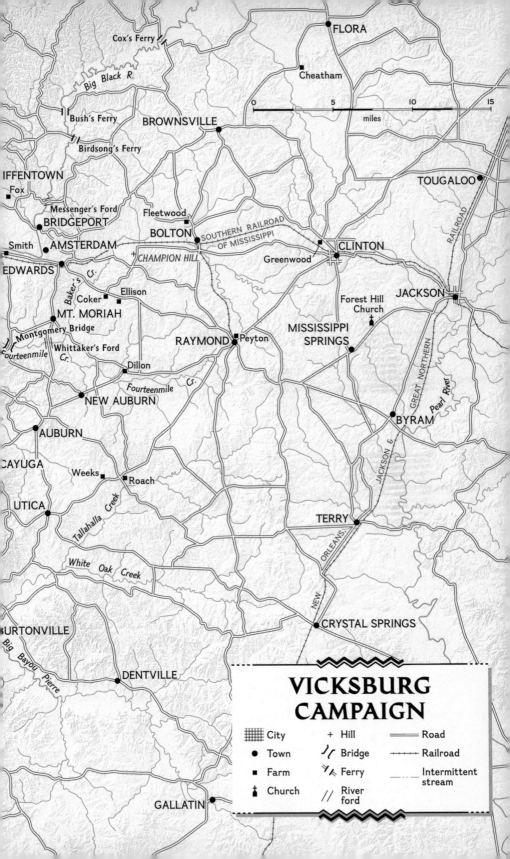

FLORA

Cox's Ferry

Big Black R.

Cheatham

0   5   10   15
miles

Bush's Ferry

Birdsong's Ferry

BROWNSVILLE

IFFENTOWN

Fox

TOUGALOO

Messenger's Ford

Fleetwood

BRIDGEPORT

BOLTON

SOUTHERN RAILROAD
OF MISSISSIPPI

CLINTON

Smith

AMSTERDAM

Greenwood

CHAMPION HILL

EDWARDS

JACKSON

Baker's Cr.

Coker

Ellison

Forest Hill
Church

MT. MORIAH

Montgomery Bridge

RAYMOND

Peyton

MISSISSIPPI
SPRINGS

Fourteenmile

Whittaker's Ford
Cr.

Dillon

GREAT NORTHERN

Pearl River

NEW AUBURN

Fourteenmile Cr.

BYRAM

AUBURN

CAYUGA

Weeks

Roach

JACKSON &

UTICA

Tallahalla Creek

TERRY

White Oak Creek

NEW ORLEANS

URTONVILLE

Big Bayou Pierre

CRYSTAL SPRINGS

DENTVILLE

VICKSBURG
CAMPAIGN

▦ City   + Hill   ═══ Road

● Town   )(Bridge   +++ Railroad

■ Farm   ⚓ Ferry   ─·─· Intermittent
                                stream

⛪ Church   // River
                 ford

GALLATIN

Sherman is unconvinced. After Grant issues the order to move to New Carthage, Sherman sends a letter to Lt. Col. John Rawlins, Grant's chief of staff, saying that Grant should hold a council of war to ask his corps commanders what to do. Years later, in his memoirs, Sherman penned that he wrote this letter after one of the sessions at Grant's headquarters, where he said the officers "openly talked about such things." He denied that it was any kind of a protest, and Grant, in his later writings and interviews dismisses the letter as a note from one friend to another. But Sherman has already told Grant that he thought the move would be a mistake, and when Grant orders it despite Sherman's advice, Sherman then puts his concerns in writing. In the military this is known as a CYA (cover your ass) letter, but Grant ignores it.

Sixteen years later, Grant commented on his decision: "War has responsibilities that are either fatal to a commander's position or very successful."

When Grant issues the marching order to McClernand, he writes to Porter asking if he can get "one or two vessels" past the batteries of Vicksburg and downriver to New Carthage.

Grant writes to Porter: "Without the aid of gunboats it will hardly be worth the while to send troops to New Carthage." Porter replies the same day that he is ready to cooperate in the move, but he reminds Grant, "When these gunboats once go below, we give up all hopes of ever getting them up again."

Porter has concerns based on the power of the gunboat engines. The Eads ironclads have a maximum sustained speed of six knots, and the current of the Mississippi near the west bank flows at four knots. At the combined speed of ten knots the boats will be under the Vicksburg guns for 20 minutes. But, if the gunboats have to travel back upstream, their speed will be reduced to two knots, placing them under fire for 90 minutes. Even the sturdy Eads ironclads, Porter knows, can't take that kind of pounding, and now Porter has placed this caveat in writing. Porter, like Sherman, has a CYA letter on file. Still, Grant is willing to accept the risk.

While McClernand moves south, Grant has Sherman send a diversionary raid north to Greenville in the Mississippi Delta. This raid is designed to convince the Confederates that the Yanks are again attempting to flank Vicksburg from the north. On April 2, Gen. Frederick Steele's division leaves its camps at

Young's Point aboard a fleet of transports, and two days later his men go ashore at Greenville. By April 8 they have penetrated southward along the banks of Deer Creek to within 20 miles of Rolling Fork.

The Confederates take the bait. Gen. Carter Stevenson, Pemberton's commander in Vicksburg, sends Gen. Stephen D. Lee's reinforced brigade of infantry to Rolling Fork to oppose Steele's expedition, and Gen. William W. Loring, commander at Fort Pemberton in Greenwood, rushes Gen. John C. Moore's brigade to assist. Grant now has Pemberton looking north in Mississippi while McClernand's men are marching south in Louisiana.

After the failure of Grant's bayou expeditions, Pemberton is pleased with himself, but he now begins to read the tea leaves the wrong way. When he learns on April 2 from General Stevenson in Vicksburg that large numbers of Federal boats loaded to the gunwales with troops are going up the Mississippi River, he concludes that Grant must be withdrawing before the summer miasmas set in.

For the movement south, Grant's choice of McClernand to lead the march is not popular with his other senior officers, but McClernand, unlike Sherman and McPherson, believes in Grant's idea of marching south for a crossing of the Mississippi. Grant, although he and McClernand don't like each other, wisely chooses the politician-general to lead the way.

The tip of McClernand's spear is Col. Thomas W. Bennett's 69th Indiana Infantry of Gen. Peter J. Osterhaus's division. Osterhaus's men have to build bridges and corduroy roads along the way, so they have with them Capt. William F. Patterson's Kentucky Company of Engineers and Mechanics. They also have two companies of the Second Illinois Cavalry and a detachment of the Sixth Missouri Cavalry. The cavalry has two mountain howitzers—which are light in weight but pack a good punch. This task force is about 1,000 men, and after they blaze the way, McClernand's 17,000-man corps follows.

Osterhaus's men move quickly, and by April 4 they are at Pointe Clear Plantation, two miles north of New Carthage, where Roundaway Bayou debouches into Bayou Vidal. But here the bottom seems to fall out of Grant's plan, because at this point McClernand sees that everything is flooded between Pointe Clear and New Carthage. Thus, the planned staging area around New Carthage is underwater, and it looks like Sherman was right.

Downriver, at the newly built earthen fortifications of Grand Gulf, an aggressive Gen. John Bowen is worried about what Grant is doing. He gets his hands on two small steamers, *Hine* and *Charm,* and quickly sends two regiments of Col. Frank Cockrell's Missourians from Grand Gulf across the Mississippi River to

Louisiana to see what the Yanks are up to. Cockrell's men make contact with the head of the Union column and soon report the Federal march south to Bowen. The general burns up the telegraph lines with warnings to Pemberton in Jackson.

On April 4 in Tennessee General Rosecrans telegraphs his own very limited plan of attack to General Halleck. Rosecrans, like Grant, wishes to sever his enemy's line of communication, and General Bragg's is the Western and Atlantic Railroad, which runs from Chattanooga to Atlanta. Rosecrans proposes to send 1,500 horse soldiers to Eastport, Mississippi, on the Tennessee River, where the Mississippi, Alabama, and Tennessee borders coincide. There the raiders will need to be reinforced by soldiers from General Hurlbut's XVI Corps of Grant's Army of the Tennessee. The combined force will then head east into Alabama, and from there sweep across northern Alabama into Georgia to cut the Western and Atlantic Railroad.

A usually cautious Halleck approves Rosecrans's risky plan, probably just to see some action from that quarter. Rosecrans then requests assistance from Gen. Grenville Dodge, who is a subordinate of Hurlbut and is stationed at Corinth. Dodge properly refers the matter to Hurlbut in Memphis, who promptly approves the plan and instructs Dodge to take "force enough to do it thoroughly." Hurlbut knows that Grant is planning the same thing in Mississippi, so he feels sure that his boss will sustain this decision. He is right.

Meanwhile, Rosecrans continues to request reinforcements for his Army of the Cumberland and to strengthen his massive, fortified supply depot in Murfreesboro. General Halleck, upon receipt of another request for large guns for Fortress Rosecrans, is concerned that Rosecrans is not thinking offensively. He tries to motivate Rosecrans to move.

Halleck telegraphs Rosecrans on April 9, saying, "If you fortify too many places you will destroy the mobility of your forces." The next day Secretary of the Treasury Salmon P. Chase, former Governor of Ohio and a friend of Rosecrans, writes to the general: "The country is longing for . . . some victory with results. . . . I contemplate little of importance achieved since your success at Murfreesboro."

But Rosecrans ignores the advice. Old Rosy is not ready to move, and he will miss the brass ring because of his indolence.

About the same time that McClernand finds nothing but water to his front in Louisiana, Abraham Lincoln is on a journey of his own into Virginia. On Sunday, April 5, 1863, the President visits the Army of the Potomac, arriving by special train at Falmouth, Virginia, at noon. During his six-day stay, Lincoln visits disabled soldiers, receives officers in his tent, and attends various social functions. Lincoln is pleasantly surprised at the condition and morale of the army.

The President meets with General Hooker and General Couch, Hooker's second in command. Hooker is concerned about intelligence leaks and he will not reveal his plans, even to Lincoln.

Lincoln remains nonplussed and offers a piece of advice to the generals: "I want to impress upon you two gentlemen: in your next fight, put in all of your men."

During the conference Hooker confidently talks about what he will do when he gets to Richmond. This braggadocio causes Lincoln to worry about a general who, like the press and the public, seems to be focused on capturing Richmond and not on destroying Robert E. Lee's army.

As for Hooker's actually getting to Richmond, the President remarks to his secretary, "The hen is the wisest of all the animal creation because she never cackles until the egg has been laid."

While Lincoln visits with his generals, just across the Rappahannock River from Falmouth is a downsized Army of Northern Virginia—downsized due to the absence of Longstreet's two divisions. Robert E. Lee is there, and though he has been sick for a week, he is feeling better.

On April 6, Lee receives a message from Secretary Seddon, asking if it would be possible to send part of Longstreet's command to Tennessee to reinforce Bragg. Lee replies that he will, of course, do as he is ordered, but that Longstreet's mission of gathering supplies is of vital importance. He also states that, if the Army of the Potomac remains on the defensive, he would like to have Longstreet rejoin him and again invade Maryland. This, of course, would be impossible if Longstreet's troops were sent to Tennessee. Seddon defers to Lee's judgment, and Lee makes plans for an offensive on May 1, barring any Federal initiative.

Lee has a valid argument about Longstreet's mission to gather provisions, because the army still has severe shortages of rations and forage. His men have been on half rations for weeks, and scurvy has broken out in the ranks. He has to depend on Longstreet to forage the necessary foodstuffs in southeast Virginia and northeast North Carolina, despite the risk of Hooker going on the offensive. To that end, with a supply expedition as the main objective, Longstreet leaves Petersburg and heads southeast toward Suffolk, Virginia, 20 miles from Norfolk.

In Mississippi, on April 6, John Pemberton is convinced that Grant is withdrawing, and Bowen's warning of Grant's southward march falls on deaf ears. After all, there is a mass Yankee exodus to the north in progress. Steele's Federal troops have been seen going north on the Mississippi on April 2 and 3, and troops have been seen going north on the Tallahatchie on April 5 as they withdrew from in front of Fort Pemberton. These movements cause Pemberton to misread Grant's southward march as a diversion. Grant's real intent, Pemberton believes, is to send troops to Tennessee to reinforce Rosecrans's Army of the Cumberland.

McClernand's column in Louisiana, aside from being seen by Colonel Cockrell's men out of Grand Gulf, is also being observed by Maj. Isaac Harrison's 15th Louisiana Cavalry Battalion of Gen. E. Kirby Smith's Trans-Mississippi Department. Kirby Smith has replaced the elderly, deaf, and unhappy Theophilus Holmes in February. Major Harrison has been reporting the Federal movement to Smith and has wisely been sending copies of his reports to Bowen at Grand Gulf. Bowen then sends those reports by telegraph to Pemberton in Jackson, who forwards them to Richmond. So, as early as April 7, Jefferson Davis knows of the Yankee move southward from Milliken's Bend.

Grant, during this move south, has to contend with a lot of distractions, ranging from disbelief of subordinates to high water. And, it seems that commanders, when they are undertaking something risky, often have the additional burden of intrusion from higher headquarters. Grant is no exception.

Arriving at Milliken's Bend on April 6 is Assistant Secretary of War Charles A. Dana, who was recently the number two man at Horace Greeley's *New York Tribune*. Dana was canned by Greeley over politics in the spring of the previous year, and now he has gone west. Dana is one of the founders of the Republican Party, so he has some pull in Washington, and Secretary of War Stanton offers him a job to settle some claims in Cairo. Dana does that work and moves on to other things, but a year later he's back on Stanton's payroll and shows up at Milliken's Bend as Lincoln's "eyes at the front."

What is Dana's mission? Officially, it's to investigate the army's pay service, but his true mission is to send reports on Grant back to Washington. After all, Grant is way out in the West—out of sight, so to speak—and his bayou expeditions have failed. Grant has his detractors, and soon the press decides that he is a good target. There are printed accusations that Grant is lazy, incompetent, a drunkard, and "a jackass in the original package." Treasury Secretary Salmon P. Chase advises President Lincoln to take Grant's men and send them to Rosecrans. Abraham Lincoln has never met Ulysses Grant, and not knowing the man, he needs to cover his bases just in case the drinking rumors happen to be true. That's where Dana enters the picture.

Grant knows Dana's real purpose, yet he greets him warmly and makes friends with him. Grant did the same thing back in early 1862 when Halleck sent James McPherson to serve on Grant's staff and report on Grant's drinking. Wisely, Grant turned McPherson from a spy into a protégé. So, once again in 1863, Grant tells his skeptical chief of staff, John Rawlins, to take good care of Dana. By 3 p.m. on the day he arrives, Dana has been fully briefed, and he feels important. He sends back glowing reports on Grant to Washington. That's making lemonade out of lemons.

In Virginia, Longstreet marches toward Suffolk on April 8. He assures Lee, "I do not propose to do anything more than draw out the supplies from that country, unless something very favorable should offer." The phrase "unless something very favorable should offer" portends a bit more than gathering provisions. Aside from foraging the countryside for supplies, Longstreet is also looking for a taste of military glory by capturing the Suffolk garrison.

But Suffolk is well fortified, with the Nansemond River protecting the western flank and the Great Dismal Swamp on the eastern flank. To the north are two naval flotillas. In this venture, Longstreet could have used well the advice of the Chinese general Sun Tzu: "The highest realization of warfare is to attack the enemy's plans, . . . and the lowest is to attack their fortified cities."

In Tennessee, Rosecrans continues to refuse to move southeastward from his Murfreesboro stronghold. Rosecrans later wrote: "The winter rains made the country impassable for large military operations. . . . Meanwhile, we hardened our cavalry, drilled our infantry, fortified Nashville and Murfreesboro for secondary depots, and arranged for our plans for the coming campaign upon the opening of the roads, which were expected to be good by May 1, 1863."

Rosecrans reports to Washington that his army does not have to attack, it is serving its purpose by preventing Bragg from sending reinforcements to Mississippi to oppose Grant in the campaign against Vicksburg. Rosecrans describes Bragg's actions: "Holding this army [the Army of the Cumberland] in check . . . is the most important service Bragg can render to his cause. . . . In fact, he is now holding us here by his nose, which he has inserted between our teeth for that purpose. We shall keep our teeth closed on his nose by our attitude, until we are assured that Vicksburg is within three weeks of its fall."

While Rosecrans remains motionless and "keeps his teeth closed on Bragg's nose," on April 10 he finally initiates his cavalry raid against Bragg's railroad line of communications. He places Col. Abel Streight in command of the raid, and Streight leaves Nashville for Fort Henry.

On April 11, in Virginia, Longstreet decides, not surprisingly, that he will move to capture Suffolk. He has also sent two spies out to gather information on the road network to the southeast and on the garrison at Suffolk. One of these spies is a man named Henry Thomas Harrison.

Longstreet later wrote that Harrison "proved to be an active, intelligent, enterprising scout, and was retained in service. The accounts that we gained indicated that Suffolk could be turned and captured with little loss."

But, to capture Suffolk, Longstreet will need the help of the Confederate Navy, because of the Union gunboats that can come to the garrison's aid via the Nansemond River. He sends his request to Richmond for the support of C.S.S. *Richmond,* an ironclad, to block the mouth of the Nansemond River so that Federal gunboats cannot come to the aid of the Federal garrison in Suffolk.

At the same time, Joe Hooker, with his reorganization complete, decides to go on the offensive, beating Lee to the punch. His plan is designed to force General Lee to abandon his Fredericksburg fortifications and, if all goes as he has planned, the road to Richmond will be open. Through Colonel Sharpe and his intelligence network Hooker knows that Longstreet is 130 miles southeast, near Suffolk, and that Lee's forces are greatly reduced in number. In fact, Lee has about 60,800 men facing the 130,800 soldiers of the Army of the Potomac. Hooker thinks the time is perfect to move on Richmond.

Lincoln wants Joe Hooker to understand the intent of the offensive move and sends him a telegraph on April 11: "Our prime objective is the enemy's army in front of us, and is not with or about Richmond at all, unless it be incidental to the main object."

Colonel Sharpe tells Hooker that Lee is having problems keeping more than four days' rations on hand. Hooker reasons that if Lee's supply line can be severed he will be compelled to either withdraw or starve. To sever Lee's supply line, Hooker sends Gen. George Stoneman's cavalry corps on a raid to get between Lee and Richmond. For maximum effect, this cavalry raid is to precede the infantry movements by two weeks.

On the morning of April 13, General Stoneman rides out with his 10,000 troopers, planning to move westward and then sweep southeast toward Lee's vital supply line. Before Stoneman departs, Hooker gives him a pep talk. "Celerity, audacity, and resolution are everything in war. Let your watchword be fight, fight, fight."

On April 14, in Mississippi, Pemberton, although he has been repeatedly warned by Bowen of Grant's move south, still does not accept this thrust as anything but a diversion. To reinforce Bragg's Army of Tennessee, Pemberton pulls Gen. Abraham Buford's 4,000-man brigade out of Port Hudson so that they can be sent back to Bragg. This was to partially replace the 9,000 men of Stevenson's division sent in mid-December to reinforce Pemberton in Mississippi. Soon, Buford's men leave Jackson for Chattanooga. Pemberton orders Gen. John C. Vaughn's brigade to be ready to pull out of Vicksburg to go back to Tennessee. He telegraphs Gen. Simon Bolivar Buckner, commander of the Department of the Gulf, advising that he is sending troops to Tennessee because he is satisfied that a large portion of Grant's army is reinforcing Rosecrans. And since Gen. Isaac Quinby's Federals, like Ross's people earlier, had been checkmated in front of Fort Pemberton and have steamed back up the Tallahatchie, General Tilghman's Confederates are removed from Fort Pemberton at Greenwood and arrive in Jackson on April 18.

All this time, Pemberton is headquartered in Jackson, the fourth largest city in the state. Here he commits the cardinal sin of a commanding officer: becoming too comfortable. He is cozy. He has with him his wife, Pattie, and he is following the events in Louisiana and on the Mississippi River through the eyes of his commander in Vicksburg, Carter Stevenson. Pemberton reasons that Stevenson is a fellow West Pointer and a senior general, so he must be assessing the situation correctly.

In Virginia, after Stoneman's cavalry rides south, on the night of April 14 the bottom falls out of the skies. The rain starts and continues to fall for 36 hours. The rivers rise, and Stoneman's horsemen cannot cross the flooded Rappahannock. As it turns out, the troopers do not cross until almost the end of the month on pontoon bridges. Cutting off Lee's "hogs and hominy" doesn't happen as planned, and Stoneman's cavalry raid will not be a factor in the Chancellorsville Campaign.

On April 15, in Pemberton's Jackson headquarters, reports of Federals marching south in Louisiana continue to arrive from Bowen at Grand Gulf. The Yankees have not gone north, Bowen says, they are marching south. Finally, Pemberton begins to have his doubts about Stevenson's reports. Unfortunately for the Confederate cause, Stevenson has been misreading Grant's intent, and worse, Pemberton does not follow his instinct when he begins to suspect this. He hesitates to act, and Grant steals a march on him.

Early in April, Grant sends a message to Porter. "To-morrow I shall have work commenced to prepare at least six steamers to run the blockade," he wrote. "I would, admiral, therefore, renew my request to prepare for running the blockade at as early a day as possible." The time to run the blockade is determined to be the night of April 16.

Porter agrees, and his plan for running the 37 big guns of the Vicksburg batteries is to place in the vanguard the slowest of the gunboats, the ponderous but well-protected ironclad *Benton,* an Eads-converted catamaran snag boat with 16 guns that now flies the pennant of Porter's flagship. Her boilers are below decks, making her safer in combat, and she is known as the Old Warhorse. Because she is the slowest of the boats, all the others can keep up with her. Lashed to *Benton* on her starboard beam will be a tug, *Ivy,* which is needed to assist the underpowered ironclad.

Behind *Benton* is *Lafayette,* with eight guns. *Lafayette* is another Eads-converted riverboat, formerly a steamer purchased for use as an army transport. Attached to her starboard beam is a captured Confederate ram, *General Price.*

Next come four of the Eads city-series ironclads, *Louisville* with 12 guns, *Mound City* with 14 guns, *Pittsburg* with 13 guns, and *Carondelet* with 11 guns.

The ironclads are followed by three transports, *Silver Wave, Henry Clay,* and *Forest Queen.* Bringing up the rear is *Tuscumbia* with five guns. Like *Chillicothe, Tuscumbia* is another one of Joseph Brown's poorly constructed gunboats, this one from the New Albany, Indiana, boatyard. *Tuscumbia* is in the rear to prevent any of the transports from deliberately falling behind. The transports have barges filled with forage lashed to each beam for some protection, and the seven gunboats have a barge filled with 10,000 bushels of coal lashed to the port side for fuel and added protection.

The lines of the fleet are cast off at 9:15 p.m. As the gunboats round the river bend above Vicksburg, Confederate volunteers in small boats struggle through the current of the Mississippi to Delta Point on the Louisiana side. Here these intrepid Rebels torch barrels of turpentine that will light up the Louisiana shore to illuminate the gunboats as they pass down the river. At 10:30 p.m., the Confederates spy their shadowy targets and the shore guns begin to roar. The Union tars aboard the gunboats return the fire, and the boats are close enough to the Vicksburg shore for the sailors to hear the shells smacking into brick buildings. The sailors hear the Confederate officers shouting commands, and they can hear the curses of the Rebel artillerists.

By 11:11 the fleet is under heavy fire in front of Vicksburg. When the transport *Henry Clay* is halfway past the river city, she is hit and set afire. Her engines are knocked out and she drifts aimlessly, a wreck. But, despite the prolific pyrotechnics, *Henry Clay* is the only casualty, and two transports and all of the gunboats successfully run the Vicksburg gauntlet. Grant now has the means to cross the Mississippi below Vicksburg.

At 2:30 a.m. on April 17, Pemberton in Jackson receives a telegram from Stevenson that at least five Federal gunboats have run past the batteries. By the middle of the morning Pemberton knows that he has a serious problem now that Grant has boats south of Vicksburg. Pemberton telegraphs Johnston, advising him that he needs Buford's brigade back, and that he will have to renege on the plan to send help to Bragg. Poor old Abe Buford! He and his tired men have already passed through Atlanta on the last rail leg to Chattanooga, and they have to turn around and make the return trip in boxcars or on flatcars.

Grant's many movements have the Confederates constantly shifting troops. Grant also receives assistance from an unexpected quarter—the Confederate command structure. The departmental dividing line between Pemberton's Department of Mississippi and East Louisiana and the Trans-Mississippi Department is the Mississippi River, and no one has responsibility for the river itself.

Johnston had earlier tried to fix the Confederate problem by suggesting that the Trans-Mississippi provide support for Pemberton, but it wasn't done, and now it is too late. So who is to blame for this terrible organization? The person to blame occupies the White House of the Confederacy, and that person is Jefferson Davis, the man who is working with his fourth Secretary of War in two years.

Grant doesn't have that command problem, because he owns all the ground he's operating on, and he has a naval officer—a naval officer who willingly cooperates with him—and a fleet of gunboats and steamboats that is operating on the river. Grant has a river line of communications back to Memphis, which is infinitely more secure than the railroad he relied upon back in December.

There is another factor which will work to Grant's advantage. After Porter's fleet runs the Vicksburg batteries, Union gunboats can now run freely between the waters below Vicksburg and above Grand Gulf. So, on April 17, Col. Francis M. Cockrell is told to get his men back across the Mississippi River on the boats *Hine* and *Charm* as fast as possible before the gunboats can cut them off or, even worse, sink one or both of the Confederate boats loaded with troops. With Cockrell's withdrawal from Louisiana, that leaves only Major Harrison and his 240 Louisiana cavalrymen to observe the Federal march southward, and they will be quickly pushed aside by Grant's powerful advance.

After the successful run of the boats past the Vicksburg batteries, McClernand's men at Joshua James's Ione Plantation south of New Carthage gleefully watch as the fleet arrives during the afternoon of April 17. Grant rides south from Milliken's Bend to inspect the boats that afternoon and to talk to McClernand. With Grant are his 12-year-old son, Fred, several staff officers, and a cavalry escort. Grant has a rough time during this 30-mile circuitous horseback ride, because he has either the piles—he writes to Julia on April 6 that he can "scarcely sit, lay, or stand"—or he has a bad case of boils, which is what Col. Adam Badeau says when he writes Grant's biography. Either way, Grant must have experienced a rough, painful ride from Milliken's Bend to Ione Plantation along the muddy roads, which have been corduroyed by laying a carpet of logs across them.

Regardless of his painful condition, Fred Grant recalls that along the way Grant couldn't resist making "one of his daring leaps" on horseback across a slough, rather than wait to cross a busy, narrow bridge. Fred said, "The rest of us preferred to wait our turn at crossing by the bridge, over which a wagon was slowly passing."

At Ione Plantation, Grant realizes that Warrenton is no good as a landing area, because its batteries are 17 miles upriver from Ione, and it will take at least three hours to steam that distance. The gunboats will have to silence the guns at Warrenton, and that will take some doing. The Confederates at Vicksburg can use all that time to shift troops south to oppose a landing. So Warrenton is out of the question. That leaves Grand Gulf, located 24 river miles south of Ione, as the place to land the Federal troops, and Grant tells McClernand to work on getting his men farther south, to a point in Louisiana opposite Grand Gulf so that they can land quickly once the Federal Navy silences the Confederate guns there. McClernand assures Grant that he has already found a new route south. Grant rides back to Milliken's Bend, secure in the knowledge that he chose the right man to lead the march.

From his headquarters boat at Milliken's Bend, Grant sets to work bringing up McPherson's XVII Corps to support McClernand. The advance elements of Isaac Quinby's division are already arriving by steamboat at Milliken's Bend from their Yazoo Pass Expedition misadventure, but Quinby is not aboard. He has been on sick leave since April 14, and Col. John Sanborn is in temporary command of the division.

Sanborn, upon his arrival at Milliken's Bend, notes that "the greatest activity prevailed. . . . Everything indicated that a campaign was to open with utmost vigor." He also observes his West Point classmate Grant, and recalls, "None who had known him previously could recognize him as the same man. . . . His energies seemed to burst forth with new life."

Grant also has General Hurlbut in Memphis working on the cavalry raid to strike Pemberton's railroads and to divert attention away from his move south in Louisiana. When he learns of the Federal march south, Hurlbut writes to Grant, "This cavalry dash I desire to time so as to co-operate with what I suppose to be your plan to land below Vicksburg, on south the side of Black River, silencing the Grand Gulf batteries." The time for that cavalry dash has come.

On Wednesday, April 15, Hurlbut sends orders to Gen. William "Sooy" Smith, commanding the Federal base at La Grange, Tennessee, that the cavalry raid is to "start sharply at or before daylight on Friday morning." Col. Benjamin H. Grierson, a Pennsylvania-born, now Illinois resident, music teacher who hates horses, arrives from personal leave just in time to command the raid. His jaunt through the heart of Mississippi will literally become the stuff that films are made of, and Grierson will sever both the Southern Railroad of Mississippi, which connects Pemberton with the east, and the New Orleans, Jackson and Great Northern Railroad, which connects Pemberton with the south. But the most important aspect of this raid, which will end on May 2 in Baton Rouge, is that it causes Pemberton to once again look in the wrong direction.

Three Federal commanders, on three fronts, attempt to sever their opponents' railroad lines of communication. Rosecrans sends Colonel Streight to cut Bragg's Western and Atlantic Railroad. Hooker dispatches General Stoneman to cut Lee's Fredericksburg and Richmond connecting railroads. Grant orders Colonel Grierson to severe Pemberton's Southern Railroad of Mississippi.

On April 18, the day after Grierson departs La Grange for the raid into Mississippi, Gen. James Longstreet, who is advancing on Suffolk, Virginia, hears from Richmond that the naval support of C.S.S. *Richmond* is not approved for his planned capture of the Suffolk garrison. Longstreet is told that the Confederate ironclad is behind the obstructions that protect the southern capital city on the James River. If the obstructions are opened to let the ironclad out, then Federal gunboats might suddenly force their way in, so Longstreet will have no help against the Union Navy on the Nansemond River. Without naval aid, Longstreet decides to lay siege to Suffolk rather than attack its eight fortifications.

In Louisiana that same day, McClernand has been told by Grant to prepare for a Grand Gulf landing, so he marches south in search of a staging area nearer to Grand Gulf. His scouts tell him that Judge John Perkins's Somerset Plantation, about three miles south of Ione, is one possible staging area, and the other is the Hard Times Plantation of Dr. J. Y. Hollingsworth, just five river miles above Grand Gulf. A route to Somerset runs along the west bank of Bayou Vidal, but it will need considerable corduroying and bridge building. From Somerset to Hard Times there is a good road that goes south and runs along the west bank of Lake St. Joseph, but that road will require extensive work to rebuild four bridges which the Confederates have burned across Holt's Bayou, Bayou DuRossett, Phelps's Bayou, and Clark's Bayou. McClernand's Yanks barely pause. McClernand puts the men from Gen. Alvin P. Hovey's division to work on the Bayou Vidal road on April 22, and the work is completed in four days.

While McClernand is working on the roads south, Grant knows that he needs more transports to cross the Mississippi with enough speed and strength to achieve the element of surprise. Encouraged by Porter's success in running the Vicksburg batteries on the night of the 16th, Grant is cocky, and he decides to try it again. But this time he will run the batteries with transports only. Six of them are loaded with 600,000 rations for McClernand's men, and they are reinforced with cotton bales and barrels of beef. At eleven o'clock on the night of April 22 the transports *Tigress, Anglo-Saxon, J. W. Cheeseman, Moderator, Horizon,* and *Empire City* round De Soto Bend in front of Vicksburg and brave the fire of the Confederate cannoneers. Only *Tigress,* Grant's former headquarters boat at Shiloh, is destroyed under the guns of Vicksburg, and by noon on April 23, five more transports—battered but still afloat—arrive at New Carthage. Grant now has seven transports, seven gunboats, a ram, and a tugboat downriver for the upcoming river crossing. He moves his headquarters from his boat at Milliken's Bend south to Pointe Clear Plantation, two miles north of New Carthage.

On April 23, McPherson's XVII Corps, which has since arrived at Milliken's Bend from Lake Providence, begins the march south. Sherman then orders Steele's division, fresh from its Greenville Expedition, downriver from Greenville to Young's Point on the 24th, and they arrive the next day. Grant, now at Pointe Clear, sends a message to Sherman at Young's Point, asking him to remain in the rear and improve the road network because the wagons and artillery are having a rough time. That'll teach Sherman not to write CYA letters.

Meanwhile, Osterhaus's men start work on the Lake St. Joseph road on the 25th. At Holt's Bayou they tear down the plantation buildings at George Douglas's Shady Grove Plantation to rebuild the bridge, and at Bayou DuRossett John Ogden's Wyoming Plantation buildings are stripped to supply the needed lumber. At Phelps's and Clark's Bayous, pontoons are placed in the water and covered with lumber stripped from the Routh family's Kenilworth Plantation, located in the quarter-mile-wide strip of land between the two watercourses.

Grant is pleased with the progress, and later wrote that "the ingenuity of the 'Yankee soldier' was equal to any emergency."

On April 27, Grant decides that, in addition to Grierson's raid, he needs another diversion to keep the Confederates guessing. Grant asks Sherman to consider making a diversion up the Yazoo River toward the Snyder's Bluff fortifications, but he doesn't order him to do it. He makes it a point to tell Sherman that it is a request, and not an order, because the ever present reporters will certainly call it a repulse when Sherman falls back. Grant is using psychology on Sherman.

Back in December, Sherman's men took a beating at the same place Grant now wants him to make a demonstration—the Chickasaw Bayou area. When

Sherman was beaten back by the Confederates, reporter Thomas Knox wrote an article that revived the old "Sherman is insane" accusation. Grant knows that Sherman is extremely sensitive about this. So Grant is daring Sherman by implying that he might be afraid to be the victim of more negative press. Sherman accepts the dare, saying he will make the diversion.

He writes to Grant, "As to the reports in the newspapers, we must scorn them, else they will ruin us and our country. They are as much enemies to good government as the secesh, and between the two I like the secesh best, because they are a brave, open enemy, and not a set of sneaking, croaking scoundrels."

Grant's multiple approaches have thoroughly confused Pemberton. For the past six days Grierson's cavalry has captured Pemberton's attention as the Yankees cut a path through Mississippi, having on April 24 cut the east-west Southern Railroad of Mississippi at Newton Station. Now, even though Ben Grierson doesn't look and walk like John Wayne, he fits the part, and on April 27 he sends his "butternut guerrillas"—Union troopers wearing Confederate uniforms—into Hazlehurst. Two of these men saunter into the telegraph office and send a counterfeit telegram to Pemberton in Jackson, saying that Grierson's Yankees are headed toward the capital city. The timing surely isn't scripted, but it couldn't have been more perfect, because that telegram causes Pemberton to order the Confederate cavalry away from the Mississippi River just as Grant is assembling his troops at Hard Times, opposite Grand Gulf.

On April 27, Pemberton orders General Bowen at Grand Gulf to call in his "eyes and ears," Col. Wirt Adams's Mississippi Cavalry, and send the troopers east toward Union Church, Mississippi, to intercept Grierson's cavalry. Adams has been patrolling along the Mississippi River on the east side to try to fathom Grant's intent. Bowen protests, advising Pemberton that the enemy's movements of the past 24 hours indicate the intent to march lower into Louisiana, run the steamers past Grand Gulf, and cross the Mississippi downriver, possibly at Rodney or St. Joseph. Pemberton misses the big picture. He insists that Bowen dispatch the cavalry eastward toward the pesky Ben Grierson.

Colonel Grierson's raiders, after successfully cutting the Southern Railroad of Mississippi at Newton Station, ride westward through Hazlehurst, where they cut the north-south New Orleans, Jackson and Great Northern Railroad, and soon pass through Gallatin. A mile west of Gallatin they capture a Confederate ordnance train with a 65-pounder Brooke rifle, which is en route for Grand Gulf, and Grierson realizes that the Confederates must still hold that site. He decides to turn southwest to Natchez.

On April 27, Joe Hooker in Virginia, after sending General Stoneman's cavalry to sever Lee's railroads, plans to cross the Rappahannock and Rapidan Rivers to go around Lee's left. He intends to do this with three of his seven infantry corps by marching west to Kelly's Ford on the Rappahannock River, 25 miles northwest of Fredericksburg. The three corps that Hooker will send on this mission are the V Corps commanded by Gen. George G. Meade, the XI Corps commanded by Gen. O. O. Howard, and the XII Corps commanded by Gen. Henry Slocum. Hooker, with part of his headquarters, will accompany the column of maneuver, riding with Meade. They start that morning.

At Hard Times, Louisiana, on April 28, Grant has McClernand's XIII Corps in position for an attack on Grand Gulf, with McPherson's XVII Corps in supporting position, and Sherman's XV Corps upriver creating a diversion near Vicksburg. He also has Porter's gunboats ready for the attack on Grand Gulf.

On April 28, Bowen telegraphs Pemberton: "Reports indicate an immense force opposite me. . . . I advise that every man and gun that can be spared from other points be sent here."

When Bowen asks Pemberton to send additional troops to Grand Gulf, Pemberton telegraphs General Stevenson in Vicksburg, telling him to get 5,000 men ready to rush to Grand Gulf upon Bowen's request. But Stevenson does not want to release these men because he is convinced that the Union movement south is a feint designed to draw troops away from Vicksburg, where he thinks the main assault will take place. General Pemberton then gets around to sending telegrams on the 28th to President Davis and General Johnston, advising them that the Yankees are at Hard Times.

Late on the 28th, Grant prepares to make his amphibious assault on Grand Gulf. That evening at Hard Times Landing, more than half of McClernand's 17,000-plus man XIII Corps are aboard the transports and barges that were lashed to the boats on the run past Vicksburg. These are soldiers of Hovey's division, as well as men belonging to Osterhaus's division and four regiments of Gen. Stephen G. Burbridge's brigade, which are temporarily attached to Osterhaus. Many of the barges are full of shell holes from the Vicksburg passage, and the men in the leaky barges have no choice but to stand in almost knee-deep water.

Grant has issued his orders to McClernand: "The plan of the attack will be for the navy to attack and silence all the batteries commanding the river. Your corps will be on the river, ready to run to and debark on the nearest eligible land below the promontory [Point of Rock]. . . . The first object is to get a foothold where our troops can maintain themselves until such time as preparations can be made and troops collected for a forward movement."

On the 28th, Grierson's horse soldiers arrive at Union Church, where they are weakly confronted by advanced elements of Col. Wirt Adams's cavalry. Grierson thinks the situation over. He doesn't know when Grant will land at Grand Gulf, and he knows there are Confederates between his men and that point. He decides to create the impression that he is headed southwest toward Natchez, but he will turn southeast, and then go south to Baton Rouge.

On April 29, Sherman steams up the Yazoo River on ten transports, with ten regiments from Gen. Frank Blair's division, escorted by ironclads *Choctaw* and *Baron de Kalb;* tinclads *Linden, Signal, Romeo,* and *Petrel;* timberclad *Tyler;* Porter's huge flagship, *Blackhawk;* and three scows with 13-inch mortars.

At 7 a.m. at Grand Gulf, Porter's gunboats pull away from Hard Times Landing and steam downriver. Porter has reconnoitered the Grand Gulf batteries from upstream, and he knows roughly what he will face because he drew some fire on his reconnaissance. With his experienced eye, he gauged the size of the shell splashes in the water to determine the caliber of the Confederate guns.

Leading the attack will be *Pittsburg,* because its skipper, Lt. William Hoel, was a river pilot before the war. Hoel knows the Mississippi better than anyone else in the fleet. Grant, meanwhile, will board the tug *Ivy* and take station midstream behind the fleet. Behind Grant's tug, the speedy ram, *General Price,* will escort the packed transports and invasion barges after the Confederate guns are silenced.

At Grand Gulf, Bowen has a two-brigade division of Confederates—about 4,000 men. Other than the earthworks, there is not much at Grand Gulf. The town was burned by Flag Officer David Farragut when his blue-water fleet came upriver in late spring of 1862, so only a couple buildings are standing, and they are well back from the river. The lower fort is behind the fire-gutted town, on a 20-foot-high protrusion of a bluff. It will become known as Fort Wade after Col. William Wade, the fort commander, is killed there. Here Bowen positions four big guns of Company A, First Louisiana Heavy Artillery—a 100-pounder Blakely rifle, two rifled 32-pounders, and one VIII-inch Dahlgren shell gun.

Fort Cobun, located 1,500 yards north of Fort Wade, is a more formidable fortification. Fort Cobun commands the broad, open waters of Grand Gulf. The "gulf" is the swirling, whirlpool-like current caused by the conjunction of the Mississippi and Big Black Rivers just north of the fort. Fort Cobun's guns also belong to Company A, First Louisiana Heavy Artillery, and they are 40 feet above the river and dug into the side of the cliff of Point of Rock, similar to the guns in the 1961 movie *Guns of Navarone.* These guns are two 32-pounders, one VIII-inch Dahlgren, and a 30-pounder Parrott rifle, all firing through the narrow embrasures of a 40-foot-thick earthen parapet.

Embrasures in the parapet provide protection for the gun crews, but they severely limit the elevation and deflection of the cannon. This means that the tubes can't be raised or lowered, and they can't be sighted more than several degrees to the left or right.

Both Cobun, the upper fort, and Wade, the lower fort, were quickly constructed when Bowen arrived at Grand Gulf in mid-March. The forts are connected by a three-quarter-mile-long double line of rifle pits and a covered, or sunken, way. A secondary fighting line of rifle pits begins above the Grand Gulf Cemetery, which is about one-half mile behind the town site, and extends along the line of the bluffs. On top of Point of Rock, 170 feet above the river, Bowen has a wooden observation tower. From this perch he can see across the Louisiana floodplain to the west, and he used this vantage point to watch the Federal movements.

As Porter's fleet steams downriver to attack Grand Gulf, the four city-series ironclads open fire on Fort Cobun at 7:50 a.m. By 8:15 the Confederate guns return fire.

Porter has the fleet divide into two flotillas. The vessels attacking Fort Wade consist of the city-series gunboats—*Pittsburg, Louisville, Mound City,* and *Carondelet,* in that order. When *Pittsburg* reaches Fort Wade, she rounds to and takes position close in to the bank with her bow upstream. Her engines churn at the same speed as the current, thus providing a stable firing platform. The other three ironclads perform the same maneuver, each falling in immediately astern of one another. By doing so, they shower Fort Wade with shot and shell from 16 guns—four on the starboard side of each boat.

At 9 a.m. one of the gun carriages of Fort Wade is disabled, then another, and Colonel Wade is killed at one of the guns with his "head torn off by an immense shell." A Federal shell also lands in the Confederate rifle pits, killing two men and wounding nine.

While Fort Wade is under heavy fire, Porter's upstream flotilla attacks Fort Cobun at 8:25 a.m. This group has *Benton,* the flagship, with 16 guns. *Lafayette* takes position in an eddy northwest of the fort, and opens fire with her huge stern guns—100-pounder Parrott rifles. She attempts to enfilade the fort—that is, she is shooting down the line. After firing 35 rounds from her stern guns, *Lafayette* rounds to and gives the fort blasts from her broadside guns. As she continues her turn, she blasts the fort from her two bow XI-inch Dahlgrens.

The third ironclad attacking Fort Cobun is the "miserable"—as Porter calls her—*Tuscumbia*. When the boatbuilder secured the armor plating to *Tuscumbia's* wood backing, he fastened the plates with spikes, rather than with bolts secured by nuts inside the bulkhead. When a round hits the armor, the spikes start and eventually loosen, then the heavy armor slides off. *Tuscumbia* isn't a very good vessel, and the Confederates know it, so they single her out. She is hit 81 times.

At ten o'clock Porter hears the fire of only two guns in Fort Wade, so he orders *Lafayette* to drop downstream to add her fire to the four city-series ironclads, leaving *Benton* and *Tuscumbia* in front of Fort Cobun. At 10:10 a.m. a shot from Fort Cobun enters the pilothouse of *Benton,* wounds the pilot, shatters the wheel, and wounds Porter.

Young Fred Grant, who is with his father on Ivy *during the battle, sees Porter later that day aboard* Benton *and says the admiral was hit on the back of the head by a shell fragment and that his face showed the agony he was suffering.*

Benton has one of her steering cables cut by a lucky Confederate shot, and she drifts out of control for 1,500 yards downstream, striking the riverbank on the Confederate side just under Fort Cobun. But the thick parapet of the fort does not allow the fort's guns to be depressed. *Benton* makes repairs in relative safety and withdraws, but while she is out of action *Pittsburg* takes her place in line at Fort Cobun.

By noon the guns of Fort Wade are silenced, so *Louisville, Carondelet, Mound City,* and *Lafayette* steam upriver and circle in front of Fort Cobun several times, firing with all guns and closing to within 300 yards of the fort. *Lafayette* resumes her original position, trying again to enfilade the fort. At 12:30, *Tuscumbia's* port engine is disabled and she drifts downriver, out of action. But *Benton* chuffs upstream to replace *Tuscumbia.*

At 12:50, Porter goes over to the middle of the river to talk with Grant. They realize that the Confederate guns of Fort Cobun are still very much in action, and that the rifle pits have hardly been touched. Taking unarmored transports, loaded to the gunwale with troops, into such fire would be murder. So at 1:15 the fleet withdraws to Hard Times Landing with 18 killed and 57 wounded, compared to the Confederate casualties of three dead and 19 wounded. Grant has to come up with another plan.

As the Federals withdraw to Hard Times Landing and McClernand's tired, wet troops disembark from the porous transports and barges, Confederate fatigue parties scramble over Grand Gulf's forts, repairing the works. *Lafayette,* since she is virtually invulnerable, is ordered back downriver to stop the Rebel working parties. From the middle of the Grand Gulf her hundred-pounder Parrotts keep up a steady fire against Fort Cobun at five-minute intervals until 8 p.m.

Meanwhile, at 7:45 the fleet casts off again from Hard Times with *Benton* taking the lead, followed by the other gunboats and the transports and barges, the latter now emptied of their human cargo. The gunboats pound away at the Confederate batteries, which fire back with unexpected vigor. But the transports and barges, with their lights out and covered by the shadows of the Louisiana shore, slip behind the screen of gunboats with no losses. The covering gunboats then break contact with the Confederate cannon and follow, tying up on the Louisiana shore four miles below Grand Gulf. In this passage one man aboard *Carondelet* is killed.

All that day, General Stevenson in Vicksburg still believes that Vicksburg is to be the real point of attack, and Sherman's men on the Yazoo River add credence to that belief. Although Stevenson hears the booming of the big naval and land guns just 20 miles downriver, he does not receive a request from General Bowen for the 5,000 troops that were to go to Grand Gulf because the telegraph line between the two fortified positions is down. He waits until late in the day to release two brigades to go to Bowen's aid.

The first troops that leave Vicksburg are Gen. Edward D. Tracy's Alabama Brigade. These troops leave Warrenton, south of Vicksburg, at 7 p.m., and they march all day and night to support Bowen's troops. Tracy is a lawyer from Georgia, and he fought at First Manassas before being sent to the West, where he took part at Shiloh. Little does he know he is going to meet the grim reaper at Port Gibson. Gen. William E. Baldwin's brigade of Mississippians and Louisianans, which is encamped north of Vicksburg, follow Tracy's men at 9 p.m. Neither of these two units will arrive in time to oppose Grant's crossing of the Mississippi. Even if they had, Bowen had no cavalry to determine where the crossing will be, and he could not have left Grand Gulf to march south to try to oppose a crossing. If he did, the Union Navy could have pulled to and occupied the fort.

At Hard Times, McClernand—with his men now disembarked—is ordered to march his corps southward across the base of Coffee Point. His men stay on a farm road just out of range of the big guns of Grand Gulf.

Grant is running out of options because he is running out of dry land. The road taken by McClernand's men south from Hard Times is described by a resident of Elk Ridge Plantation at Lake St. Joseph, Sarah Dorsey, who wrote: "The only road for Grant's land forces lay down the Hard Times Levee. The country on every side was under water, and this narrow dyke, broad enough for a single carriage to drive on, was the only Ararat, standing out from the sea of waters."

By dark the leading elements of McClernand's XIII Corps reach Disharoon Plantation, three miles south of Hard Times. The plantation has a single-balconied white house, shaded by magnolias on a high natural levee. It has cleared fields west of the levee—a good campground for McClernand's worn-out soldiers. Many of these men had spent more than 18 hours standing in water in the leaky barges at Hard Times, getting their feet and their shoe-leather soaked. Then they had to commence marching with wet feet, which guarantees some nasty blistering on the softened skin.

Grant plans to embark his troops at Disharoon Plantation the next morning, and then steam 11 miles downriver to Rodney, where the maps show a good road leading to Port Gibson. From there Grant hopes to flank Grand Gulf, taking it from the land side. If he succeeds, he will have a base from which to operate on the Mississippi River. His supplies can be taken by the road from Milliken's Bend to Somerset Plantation, and then delivered by boat to Grand Gulf. If Grant doesn't capture Grand Gulf, supplies will have to travel from Milliken's Bend all the way to Disharoon Plantation, and this is too far to be practical. But he is confident of success.

Grant is so sure that he will successfully cross the Mississippi River the next morning that he writes to Sherman to march two of his three divisions south. Grant writes to Halleck that he feels like the "battle is now more than half won," a statement that has to be taken in view of the long, hard winter Grant's army has spent in Louisiana and Mississippi.

But why is Grant so confident? How does he know on the night of April 29 that he will be able to make a successful river crossing the next morning?

Five days earlier, Grant ordered McClernand to have General Osterhaus, who was leading the expedition south, conduct a cavalry reconnaissance of the

Louisiana shore opposite Bruinsburg. Numerous plantation owners and slaves were then questioned about the road network leading inland from the bluffs around Bruinsburg, and Grant has that information. The next day, Grant orders Col. Harry Wilson to cross the Mississippi and perform a reconnaissance in the area north of Grand Gulf, and Grant has that information. So Grant knows what is above and what is below Grand Gulf—he has not been blindly marching his army south.

Grant garners all the information he can, and in the end he decides on Bruinsburg as the landing area, because it is only five miles downstream, instead of the 11 miles to Rodney. It would take almost three hours to get to Rodney, and a landing at Bruinsburg would cut his travel time in half. This will get his army ashore in Mississippi much faster, and Grant needs to secure a foothold before the Confederates can contest his crossing.

While Porter duels with Grand Gulf, Col. Ben Grierson bluffs a full-scale attack on Adams's men at Union Church on the 29th. The wily Federal colonel then breaks contact and heads back southeast to Brookhaven to do more damage to the New Orleans, Jackson and Great Northern Railroad. He then rides hell-for-leather to Baton Rouge, which is in Federal possession.

In Virginia, on April 29, Hooker plans to keep Lee's army in its defensive posture by having two of his corps demonstrate, or feign an attack, in front of Fredericksburg. While Hooker's three maneuver corps tramp northwest, screened by the topography, the two demonstration corps cross the Rappahannock River at the site of Franklin's December crossing, two and one-half miles below Fredericksburg. This force makes a strong demonstration in front of the Confederates to divert Lee's attention away from the force making the turning movement. Early on the morning of the 29th the three maneuver corps cross the Rappahannock River at Kelly's Ford. Hooker then marches Meade's V Corps to Ely's Ford on the Rapidan, and Slocum's XII Corps and Howard's XI Corps to Germanna Ford, five and one-half miles west of Ely's Ford on the Rapidan. When these three corps cross the Rapidan River, they continue southeast toward Chancellorsville.

Robert E. Lee is awakened early on the foggy morning of April 29 and is advised that the Federals are crossing the Rappahannock just below Fredericksburg. This is Hooker's demonstration. As the day progresses and the Federals fail to attack, Lee recognizes that the movement is designed to draw his attention from the real effort—the principal attack is to come from another direction. He looks at his maps and realizes that Chancellorsville is the point where the Federals will converge after crossing the river, because several roads lead from the Chancellor house to Fredericksburg and to the rear of his army. Both Gen. Richard Anderson's and Gen. Lafayette McLaws's divisions have been left at Fredericksburg when Longstreet went to Petersburg, so they are available to Lee. At 6:45 p.m. Lee orders Anderson's division to march westward toward Chancellorsville. Anderson moves out in a driving rain at 9 p.m. to a position at Zoan Church.

When Hooker initiates his demonstration at Fredericksburg, messages go out to Longstreet near Suffolk to return to Fredericksburg as soon as possible. This means, of course, that Longstreet's siege of Suffolk has to be terminated. But Longstreet is slow to respond, and he receives repeated appeals from Lee and from Richmond to pull away from Suffolk and return to Fredericksburg. Still, he does not come, citing problems in getting his heavily laden supply wagons collected. Finally, he is peremptorily ordered to return to Fredericksburg. He does not report back to Lee until May 9—far too late to assist the Confederates at Chancellorsville.

On April 30, in Louisiana, reveille sounds well before dawn for Grant's troops. By 8 a.m., after a signal from flagship Benton, *the invasion armada heads downstream.*

Grant is riding with Porter on *Benton* in the armored pilothouse when a strange thing happens. A band on board strikes up the martial air "The Red, White, and Blue," and thousands of soldiers and sailors cheer. Now, that's something you don't do if you are trying to surprise the enemy, unless you know there is no enemy in front of you. Grant must have known this, or he would never have let those musicians get their fifes in tune, to paraphrase Bedford Forrest.

At Bruinsburg, *Benton* rounds to, and her bow thuds against the mud bank. Grant gives the task of landing the first of his soldiers to John McClernand, a man whose heart is in the mission. Maybe Grant remembers that during the Revolutionary War, George Washington's biggest mistake was at the Battle of Monmouth, when he gave Charles Lee the mission to attack the British. Charles Lee, a man who only liked his dogs and only his dogs liked him, did not have his heart in the mission. On June 28, 1778, when the British turned to face Lee's attack, he ingloriously retreated. Never delegate authority to someone who does not share your vision.

To ferry McClernand's men across the Mississippi, Grant uses the gunboats and the seven transports, as well as the coal and hay barges. The first to land are infantrymen of the 24th and 46th Infantry of Gen. Alvin Hovey's division. By noon on April 30 most of the XIII Corps is ashore—around 17,000 men.

Grant wrote, "When this was accomplished I felt a degree of relief scarcely ever equaled since. Vicksburg was not yet taken it is true . . . but, I was on dry ground on the same side of the river with the enemy."

Although Grant is relieved when McClernand's men land unopposed, he will soon be unhappy when he learns that McClernand's staff has not issued rations to the troops. The men are supposed to have three days' rations in their haversacks, but someone has forgotten to take care of this. A four-hour delay ensues while rations are brought downriver and issued to the men. This oversight could have been disastrous.

After the rations are delivered, McClernand's men don't have time to break the provisions down and issue them. The troops have to get to the high ground soon, and they begin the march at 4 p.m. They march almost a mile and then climb up the steep hundred-foot escarpment for one-quarter of a mile. All the while details of men are rolling heavy barrels of salt pork and lugging boxes of hardtack.

Leading the march is Gen. Eugene A. Carr's division of McClernand's XIII Corps. Carr is a West Pointer, class of 1850, who will be awarded the Medal of Honor in 1894 for his leadership at Pea Ridge in 1862. When the Medal of Honor list is reviewed in the 1890s, it is decided that the medal can only be awarded for gallantry and intrepidity above and beyond the call of duty. So if a soldier wants to receive the medal for action in the Civil War, he will have to be long-lived, because he will have to submit documentation. The ones that get the belated medal have to be rather fortunate to be still alive in the 1890s so that they can write their puff pieces.

Carr is riding an old mule, and, since he has no cavalry to detect an ambush, he orders the 11th Wisconsin of Col. Charles Harris's brigade forward. At least it is Harris's brigade until he gets stomach cramps about 10 p.m., and then Col. William M. Stone, the future governor of Iowa, takes his place. Stone will get to command the brigade for one day and fight at Port Gibson before Gen. Mike Lawler, wearing a brand-new star, arrives to assume command on May 2.

When the soldiers reach the top of the bluff overlooking the Mississippi River that afternoon, they soon march under the shade trees south of the Widow Smith Coffee Daniell's Windsor Plantation. It is late in the day, and the men are ordered to halt for supper south of the mansion.

One of Carr's officers says that the big house at Windsor is the most magnificent house he has ever seen. It took two years to build Windsor, from 1859 to 1861, and the house has 22 rooms. But the planter, Smith Daniell, died at the age of 34, only a few weeks after Windsor was completed. So only the Widow Daniell is here with her eight young children when Grant and McClernand arrive.

Colonel Warmouth of McClernand's staff describes the Daniell family in his diary: "The whole set are rebels. The old woman and the young ones, too, are spitfires."

Windsor Mansion survives the war because once Grant captures Grand Gulf, the remaining Federals cross upriver, so the stragglers were not in the area. The stragglers are the ones that do the burning, as they do over in Louisiana. But, during a party on February 17, 1890, a man will drop a lighted cigarette in a trash can and Windsor will burn to the ground. All that is left today are the 23 stately Corinthian columns, a couple of giant live oak trees, and traces of the brick foundation.

The largest group by far that will ever visit Windsor will be the Yankees in 1863. But the second largest crowd to assemble at Windsor was in July 1956, when Hollywood filmed part of the movie *Raintree County*, with Monty Clift, Liz Taylor, and Eva Marie Saint. So Windsor, even though no one has found a photograph of the house before it burned, becomes famous on film as a Civil War ruin, even though it survived another 35 years after the war.

At Windsor, McClernand's panting, sweaty soldiers break open the rations that have been manhandled from the river and up the bluff, and wolf down their suppers. While the men gobble crackers and pork, McClernand rides up and decides that, even though it is late in the day, the march needs to be resumed to surprise the Confederates and to stop them from burning the bridges over Bayou Pierre. Grant agrees, and the march resumes at 5:30 p.m. Since the men barely have had time to break open their rations, they fix bayonets and have extra rations of meat impaled on the steel spikes.

Moving out behind Carr's division is Gen. Peter J. Osterhaus's division. Osterhaus is a former Prussian Army officer who fled to the United States after the 1848-49 revolutions in the German states.

Taking up the march behind Osterhaus is Gen. Alvin P. Hovey's division. Hovey, a lawyer, is a peculiar man who believes he is the reincarnation of Napoleon Bonaparte. In 1888 he will be elected governor of Indiana.

Following Hovey's division is Gen. Andrew Jackson "Whiskey" Smith's division. Whiskey Smith comes by his moniker honestly, but he is a good fighter. He is 48 years old, a West Pointer, class of 1838. Hovey and Smith are not going to reach the area of the A. K. Shaifer house until late morning of May 1, after the battle has begun.

During the night of April 30, Grant decides to keep the vessels running on the Mississippi River to shuttle McPherson's men across. About the same time that McClernand's men leave Windsor with their pork-decorated bayonets, two of Gen. John Logan's three brigades, commanded by Gen. John E. Smith and Gen. John D. Stevenson, begin to cross the Mississippi River. Grant has successfully crossed McClernand's 17,000 men of the XIII Corps, and soon he will add an additional 5,000 soldiers from McPherson's XVII Corps to his fighting force.

The Union night march heads through unusual territory. Grant has probably the best description of this area in his *Memoirs,* where he writes that "the country in this part of Mississippi stands on edge." He says the roads run along ridges, and the ravines are filled with impenetrable growth of wild cane, underbrush, and vines. But the ridge tops are clear, because they are cultivated.

The Bruinsburg Road crosses four major creeks and is in poor condition, so it is not used by Grant to go inland. He takes the Rodney Road instead, even though it is a longer and more circuitous route.

Grant's column moves southward two miles to Bethel Church, where the Bruinsburg Road and the Rodney Road join. At this junction the column turns east.

When Grant's column first marches south from Windsor, it appears to the Union soldiers that they are marching away from Vicksburg toward Port Hudson. But when the procession turns east toward Port Gibson, the morale of the soldiers soars. The difficult winter months in Louisiana and the Mississippi Delta are quickly forgotten.

The deeply sunken roadbed, worn by generations of farm wagons and dray animal hooves and sheltered by a canopy of oaks, makes a lasting impression on the Yankee soldiers, especially after months in the pancake-flat bayou country of Louisiana. Even though it is a forced night march, the men seem happy. First Sgt. Charles Hobbs of the 99th Illinois writes that as they march along, "The moon is shining above us and the road is romantic in the extreme."

On the morning of April 30, Bowen knows what's coming. He has seen the Yankee gunboats and steamers pass Grand Gulf early the previous night. He has seen Yankee soldiers march across the base of Coffee Point. Bowen can't pull all his men out of Grand Gulf to go south and oppose Grant's crossing because the Yankees have a fleet, and if he pulls out, the Yankees will come back upstream and take Grand Gulf. He is waiting for reinforcements from Vicksburg, and they are slow in coming. Nevertheless, he knows he has to do something.

In desperation, after the gunboats ran past his batteries the previous night, Bowen ordered Gen. Martin E. Green to send a strike force of 500 men down to Port Gibson to at least slow the Yankees down. Then, at 1 a.m., Bowen orders Green to march to Port Gibson with the remainder of his brigade of Arkansas and Missouri troops. Green is a Virginian who transplanted to Missouri and was operating a sawmill when the war started. Though not a professional soldier, he has been at Lexington, Pea Ridge, Iuka, and Corinth.

Green marches down to Port Gibson and finds that Col. J. E. Cravens, commanding the 500-man strike force, is on the wrong road. Bowen's cavalry has been ordered east to pursue Grierson's raiders, and Cravens doesn't know his ground. A frustrated Martin Green orders Cravens to the west of town to the junction of the Rodney and Bruinsburg Roads. Here, at a Y intersection, the roads from Rodney and Bruinsburg converge to form one road into Port Gibson from the west. Green posts his men at the intersection, because he doesn't know which road Grant will take. Still, he believes he has time because he doesn't think Grant is going to make a night march. He makes a classic mistake—he underestimates his enemy.

Green then rides down the Rodney Road and selects a defensive position near Magnolia Church about one-third mile east of the Shaifer house. In selecting his position, General Green makes a critical tactical error. He posts his men east of the intersection of a road—the Plantation Road—that connects the Rodney and Bruinsburg Roads; thus, he voluntarily surrenders to an approaching enemy the ability to shift troops between the Rodney and Bruinsburg Roads.

Late on the afternoon of April 30, Bowen rides to Port Gibson to discuss the situation with General Green. They decide to post two or three companies on the Bruinsburg Road with the rest of Green's command on the Rodney Road. Neither Green nor Bowen knows that Grant is not using the Bruinsburg Road.

At last, around 6 p.m. reinforcements begin to arrive from Vicksburg. The help comes from Tracy's Alabama Brigade, 1,500 strong. With Tracy are two sections—four guns—of the Virginia Botetourt Artillery. The other section, which was on detached duty from the battery, is still en route. The Alabamians and Virginians have marched 40 miles in 27 hours, with only a brief rest on their arms.

When Tracy's brigade arrives, Green decides to place the Alabamians in a position to block the Bruinsburg Road, while Green blocks the Rodney Road with his men. This will place half of the available Confederate force on a road that is not being taken by the Federals. Grant, whether he knows it or not, is making use of a lesson from Julius Caesar—"Divide and conquer!"

Grant has thoroughly confused the Confederates. He has stolen a march on Pemberton through Louisiana because Steele's diversion to Greenville has been interpreted as a retreat. He has crossed the Mississippi River unopposed, because Sherman's diversion on the Yazoo River has caused Stevenson to delay the departure of reinforcements from Vicksburg. Now, the route of his movement inland is unknown to Bowen because Grierson's horse soldiers' raid has drawn the Confederate cavalry away from the river.

In Virginia on the morning of April 30, Dick Anderson's two Confederate brigades are concentrated in the Zoan Church area and are digging in. By early evening on April 30, Joe Hooker is encamped at the rendezvous point, a rambling inn and farmhouse belonging to the Frances Chancellor family.

Hooker's move has been brilliantly executed, and Fighting Joe Hooker now has a reason to be proud. He has flanked the aggressive tactician Robert E. Lee. Hooker boasts, "I have Lee in one hand and Richmond in the other."

Even General Meade, no fan of Hooker, exclaims, "Hurrah for Joe! We're on Lee's flank and he doesn't know it." Hooker's plan, however, is based on Lee doing what Hooker expects him to do.

One of Napoleon's maxims is that "time is invaluable for a soldier," and Hooker has two hours of daylight remaining when he arrives at Chancellorsville on April 30. But he decides to wait until morning. Hooker is intractable in his belief that Lee will retreat, so he waits for that retreat to begin. Hooker is in for a surprise.

Late on April 30, Lee's suspicion of a turning movement by Hooker is confirmed when his cavalry chief, Jeb Stuart, reports to him that a large federal force has crossed the Rappahannock at Kelly's Ford. At midnight on April 30, Lee orders McLaws west toward Chancellorsville. Stonewall Jackson follows soon afterward. Jackson will be Lee's eyes at Chancellorsville, and Lee gives his attack-minded subordinate discretionary authority to act as the situation requires. The one option that Robert E. Lee is not considering on April 30 is retreat. This will rattle Fighting Joe Hooker, resulting in perhaps the most lopsided Confederate victory of the war.

Chapter 4
WHAT WILL THE COUNTRY SAY?

May 1–6, 1863
During the first few minutes of Friday, May 1, Grant's lead
elements are five and one-half miles east of Windsor Plantation,
marching toward Port Gibson in the darkness. The shadows of the
deeply cut Rodney Road are intensified by the canopy of trees, and
the soldiers are understandably nervous.

THE VANGUARD OF THE MARCH IS COMPOSED OF LT. COL. CORNELIUS
Dunlap of the 21st Iowa and a 16-man patrol supported by four companies
of the regiment. Suddenly, the night march ends and the fighting begins at
12:30 a.m. at the house of A. K. Shaifer, one-third mile west of Magnolia Church.

Confederate Gen. Martin E. Green has posted his defensive line behind a rail
fence along the ridge between Magnolia Church and the Foster house, a modest structure 250 yards to the east of the church on the north side of the road.
He has about a thousand men of the 15th Arkansas, the 21st Arkansas, and the
12th Arkansas Sharpshooter Battalion, and he has been reinforced by the Sixth
Mississippi and four guns of the Pettus Flying Artillery. Green has positioned the
12th Arkansas Battalion astride the Rodney Road. The 15th and 21st Arkansas regiments extend the line south in the direction of Widows Creek, and the
Sixth Mississippi has been posted to the north. The four guns of the Pettus Flying
Artillery are positioned around the Foster house. For security Green has an outpost of four men under Lt. William D. Tisdale from the 12th Arkansas Sharpshooter Battalion in the Rodney Road in front of the Shaifer house.

Around midnight, Green gets nervous and rides forward to his Shaifer house
outpost. In front of the house he finds Mrs. A. K. Shaifer and her sister packing

their things in a wagon. Mrs. Shaifer is an older sister of Col. Benjamin G. Humphreys of the 21st Mississippi. (Humphreys will take command of Gen. William Barksdale's brigade after Barksdale is shot down at Gettysburg on July 2.) She and her sister are better informed than Green, because they know the Yankees are coming. The general assures the two ladies that soldiers don't march at night.

About that time, Lieutenant Tisdale in the outpost hears some clinking of metal along the Rodney Road to the west, where the road ascends the ridge out of the Widows Creek bottom. The lieutenant challenges the strangers in the darkness, and he is answered with muzzles flashes and bullets whizzing past, smacking into the side of the Shaifer house. One of the minié balls rips through the west wall and lodges in the frame of a portrait of Mrs. Shaifer. The women make a beeline for Port Gibson, leaving Green a bit ruffled.

Tisdale and his men, after exchanging fire, fall back with Green to Magnolia Church. Now the unheard-of happens: A nighttime battle opens. Colonel Stone aggressively orders his Yanks to attack. He has Col. Samuel Merrill bring up the remaining six companies of the 21st Iowa. Meanwhile, Stone forms a skirmish line with his four point companies and advances in the dark. The Yanks move to within 50 yards of the Confederate line on the ridge east of Magnolia Church. The Arkansas soldiers patiently wait before they light up the night with their volley.

The Iowa boys fall back to take cover west of Magnolia Church Ridge, and a 12-pounder howitzer of the First Iowa Battery is unlimbered in the road. The road has high banks on both sides, so the banks provide protection from small-arms fire from the flanks. However, 300 yards to the east the Confederates have sighted the four guns of the Pettus Flying Artillery to fire down the road, and before the Hawkeyes can go into action, they are swept in the defile of the road by shot and shell. Still, Sgt. William Leibert holds the blue-coated artillerymen to their gun, and the 12-pounder starts barking defiantly in the darkness. The other five guns of the Hawkeye battery arrive and drop trail on a knoll north of the road, 175 yards east of the Shaifer house. When this happens, Leibert wisely withdraws his lone gun from its hazardous position and joins the battery 300 yards to the rear.

Stone then deploys his men, the 21st Iowa, north of the road and 23rd Iowa to the left of the 21st. The 22nd Iowa and 11th Wisconsin form a second line behind the guns. Then the horses pulling three cannon of the First Indiana Battery pound their way up the road, and Stone places these guns in battery in line with the Iowa guns, south of the road. The cannon of both sides blast away at unseen targets in the moonlight.

The moon soon sets and the night turns inky black, except for muzzle flashes. The Confederates seem to be good at this kind of night fighting, and their artillery shot, shell, and canister raise hell in the Yankee lines. Stone pulls two of his regiments back behind the ridge to get them out of the line of fire. General Carr has Gen. William Benton's brigade cross Widows Creek, and Benton's men neatly stack their haversacks south of the road before rushing up the steep road grade to support Stone. Then Carr decides discretion is the better part of valor, and he has Benton's men pull off the road and wait for dawn. Carr is the senior man on the field at this time, and he is worried about a Confederate trap. Finally, at 3 a.m. both sides break off the engagement, but this action will long be remembered by those who fought in the night at Magnolia Church.

Grant's crossing of the Mississippi continues that night, but at 3 a.m., the transports *Moderator* and *Horizon* collide, and *Horizon* is no more. She sinks, taking the guns, limbers, caissons, and horses of Company G, Second Illinois Light Artillery, to the bottom of the Mississippi River. Grant doesn't appreciate losing a steamer and an artillery battery at the same time, so he suspends the crossing of the rest of McPherson's men until daylight on May 1.

Gen. John A. Logan watches his men cross at daybreak. Logan is swarthy, with a big walrus mustache and long black hair hanging over his collar. He was a Democrat in Congress before the war, and a dough-faced Democrat at that—one that voted with the Southerners on sectional issues. But Logan knew that his constituents were unhappy having an unfriendly power control the lower Mississippi River, so he warned the Southerners, as their states seceded and they walked out of Congress: "The people of the old Northwest will hew their way to the Gulf with their swords." He then joined the army and served at First Manassas as a private. But he came back as colonel of the 31st Illinois, only to be wounded at Fort Donelson. Now he is a division commander, and he plans to hew his way.

While Grant continues to get men across the Mississippi River, what is John Pemberton doing? Pemberton finally moves his headquarters from Jackson to Vicksburg on May 1. But before he leaves Jackson, he orders his detached units, which have been scattered due to Grant's many diversions, to rendezvous in Jackson. Gen. William Loring, fresh from an unsuccessful pursuit of Grierson, travels from Meridian to Jackson and then to Big Black Bridge to take charge of Gen. Lloyd Tilghman's command of two infantry regiments and a battery of artillery. They are then to go to John Bowen's support, but these soldiers will arrive too late to assist Bowen at Port Gibson.

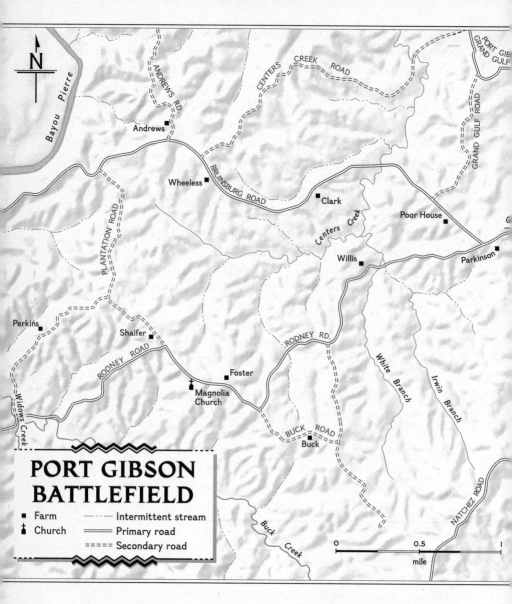

PORT GIBSON
BATTLEFIELD

- Farm
- Church
- - - Intermittent stream
- === Primary road
- ===== Secondary road

By daybreak, General McClernand, who remained at Windsor until 2 a.m., arrives at the Shaifer house with his staff and establishes his headquarters in the yard. He learns of a road that runs north and south, only a hundred yards east of the Shaifer house. Known locally as the Plantation Road, the farm path connects the Rodney Road to the Bruinsburg Road just a little more than a mile to the north, and his men have access to it. McClernand makes a personal reconnaissance of the road, and lo and behold, where the road meets the Bruinsburg Road he uncovers another Confederate battle line. This is General Tracy's Alabama Brigade.

Tracy's men have shifted their line to the sound of the guns and are now parallel to, rather than astride, the Bruinsburg Road facing south. Tracy receives a request from Green for reinforcements and a section of artillery. He reluctantly sends the 23rd Alabama and two brass 12-pounder howitzers of the Botetourt Artillery to Green's aid, but because the Plantation Road now has Federal forces on it, the soldiers and guns travel two miles east to the Y intersection and then move two more miles back west on the Rodney Road to Green's position. The Confederates have sacrificed their interior line—the Plantation Road—to the Federals. So the reinforcements for Green take at least an hour to arrive.

Now there are two separate Confederate lines. Four regiments are on the Rodney Road under Green—about 1,000 men with four guns, with one regiment and two guns of Tracy's brigade on the way—and four Confederate regiments are on the Bruinsburg Road under Tracy. After sending reinforcements to Green, Tracy has about 1,200 men, and only two 12-pounder Napoleons.

Neither Confederate force can go cross-country to support the other because of the deep ravine of Centers Creek that runs between the roads. The total Confederate force is about 2,200 officers and men facing the 17,000-strong XIII Corps of John McClernand. And 5,000 more men of John Logan's division are hurriedly crossing the Mississippi River to join McClernand.

At 5:30 a.m., when Osterhaus's division arrives behind Carr's, McClernand orders an attack. Osterhaus takes 4,000 men and 12 cannon and attacks Tracy's men northward up the Plantation Road, while Carr assails Green's men eastward on the Rodney Road. Osterhaus's division has Gen. Theophilus T. Garrard's brigade in the lead, and Garrard brings six ten-pounder Rodman rifles, also called three-inch ordnance rifles, of the Seventh Michigan Battery up the Plantation Road and places them on a hilltop 800 yards northwest of the Shaifer house. So the Michiganders have six rifled guns blasting away at the two smoothbores of the Virginians. Even so, the Virginians get the upper hand in the artillery duel, and the Michiganders suffer two dead and two wounded.

While Osterhaus's artillery blasts away at the Virginia gunners, Garrard's infantry forms a double line of battle and attacks Tracy's infantry at 8:30. But the terrain, vines, cane, and cat's claw briars in the ravines confound Garrard's men, and when they reach the main Confederate battle line, the attack stalls. Nevertheless, Yankee sharpshooters creep forward and pick off the Virginia artillerymen one by one. Tracy rides forward to the Virginia artillerymen and is shot in the throat. He dies instantly. Col. Isham W. Garrott of the 20th Alabama then assumes command. Garrott has been a lawyer and a politician in Mobile, and he doesn't know Tracy's battle plan, or even if Tracy had one. So Garrott sends a courier on the four-mile-ride to Green to ask for instructions. Two hours later, the courier returns with a message of little value. Garrott is to hold his position "at all hazards."

While Garrott is waiting for instructions from Green, Osterhaus brings up his other battery, the First Wisconsin Light Artillery, which has six 20-pounder Parrott rifles. Four of these big guns join the Wolverine battery of 10-pounder rifles in counterbattery fire against the two 12-pounder Napoleons. Shells screech in, and Lt. Phillip Peters's two smoothbore Napoleons take terrible punishment just as two detached 6-pounder guns of Lt. William Douthat of the Botetourt Artillery arrive. The timing of the arrival of these two guns is terrible due to the incoming fire, which panics the horses as the shells burst behind them. About the same time, the battery commander, Capt. John W. Johnston, the nephew of Gen. Joseph E. Johnston, arrives. Johnston has been left behind in Vicksburg on court-martial duty, but now he catches up to his battery. A 20-pounder shell from the Badger battery screams in and decapitates Peters and Douthat as they discuss the situation. Other incoming shells shatter a Napoleon and a 6-pounder. Soon Captain Johnston has to leave the field because of illness, and that leaves Sgt. Francis Obenchain in command of the two remaining guns—one Napoleon 12-pounder and one 6-pounder.

Although the Botetourt Artillery is taking a terrible beating under the intense counterbattery fire, Osterhaus's infantry attack has stalled. The Prussian then decides to move his troops around to the Confederate right, which is anchored on Bayou Pierre. He will threaten there, but he plans to have the main thrust go against the center of the Confederate line. By noon Osterhaus is redeployed and ready. Then, without explanation, he decides he cannot attack without reinforcements, despite three-to-one infantry odds and ten rifled guns against two smoothbores.

At two o'clock, McPherson arrives on the field at the head of Logan's division with J. E. Smith's and John Stevenson's brigades. Grant sends Stevenson's brigade down the Rodney Road, while Smith is sent to reinforce Osterhaus on the Plantation Road. Smith moves northward up the trace and forms on Osterhaus's left. McPherson goes with Smith, getting into position at 3 p.m.

On the Rodney Road, General Bowen arrived on the field at 7:30 a.m. at Green's position, having ridden hard from Grand Gulf. Bowen sees that the

WHAT WILL THE COUNTRY SAY?

Union forces are threatening east of Magnolia Church Ridge. At 8:30 the reinforcements and two guns arrive from Tracy's brigade, and Bowen sends the 23rd Alabama and the Sixth Mississippi forward to drive the Federals back. He then races to the rear to try to hurry up more help for Green's outnumbered men. When Bowen rides off, he asks Green to hold on for another hour, and he sends an urgent message to Grand Gulf for Col. Frank Cockrell to bring his Missourians to the battlefield.

McClernand intends to settle the issue on the Rodney Road before Bowen can find help. Although McClernand sent Osterhaus up the Plantation Road to face Tracy's men, he plans for the main thrust to be against Green. When McClernand hears the sound of Osterhaus's guns from the north, he orders Carr's division east on the Rodney Road to attack Green's position. At the same time Hovey's division receives orders to move up and take a position south of the Shaifer house. Then Hovey's people march past the house, and McClernand tells him to deploy, but not to get into the fight until A. J. Smith arrives with his division. Smith's lead brigade, commanded by Stephen Burbridge, arrives at 8 a.m. and Col. William Landrum's brigade arrives 30 minutes later. Soon, the ridgeline east of the Shaifer house is crowded with soldiers who are standing shoulder-to-shoulder like pods of okra.

At 10 a.m. Hovey's Federals attack head-on into the Confederate guns, which have now been loaded with canister for the close-in work. The blasts of flying, bounding, and ricocheting iron balls are too much for the Federals, and the blue attack breaks 80 yards short of the guns. But soon Carr's men join the attack and the huge Union line extends far beyond the Confederate right flank. The long lines of Yankees surge forward, and Lt. William Norgrove's two 12-pounder howitzers of the Botetourt Artillery are overrun when all of his gunners are shot down. The lieutenant tries to load and fire his cannon alone and is mortally wounded as he is about to pull the lanyard. The Yanks roll over the guns like a giant wave. So many bluecoats storm the position that no one really knows who captured the guns, but many of the Federals remember Norgrove as one of the bravest men they ever saw.

After Green's line collapses, his men fall back down the Rodney Road for a little over a mile, where they meet Gen. William Baldwin's brigade, which is deploying across the road at Centers Creek. Baldwin's brigade arrived in Port Gibson early that morning, and now, just west of town, they meet General Bowen, who urges them forward. Bowen then races back down the Rodney Road in time to see Green's line collapse. He realizes that the men must have time to reorganize, so he orders Green to march his men east to the Y intersection and then back west to the Confederate right wing to support Colonel Garrott, who by now is also hard-pressed.

The fire-eating Colonel Frank Cockrell at Grand Gulf receives Bowen's urgent summons at 10 a.m. and immediately moves out. His troops quickly march the eight miles to the intersection of the Rodney and Bruinsburg Roads, where Bowen meets them at 12:30. By then Green's line across the Rodney Road near Magnolia Church has been broken, but Baldwin's brigade has arrived at the Y intersection a few minutes earlier, and has been sent out the Rodney Road to try to delay, or even hold, the Yankees. Bowen quickly sends one of Cockrell's regiments, the Sixth Missouri, westward on the Bruinsburg Road with Green's battered men to help Garrott fight Osterhaus and Logan, and he rushes Cockrell's remaining two regiments, the Third and Fifth Missouri, and his artillery down the Rodney Road to help Baldwin stop McClernand's advance.

Green's men march down the Bruinsburg Road and arrive at Garrott's position at 2:30 p.m. Green, as ranking officer on the Confederate right, decides he doesn't want to assume any more responsibility. Instead of advising Colonel Garrott that his reinforcements have arrived and assuming command, he simply puts the Sixth Missouri into line on Garrott's left and keeps his men out of the fight. But the Union attack is pressuring Garrott's right, not his left, so when Garrott finally realizes the Missourians were placed on his left, he shifts the 46th Alabama from his left flank to his right. Luckily, he accomplishes this just as the Yankees attack.

Anchoring the right flank of Garrott's position down the bluff to Bayou Pierre is the 20th Alabama, but these men are stretched too thin. The Federal attack soon breaks their line. This leaves the right flank companies of the 30th Alabama stranded on the hilltop to the right of the Bruinsburg Road, and they receive fire from both flanks as the Yanks move around the hill.

Although the unfortunate Botetourt Artillery has lost all its officers, four of its guns, and many of its horses and men, Colonel Garrott asks Sergeant Obenchain if he can go back into action. Obenchain says he can, and places his two remaining guns on the crest of a small hill 600 yards east of the Andrews house. He fires down the Bruinsburg Road so the shells burst over the heads of the blue-coats swarming through the hollows on both sides of the road, blunting the attack. Sergeant Obenchain has risen to the occasion.

While Obenchain blasts away, Col. Eugene Erwin's combative Sixth Missouri slips over to Garrott's right to help plug the gap, and Green timidly shifts

his badly beaten and shaken men to the left to fill the gap, where there is almost
no action. General Green is still content to let Colonel Garrott command.

The Yanks reform and attack again. The 120th Ohio of Garrard's brigade,
led by Col. Marcus M. Spiegel, leads his men against the strategic knoll on the
north side of the Bruinsburg Road and takes the crest. Spiegel, a German-Jewish
immigrant, will be killed during the Red River Campaign in May 1864, and his
brother, Joseph, who was a sutler during the war, will open a dry goods store in
Chicago that will become the catalog giant Spiegel & Company.

*Colonel Spiegel reported: "When I had obtained possession of the knoll, I did
not deem it prudent to pursue them any farther, being at least 300 yards in
advance of any of our troops, and in danger of meeting the enemy's entire
right wing massed behind a number of old buildings directly in front of me.
I deployed my regiment on the knoll, in order to punish the retiring force."*

Spiegel's successful attack endangers the Confederate right flank, and Colonel Erwin decides he has to do something. He takes action. Without orders,
Erwin counterattacks, and his 400-man Sixth Missouri charges into the 49th
Indiana. Col. James Keigwin of the 49th said they found the Missourians coming
up at them with bayonets fixed. But Erwin's courageous counterattack is turned
back by the overwhelming numbers of Yanks.

By 5 p.m. Colonel Garrott knows he cannot hold any longer. His right flank
has collapsed and Erwin's counterattack has failed. At the same time General
Green receives a message from General Bowen to hold "until near sunset." Green
decides that five o'clock is near enough to sunset. He assumes command, and
his first order to Colonel Garrott is to retreat. The last two guns of the Botetourt Artillery, under the command of the intrepid Obenchain, pound away
to cover the retreat. Garrott leads the retreat up the Andrews Farm Road, followed by Green, en route to the Bayou Pierre suspension bridge. After they cross
the river, the exhausted and bloodied soldiers fire the bridge and bivouac on the
north bank.

But as Green and Garrott retreat, Colonel Erwin doesn't receive the order,
probably because his Sixth Missouri belongs to Cockrell, but has been attached
to Green. At 5:30 Erwin realizes his Confederates are the last on the field, and
he is about to be flanked and surrounded. He decides to bluff his way out of the
predicament and boldly bellows out, "Fix bayonets!" as though his men are going
to charge. Henry Clay, his grandfather, would have been proud of Erwin. The

Yanks, recalling Erwin's first bayonet charge, buy into this bluff and stand fast. Erwin's men then slip away, but as they do, the Yanks realize what is happening and capture 46 of Erwin's men. Gen. John E. Smith's brigade of Logan's division then advances to the Confederate position, but there is no pursuit. The Yanks have had enough of the Rebs on the Bruinsburg Road.

On the Rodney Road, Bowen has Baldwin's brigade and two regiments of Cockrell's brigade to hold the Yankees. In the morning fight, Green's men held the high ground along the road and were beaten back, and Bowen has learned a lesson from this. The ridgetops are bare and offer little cover for the defenders, especially against all that Yankee artillery. Plus, the defenders on a ridgetop are silhouetted against the skyline, while the attackers in the ravines are concealed in the underbrush. So Bowen places his men down in the hollows, among the woods and canebrakes of Centers Creek bottom. This, he believes, will help nullify the Union artillery superiority.

One-half mile west of the Y junction, Centers Creek crosses the Rodney Road and then divides into two branches south of the road to go around a thinly wooded ridge. White Branch runs west of the ridge and Irwin Branch flows to the east. The western bluff above White Branch is higher than the ridge between the branches; thus the approaching Federal troops will have the high ground. But they will be in the open on the ridgetop and will be silhouetted by the afternoon sun. With this in mind, Bowen forms the center of his line on the lee side of the low ridge between the two branches, with the two 24-pounder howitzers of Landis's Missouri Battery just south of the Rodney Road in position to fire down the valley of Irwin Branch. In reserve on a hilltop 800 yards behind the battle line are two guns of the Pettus Flying Artillery. The four 12-pounder howitzers of Guibor's Missouri Battery drop trail on a ridge 350 yards behind the battle line in a position to fire over the low ground to the front, and to sweep the western ridge of White Branch. As soon as Cockrell's two remaining regiments arrive, they are concealed in the woods south of the Mississippians.

Meanwhile, McClernand's men celebrate their victory over Green's men at Magnolia Church. Just after Green's line collapses, Grant arrives at the Shaifer house and rides eastward down the Rodney Road to the church with McClernand and Governor Richard Yates of Illinois. The two politicians stop at the church to make stump speeches to the soldiers. McClernand yells out, "It's a great day for the Northwest!" Grant, though he must have been quite irritated at the speeches being made while a battle is still being fought, sits while the hot air blows, and then suggests that there is still work to be done. While the politicians talk, the troops have a drink of water and rest their feet. Then, around noon, they move east with four brigades.

The men of Hovey's division reach the western ridge of White Branch of Centers Creek and immediately come under fire from the two 24-pounders across the hollow. Union artillery is brought up and a duel begins, while McClernand and his division commanders evaluate the situation. The Confederate line seems disjointed, with gaps along it, and McClernand fears a trap. Finally, the Federals drop down into the bottom of White Branch, and as they climb the ridge between the two branches, they receive flanking fire from the 24-pounders. The Federals dive for cover and for an hour and a half can't move forward.

Finally, McClernand decides to crush the Confederates with overwhelming numbers. He lines up Hovey's division, Carr's division, Smith's division, and Stevenson's brigade of Logan's division. In all, 21 regiments are positioned from end to end in a half-mile-long formation.

When Bowen sees this massive line, he knows he has to do something. He sends his Missourians to his left with the mission of turning the Union right flank. Bowen is also concerned that the Federals might discover the Natchez–Port Gibson Road, barely 1,200 yards from the Union right, and that road leads into the Confederate flank and rear. Bowen has Cockrell march his two regiments south along Irwin Branch, where they form behind a knoll, several hundred yards behind the enemy right flank. As Cockrell's men move into position, Alvin Hovey spies the movement and makes preparations to oppose it.

Due to the urgency of the situation, Hovey doesn't have time to report to McClernand. Instead, he personally rides to the right flank and places every gun of his division—four batteries, totaling 22 guns—on his right flank. Soon the Missourians appear over the crest of a ridge 300 yards away and make a dash for the Union right flank. Hovey's guns blast into them, but despite the heavy artillery fire, Cockrell's combat-hardened soldiers smash through Col. James R. Slack's brigade. Then Gen. George McGinnis's and Gen. William Benton's brigades rush to the fight, followed by the reserve troops of General Burbridge's brigade. Even though Cockrell's men fight like demons, they are finally overwhelmed by sheer numbers and are forced to withdraw.

There is no Union counterattack, which puzzles Bowen. He is still concerned that the Yanks might be trying to outflank him on the Natchez Road, and that the force to his front is only a demonstration. At 4 p.m. he has General Baldwin attack to see what develops. The attack is preceded by a barrage from Bowen's eight guns, yet once the Mississippians and Louisianans charge across Centers

Creek, they are quickly driven back by overwhelming numbers. Bowen realizes that the principal Union force is still to his front, and soon that massive force begins to press slowly forward. Bowen's men have to give ground.

As the Union troops cross White Branch, Capt. Samuel De Golyer, who commands the Eighth Michigan Battery in McPherson's XVII Corps, manhandles his six guns—two 12-pounder howitzers and four 12-pounder James rifles—across the branch and up the west face of the ridge between the two branches. The Confederates are hunkered down on the east face of the ridge, and De Golyer's guns suddenly appear atop the ridge. The Yanks depress the muzzles and blast canister down on the unsuspecting foe. Despite counterbattery fire from the Confederate cannon, the ridge has to be abandoned by the Confederates.

Bowen now knows that he cannot hold out against such odds, and at 6 p.m. he orders a retreat. Cockrell's men take the Grand Gulf Road, located less than half a mile west of the Y intersection, and retreat north to the Bayou Pierre suspension bridge. But by the time Baldwin's men can withdraw, they learn that Union infantry on the Bruinsburg Road has moved eastward and blocked the Grand Gulf Road intersection. Thus, Baldwin's men travel east on the Bruinsburg Road and go through Port Gibson at 9 p.m. They cross to the north side of Little Bayou Pierre and torch the bridge behind them as they continue north to Grindstone Ford, where they arrive at midnight and cross Big Bayou Pierre on a suspension bridge. After they cross the river they fire the bridge, but don't stay to ensure it is destroyed. They then march to join Bowen's command.

Meanwhile, late on the afternoon of May 1, the railroad trains bearing the troops of Confederate General Loring arrive at Big Black Bridge. Here Loring meets General Tilghman. The two generals then head southwest toward Port Gibson with the 15th and 26th Mississippi and Company C, 14th Mississippi Artillery Battalion.

Grant has beaten Bowen, and his beachhead on the east side of the Mississippi is secure. The Confederates have retreated across Bayou Pierre, but the Federals do not pursue because they've won a hard-fought battle, and they believe that is enough for one day. They've lost 875 men—killed, wounded, and missing—and captured four Rebel guns. The Confederates have done pretty well in the fight, but in the loss Bowen suffers 787 casualties. They had 6,800 men and 16 guns, and they battled 23,750 Yankees with 58 guns, and held them off for one day. But their effort was too little, too late.

WHAT WILL THE COUNTRY SAY?

On May 1, in Virginia, at 11 a.m. Hooker finally orders a movement toward Fredericksburg. His plan is to advance on the three roads that lead from Chancellorsville to Fredericksburg and "to take up a line of battle about two and one-half miles in front, preparatory to a simultaneous advance along the line at 2 p.m." By 11:30, three Federal divisions are moving east on the Orange Turnpike and Orange Plank Road toward the Confederate position near Zoan Church.

While Hooker pauses, Stonewall Jackson has arrived at Zoan Church, and after assessing the situation, he, too, decides to move forward at 11 a.m.

General Anderson, whose men have been digging in at Zoan Church, recalled that, by Jackson's orders, "the work on the trenches was discontinued, and the troops were put in readiness for an advance." Jackson's bold decision to advance on the enemy, rather than await an attack, is in marked contrast to Hooker's inaction when he arrived at Chancellorsville.

Jackson is a fighter, and he is not about to sit and wait for the Federals to strike him—he is going out to hit them first. The Federals soon see the initiative passing from them, and Hooker, from his headquarters at the Chancellor house far to the rear, orders his troops to withdraw. Hooker now shifts to a defensive strategy in which he plans to let the enemy assail him.

The Confederates then move up, and they continue doing something that they would not have done a year before. They have since learned the value of breastworks, and they dig in. The Confederates then use their newly gained high ground to train their guns on Chancellorsville.

Hooker's men pull back almost all the way to the Chancellorsville intersection. Under Hooker's orders the Army of the Potomac has given up the offensive, pulled back into a strong defensive position, and likewise is entrenching and throwing up breastworks.

When Gen. Darius Couch returns to Hooker's headquarters, Hooker says to him: "It is all right, Couch, I have got Lee just where I want him; he must fight me on my own ground." Couch later wrote, "I retired from his presence with the belief that my commanding general was a whipped man."

In truth, Hooker has taken up a strong defensive position—except for his right flank, which is held by Gen. Oliver O. Howard's XI Corps. Howard's position would be much better if his right flank were anchored on Hunting

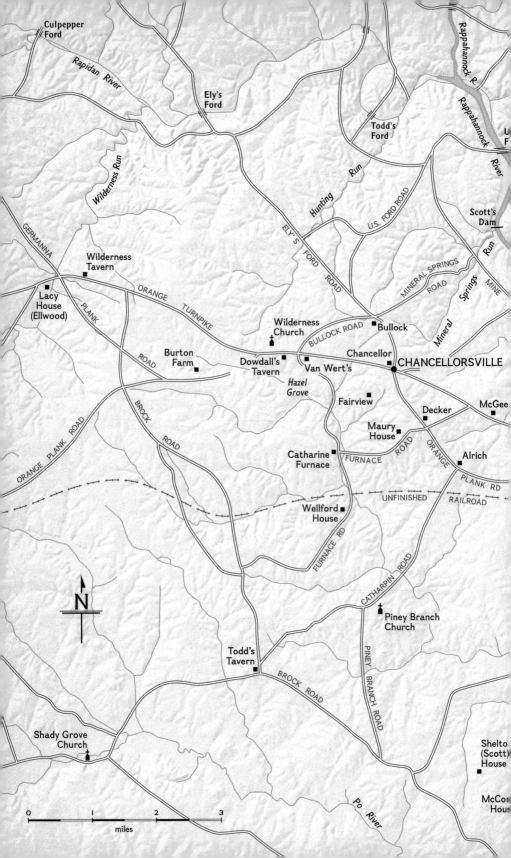

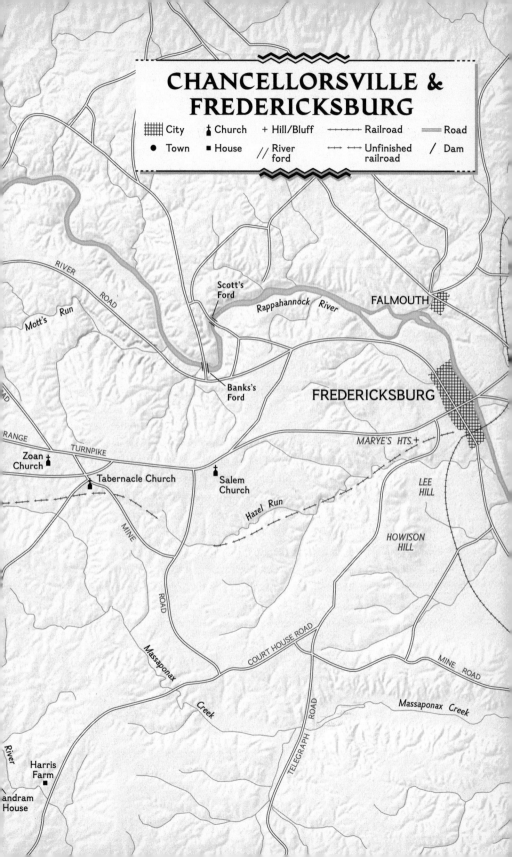

CHANCELLORSVILLE & FREDERICKSBURG

▦ City	⛪ Church	+ Hill/Bluff	┼┼┼┼┼ Railroad	═══ Road
● Town	■ House	∥ River ford	┼┼┼┼┼ Unfinished railroad	╱ Dam

RIVER ROAD

Mott's Run

Scott's Ford

Rappahannock River

FALMOUTH

Banks's Ford

FREDERICKSBURG

RANGE

TURNPIKE

MARYE'S HTS.+

Zoan Church

Tabernacle Church

Salem Church

LEE HILL

MINE

Hazel Run

HOWISON HILL

ROAD

COURT HOUSE ROAD

MINE ROAD

Massaponax

Creek

TELEGRAPH ROAD

Massaponax Creek

River

Harris Farm

andram House

Run, a stream to the north, but he doesn't do this. Instead, he leaves it "in the air," or unsecured.

Howard is from Leeds, Maine, and graduated from West Point in 1854. He was number four in a class of forty-six. At West Point he and Custis Lee, Robert E. Lee's eldest son, were close friends, and Custis finished number one in the class. The superintendent at West Point in 1854 happened to be Robert E. Lee, and Howard, who wrote to momma frequently, whined in his letters that he would be number one in his class, provided there wasn't some nepotism on the part of the superintendent. But Howard never explained, and the question was never asked, why Oliver graduated number four, not number two.

While Hooker digs in late on May 1, Lee conducts a night reconnaissance, just as he did at the Pedregal in the Mexican War. Lee goes to the Union left, and he sends one of his aides, Maj. T. M. R. Talcott, who is an engineer officer, and Capt. James Keith Boswell, Jackson's chief engineer, to reconnoiter the Union center. Meanwhile Gen. Fitz Lee's cavalry brigade conducts a reconnaissance of the Union right.

After Lee surveys Meade's defenses on the left, he realizes that he cannot go around those breastworks or across that terrain. Not only is the Union Army entrenched, but it is behind an imposing physical barrier, Mineral Spring Run, and the army's left flank is anchored on the Rappahannock River at Scott's Dam, a bit over a mile downstream from U.S. Ford.

About 10 p.m. Major Talcott and Captain Boswell return with their report. They have heard the thud of Federal axes felling trees and the sound of spades used to dig rifle pits. They report that the Union center is too strong to attack.

At nearly the same time Fitz Lee's report arrives. Fitzhugh Lee is a rather svelte gentleman in 1863, not the giant he will become. When he goes back in the service in the Spanish-American War in 1898, he's so big that he should be riding a Clydesdale. Fitz Lee has reconnoitered the Union right and has discovered that the XI Corps flank is not secure. The problem is, how to get there? Robert E. Lee discusses it with Stonewall Jackson under a grove of pine trees.

Major Talcott recalls: "At this time Lee and Jackson were together, and Lee, who had a map before him, asked Jackson: 'How can we get at these people?' To which Jackson replied, in effect, 'You know best. Show me what to do, and we will try to do it.' General Lee looked thoughtfully at the map; then indicated on it and explained the movement he desired General Jackson to make, and closed by saying, 'General Stuart will cover your movement with his cavalry.' "

Stonewall Jackson would follow Lee anywhere, and he listens attentively to Lee's plan. Then, his face lights up as he smiles. He rises, touches his cap in a salute, and says, "My troops will move at four o'clock."

That night in Mississippi, after the Battle of Port Gibson, Grant's men sleep on the battlefield and arise on the morning of Saturday, May 2, to a breakfast of hardtack and coffee.

Grant's soldiers march into Port Gibson, and from the hilltop west of town they see the church steeples of the Methodist church, the Catholic church, and, especially, the Presbyterian church, with its index finger pointing skyward on the top of the steeple. This church, completed in 1860, is one of several in North America today that, instead of a cross on the steeple top, portrays a closed hand with the index finger pointing skyward, as if to remind the viewer to focus on the heavenly goal.

After his victory at the Battle of Port Gibson, Grant next intends to capture Grand Gulf. On April 28, before he crossed the Mississippi River, he wrote to his wife, Julia: "Possession of Grand Gulf, too, I look upon as virtual possession of Vicksburg and Port Hudson and the entire Mississippi River." In his memoirs, he wrote, "My first problem was to capture Grand Gulf to use as a base."

Grant has a major river, Big Bayou Pierre, between his army and Grand Gulf. There are two suspension bridges over that river, and Grant needs possession of at least one of them. Where Little Bayou Pierre joins its big sister, two miles northwest of town, the Port Gibson–Grand Gulf road crosses Big Bayou Pierre with a suspension bridge and a railroad bridge. To the northeast, almost four and a half miles from Port Gibson, the Port Gibson–Vicksburg Road crosses Big Bayou Pierre on a suspension bridge at Grindstone Ford. The two bridges are the keys to getting to Grand Gulf. If Grant crosses Big Bayou Pierre, he can box Bowen in at Grand Gulf, with the Mississippi River to the west, Big Black River to the north, and Big Bayou Pierre to the south. There is also a suspension bridge over Little Bayou Pierre in Port Gibson, which will give Grant access to the road leading to the bridge at Grindstone Ford. All three of these suspension bridges have been built by the same contractor, so they are virtually identical.

By 10 a.m. Burbridge's men occupy Port Gibson. Grant soon learns that the suspension bridge on the north edge of town over Little Bayou Pierre has been burned by the retreating Confederates the night before. Details are put to work building a new bridge—a raft floating bridge—and Lt. Col. Harry Wilson of Grant's staff is in charge. Grant orders McPherson to have Logan send one brigade up the northwest road leading to the suspension bridge over Big Bayou Pierre and to Grand Gulf. The brigade chosen is General Stevenson's brigade, and Stevenson soon finds the railroad and suspension bridge burned and the Confederates on the other side in a blocking position. General Bowen has established a strong position on the north shore of Big Bayou Pierre with three regiments and six guns under the command of Colonel Cockrell.

While Grant is waiting in Port Gibson for the work parties to build a new bridge across Little Bayou Pierre, he orders McPherson to send one brigade upstream, to the east, along the south bank of Little Bayou Pierre to try to find a ford. A local black shows them a cattle crossing, three miles east of Port Gibson, with a road on the other side of the river leading northward. McPherson sends General Smith's brigade and General Dennis's brigade for support, in the event there is trouble.

Smith's and Dennis's brigades soon cross Little Bayou Pierre at Askamalla Ford and take the road to its intersection with the old Natchez Trace, or the Port Gibson–Vicksburg Road, where they come across a Confederate commissary that has been secreted on Lucknow Plantation, one of Colonel Humphreys's Claiborne County properties. Humphreys is serving at Marye's Heights in Fredericksburg, so he has no idea that the Yankees are rummaging through his buildings and confiscating 8,000 pounds of bacon in his barns. The men of the two Federal brigades quickly fill their haversacks to near bursting with pork and then await the arrival of their comrades.

Meanwhile, John Stevenson's Yanks on the Port Gibson–Grand Gulf Road are unable to force a crossing of Big Bayou Pierre in front of Cockrell's stubborn Missourians. The Yanks are reinforced by the four rifled Model 1841 bronze 6-pounders, called 12-pounder James rifles, and the two 12-pounder howitzers of the Eighth Michigan Battery. They are also bolstered by the big 20-pounder Parrotts of the First Wisconsin Battery, and about 4 p.m. the artillerymen of both sides blast away at each other across the river. Stevenson, who has been joined by John Logan, then learns that the raft bridge in Port Gibson has been completed, and the Federals withdraw.

By late afternoon the Yanks in Port Gibson cross Little Bayou Pierre on the newly constructed raft bridge, with McPherson's XVII Corps out in front. The

Seventh Division, which missed the Port Gibson battle, is in the lead. The division is now commanded by hard-fighting and hard-cussing Marcellus Monroe Crocker, who has just arrived from the north to replace Col. John. B. Sanborn as commander. Crocker suffers from tuberculosis, but he is not about to let some minor problem like that slow him down, and he endures until war's end, when he "joins the great majority" in August 1865. John Stevenson's brigade follows Crocker over the bridge, while Grant sits on the bank in his dusty uniform, resting and watching. He has allowed McClernand's men to spend a quiet day in Port Gibson.

McPherson's men march up the deeply cut Port Gibson–Vicksburg Road toward Grindstone Ford to the third suspension bridge, which they hope to find intact. Along the way, the column passes Humphreys's plantation, where Smith's and Dennis's brigades are issuing the confiscated Confederate bacon to passing soldiers. The two meat-dispensing brigades then fall in at the rear of the column.

Crocker's vanguard arrives at Grindstone Ford at 7:30 p.m. to find the remains of the suspension bridge over Big Bayou Pierre still smoldering. On each end of the bridge there are two large cast iron circular towers, at least 30 feet high, and the suspension is swung from these towers. The suspension consists of straps of iron tied together, much the same as the springs on a Model T automobile. That's what was used instead of cable. When Baldwin's men burned this bridge, they could not burn the cast iron leaves that form the suspension, and they could not burn the towers. All they did was burn the wooden roadway, and because they were in a hurry, they did not do a good job of that. So, much of the roadway is still on the suspension when the Federals arrive. Still, Grant has to pause to have the bridge repaired.

When Confederate General Loring and General Tilghman arrive at Rocky Springs that morning, they learn of the Confederate defeat at Port Gibson. Loring knows that if Grant crosses Big Bayou Pierre at Grindstone Ford Bowen will be trapped in a cul-de-sac, so he sends an artillery battery and two regiments toward Grindstone Ford under the command of Col. Arthur E. Reynolds of the 26th Mississippi. Loring takes Tilghman with him and rides to see Bowen.

Loring and Tilghman ride hard and find Bowen between Grand Gulf and Big Bayou Pierre at 11 p.m. The three generals have a pre-midnight conference, and Bowen advises Loring of the situation and offers him command. Loring, however, doesn't want to assume command at the moment the only option open is to abandon Grand Gulf. Who wants the loss of a fortified position on their résumé? So Bowen retains command and orders his four brigade commanders to abandon the Grand Gulf enclave and withdraw to the flatboat bridge over Big Black River at Hankinson's Ferry.

When Bowen returns to Grand Gulf to oversee the evacuation, a brigade of Tennesseans, commanded by Col. Alexander W. Reynolds, arrives. They have been sent to Grand Gulf by Gen. Carter Stevenson in Vicksburg, and they have arrived a day late and a dollar short. So Bowen sends them east in the darkness toward Grindstone Ford to help Col. Arthur Reynolds prevent the Federals from crossing Big Bayou Pierre.

While Bowen is working feverishly to abandon Grand Gulf, at Grindstone Ford, Ulysses Grant goes to a little log cabin by the side of the road to catch some sleep.

In Virginia, although Stonewall Jackson promised Robert E. Lee a 4 a.m. start, his troops don't get moving early on May 2. They begin their march shortly after 7:20 a.m., because Jackson is tired, and he is ill, and his men had marched for much of the previous night to get to Zoan Church. Then he and Lee stayed up very late with their night conference. Still, this delay will mean that Jackson will not attack until late afternoon, with only about two hours of daylight remaining.

Major Talcott recalled that "on the morning of May 2nd, Jackson was the first to arise from the bivouac . . . and, observing a staff officer without cover, he spread over him his own overcoat. The morning being chilly, he drew near a small fire that had been kindled by a courier, and the writer, who soon after sought the same place, found him seated on a cracker-box. He complained of the cold, and, as cooks prepared breakfast, I managed to procure him a cup of hot coffee, which by good fortune our cook was able to provide. While we were still talking the general's sword, which was leaning against a tree, without apparent cause fell with a clank to the ground. I picked it up and handed it to him. He thanked me and buckled it on."

At the time that Jackson's sword falls to the ground it occurs to Major Talcott that this event has some symbolic meaning, such as seeing a picture or a mirror fall. To Talcott, the falling of the sword is an omen of the coming fall of his illustrious leader.

As Jackson's column moves toward the Union right flank, it is spotted. Hooker's first alert is at 9:30 a.m., and it is relayed to Howard on the right flank. This is Hooker's version of what, in WWII, was called a "condition red." The Yanks are to be on the lookout because Hooker has "good reason to suppose that the enemy is moving to our right." Hooker writes to Howard that he doesn't think the right of the line is strong enough; that is, "no artificial defenses worth naming" have been constructed and there are too few troops at that point. He also suggests that there be "heavy reinforcements well in hand."

Whether Howard gets the message or not, he sends a message to Hooker at 10:50 that he "can observe a column of infantry moving westward on a parallel road with this ridge about 1½ to 2 miles south of this. I am taking measures to resist an attack from the west."

Jackson's march, which appears to be away from the battlefield, is exactly what Hooker is expecting Lee to do. He boasts that Lee has but two options. Option one is to abandon his works and flee ingloriously. Option two is to come out of his works and fight on ground of Hooker's choosing. Hooker decides that Lee must be fleeing ingloriously. But Hooker is dead wrong.

Darius Couch goes to the Chancellor house at 2 p.m., and Hooker greets him with the news that "Lee is in full retreat toward Gordonsville, and I have sent Sickles out to capture his artillery." Couch thinks to himself that if Hooker's conception is correct, "It is very strange that only the Third Corps should be sent in pursuit."

Now, what is the length of Jackson's marching column? A major problem with this body of 29,000 to 30,000 soldiers and 112 cannon is the narrowness of the road. The men are moving in columns of fours. And there are 112 cannon, which if they have their units of fire, would have 224 units, because each gun and caisson is pulled by a limber and six horses. A limber, with an ammunition chest for a six-pounder gun, carries 50 rounds. So that's the first unit of fire. The other three units of fire are a caisson with two ammunition chests, pulled by a limber with one ammunition chest and a team of six horses, for another 150 rounds. Using a six-horse team on a limber and gun will take about 50 feet of road space, about the length of a modern passenger bus. And considering the limber and caisson, that is a minimum of 100 feet of road space for every gun. Thus, 112 guns with limbers and caissons equal the length today of 224 passenger buses bumper-to-bumper, which is 11,200 feet—or over two miles of road space at a minimum, and the 29,000 soldiers haven't even been considered. Add the soldiers into the column and you have a marching order six to seven miles long.

And—however distasteful it might be to consider—another factor must be added to the equation, which is that equines cannot walk and urinate at the same time. They can defecate when they walk, but they have to stop to urinate. Farm boys learn that, and farm boys also learn that equines work as a team; if one stops when Mother Nature calls, the entire team stops. So it's a long, long column, which is constantly stopping and starting, and it will take four to five hours for this column to pass any given point. In fact, when Jackson attacks at 5:30 p.m., the trailing brigade is going to be two miles away down the Brock Road.

As the head of the column is approaching the crossing of the Brock Road with the Orange Plank Road, it is after 2 p.m. At the crossing Jackson meets Fitz Lee, who has been out reconnoitering, and Fitz asks Jackson to ride with him for about a mile to the northeast up the Orange Plank Road, because there is something Jackson needs to see. Fitz barely knows Jackson, so Jackson knows this must be important.

Now when Jackson left Lee that morning, the plan was that when Jackson reached the Orange Plank and Brock Road intersection, he would turn his column right onto the Orange Plank Road and proceed back to the northeast to the Union right flank. At that time they believed the Union right did not extend as far west as the point where the Orange Plank Road and the Turnpike Road diverge, which is just west of Dowdall's Tavern. Jackson's men would then be deployed in an angle to the Union front, but in essence it would be a flank attack against the Union front. But the situation is different than anticipated, says Fitz, so he asks Jackson to ride up the Orange Plank Road with him.

In 1879, Fitzhugh Lee recalled his remarks to Jackson: "General, if you will ride with me, halting your column here, out of sight, I will show you the enemy's right, and you will perceive the great advantage of attacking down the Old turnpike instead of the Plank road, the enemy's lines being taken in reverse. Bring only one courier, as you will be in view from the top of the hill."

Fitz Lee is not sure what the general might think when he makes the suggestion, but Jackson quickly agrees to take a look. Jackson is riding Little Sorrel. Little Sorrel is small, dumpy, and even homely, but he is tough, has a smooth gait, and is an intelligent, comfortable little horse. He is Jackson's favorite mount. But, after Little Sorrel dies in 1886, he is sent to the taxidermist, and now he looks somewhat sorry and flea-bitten in the VMI museum in Lexington, Virginia.

WHAT WILL THE COUNTRY SAY?

Fitz Lee and Stonewall Jackson ride up the Orange Plank Road to the Burton place, which is to the north of the Orange Plank Road, about a mile southeast of Dowdall's Tavern. And just to the south of the road at Burton's is a hill—a perfect observation site. Fitz Lee and Jackson and their orderlies ride up the hill and look due north. The position of the enemy is not what Jackson thought it was. The Federal line extends well to the west, past the area of Dowdall's Tavern where Lee and Jackson thought the line ended, for another mile to the area of the Hawkins and Talley farms, which is open ground. Even so, Jackson, who is only going to stay on the hilltop for four or five minutes, sees the Federal line at a distance of one-half mile or less, and he pictures an army that is not alert. He can see the line is parallel to, and immediately south of, the turnpike. He sees a butcher stringing up beeves and slitting them. He sees soldiers walking around and talking. He sees arms stacked. There are card games going on, there's coffee being boiled, and the Union soldiers are laughing and are relaxed—these are soldiers that nobody has told to be on the alert.

Fitzhugh Lee described Jackson's countenance while on the hill at Burton's, saying, "His eyes had a brilliant glow. The paint of approaching battle was coloring his cheeks, and he was radiant to find no preparation had been made to guard against a flank attack. He made no remarks to the officer with him; his lips were, however, moving, for, sitting on his horse in sight of and close to Howard's troops, he was engaged in an appeal to the God of Battles."

Jackson agrees with Fitz that he should continue marching his men up the Brock Road to the Orange Turnpike, which will put him beyond the Union right flank. He will then turn east onto the turnpike and deploy his units facing east. This extended move, another two and one-half miles of marching, will cost him about two more hours, but the attack will be that much more decisive and terrible, providing the Yankees do not take alarm.

As Jackson's men arrive on the Orange Turnpike, they form their battle lines on the Luckett farm. Their total march has been about 12 miles. As the Confederates deploy for battle, their vedettes and skirmishers are fired upon by Col. Leopold von Gilsa's pickets at 4 p.m. This is followed by a skirmish in which the two guns on the Union right flank fire two rounds without being ordered to do so.

At 5 p.m. Jackson asks one of his commanders, "Are you ready, General Rodes?" "Yes, sir!" answers Rodes. "You can go forward, then," replies Jackson. A single bugle blasts, followed by bugles on the left and right, and the line starts forward. From the long Confederate line, bugle calls ring in the evening air, causing the Federal soldiers of the XI Corps to look to the west. The thousands of Rebel yells cause the deer and rabbits to race out of the woods eastward into the Federal lines, followed by Confederate soldiers. The brush is so thick that it rips the uniforms of the Rebels, but still they come. The retreating Federals fall back ingloriously, and by 6 p.m. one division of the XI Corps has been wrecked and Jackson is rolling up the Union line.

Jackson's attack is pushing east, and just after 9 p.m., he barks the orders: "Press them! Press them!" But it is now dark, and his commanders are confused. Jackson rides forward to conduct a reconnaissance. He has seized the initiative. He's driven the Yankees back almost two miles. He's routed one Union corps. In spite of the dangers of a night attack, he wants to continue. His reconnaissance party rides forward into the night, led by Pvt. David Kyle and trailed by eight men, in a column of twos. They are so quiet that their own infantry officers do not hear them and are not told of their passage to the front. This secrecy will be Jackson's undoing. They get nearly to the 33rd North Carolina's skirmish line, and Jackson decides to stop and listen. He hears the Federal axes, *whack, whack!* He hears the commands of the Yankee officers as they form their lines 400 yards to the east. Jackson, an old artilleryman with bad ears, listens for a few minutes to make sure of what he is hearing. He then pulls back on the reigns of his horse, Little Sorrel, and turns him around. The time is 9:15.

As Jackson rides back toward the line of the 18th North Carolina, a single shot rings out, followed by a volley fire. As the firing erupts, both parties race toward the Confederate lines. Fearing an enemy charge, Maj. John D. Barry of the 18th North Carolina orders his men to fire. Many of the North Carolinians carry smoothbore muskets. Jackson is struck by the volley. A buckshot strikes him in the palm of his right hand between the thumb and forefinger and lodges just beneath the skin. A .69-caliber musket ball strikes him just below the left elbow and runs downward, exiting near the left wrist. The final musket ball strikes him in the left humerus—the long bone of the arm—where the bone flares out several inches below the shoulder joint. Terrorized, Jackson's horse spins around, and then races away from the firing toward the Federal lines. An overhanging branch hits Jackson and lacerates his face, but he is able to stay in the saddle and grab the reins with his bleeding hand. He turns his horse around and rides to his aides. Jackson's broken left arm is quickly bound with a handkerchief, and soon he is being helped back to the Confederate lines. But as the party around the wounded Jackson grows in size, it attracts the attention of two Federal cannon. They open fire and the area is raked with canister.

Federal iron missiles scream in on the party of Confederates, creating confusion among them. Despite the deadly stream of canister flying overhead, Jackson raises himself and emphatically yells, "You must hold your ground!"

When Jackson finally reaches a field hospital, Dr. Hunter McGuire administers chloroform to him. As his pain begins to subside, the general whispers, "What an infinite blessing!" McGuire removes the buckshot from Jackson's right hand, and notes that two bones in the hand were broken. In the last hours of May 2, the shattered left arm is amputated about three inches below the shoulder. Lee upon learning this, metaphorically states, "Jackson has lost his left arm, but I have lost my right."

Early on May 3 in Mississippi, Grant's men are tramping across the repaired suspension bridge at Grindstone Ford. In his engineering report, Colonel Wilson wrote: "By 5:30 a.m. . . . the bridge was completed and the army in full march." In 1885, Wilson commented in more detail, "Breakfast was ready and eaten before daylight, and Grant and the rest of the staff moved out as soon as they could see the road and the marching soldiers."

When McPherson's two divisions cross Big Bayou Pierre on the repaired Grindstone Ford suspension bridge, Bowen's Confederate position at Grand Gulf is flanked. Grant's second objective is all but achieved.

Gen. John Bowen knows he has been flanked, and Lt. Col. Pembroke S. Senteny, whose Second Missouri has been garrisoning Grand Gulf, is ordered by Bowen to spike the guns and blow the three magazines, which Senteny does just before dawn. Loring finally assumes command of Bowen's retreating columns and races toward the Hankinson's Ferry floating bridge. As the column marches to the northeast, the vanguard runs into Alexander Reynolds's Tennessee Brigade, which has gotten lost in the maze of back roads in the inky blackness of the night and has failed to go the assistance of Col. Arthur Reynolds's men at Willow Springs. An exasperated Loring knows that if Grant gets across Big Bayou Pierre, the Yanks will have a shorter distance—about eight miles from Grindstone Ford to Hankinson's Ferry—than the Confederates' 12-mile route from Grand Gulf to Hankinson's, so he sends General Tilghman with the Alabama Brigade to help the Mississippi regiments delay Grant at Willow Springs. The Alabamians have just received a new commander, Gen. Stephen D. Lee, to replace the dead

General Tracy, so the temporary commander, Colonel Garrott, reverts back to command of the 20th Alabama.

When Loring's column reaches Hardscrabble Crossroads, where the Vicksburg–Grand Gulf Road meets the Vicksburg–Port Gibson Road halfway between Willow Springs and Hankinson's Ferry, Loring places Colonel Cockrell's hardfighting troops at the intersection. Cockrell is in position to protect the right flank of the main Confederate body as it passes through the intersection. He can also move south toward Willow Springs to provide support for the Confederates there if he is needed.

Spearheading the Union march north of Grindstone Ford is Gen. J. E. Smith's brigade, and the soldiers soon climb up the steep watershed on the north side of the river, using the deeply cut roadbed of the old Natchez Trace. Before the Yankees can travel a mile, the resounding boom of artillery breaks the morning calm. The rounds have been fired from a masked battery at the crest of the escarpment, and the guns belong to Arthur Reynolds's Mississippians. But Reynolds only has two regiments and a battery, and he posts them about a mile south of the community of Willow Springs and opens fire. Greatly outnumbered, Reynolds fires one volley and then withdraws two miles north to form a roadblock on the high ground of Alfred Ingraham's Ashwood Plantation, between the roads to Grand Gulf and Hankinson's Ferry. Here he is joined by Lee's Alabama Brigade, which forms on Reynolds's left to block the Hankinson's Ferry Road while Reynolds plans to block the road to Grand Gulf. General Tilghman, the senior officer, then assumes command of the troops.

McPherson, at Grindstone Ford, hears the guns and rushes Crocker's division across the bridge over Big Bayou Pierre to support Logan, who is moving forward with Smith's brigade. Smith forms a battle line and advances through the community of Willow Springs. After a brief skirmish north of Willow Springs, the Confederates retire, giving the Yanks possession of the heights at Ingraham's and, most importantly, control of the vital crossroads. Thus the Yanks gain access to the roads to Grand Gulf and Vicksburg. Tilghman's Confederates retreat up the road to Grand Gulf, pursued by Elias Dennis's brigade of Logan's division, while Stephen Lee falls back on the road to Hankinson's Ferry with Sanborn's brigade of Crocker's division hard on his heels.

Lloyd Tilghman, the first Confederate general captured in the Civil War at Fort Henry on February 6, 1862, has had enough of the Yankees on May 3. He retreats from Willow Springs west toward Grand Gulf until he reaches the intersection with the Vicksburg–Grand Gulf Road. At this intersection he turns his men north toward Vicksburg to follow General Loring and General Bowen and the retreating Confederates from Grand Gulf.

The race is now on to Hankinson's Ferry. If Grant's men can get there first—and they have the most direct route from Willow Springs to Hankinson's—they have the Confederates boxed in. But the combative Stephen Lee, showing the traits that will eventually make him the Confederacy's youngest lieutenant general, falls back for three-quarters of a mile to the high ground north of Kennison Creek and forms a battle line. Lee knows that he has to hold his blocking position long enough for Loring's and Bowen's column to pass through Hardscrabble Crossroads behind him and turn north toward Hankinson's Ferry. Lee is soon joined by the equally aggressive Cockrell and his ferocious Missourians, who have hustled south from Hardscrabble Crossroads to help delay the hard-pressing Yanks.

Moving north on the Vicksburg–Port Gibson Road, Crocker runs head-on into Lee's Kennison Creek line, and Crocker quickly deploys Sanborn's brigade. He places one of his regiments—his Hoosiers from the 59th Indiana—astride the road, with the 4th Minnesota on their right and the 48th Indiana on the left. After a brief spell of cannon fire, Sanborn's brigade advances across Kennison Creek.

Crocker knows the importance of this road because it is also the road to Vicksburg, so he takes his other two brigades, the Second Brigade of Col. Samuel A. Holmes and the Third Brigade of Col. George Boardman Boomer, and places them in line. Boomer masses on Sanborn's right, and Holmes on Sanborn's left.

Lee and Cockrell see that their lines are being overlapped by the oncoming Yanks. Lee orders Cockrell to cover his withdrawal, and he falls back with his Alabamians. The reliable Cockrell holds his ground long enough for Lee to retreat, and then his well-placed scouts advise him that Logan's men are advancing to his rear along the Vicksburg–Grand Gulf Road to the Hardscrabble Crossroads intersection about a mile in his rear. Cockrell then skillfully withdraws north, quickly moving through Hardscrabble Crossroads to Hankinson's Ferry, with Logan's Yankees following close behind.

Logan's division, upon advancing to Hardscrabble Crossroads, turns north toward Hankinson's Ferry in pursuit of Cockrell's retreating Confederates. After two and one-half miles, Logan's advance is on the ridge overlooking Hankinson's Ferry. At Hankinson's Ferry there occurs a coup that will take 82 years to equal. That will be when the First Army dashes across the Rhine at Remagen. Logan's people double-time down the half-mile escarpment to Hankinson's Ferry, where they capture the floating bridge over Big Black River before the Confederate rear guard can destroy it. They can do this because Capt. Samuel De Golyer's Eighth Michigan Battery gallops its teams to the front, unlimbers the guns, goes into battery, and fires rounds that scream downhill and raise geysers of water close to the unfortunate Confederate pioneers who are trying to chop the lashings holding the bridge. But the grunts grab the glory as the 20th Ohio of Dennis's brigade garners the honor of capturing the bridge.

Grant rides west from Willow Springs toward Grand Gulf. He needs to get to Grand Gulf because he has a number of things to attend to, primarily communicating with Washington. At the intersection of the Grand Gulf–Willow Springs Road and the Vicksburg–Grand Gulf Road, he sees the flotsam of a retreating army and knows that the Grand Gulf garrison has taken the road northward toward Vicksburg.

> *Governor Richard Yates of Illinois is at this intersection. He recalled the moment they realized that Bowen had retreated out of Grand Gulf. "This army of the Rebels was considered, as I now learn, invincible," he wrote. "But it quailed before the irresistible assault of Northwestern valor. I consider Vicksburg as ours in only a short time, and the Mississippi River as destined to be open from its source to its mouth."*

Grant continues west to Grand Gulf in the company of 20 cavalrymen. Accompanied by Lt. Col. John Rawlins and Assistant Secretary of War Charles Dana, he reaches Grand Gulf that afternoon to find Porter's navy already there. Early that morning Porter, at Bruinsburg, heard three gigantic explosions and saw the flashes in the predawn darkness from the direction of Grand Gulf. He knew what those explosions represented—the Confederates had evacuated the fortifications and blown their magazines. Porter headed up the river as quickly as he could to take possession of Grand Gulf before Grant could get there, because the Navy likes to play one-upmanship with the Army, and vice versa.

Porter allows his sailors at Grand Gulf to disembark and view firsthand the fortifications that gave them so much grief on April 29. After giving his tars the satisfaction of walking on the fortifications that formerly belonged to their adversary, Porter sounds recall. Obeying orders from the Secretary of the Navy to cooperate with Admiral Farragut's ships at the mouth of the Red River, Porter sends *Benton, LaFayette, General Price, Pittsburg,* and the tug *Ivy* south to the Red River. He leaves behind the damaged *Tuscumbia* as well as the

Eads gunboats, *Louisville, Carondelet,* and *Mound City.* These will be the boats moored at Grand Gulf when Grant rides down the steep bluff into the charred remnants of the town.

When Grant arrives at Grand Gulf, he does not take time to celebrate, although he has to be elated because he has achieved his second objective in the campaign for Vicksburg. But he does go aboard *Louisville* for a few creature comforts. He grabs a decent meal, a bath, and a change of underwear.

At Grand Gulf, Grant is going to make one of the great calculated risks of his career—a move with great significance for our nation as well. His orders, from no less than the United States War Department, are to remain at Grand Gulf and send one corps south to cooperate with Gen. Nathaniel P. Banks, who is supposed to be moving against Port Hudson. After Banks has captured Port Hudson, he will then come upriver, and he and Grant will strike toward Vicksburg with their combined forces. Banks has date of rank over Grant, so the political general would command this combined expedition. When Grant, however, boards *Louisville,* he realizes this plan is no longer viable. He learns, from a message given to him by the Navy, that Banks is off on an excursion trying to capture Alexandria, the new state capital of Louisiana. So Banks is nowhere near Port Hudson. He cannot be back at Baton Rouge before May 10 at the earliest, and then with only 15,000 men.

Ulysses S. Grant decides he is going to flout his orders. He has an opportunity to take Vicksburg on his own, and Banks has provided him a loophole in the contract. Even Halleck, the consummate lawyer, would have to accept that.

While at Grand Gulf, Grant sends a momentous message to Halleck: "I shall not bring my troops into this place, but immediately follow the enemy, and, if all promises as favorable hereafter as it does now, not stop until Vicksburg is in our possession."

Grant has the Confederates on the run, and he wants to continue striking. But, his boss, General Halleck, is called Old Brains, and he always believes in playing it safe. Risk taking is not in his vocabulary. In fact, Secretary of the Navy Gideon Welles made a famous diary entry about Halleck: "Knows nothing; does nothing; initiates nothing; and is good for nothing."

As Grant recalled in his memoirs: "I knew well that Halleck's caution would lead him to disapprove of this course, but it was the only one that gave any chance of success. The time it would take to communicate with Washington and get a reply would be so great that I could not be interfered with until it was demonstrated whether my plan was practicable."

Grant knows that there are no telegraphic communications south of Cairo, Illinois. Even when Halleck disapproves his plan, Grant is not going to officially learn this until the morning of May 17. By then it will be far too late to stop Grant's blitzkrieg.

Grant does intend, however, to keep Grand Gulf as a base of supplies for his army, and from Grand Gulf he sends a message to Sherman, who, per Grant's instructions, is marching the divisions of Gen. Frederick Steele and Gen. James M. Tuttle south. Sherman has left Gen. Frank Blair's division at Milliken's Bend to guard the supply depot and improve the roads from Young's Point to Richmond. Grant tells Sherman to collect 120 wagons at Milliken's Bend, load them with bacon, coffee, sugar, salt, and hardtack, and bring them and his men to Grand Gulf as soon as possible. He also tells Sherman that the enemy is "badly beaten," and that "the road to Vicksburg is open."

After writing the necessary messages, sometime around midnight on May 3, Grant rides into the darkness to Hankinson's Ferry and to the captured floating bridge, where Logan's and Crocker's divisions are encamped.

Colonel Wilson recalled that "Grant, Rawlins, and I worked until after midnight on the 3rd. . . . We mounted and rode back to the army, which we found in camp near Hankinson's Ferry at four o'clock on the morning of the 4th. As all the houses in the neighborhood were occupied by those who got there before us, we unsaddled, spread our blankets, and threw ourselves down on the porch of a plantation house for a rest. Grant was with us, tired and sleepy, but contented. We slept 'til the smell of breakfast and the rising sun awoke us."

At Chancellorsville on May 3, a Sunday morning, Robert E. Lee and Stonewall Jackson have turned the tables on Joe Hooker by flanking the Federal Army; thus making even the score after Hooker's successful turning movement of April 30. However, although Hooker's army has been dealt a staggering blow, it has not been destroyed, and Lee's army is still divided. So Lee is in peril, despite Jackson's best efforts to prevent the Federals from reorganizing. Just as important, Lee has lost Stonewall Jackson. The Army of Northern Virginia has lost its clenched fist— its thunderbolt.

When Lee hears of what happened to Jackson, he exclaims, "Thank God it is no worse! God be praised he is still alive."

Without his other corps commander, James Longstreet, who is in the Suffolk area, Lee has unfinished work. He must reunite his force in the face of Hooker's numerically superior force. With Jackson injured, command of the II Corps is given to the young, but respected, Jeb Stuart. At 3 a.m. Lee writes to Stuart that Hooker "must be pressed so that we can unite the two wings of the army. Endeavor, therefore, to dispossess them of Chancellorsville, which will permit the union of the whole army."

Jeb Stuart takes command of Jackson's corps and obeys Lee's orders to push forward. During the early morning hours, the Confederates prepare for the attack that is to begin at daylight. They begin to move forward at 5:30 a.m., but the new command structure causes confusion and orders are misinterpreted. Not until 6 a.m. do the Confederate skirmishers fronting Stuart's first battle line move forward.

About the same time, Joe Hooker orders Gen. Dan Sickles, commanding the Union III Corps, to evacuate Hazel Grove, which stands between the two Confederate wings of Lee's army. It is also the best artillery ground on the field. Sickles reluctantly obeys. Stuart's new chief of artillery, Col. Edward Porter Alexander, arrives at Hazel Grove, and he seizes the golden opportunity.

Alexander, in 1907, recalled the "gift" of Hazel Grove: "The battle was still Hooker's, had he fought where he stood. But about dawn he made the fatal mistake of recalling Sickles from the Hazel Grove position, which he was holding with Whipple's and Birney's divisions, and five batteries. There has rarely been a more gratuitous gift of a battle-field."

Of all the battles in the Civil War, both in the eastern and western theaters, this is the one in which the Confederate artillery will overwhelm their Union counterparts. Porter Alexander will use his artillery to move forward with fire and movement, which was one of Bonaparte's great secrets. Being an artillerist, Bonaparte made use of infantry and artillery in coordination. With that tactical innovation, Bonaparte became the master of most of Europe until he made the mistake of invading Russia in 1812.

Alexander quickly places his artillery on the high ground of Hazel Grove, and soon 31 cannon are blasting the Yankees. They're going to give the bluecoats payback for Malvern Hill. The Confederates, however, will receive their payback two months later at Gettysburg.

As the Confederates attack, Jeb Stuart is everywhere. He is dressed flamboyantly. Although it is rather dangerous, he is wearing a blue coat, two ostrich feathers in his hat, and a red artillery sash, having removed his yellow cavalry sash. And he's singing a song to the tune of "The Old Gray Mare," except he's using the words, "Old Joe Hooker, won't you come out of the Wilderness." While it may not be very cerebral, the men are responding to it. Stuart's a colorful, flashing figure.

Shortly after 9 a.m. Gen. Dan Sickles sends his senior aide, Maj. Henry E. Tremain, to Joe Hooker to ask for support. Hooker is on the porch of the Chancellor house when he sees Tremain coming, so he leans over the rail to hear the report in the din of battle. A solid shot hits the pillar that Hooker has just been leaning on, and it splits the column from top to bottom, just as lightning may do when it hits a tree. Hooker is brushed by half of the split column, which smacks him on his head and down his side. He is knocked senseless, and for a few minutes is thought to be dying. The rumor of his death spreads like wildfire through the army.

> *Gen. Darius Couch recalled in 1884: "I was at the time but a few yards to his left, and, dismounting, ran to the porch. The shattered pillar was there, but I could not find him or anyone else. Hurrying through the house, finding no one, my search was continued through the back yard. All the time I was thinking, 'If he is killed, what shall I do with this disjointed army?' Passing through the yard I came upon him, to my great joy, mounted, and with his staff also in their saddles. Briefly congratulating him on his escape—it was not time to blubber or use soft expressions—I went about my own business. This was the last I saw of my commanding general in front. The time, I reckon, was from 9:15 to 9:30 a.m., I think nearer the former than the latter. He probably left the field soon after his hurt, but he neither notified me of his going nor did he give any orders to me whatever. . . . Lee by this time knew well enough, if he had not known before, that the game was sure to fall into his hands, and accordingly plied every gun and rifle that could be brought to bear on us."*

General Couch, discussing the situation with Gen. John Geary, tells Geary to "fight it out." A few minutes later, a member of Hooker's staff rides up to Couch and asks him to come see Hooker. Couch turns to General Hancock, who is nearby, and tells him to "take care of things," and then rides to the rear for about a half mile to an open field with three or four standing tents. A number of officers are milling around, including George Gordon Meade. Couch finds Hooker in a small tent by himself, and when he enters, Hooker raises himself up a little, and says: "Couch, I turn command of the army over to you." But then, after turning over the command, Hooker continues, "You will withdraw it, and place it in the position designated on this map." Hooker points to a line that has been drawn on a field sketch. Hooker has lost his will to fight, and he will not allow his lieutenant to pick up the sword.

Couch later recalled that the meeting with Hooker "was perhaps three-quarters of an hour after his hurt. He seemed rather dull, but possessed of his mental faculties. I do not think that one of those officers outside of the tent knew what orders I was to receive, for on stepping out, which I did immediately on getting my instructions, I met Meade close by, looking inquiringly as if he expected that finally he would receive the order for which he had waited all that long morning, 'to go in.' Colonel N. H. Davis [Hooker's assistant inspector-general] broke out: 'We shall have some fighting now.'"

Instead of "going in" as the corps commanders expected, the army is ordered to fall back to a new defensive line. Shortly after 10 a.m. the order to withdraw is given, and between 11 a.m. and noon on May 3, 1863, the Federal troops have all pulled back to the new defense line designed to protect their escape route, U.S. Ford.

Robert E. Lee rides to the front at the burning Chancellor house, and an aide, Maj. Charles Marshall, recalled that "his presence was the signal for one of those uncontrollable outbursts of enthusiasm which none can appreciate who have not witnessed them. The fierce soldiers, with their faces blackened with the smoke of battle, the wounded crawling with feeble limbs from the fury of the devouring flames, all seemed possessed of a common impulse. One long, unbroken cheer, in which the feeble cry of those who lay helpless on the earth blended with the strong voices of those who still fought, hailed the presence of the victorious chief."

In the midst of this Lee receives a note from the wounded Jackson congratulating him on the victory. Lee replies: "Could I have directed events, I should have chosen, for the good of the country, to be disabled in your stead. I congratulate you upon the victory, which is due to your skill and energy." When

Jackson receives Lee's message, he says: "General Lee is very kind, but he should give the praise to God."

Lee then sends a "victory" message to President Davis advising him that Hooker "was dislodged from all his positions around Chancellorsville, and was driven back toward the Rappahannock, over which he is now retreating." The second part of this statement is, at the time, an erroneous assumption on Lee's part, possibly influenced by the emotion of the moment. Lee goes on to say: "We have again to thank Almighty God for a great victory. I regret to state that General Paxton was killed, General Jackson severely, and General Heth and Gen. A. P. Hill slightly, wounded."

Lee's triumphal moment is short-lived, because at 12:30 one of Jubal Early's aides arrives on a sweat-lathered horse to warn that Gen. John Sedgwick's reinforced Federal VI Corps, which Hooker has left behind to hold Lee in place, has taken the heights above Fredericksburg. Sedgwick is a Gen. Omar Bradley–type individual—a soldier's soldier. His grandfather, also named John Sedgwick, was a major in Washington's army during the Revolutionary War. Sedgwick commands nearly 22,000 men, dispersed among four divisions. And now, just as Lee is preparing to renew the attack on Hooker, he learns that he has a reinforced Federal infantry corps threatening his rear. But Lee remains calm.

A Mississippi soldier, R. W. Royall, recalled that, when he excitedly rode up to Lee with another report, Lee simply said, "We will attend to Mr. Sedgwick later."

Lee quickly assesses the situation. Of course, he has to abandon, at least for the time being, his plans to attack Hooker, but he will hold Hooker in place with a demonstration. To block Sedgwick he orders Gen. Lafayette McLaws to march his division, which has not been heavily engaged, back toward Fredericksburg. Lee then turns his attention to Hooker. He orders a demonstration toward U.S. Ford to keep Hooker in place. Then Lee gets some relatively good news. He learns that Gen. Cadmus Wilcox has moved his Alabama Brigade, which has been watching Banks's Ford, southward to block Sedgwick at Salem Church. Wilcox is a West Pointer, class of '46, and is a professional soldier. This will not be the only time in the war that Wilcox shows great initiative, but this is the perfect time and place for such an attribute, because if Wilcox can hold Sedgwick long enough at Salem Church, there are four brigades under McLaws on the way to help.

WHAT WILL THE COUNTRY SAY?

As Sedgwick moves westward from Fredericksburg on the Orange Plank Road with three brigades of Gen. William "Bully" Brooks's division—nearly 4,000 men—they make contact with Wilcox's 1,200 Alabamians. Wilcox is fighting for time until he can be reinforced. Remarkably, he delays the Federals for four hours, until a messenger rides up to inform him that McLaws is on the way. McLaws quickly moves his men eastward to Salem Church, while Wilcox deploys his men across the Plank Road in some old rifle pits dug by Gen. George Pickett's division back in January as a fallback position behind Fredericksburg.

When the Federals begin to advance, they drive in the Confederate skirmish line, and they continue advancing until they reach Salem Church. But, just as they reach the church, they are confronted by a line of five brigades—those of Mahone, Semmes, Wilcox, Kershaw, and Wofford, totaling about 10,000 men. McLaws has arrived just in the nick of time to save Wilcox from certain destruction. Even so, the fighting around the vicinity of the church is ferocious with heavy casualties on both sides. But the Confederates hold this important ground.

General Lee hears the cannonading from Salem Church just before 5 p.m., and he knows that if Hooker is ever going to attack from his defensive position in front of U.S. Ford, it is now. But, remarkably, Hooker stays in place, content to let Sedgwick fight on his own, and darkness ends the fighting.

In Tennessee, General Rosecrans is still in Murfreesboro on May 3, and his one spring offensive—the raid of Col. Abel Streight—comes to an ignoble conclusion around noon that day. Nathan Bedford Forrest's cavalry has been in pursuit of Streight's men across north Alabama since April 29, and "Old Bedford" has finally caught up with the bone-tired Yanks at Mrs. Lawrence's plantation near the Alabama-Georgia state line, 20 miles west of Rome, Georgia. Forrest has his men on both flanks of Streight's command, but before he attacks, he senses the moment. In typical Forrest fashion, he sends one of his staff officers, Capt. Henry Pointer, forward under a flag of truce, demanding Streight's immediate surrender "in order to stop the further and useless effusion of blood."

Acknowledging Forrest's flag of truce, Streight calls a council of his officers to discuss their options. Streight knows that he is almost out of ammunition, that the horses and mules are worn-out, and that the men cannot stay awake. The only option is surrender, say his officers, but Streight is opposed to that. So, accompanied by an aide, he rides out to play his hand, as best he can, with the master poker player, Bedford Forrest.

Streight says that he will not surrender unless he can be assured that Forrest has a force at least equal to the size of his. Now, Forrest doesn't have but 500 men with him, and Streight has 1,250, so Forrest decides to bluff. He makes the point that he has been driving and beating Streight's men for the past three days, and that should be proof enough of his superior numbers.

As the two commanders talk, a section of Forrest's artillery under Lt. J. G. Jones arrives at a full gallop, and Streight correctly complains that neither troops nor guns should advance during a flag of truce. Forrest agrees, and sends word to move the guns back to a ridge 300 yards in the rear. But Forrest continues his bluff. Lieutenant Jones is covertly instructed to take the guns behind the ridge and circle the two guns, first going out of sight and then reappearing. Forrest notes the look in Streight's eyes as the colonel sees the succession of guns appearing and then disappearing from the ridgetop. Finally, Streight says: "Name of God! How many guns have you got? There's fifteen I've counted already." Forrest glances over his shoulder, and, poker-faced, says: "I reckon that's all that has kept up."

Streight nervously asks Forrest again how many men he has. "Enough to whip you out of your boots," is Forrest's answer. Streight says that he wants to go back and talk with his officers again, and Captain Pointer decides to up the ante. The captain offers Streight a drink before he leaves, saying it might well be the last he will ever have. Streight is happy to accept, and, after taking a big swig, he shakes hands with his adversaries and goes back to talk to his officers.

Streight's officers vote unanimously to surrender, and Streight yields to the decision of the council. He surrenders around noon, and though his men don't know it, they outnumber Forrest's command by almost three to one.

After Streight's men are disarmed, he realizes he has been duped. He demands to have his weapons back so that they can fight it out. Forrest pats Streight on the shoulder and says, "Ah, Colonel, all is fair in love and war, you know."

On May 4, at Hankinson's Ferry on Big Black River, Grant has Capt. Stewart Tresilian busily repairing the floating Confederate bridge, and for the next few days all of the skiffs and boats in the area are gathered and roads are cut down to the riverbank in different areas to support a river crossing. As the Confederates watch, they become convinced that Grant intends to close on Vicksburg from the south. That is precisely what Grant wants them to believe.

Grant and his son, Fred, establish quarters in the home of Mrs. Samuel Pipes Bagnell, located one mile north of Hardscrabble Crossroads on the Port

Gibson–Vicksburg Road. A family member later claimed that Grant planned the next stage of his campaign on a little table in the room where he stayed.

While Grant encamps near Hankinson's Ferry, McClernand bivouacs at Alfred Ingraham's house, Ashwood Plantation, located about three-quarters of a mile north of Willow Springs. McClernand sends Osterhaus's division up the old Natchez Trace to Big Sand Creek. At Ashwood, McClernand quickly learns that Mrs. Elizabeth Ingraham is the sister of a senior officer in the Army of the Potomac, George Gordon Meade, who at that very moment is commanding the V Corps at Chancellorsville. Yes, Mrs. Ingraham has sons serving in the Confederate Army, but she lets McClernand know that McPherson's men looted her property when they came through the day before, and that she wants what's left of her home and farm protected. Word travels fast in the area, and area inhabitants are seeing the plumes of smoke from the burning plantation homes in Louisiana.

Sherman blames this wanton destruction of private property on the "cursed stragglers who won't fight, but hang behind and disgrace our cause and country."

Much of this destruction is being done by men of Sherman's XV Corps— Gen. Charles L. Matthies's brigade. In this brigade are soldiers of the Eighth and 12th Iowa who were captured at the Hornet's Nest at Shiloh on April 6, 1862. They are embittered by their six-month stay in Confederate prison camps before their exchange, and now they exact their revenge on the South.

On May 4 at Chancellorsville, Stonewall Jackson is transported in an ambulance more than 30 miles to Thomas C. Chandler's 740-acre Fairfield Plantation, where Jackson's doctor hopes to place him aboard a train for Richmond once the Confederates regain control of the rail line.

While Stonewall Jackson is being moved away from the battlefield, Lee realizes that Hooker is not going to attack, so the Gray Fox plans to destroy Sedgwick's isolated corps. All the while, Hooker somehow manages, at least in his mind, to shift the responsibility for saving his army over to Sedgwick. He will let Sedgwick with 24,000 men try to achieve what he was unable to accomplish with more than 72,000 troops.

Lee sends Gen. Richard Anderson's division to assist McLaws, and then he personally rides to Salem Church to supervise his senior division commander,

McLaws, whom he knows is a good division commander but not a man of initiative. When Lee arrives at 11 a.m. he finds that McLaws has done virtually nothing and is simply awaiting Anderson's arrival. To add to Lee's exasperation, Anderson is very slow in coming up. Lee loses his temper.

> *Col. Edward Porter Alexander of McLaws's artillery reserve wrote: "Probably no man ever commanded an army, and at the same time, so entirely commanded himself, as Lee. This morning was almost the only occasion I ever saw him out of humor. . . . Although Lee urged all possible speed, it was 6:00 p.m. when the attack commenced. Sunset was at seven. Darkness fell before the lines could be gotten into close action."*

The "fog of war" foils Lee's plan. Confusion reigns in the Confederate lines in the darkness, and under cover of night, Sedgwick's VI Corps escapes across the pontoon bridge over the Rappahannock at Scott's Ford.

Meanwhile, Joe Hooker, somewhat recovered, now wants to retreat. But, rather than accept the responsibility of a decision, he decides to hold a midnight council of war in his tent. During this council he asks his officers to vote on what course of action the Army of the Potomac should take.

> *Couch later recalled that at this meeting, "Hooker stated that his instructions compelled him to cover Washington, not to jeopardize the army, etc. It was seen by the most casual observer that he had made up his mind to retreat."*

At the council of war the officers vote, and the results are three for fighting it out, two to withdraw. Reynolds, Meade, and Howard vote to attack, and Sickles and Couch vote to withdraw. Despite the three-to-two vote to stay and fight, Hooker says the army will withdraw. The results are too close, he says, and he thanks the generals, and adjourns the meeting.

> *As Darius Couch stoops down to leave the tent, a disgusted John Reynolds says to him, "What was the use of calling us together at this time of night when he intended to retreat anyhow?"*

On May 5, Grant is still at Hankinson's Ferry on Big Black River, busily making plans and evaluating the situation. He has soldiers establishing a supply base at Grand Gulf, with Col. William S. Hillyer, one of Grant's aides, serving as the "logistics czar."

Grant sends Hillyer a message from Hankinson's, saying, "Movements here are delayed for the want of ammunition and stores. Every day's delay is worth two thousand men to the enemy. Give this your personal attention."

Grant orders McPherson to send two regiments from Boomer's brigade, along with two pieces of artillery, across Big Black River on a reconnaissance mission to determine the location and intent of the Confederates. A squadron of Missouri cavalry forms the vanguard, and the troopers soon discover, dug in along Redbone Ridge about seven miles due north of Hankinson's, a strong defensive line manned by thousands of Confederates.

Grant also has McClernand send Osterhaus's division out of Willow Springs, northeast to Rocky Springs. Three miles past Rocky Springs, at Big Sand Creek, Osterhaus's vanguard runs into a Confederate cavalry patrol and has a spirited skirmish. The Southerners make a hasty retreat, but lose 12 dead and 30 captured. Osterhaus's vanguard goes into camp at Big Sand Creek, while most of his division encamps at Rocky Springs.

Grant receives McPherson's report of the area north of Hankinson's Ferry, and doesn't feel it would be wise to go against the Confederate prepared positions, much less fight in this terrain where the country "stands on edge," so he decides on another plan. He decides to cut the railroad communications between Vicksburg and Jackson, repaying Pemberton for Van Dorn's raid back in December. Grant decides that as soon as Sherman arrives, the army is going to move in a northeasterly direction toward the Southern Railroad of Mississippi that connects Jackson to Vicksburg.

As insurance, Grant sends orders to Hurlbut in Memphis to send Gen. Jacob Lauman's division to Milliken's Bend as soon as possible. Even though Grant knows these men cannot possibly arrive in time to help him on his inland campaign, he feels sure they can be of use to him when he returns to the Mississippi River.

At Chancellorsville, it takes all day on Tuesday, May 5, for Robert E. Lee to marshal and organize his scattered forces. He plans to attack Hooker's new defensive position as soon as he can get his army organized, but that afternoon a thunderstorm moves in, flooding the roads and making any movement in the mud a monumental task. Lee has no choice but to wait for Wednesday morning to attack.

While Lee reorganizes on May 5, Hooker works on his retreat. All during the day, General Warren lays out a compact, final defensive line to protect U.S. Ford, and roads are cut leading to the ford.

Hooker has Gen. Dan Butterfield, his chief of staff, send a message to President Lincoln, breaking the news as best he can: "Position is strong, but circumstances, which in time will be fully explained, make it expedient, in the general's judgment, that he should retire from this position to the north bank of the Rappahannock for his defensive position."

The Federal artillery begins to retreat across three pontoon bridges over the Rappahannock at 7 p.m. Hooker and Butterfield are among the first to cross, leaving their corps commanders and their men to fend for themselves.

That same day, James Longstreet is en route to rejoin Lee, and he passes through Richmond, arriving late. He meets privately with Secretary of War James Seddon.

Seddon informs Longstreet that he has "in contemplation a plan for concentrating a succoring army at Jackson, Mississippi, under the command of General Johnston, with a view of driving Grant from before Vicksburg by a direct issue-at-arms."

Seddon asks Longstreet for his opinion about sending troops to Mississippi, and Longstreet advises that Grant is too strong and too well supplied via the Mississippi River. Longstreet says he believes that the best strategy is to reinforce Bragg's army and go on the offensive against the immobile Rosecrans at Murfreesboro. He then proposes that he take his two divisions, which are still en route to rejoin Lee, and entrain for a journey west to Bragg's army at Tullahoma. Bragg's strengthened army could then defeat Rosecrans and march for Cincinnati, forcing the Federals to withdraw troops from Mississippi to meet this new threat.

Longstreet later wrote that Seddon was unconvinced and that the secretary said, "Grant was such an obstinate fellow that he could only be induced to quit Vicksburg by terribly hard knocks."

Longstreet has had a taste of an independent command at Suffolk, and like any soldier with ambition, he enjoyed it. Longstreet certainly knows that General Bragg is on very shaky ground as a commanding general, so, who better to fill the bristly Bragg's shoes than Lee's Old War Horse? That thought certainly crosses Longstreet's mind during his interview with Seddon. Abraham Lincoln once described this kind of blind ambition as a "grub that gnaws deep."

On May 6, Grant sends another message to General in Chief Halleck from Hankinson's Ferry, advising him: "Ferrying and transportation of rations to Grand Gulf is detaining us on the Black River. I will move as soon as three days rations received and send wagons back to the Gulf for more to follow. Information from the other side leads me to believe the enemy are bringing forces from the Tullahoma. Should not General Rosecrans at least make a demonstration of advancing?" This message will not be received by Halleck in Washington until 1:30 a.m., May 13. It makes no difference, because Rosecrans has no intention of moving.

Grant needs rations and ammunition for his move toward the railroad. Leaving Grand Gulf for Hankinson's Ferry early on May 6 are 200 wagons of all sizes and shapes, loaded high above the sideboards with rations and ammunition. Colonel Hillyer has done his job well.

At 7 a.m. General McClernand departs Willow Springs with Hovey's division and marches to Rocky Springs, arriving before noon.

A soldier of the 24th Iowa wrote in his diary that there were "several stores and fair buildings. I called at one, where a crowd was gathering up the articles and got a couple of books."

At Chancellorsville, the Union engineers work all through the dark, stormy, early morning hours of May 6, desperately attempting to lengthen the three pontoon bridges due to the rising water. Finally, they disassemble one bridge to obtain pieces to lengthen the other two, and, though the engineers complete the work, it takes until daybreak on Wednesday, May 6, before the artillery is across. After daylight, the infantry begins to cross, and soon there are thousands of soldiers packed together, waiting to cross the Rappahannock. By 8 a.m. the exhausted and soaked army is across. The last soldiers to cross are from the brigade of Gen. James Barnes of Meade's V Corps.

General Lee, on the morning of May 6, is about to give orders to attack the Federal defensive position, when Gen. Dorsey Pender rides up and advises that Hooker is gone. Lee is frustrated, because he was surprised by Joe Hooker at the beginning and ending of this campaign.

In Washington, Abraham Lincoln begs for news of the battle. At 3 p.m. on May 6, he receives a message that the Army of the Potomac has retreated across the Rappahannock. Journalist Noah Brooks, in the White House with the President when this message arrives, wrote: "Had a thunderbolt fallen upon the President he could not have been more overwhelmed. One newly risen from the dead could not have looked more ghostlike. . . . Clasping his hands behind his back, he walked up and down the room, saying, 'My God, my God, what will the country say! What will the country say?' "

Chapter 5
TO THE RAILROAD EAST
OF VICKSBURG

May 7–13, 1863

After the capture of the Confederate raft bridge by Gen. James McPherson's XVII Corps at Hankinson's Ferry on Big Black River below Vicksburg, Grant remains at Hankinson's until the night of May 7. He anxiously waits for news that Sherman has reached Hard Times Landing and is crossing over to Grand Gulf with two of his XV Corps divisions, commanded by Gen. James Tuttle and Gen. Frederick Steele. Tuttle is a former Ohio farmer and shopkeeper and has served with Grant at Donelson, Shiloh, and Corinth. Steele is a New Yorker and an 1843 West Point classmate of Grant's. The fact that Steele is with Grant is no accident.

GRANT SEEMS TO HAVE A LOT OF HIS CLASSMATES ALONG WITH HIM. AS an army commander, he is beginning to show the problem of cronyism that is going to get him in trouble in the White House. If he likes you, he likes you. As long as he likes an able man, that's all right. But if he likes a guy that doesn't have much ability, then Grant, being the trusting soul that he is, will overlook it. This will be the seed for his problems as President.

Sherman's two divisions march south in Louisiana, taking the route pioneered by McClernand, with Steele's division as the vanguard. Steele's men arrive at Hard Times on the night of May 6, and the soldiers begin to shuttle across the Mississippi to Grand Gulf. Tuttle's men arrive on the heels of Steele's men, and shuttle across all the next day and well into the night. Gen. Francis "Frank" P. Blair, Jr., commanding Sherman's other division, leaves Milliken's Bend on the morning of the seventh and marches south. Blair is the son of the Lincoln adviser who offered Lee command of the U.S. Army on April 18, 1861. The junior Blair is a lawyer and former U.S. congressman from Missouri.

Grant wrote in his memoirs: "After McPherson crossed the Big Black at Hankinson's Ferry Vicksburg could have been approached and besieged by the south side. It is not probable, however, that Pemberton would have permitted a close besiegement. The broken nature of the ground would have enabled him to hold a strong defensible line from the river south of the city to the Big Black, retaining possession of the railroad back to that point. It was my plan, therefore, to get to the railroad east of Vicksburg, and approach from that direction. Accordingly, McPherson's troops that had crossed the Big Black were withdrawn and the movement east to Jackson commenced."

On May 7, Grant orders McPherson and McClernand to move toward the railroad, maintaining a pace that will allow Sherman's XV Corps to catch up from Grand Gulf. McPherson marches from Hankinson's Ferry to Rocky Springs with Logan's division, leaving Crocker's division at the ferry to hold the bridgehead until Sherman arrives. Meanwhile, McClernand is making room for McPherson.

McClernand marches the rest of Osterhaus's division out of Rocky Springs, and the men soon go into camp with their compatriots who had skirmished with the Confederate cavalry on the fifth at Big Sand Creek. McClernand has General Hovey's division march from Rocky Springs to Big Sand Creek, and these soldiers go into camp on the left of Osterhaus's men. Carr marches his division from Willow Springs to Big Sand Creek, and these men pass through Osterhaus's troops and go into camp in an open field near the creek. McClernand's XIII Corps also brings along a battery of 30-pounder Parrotts. Since he now has three divisions encamped at Big Sand Creek, he forms a picket line along the road with these monster guns.

A lot of horse and mule power is required to pull a 30-pounder Parrott, because it is a large gun, weighing 4,200 pounds. An artillery horse can pull an absolute maximum of 700 pounds, preferably around 600 pounds, so a two-ton gun would stretch a six-horse team to the limit. A team of six horses pulling 30-pounder Parrotts needs to be expanded to eight. Still, these guns travel all the way inland with McClernand's corps and will eventually be positioned against the Confederate fortifications at Vicksburg. They will be manned by a detachment—men who have been converted to artillery—from the First U.S. Infantry.

McClernand has a big corps of four divisions, and A. J. Smith's is his reserve division. Smith marches from Willow Springs and stops short at Little Sand Creek, one and one-half miles northeast of Rocky Springs.

McClernand accompanies a cavalry patrol to conduct a reconnaissance up the old Natchez Trace to the vicinity of Hall's Ferry on Big Black River, and he dispatches a detailed report back to Grant. McClernand will do this all the way along the Union advance—that is, he will keep Grant accurately informed of the road network in front of the army.

While Grant is moving his army toward the railroad, what are the Confederates doing? Pemberton, now with his headquarters in Vicksburg, has to keep a force stationed at Snyder's Bluff because the Yankees still have a naval fleet above Vicksburg, and if these fortifications were abandoned the boats could go up the Yazoo River and disembark troops on the high ground at Satartia, where a good road leads south into Vicksburg.

Across the Mississippi River from Vicksburg are the men of Blair's division, who remain there until the morning of May 7, handling the supply depot and maintaining the road south from Milliken's Bend. These men can be seen by the Confederates in Vicksburg, so they are a potential threat.

Pemberton also has to have forces manning the Vicksburg river defenses because the Federals have a Navy. And Pemberton has men entrenching along a line in the bluffs north of Hankinson's Ferry because he is assuming that Grant, after capturing the bridge at Hankinson's, is going to attack from the south.

Besides trying to cover all these potential Federal threats, Pemberton has an in-house dilemma, and it centers around two messages he receives. The first is a telegram sent from Gen. Joe Johnston, his military commander, advising him to abandon Vicksburg and unite all his troops to beat Grant. Johnston tells Pemberton that he can return to Vicksburg after beating Grant in the field. Pemberton then receives a message from his supreme commander, President Jefferson Davis, telling him to hold onto both Vicksburg and Port Hudson because the two points are necessary to maintain a connection with the Trans-Mississippi. So the conundrum is whether to abandon Vicksburg and go out and fight Grant, or to hold onto Vicksburg and assume a defensive role.

Pemberton can't forget that he once commanded at Charleston, and when he advocated the evacuation of that city full of blue bloods and old money, he got into deep trouble. He lost his job and ended up out west in Mississippi. So Pemberton is not about to evacuate Vicksburg, as Johnston recommends, because this would defy the president's orders and possibly court trouble with Mississippi's Governor John J. Pettus.

Not being a decisive man, Pemberton decides to try to please Johnston, Davis, and Pettus, and leaves troops in Vicksburg to defend it against the Union Navy while deploying others to face Grant's hydra-like threats. This attempt to defend all points will be Pemberton's undoing. As the Chinese general Sun Tzu wrote, "To be prepared everywhere is to be weak everywhere."

In Washington, immediately after receiving the message of Hooker's retreat from Chancellorsville, Lincoln and Halleck take a carriage to the Washington Navy Yard, board a special steamer to Aquia Landing, and then entrain to Falmouth Station to meet with Hooker on May 7.

At Chancellorsville, Hooker has lost more than 17,000 men—killed, wounded, and missing—while Lee has lost nearly 13,000. Lincoln tells Hooker, his staff, and his corps commanders that this defeat will be the most serious setback of the war, both at home and abroad. To be sure, a state of near panic reigns in Washington. But Lincoln, unlike Hooker, does not point fingers, and simply asks about the morale and condition of the army. However, when Lincoln leaves that afternoon, he has Halleck stay behind. Halleck is told to find out what happened at Chancellorsville.

On the way back to Washington that night, Lincoln writes to Hooker, "The recent movement of your army is ended without effecting its object. . . . What next?"

On the morning of May 8, Sherman is finally moving east, up the escarpment and out of Grand Gulf, with three days rations and ammunition in the haversacks of his men. He is running a day behind schedule due to delays in ferrying troops across the Mississippi, so Grant's army pauses for Sherman to catch up.

On Friday afternoon, May 8, Grant and McClernand review the divisions of Osterhaus, Carr, and Hovey at Big Sand Creek. Historians often call it a day of rest for the troops, but there is nothing restful about a soldier getting his gear and uniform cleaned and ready, polishing his brass, and cleaning his weapon, followed by standing in ranks for hours until the commanding general arrives and reviews the troops. And then, there are the speeches—the interminable speeches—which are the bane of any soldier standing in ranks.

While McClernand's three divisions pass in review, Tuttle's division of Sherman's corps leads the way up the bluffs from Grand Gulf, and marches east to Willow Springs. Steele's division follows Tuttle's, but then, after passing through the community of Ingleside, Steele turns north onto the Hankinson's Ferry. At Hankinson's he relieves Crocker's men at the bridgehead late that day.

When Grant crossed the Mississippi, Pemberton, realizing he needed more men, ordered Gen. John Gregg's brigade out of Port Hudson to Jackson. On May 2, these men marched from Port Hudson to Osyka, Mississippi, 55 miles distant on the Louisiana-Mississippi state line, expecting to take trains to Jackson. However, they found that Grierson's raiders had destroyed a 20-mile stretch of the railroad from Brookhaven south to Summit, so they marched ten miles north to Magnolia and rode the trains for another ten miles to Summit. There they detrained and marched 20 miles to Brookhaven, where they entrained and rode the last 50 miles to Jackson. Gregg's exhausted men arrive just before dark on May 8, and go into camp two miles east of Jackson.

On May 8, per President Lincoln's instructions, General Halleck, who is no fan of Fighting Joe Hooker, quickly calls the corps commanders into a conference. Gen. Darius Couch advises Halleck of the "great dissatisfaction among the higher officers at the management of Chancellorsville."

Halleck returns to Washington and advises President Lincoln and Secretary Stanton that "both the check at Chancellorsville and the retreat were inexcusable, and that Hooker must not be entrusted with the conduct of another battle."

Hooker, under fire in Washington, does not improve his standing as a commander with his fellow generals in Falmouth. He begins to openly blame Howard, Sedgwick, and Stoneman for the defeat at Chancellorsville. Reacting to this attack on their colleagues, most of Hooker's corps commanders bond against him, and they indiscreetly discuss their dissatisfaction. Henry Slocum solicits his fellow corps commanders to petition the President to relieve Hooker and place George Meade in command. Meade, who is junior in grade to Slocum, Couch, and Sedgwick, will have none of such talk.

But even Meade, along with fellow Pennsylvanian and corps commander, John Reynolds, discusses the mistakes that Hooker made at Chancellorsville with visitor Andrew G. Curtin, Governor of Pennsylvania. Curtin promptly travels to the White House and meets with President Lincoln, translating the criticism of Hooker's tactics into a statement that Meade and Reynolds "had lost all confidence" in Hooker. Also, within the ranks and the junior officers of the Army of the Potomac, there is dissatisfaction.

Lt. George Armstrong Custer, only 23 years old, writes to Gen. George B. McClellan: "Even Hooker's best friends are clamoring for his removal, saying that they are disappointed in him."

For President Lincoln, however, the dilemma is more complex than just the confidence of Hooker's subordinates. In less than two years Lincoln has relieved five eastern theater army commanders: Irvin McDowell, George McClellan, John Pope, George McClellan a second time, and Ambrose Burnside. Pressure is now being applied to relieve Joe Hooker. The President does not want the public to perceive that he has such poor judgment in selecting his commanders and that he is so capricious that he would relieve a commander after losing one battle.

More important to Lincoln, Hooker has the backing of the Radical Republicans, who insist on helping Lincoln choose a general who will prosecute the war to bring about the destruction of slavery and of the South's culture. Many of these radicals carry great influence, such as Congressman Thaddeus Stevens of Pennsylvania, who is chairman of the House Ways and Means Committee; Senator Benjamin Franklin Wade of Ohio; and Senator Zachariah Chandler of Michigan. These men control the Congressional Joint Committee on the Conduct of the War, known for its partisan politics and for judging commanders based on their politics, rather that their fighting abilities. Their principal ally is a member of Lincoln's Cabinet— Treasury Secretary Salmon P. Chase—and Joe Hooker is their man. Lincoln decides that sticking with Hooker a bit longer is better than the entanglement of another nasty political fight.

While Halleck talks to Hooker's generals in Falmouth, on May 8 Lincoln finally gets some good news. At a cabinet meeting he learns from Secretary of the Navy Gideon Welles that Adm. David Porter has captured Grand Gulf. At 4 p.m. the President telegraphs Joe Hooker and advises him of the news, describing it as "a large and very important thing." But Hooker takes little satisfaction from Grant's success.

On May 9, at dawn, Crocker's division of McPherson's XVII Corps, now relieved by Steele's division of Sherman's XV Corps, marches from Hankinson's Ferry while Steele's men dismantle the floating bridge over Big Black River at the ferry site. Crocker marches through Rocky Springs, while Logan's division, already encamped at the hamlet, breaks camp around noon and falls in behind Crocker's men as they march past the brick Rocky Springs Methodist Church.

They move northeast along the old Natchez Trace for five miles, and then turn slightly southeast toward Utica. McPherson's men reach Meyer's farm, almost six miles west of Utica, and encamp on the night of the ninth.

McClernand's XIII Corps, with the exception of A. J. Smith's division, remains in camp on the ninth. Smith's men leisurely march two miles from Little Sand Creek to Big Sand Creek to join the rest of the corps.

Tuttle's division of Sherman's XV Corps has been encamped at Willow Springs, and on the afternoon of the ninth, Sherman learns that McPherson's men have cleared Rocky Springs, so Tuttle is ordered to march six miles northeast to Logan's old camps. Sherman has now assumed McPherson's old position, with Steele's division at Hankinson's Ferry and Tuttle's division at Rocky Springs.

Sherman, still at Hankinson's Ferry, still doesn't believe in Grant's concept of operations, and he gets excited when he sees the number of wagons on the road. Sherman excitedly writes to Grant on May 9. He exclaims on paper that he has 500 wagons across the river, and each one has an officer pushing to get his wagon across first. There *are* a lot of wagons, because three days earlier Colonel Hillyer had his initial 200 wagons bring supplies to the troops at Hankinson's, and the wagons were then sent back to Grand Gulf to be reloaded. The 200 quartermaster wagons, capable of carrying 7,500 pounds of cargo, are now back on the road. And Sherman has brought at least 120 more wagons south from Milliken's Bend to Hard Times. But that is not all. To carry rations and ammunition for the army, the Yanks have also confiscated everything on wheels from the countryside, from fancy carriages to farm wagons. So the road is packed with wagons, large and small, and Sherman complains that it "will be jammed sure as life." Grant, keeping calm, tells his subordinate not to worry.

On May 9, in Tennessee, Joe Johnston receives orders from Richmond to leave Middle Tennessee for Mississippi and give his direction to what is happening there. His instructions are to "proceed at once to Mississippi and take chief command of the forces, giving to those in the field, as far as practicable, the encouragement and benefit of your personal direction." Once again, Johnston has the command opportunity he says that he wants, but, once again, he does not wish to assume that command. He has been sick for more than a month, and that is his excuse. Still, he reluctantly boards a train out of Tullahoma. As he leaves the Tullahoma area, he has the two Confederate brigades of Gen. Matthew D. Ector and Gen. Evander McNair board trains for Mississippi.

In Virginia, when Longstreet reports back to Lee in Fredericksburg on May 9, he finds the general much depressed over the condition of the wounded Stonewall Jackson. Still, Longstreet tells Lee about his meeting with the secretary of war. Longstreet later wrote that his idea of sending troops to Bragg was a new one to Lee, and that Lee was "evidently seriously impressed by it." Lee, however, does not want to divide his army. Longstreet wrote that they discussed the proposed plan "over and over," and on one matter Lee left no doubt—he wanted to conduct an offensive campaign.

On Sunday, May 10, in Mississippi, McClernand again leads the way. His men have encamped for two days at Little Sand and Big Sand Creeks, and he now marches on the old Natchez Trace to the village of Cayuga. A. J. Smith's division halts at Cayuga, while the divisions of Osterhaus, Hovey, and Carr pass through town and encamp at Fivemile Creek, two miles east of town. Grant moves his headquarters from Rocky Springs to Cayuga on May 10.

That same day, Sherman accompanies Steele's division, and they march from Hankinson's Ferry to McClernand's former campground at Big Sand Creek. Tuttle's division gets a day of rest, remaining in camp at Rocky Springs, and the men watch Steele's troops march through the community.

McPherson's XVII Corps marches to Utica the same day, and then turns to the northeast toward Raymond. The troops continue only a short distance north of town and go into camp at the A. B. Weeks plantation. The men and the animals are thirsty, and the XVII Corps has crossed few watercourses.

As Grant marches inland, a new factor enters his planning. No significant rain has fallen since the night of the 27th and 28th of April, and the army will have to move from creek to creek for water. Water is a big problem for horses and mules. The equines require four gallons of water per day. Horses and mules, being dumb beasts, don't have the fear of the sergeant telling them to observe water discipline, and the creeks are going to be important sources of water for Grant's army in his early movements.

The historic Natchez Trace—that is, the 50-mile stretch of that road used by Grant—follows the ridgeline because pioneer travelers did not like to ford creeks. And along the old Trace are strange names for the watercourses, such as Commissioners Creek, Fivemile Creek, and Fourteenmile Creek. These names date back to October 18, 1820, when the Treaty of Doak's Stand was signed with the Choctaws, who—after being threatened by Andrew Jackson—ceded five and a half million acres to the whites. The boundary line between the Choctaw lands and the Anglo lands struck Big Black River at the point where one of its feeder creeks entered the river, so the watercourse was called Commissioners Creek. Five miles upstream, or northeast, of Commissioners Creek is another creek that flows into Big Black River, so that creek was dubbed Fivemile Creek. Not very original, but that's how the creek got its name. Then 14 miles upstream from Commissioners Creek is, naturally, Fourteenmile Creek.

Because the routes Grant travels were dirt roads at the time of the Civil War, if Grant had gotten several days of hard rain, his army would have had severe problems with the mud. But fortune favors the brave, because Grant is not going to get any significant rainfall until the night of May 13.

At 3:15 on the afternoon of May 10, eight days after being shot at Chancellorsville, Stonewall Jackson dies from pneumonia. In a very light voice, he utters, "Let us cross over the river and rest under the shade of the trees." And then he is gone.

Lee announces the death of Jackson to his army and issues General Orders Number 61, saying that Jackson's spirit still lives and will inspire the whole army. "Let his name be a watchword," he tells his men. But privately, Lee writes to his son Custis, saying, "It is a terrible loss. I do not know how I will replace him."

The same day that Jackson dies, Lee's staff deciphers a telegram sent the day before by Confederate Secretary of War Seddon in Richmond. He suggests that Lee send troops to Mississippi to aid John Pemberton against Grant's invading army. Lee does not like the idea, but immediately replies in a short telegram that, if it has to be done, Pickett's division should be sent.

Despite the anguish that he is feeling over the news of Jackson's death, Lee writes to Seddon in greater detail, saying: "If you determine to send Pickett's division to General Pemberton, I presume it could not reach him until the last of this month. If anything is to be done in that quarter, it will be over by that time, as the climate in June will force the enemy to retire. The uncertainty of its arrival and the uncertainty of its application cause me to doubt the policy of sending it. Its removal from this army will be sensibly felt. Unless we can obtain some reinforcements we may be obliged to withdraw into the defenses around Richmond. We are greatly outnumbered by the enemy now."

On May 11, Grant has McClernand's XIII Corps remain in camp at Fivemile Creek and at Cayuga so that Sherman's XV Corps can pass through his lines. While at Cayuga, the Federal soldiers find Southern newspapers that report

Hooker's defeat at Chancellorsville. This news increases Grant's sense of urgency, because he knows that the Lincoln Administration might not survive another major defeat. Still, he must be feeling optimistic about his chances, because so far he is going wherever he wants without serious opposition.

Per Sherman's orders, Steele's division departs from Big Sand Creek and Tuttle's division leaves Rocky Springs at dawn. They march through Cayuga and pass through McClernand's lines at Fivemile Creek. There are catcalls and good-humored bickering as Sherman's men march through McClernand's camps, especially between soldiers who had fought at Pea Ridge and in the Trans-Mississippi in early March 1862. Three regiments of Col. Charles Woods's brigade of Steele's division in Sherman's corps served with Osterhaus at Pea Ridge. Osterhaus is popular with these men, and they exchange greetings, mixed with insults, as soldiers are prone to do. Finally, Sherman's men go into camp at dusk at Old Auburn, now an extinct town where modern Highway 27 crosses the Old Port Gibson Road. Fortunately, there is a large pond nearby for water.

McPherson's command is short of water and moves only a mile on May 11, going into camp at the J. Roach plantation, where Tallahala Creek is only one-half mile away. McPherson knows this is the last water he will see for another nine miles until he gets to Fourteenmile Creek, two miles southwest of Raymond. The Roach plantation is relieved of its stockpiles of bacon, hams, sugar, and molasses, and the chicken houses are quickly depopulated. While the infantry forages, McPherson sends Col. Clark Wright's cavalry to Crystal Springs to further damage the railroad that runs from Jackson to New Orleans. Grierson's raiders had previously burnt bridges and twisted rails along that line, first at Hazlehurst and then from Brookhaven south to Summit.

McPherson's instructions from Grant are to "occupy something near the same east and west line with the other army corps," and on Monday night, May 11, the young general is still about five miles farther south than McClernand and Sherman. To rectify this, Grant sends McPherson a message, telling him to move his command "tomorrow with all activity into Raymond."

Besides water, Grant needs rations, and he knows he will soon need ammunition. On May 11, two brigades of Blair's division—Col. Giles Smith's and Col. T. Kilby Smith's—depart Grand Gulf with 200 supply wagons. Grant is counting on the timely arrival of these needed supplies.

Grant plans to move toward the Southern Railroad of Mississippi on three axes of advance, with McClernand's XIII Corps on the left, Sherman's XV Corps in the center, and McPherson's XVII Corps on the right. This movement in three columns will place the army in position to cross the last east-west water barrier, Fourteenmile Creek, on the same day, May 12. From this creek three roads will take Grant's army directly to the railroad, about nine miles to the north. If all goes as planned, they will strike the railroad at Edwards; at Midway Station, three miles east of Edwards; and at Bolton, three miles east of Midway Station.

After the army divides into three columns, McClernand—the man whom Grant likes the least but who believes in the mission and has led the march all the way from Louisiana to this point—is on the left and is closest to the enemy. The person in the center with Grant is Sherman, whom Grant likes the best and who believes that Grant is placing his army in a dangerous position. In the least dangerous position on the right, and presumably farthest from the enemy, is the young, inexperienced corps commander, James B. McPherson. Grant never explained these dispositions, but this must have been what was in his mind.

Up until now Pemberton has sent optimistic reports of success to Richmond and occasionally to Johnston. But as Grant unexpectedly moves north and east, it causes confusion in Pemberton's headquarters. Pemberton thought that surely Grant would cross the captured bridge at Hankinson's Ferry and attack Vicksburg from the south. But now that Grant is not acting predictably, Pemberton's uncertainty means the Confederates are going to be responding to Grant's moves. Grant has the initiative.

But help is on the way for Pemberton. When Richmond learns that Grant has secured his beachhead in Mississippi, Secretary of War Seddon sends an order to P. G. T. Beauregard, who now commands the Department of South Carolina, Georgia, and Florida. Beauregard is told to rush 8,000 to 10,000 men to Mississippi to help Pemberton. Beauregard quickly forms a brigade in Charleston and places Gen. States Rights Gist in command. Some wag said that, with a name like States Rights and a brother named Independent, Gist had to fight for the South. Gist is ordered to entrain his newly constituted brigade in Charleston and proceed to Mississippi.

Beauregard also orders Gen. William Henry Talbot "Shot Pouch" Walker, whose brigade is in Savannah, to entrain his men and head for Mississippi. Walker, a West Pointer, class of '37, had been wounded so often in the Second Seminole and Mexican Wars that he is called Shot Pouch; he has to sleep sitting up because of the pain in his back. He's one of those guys one doesn't want to be near during a battle, because he attracts metal like a magnet.

The two brigades of Gist and Walker number about 5,000 troops, which is a far cry from the 8,000 to 10,000 men requested by Seddon. But Richmond is trying to do something, and the first of the troops arrive in Jackson late on Monday, May 11.

At 3 a.m. on Monday, May 11, Gregg receives orders. His people, who arrived in the capital city late on Friday after their tiresome trek from Port Hudson, are ordered to march from Jackson to Raymond, 15 miles southwest.

Pemberton's order to Gregg reads: "Move your brigade promptly to Raymond, taking three days' rations, and carrying only cooking utensils and ammunition; no baggage. Let no one get ahead of you, or through your lines to the enemy, or know of your movements. Use Wirt Adams's cavalry at Raymond for advanced pickets."

Pemberton wants Gregg to move as rapidly as possible, and he wants him to achieve the element of surprise. Little does Pemberton know, the surprise will be on Gregg, because Pemberton has also sent an order to Col. Wirt Adams—an order that is a masterpiece of ambiguity.

Pemberton's order to Adams reads: "Proceed at once to Edwards Depot, and take command of all the cavalry there and at Raymond, for operation against the enemy. Report to me your arrival there. Your command will remain at Raymond."

Adams reads and re-reads his order, and due to the wording he doesn't know if he is to go to Edwards or Raymond. So he goes to Edwards. But, Pemberton wants Adams to go to Raymond to support John Gregg. Still, Adams does his best to cover his bases, He scatters his men to have a presence on the approaches from the southwest.

When Gregg arrives in Raymond on the afternoon of the 11th, he is disappointed to find that Adams's cavalry is not waiting in town to support him. But Adams does have Sgt. J. L. Miles and four privates in Raymond, along with Capt. J. M. Hall commanding a company of Mississippi State Troops, who are too young, too old, or too feeble to serve in the Confederate Army.

Gregg finds another order from Pemberton awaiting him in Raymond: "From information from General Tilghman of the enemy being in force opposite the ferry at Baldwin's, it is very probable that the movement toward Jackson is in reality on Big Black Bridge, in which case you must be prepared to attack them in rear or on flank."

Pemberton has correctly guessed that Grant is moving to the railroad at Edwards, but he has not fathomed that Grant is moving his army in three separate columns. Thus, he asks Gregg to make a rear or flank attack on what he believes to be a single Union column on the Telegraph Road. As a result, his orders send Gregg's lone brigade directly into the path of six Union brigades of McPherson's approaching XVII Corps.

In Virginia, on May 11, Lee thinks more about Secretary Seddon's proposal and likes it even less, so he writes to President Davis, saying that he has read the Northern newspapers, which report that Hooker's Army of the Potomac is going to be reinforced with 30,000 more men. Lee reasons, "Virginia is to be the theater of action," and his army should be strengthened so that he can "advance beyond the Rappa-hannock." Lee believes that by going on the offensive, he can draw Union troops out of the South; however, now he is under pressure to send troops to the western theater to help defend the line of the Mississippi River. Lee does not like the idea of losing any of his men and is not so sure that any troops he sends to Mississippi will be properly used. So he adds that he does not believe that any more troops should be sent to Vicksburg than are needed to "maintain the water batteries."

On the morning of May 12, as Sherman advances from Old Auburn, Grant travels with him. Sherman's men arrive at a bridge across Fourteenmile Creek, and at the crossing the men of Steele's division and Lt. Col. Simeon Swan's Fourth Iowa Cavalry, leading Sherman's column, butt heads with a detachment of Adams's Confederate cavalry. Sherman won't be denied. He sends for Capt. Clemens Landgraeber, who is dubbed the Flying Dutchman because of his heritage and the battery he commands. Landgraeber's battery is light, or flying artillery, which is organized for speed and mobility in order to keep up with cavalry. A battery of flying artillery has up to 146 horses, so almost all of the men are mounted. Landgraeber's moniker is that of Richard Wagner's 1843 opera, a masterpiece that is the rage in 1863.

The Flying Dutchman hastens forward to break the Confederate roadblock. Outgunned, the badly outnumbered Confederates withdraw. Sgt. Maj. Edward Reichhelm, of the Third Missouri Infantry in Steele's division, recalled that, after the fight, one of his men found his brother among the wounded Confederates.

Reichhelm remembered that he saw his soldier "kneel beside a badly wounded Confederate with tears in his eyes and full of tenderness try to make him comfortable as possible."

But the Confederate roadblock has been broken. Grant and Sherman's two divisions push forward another mile to Dillon's plantation to encamp for the night.

At 5:30 a.m. McClernand, who for the first time in the campaign is behind Sherman's men, begins his march from Fivemile Creek. The three-division column is led by Alvin Hovey's men and in a mile and one-half the troops pass through Sherman's former camp at Old Auburn. Just under two miles east of Old Auburn the column turns north on the Telegraph Road. They are now only nine miles south of the railroad at Edwards Depot.

McClernand continues north for four miles to Whitaker's Ford at Fourteenmile Creek, where his men have a savage skirmish with Col. Elijah Gates's First Missouri Cavalry (dismounted), and three companies of infantry bolstered by two cannon. Pemberton has ordered General Bowen to send these troops to Whitaker's Ford to detect any movement toward the railroad along the Telegraph Road.

McClernand sends in the Second Illinois Cavalry, but the horse soldiers are unable to dislodge the hardened Missouri boys, so he sends in Gen. George McGinnis's brigade and two artillery batteries—the Second Ohio and 16th Ohio. When the smoke clears, McClernand has crossed Fourteenmile Creek.

While McClernand took three of his divisions east to Whitaker's Ford, he sent his remaining division, A. J. Smith's, which was at Cayuga, northeast from the village to seize Montgomery Bridge, two and a half miles west of Whitaker's Ford on Fourteenmile Creek, so that the left of the line will be anchored when Grant's army moves north to the railroad. Smith's men surprise some unwary Confederate pickets at Montgomery Bridge, who flee in dereliction without bothering to set fire to the structure.

Events are going just the way Grant has planned. By midafternoon on May 12, McClernand's XIII Corps and Sherman's XV Corps have established bridgeheads over Fourteenmile Creek. As soon as McPherson establishes his bridgehead on the right flank, the Army of the Tennessee will be in position to move northward to cut Pemberton's railroad lifeline on May 13.

At 3:30 a.m. on May 12, as a result of Grant's "hurry up" message sent from Cayuga the night before, McPherson has his corps on the road to Raymond. Soon skirmishing erupts at the front of the column as Southerners fire their muskets at the horse soldiers of Capt. John S. Foster. At 9 a.m., Gen. Elias Dennis, commanding the lead Union brigade of Logan's division, orders the 20th Ohio to deploy to the right of the road and the 78th Ohio to the left. Both regiments throw out a four-company skirmish line, and a little before 10 a.m., the lead elements of McPherson's XVII Corps cross the top of a commanding ridge, three-quarters of a mile south of Fourteenmile Creek, and descend the watershed to cross the open, grassy fields. The regiments to their rear, still in column formation, have strung out like an accordion, letting large gaps form between the units, in an attempt to escape the smothering dust clouds raised from thousands of feet and hooves.

A sergeant with the Fifth Iowa was near the end of the marching column. He recalled the stifling dust, writing: "My regiment, like all the others, hurried along the country roads through dust that came to the shoe top. The atmosphere was yellow with it. The moving of a column far away could be traced by it. We followed it in the way that Joshua's army followed the mighty cloud."

The Federal skirmish line pushes its way through the tall grass of the unplanted fields. The men, covered with grass seed and sweat, move toward the shade of a belt of timber bordering the creek. They have been on the march since 3:30 a.m., and the hot, tired soldiers plan to stack arms and fill their canteens, not knowing that all hell is about to break loose.

Pemberton has fathomed, more or less, Grant's intent, so he is pivoting his army to face the threat. Pemberton now has his men positioned with his right guarding the raft bridge at Baldwin's Ferry, and his left watching the railroad bridge over Big Black River. He orders Gen. John Bowen to construct a *tête de pont* east of the Big Black Bridge. Tête de pont is French for "bridgehead," a work thrown up at the end of a bridge, nearest the enemy, so that this work will cover the bridge. The Confederates use cotton bales to build the works. They are thrifty with these cotton bales—the Yankees aren't going to get them all. Pemberton's people use 1,800 bales of cotton throwing up this line of breastworks, and his plan is to hold this position to wait for Grant to attack it.

Pemberton has five divisions, but he leaves two of them—12,000 men— in the Vicksburg area to guard the approaches from Hankinson's Ferry to the south and from the Yazoo River to the north. To protect the city from Porter's fleet, he has Col. Edward Higgins's river defenses. On May 12, Pemberton moves his headquarters from Vicksburg to Bovina to be with his other three divisions.

The two divisions in the Vicksburg area are commanded by Gen. John H. Forney and Gen. Martin L. Smith. General Forney is from Lincolnton, North Carolina, and he is a harsh disciplinarian—not well liked by his troops. General Smith, like Pemberton, is a Northerner. He is a New Yorker and a West Point-trained engineer, but his connections, through his life, marriage, and military stations, have been in the South.

On May 12 Pemberton telegraphs Johnston, who receives the message at Lake Station, Mississippi, while en route to Jackson: "The enemy is apparently moving his heavy force toward Edwards Depot, on Southern Railroad; with my limited force I will do all I can to meet him. That will be the battlefield if I can carry forward sufficient force, leaving troops enough to secure the safety of this place [Vicksburg]."

That same morning, at Raymond, General Gregg sends his makeshift cavalry force of five of Wirt Adams's cavalrymen and all of Captain Hall's state troopers down the Utica Road to see what they can find. Hall soon runs into veteran Federal troopers—that is, a 160-man provisional cavalry battalion with Captain Foster in command. McPherson had organized this battalion that day, and it includes Foster and his Fourth Independent Company of Ohio Cavalry, as well as two companies of Illinois cavalry and one of Missouri horse soldiers. Of course, Hall's men are not able to penetrate Foster's screen, so all they can do is fall back with the news that the enemy is coming. They did see the head of the Union column enshrouded in dust, so they report 2,500 to 3,000 Yankees coming down the road. This information seems to confirm what Gregg believes. He knows that scouts usually pad the numbers a bit, so his mind is made up that he's facing a lone Union brigade with a heavy cavalry screen to cover the feint. Ever combative, he says to his commanders, "We're going to wreck 'em, boys."

Gregg sets a trap. He sends out Colonel Granbury's Seventh Texas to a position on the Utica Road covering the Fourteenmile Creek bridge, and he places Maj. Stephen H. Colms's First Tennessee Battalion near a piece of high ground where the Port Gibson Road meets the Utica Road, so that the Tennesseans can support Capt. Hiram W. Bledsoe's three Missouri guns unlimbered on that elevated position. "Old Hi" Bledsoe is a longtime soldier who served in the Mexican War. He has two 12-pounder smoothbores and a 12-pounder Whitworth rifled gun, and his guns are posted to cover the bridge over Fourteenmile Creek.

Gregg tells Col. Calvin H. Walker, "I want you to post your Third Tennessee on the left of the Texans, and I want you to conceal your men behind the ridge, just north of Fourteenmile Creek." He then goes to Lt. Col. Thomas W. Beaumont and says, "I want you to take the 50th Tennessee, and I want you to move down the Gallatin Road, about one and one-half miles south of town, and deploy on high enough ground that you can guard the road." Gregg adds, "When the time comes, I want you to swing to the west and hit that Yankee brigade in the flank and rear while the Texans and the Tennesseans hit it in front."

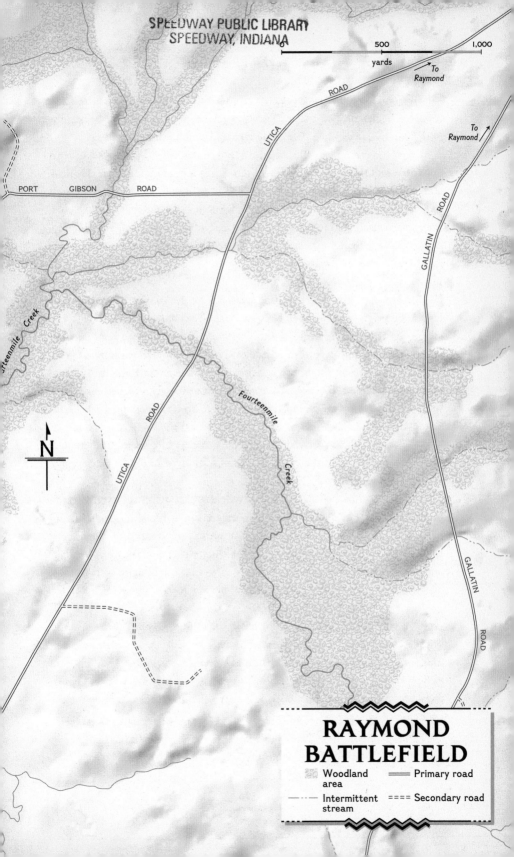

0 500 1,000

yards

To
Raymond

To
Raymond

ROAD

UTICA

PORT   GIBSON   ROAD

GALLATIN   ROAD

Greenmile Creek

Fourteenmile

Creek

UTICA   ROAD

GALLATIN   ROAD

N

RAYMOND
BATTLEFIELD

Woodland
area

Primary road

Intermittent
stream

Secondary road

To Col. Randall MacGavock, who commands the 10/30th Tennessee Consolidated Regiment, Gregg says, "Post your men about one-half mile behind the 50th Tennessee, and when they swing west and attack, you follow."

Gregg has one more regiment, the 41st Tennessee, led by Col. Robert Farquharson, and he leaves that regiment in town as a reserve, or to cover his flank and rear in case he is unexpectedly attacked from another direction. His plan is to draw the enemy into position with the Seventh Texas and then trap the bluecoats in the pocket formed by a U-shaped bend in Fourteenmile Creek. The Seventh Texas is the bait for the trap. After the Yanks have taken the bait, Gregg will then send in the 50th and 10th and 30th Tennessee regiments, swinging like a gate, onto the flank and rear of the enemy. Since Gregg has a large, 3,000-man brigade, this is a very good trap if he is attacking a 1,500-man Federal brigade. It's grabbing a tiger by the tail if he is assailing a 12,000-man corps.

Gregg starts getting his men into position at 9 a.m., and an hour later the Federal advance moves into the shade of the trees along Fourteenmile Creek. Col. Hiram Bronson Granbury, commander of the Seventh Texas, was captured in February 1862, as a major of the Seventh at Fort Donelson, and he was exchanged for two Union lieutenants. Granbury orders up Capt. T. B. Camp with some volunteers to go in the brush near the bridge over Fourteenmile Creek, and there they wait. As the Yanks are looking forward to taking a break, they move up to the shade trees, and Captain Camp's Texans open fire at a hundred yards.

At the same time Captain Bledsoe's three guns roar out from 800 yards behind the Texans—boom, boom, boom! The rounds scream over the Texans' heads and burst in the hot air over the cornfields 400 yards to the south. Col. Manning F. Force of the 20th Ohio happens to be on the high ridge, now known as McPherson's Ridge, overlooking the scene three-quarters of a mile south of the bridge over Fourteenmile Creek, and he glances at his watch. The time is ten o'clock.

Logan, commanding the lead division, is up near the front of the blue column, and he rides up to the crest of McPherson's Ridge to confer with one of his brigade commanders, General Dennis. McPherson is in the middle of the column, down the Utica Road with J. E. Smith's brigade, and he spurs his horse and gallops to the crest of the ridge. He finds Logan and Dennis ordering the deployment of Dennis's four regiments, with the 30th Illinois and the 78th Ohio moving to the west of the road, and the Illinoisans deploying to the left of the Ohioans. The 68th Ohio and the 20th Ohio are sent to the east of the road with the 78th forming on the right of the 20th. As McPherson looks to the north, he sees the smoke from three Confederate cannon more than 2,000 yards away, and he turns to Logan for a report.

While McPherson looks the situation over from the ridgetop, De Golyer's Eighth Michigan Light Artillery races up the road in a cloud of dust and goes into battery on a slight rise of ground 150 yards south of Fourteenmile Creek, close enough for the Wolverine guns to blast canister into the Texans. That's why the Yankee infantry loves De Golyer—he's always up front, he's up quick, and he's where the action is. De Golyer only has a little more than two weeks to live, because he will be mortally wounded by a sniper in front of Vicksburg on May 28.

The young De Golyer places his two 12-pounder howitzers to the left of the road and his four rifled bronze Model 1841 6-pounders to the right. De Golyer's sweating redlegs then fire across the creek at the Texans, and the muzzle blasts and the iron balls ricochet off the ground and raise huge clouds of dust. In the still, hot air, the powder smokes hangs over the low ground of the creek and covers the grass like a gray shroud, so visibility soon becomes almost nonexistent.

After Dennis's regiments go into line, Logan tells J. E. Smith, "I want you to move your five regiments up to the crest of this ridge; move to the right of the road, face left, and deploy on Dennis's right." Smith's real name is Schmidt; he was born in Switzerland and has Anglicized his name.

Stevenson's brigade—Logan's third brigade—isn't up yet, and Marcellus Crocker's division is strung out for miles because the dust is suffocating. Since Crocker is a "lunger," the dust plagues him.

Dennis's four Union regiments reach the skirt of woods at the creek and take a break in the shade of the tall trees while their skirmish line pops away at the bothersome Texans on the other side. It is now high noon, and Gregg decides to spring his trap on what he thinks is a four-regiment brigade with a battery of artillery. He orders the Texans forward, across the creek, straight at the Yankees. The Union skirmishers see the solid line of butternut and gray advancing, and they skedaddle like rabbits south through Dennis's resting troops. The Buckeyes of the 20th Ohio on the east side of the road quickly grab their stacked rifle-muskets and dash forward to take cover in the creek bed. But the 68th Ohio, to their right, runs the other way, south across the open fields toward the ridge. The right flank of the 20th is in the air, but because of a meander in the creek, the men there are facing east, not north.

Smith's brigade has come up to the east of Dennis's men, crossed the open fields, and entered the woods bordering the creek, which turns southeast to form the eastern arm of the cul-de-sac. Then the five regiments move forward to the creek, but the banks are steep—about 10 to 15 feet vertical—and covered with thick brush and vines.

Smith's right flank regiment, the 31st Illinois, swings farther to the right, facing east, to guard the flank. The 31st then strikes the deep creek bed as it runs southeast. The men become confused, turn back, and halt in the woods without crossing the creek.

Smith's left flank regiments—the 45th, 124th, and 20th Illinois—become separated and confused in the woods, and they don't cross the creek. Only the 23rd Indiana, after a tough time, finds itself on the north side of the creek, separated from the rest of their brigade. One wouldn't want to have been with those Hoosier lads. When they come out on the other side of the creek, they are confused.

To make matters worse for the Indianians, Gregg now springs his trap. Over on the other side of the commanding ridge that runs north of the creek is Colonel Walker's numerically strong Third Tennessee, composed of 548 men, and these soldiers burst over the top of the ridge. Seemingly out of nowhere they charge down the south face of the ridge into the Hoosiers' faces, crashing into the Yankees like a tidal wave. The Indiana boys break. They panic. They flee back across this creek, pursued by Walker's people, and this is what the boys on the right flank of the 20th Ohio see as they look to the east from their creek meander. The 20th Ohio sees their right flank uncovered, with the Rebs coming through the gap, and the Ohioans begin to think that discretion is the better part of valor. They think about retreating.

> A sergeant in the 20th Ohio, Osborn H. Oldroyd, recalled that "The regiment to the right of us was giving way, but just as the line was wavering and about to be hopelessly broken, Logan dashed up, and with the shriek of an eagle turned them back to their places, which they regained and held. Had it not been for Logan's timely intervention, who was continually riding up and down the line, firing the men with his own enthusiasm, our line would undoubtedly have been broken at some point. . . . The creek was running red with precious blood spilt for our country."

The Confederates—Walker's men—have crossed the creek. Who has the initiative now? The Rebels so far have committed two regiments, stymied nine, and badly chopped up the 23rd Indiana. Now Gregg plans to slam into the Union flank and rear with his Gallatin Road regiments—the 50th Tennessee and the 10th and 30th Tennessee. The first priority of these two Confederate regiments is to capture De Golyer's guns, which have now fallen back about 240 yards to slightly higher ground in an open field just to the west of the Utica Road.

The 10th and 30th Tennessee moves up from its supporting position and forms on the left of Colonel Beaumont's 50th Tennessee, and Beaumont's men advance into the woods and cross Fourteenmile Creek, but they drift to the left in the woods and form on the south side of the creek, wandering almost in front of Colonel MacGavock's 10th and 30th Tennessee. Beaumont hears the firing to his right as Granbury's Texans and Walker's Tennesseans smash into the Union lines, and he knows that it is his turn to take up the *en echelon* attack. This is a word based on the French word for ladder and is used to describe an attack with one unit attacking immediately after another, like a wave rolling up a beach.

But Beaumont is south of the fighting, with all its dust and smoke, and he is looking west across the open fields south of Fourteenmile Creek. He comes out of the trees onto a small hill, and he has a view of the action. What does he see? He sees lots of Yankees. The Utica Road is lined with bluecoats for miles. He says to himself, "Hell, that's no brigade. There's at least a division out there." He sends a message to tell Gregg that they have big problems, and he doesn't attack.

But the messenger, Maj. Christopher Robertson, can't find Gregg in all the confusion. So Beaumont performs what was called in Korea a bugout. He withdraws without orders. And MacGavock with his consolidated 10th and 30th Tennessee has been ordered to await his turn in the en echelon attack, so he can't attack until Beaumont does. This means that the Seventh Texas and Third Tennessee are now in a real pinch as regiment after regiment of Union soldiers double-time north, up the Utica Road, across the fields, and jump into the fight.

To add to the problems of the Confederates, Gen. John Stevenson's brigade marches up the dust-choked Utica Road and arrives on the field. If some historian wants to pick a Union brigade that wrecks the Confederates during the Vicksburg Campaign, that brigade is Stevenson's. He receives orders from Logan to send the 81st Illinois to support the left of Smith's line, in order to stop Walker's Tennesseans. Stevenson is then ordered to rush a regiment to the right flank of Dennis's brigade to help fight the Texans, so the Eighth Illinois is sent. Logan then places the 81st Illinois on the right of the beaten-up 23rd Indiana, and the 81st closes the gap between the 23rd Indiana and the 31st Illinois. Stevenson sends his last two regiments, the Seventh Missouri and 32nd Ohio, to the right of the 31st Illinois, making these two regiments the far right of the Union line. McPherson now has almost the entire oxbow bend of the creek covered.

Along with Stevenson comes a battery of 24-pounder howitzers, which is Company D, First Illinois Light Artillery, and these four guns take De Golyer's position on the rise just to the left of the Utica Road. De Golyer shifts his six guns almost 200 yards to the left to cover the left flank of Dennis. The ten guns of the two batteries continue to raise huge clouds of dust and smoke, and the artillerymen are firing blindly with only occasional glimpses of targets on the ridge and in the fields to the north of the creek.

The right flank companies of the Seventh Texas hold back at the creek—they have two Federal regiments firing at them and ten Federal guns blasting canister at them from their front. But the left flank companies cross Fourteenmile Creek, make their way through the timber, and enter the open field south of the creek. Here they are hit by a counterattack from the 20th Illinois, which had reformed in the field after failing to support the left flank of the 23rd Indiana. Lt. Col. Evan Richards, commanding the 20th Illinois, is killed during the counterattack, but the Texans fall back and take cover in the creek bed. Suddenly, Texans and Ohioans are mingled in the meandering creek bed, firing at each other over the bank tops.

On the Texans' left, Walker's Tennesseans charge across the creek into the woods, and Colonel Walker listens in vain for the sound of Beaumont's guns to his left, because the 50th Tennessee is supposed to pick up its assignment in the en echelon attack. Instead of Beaumont's firing, however, what Walker receives is a point-blank volley into his left flank from Col. Edwin Stanton McCook's 31st Illinois on the Union right. McCook is a member of the famous "fighting McCook" family, and he attended the U.S. Naval Academy for two years. This will be his last battle, because he will be shot in the foot and hobble off the field using two rifles as crutches. Foot wounds are slow to heal, largely because of poor blood circulation and the number of bones in the foot, so this wound ends his military career.

McCook's men have recovered from their escapade in the thick woods when they were trying to cover Smith's right flank on the eastern edge of the cul-de-sac. His Illinoisans have reformed in the edge of the woods by the field, and when the Tennesseans exit the woods in the U of the cul-de-sac, the Illinois soldiers simply about-face, and Walker's men are like tin ducks passing down a shooting line in a county fair.

The regimental history of the 31st Illinois states, "The companies fired in a manner resembling the firing by file, for as they [Walker's Tennesseans] came first within range of the right of the line they encountered a continuous fire until they reached the left. . . . It seemed an ambuscade, but it is probable that neither part knew the position of the other, till the enemy made his wild dash across the field."

Gregg, when he doesn't hear the sound of firing way off on his left flank, knows something is wrong. The Seventh Texas and the Third Tennessee are taking a beating in their frontal assault, so where is the flanking attack of the 50th Tennessee and the 10th and 30th Tennessee? Gregg orders up his reserve regiment, the 41st Tennessee, but these men are in the Raymond Cemetery, almost a mile and a half away.

If things aren't bad enough for the Third Tennessee, Smith's Federal brigade has been bolstered by Stevenson's newly arrived 81st Illinois, commanded by Col. James J. Dollins, a sociable man, but with a terrible temper. Dollins will die at the head of his regiment, in front of the Great Redoubt, during the second assault on Vicksburg on May 22.

Walker's Tennesseans, after being savaged by the flanking fire of the 31st Illinois, are also hit head-on by the 45th Illinois and the 23rd Indiana of Smith's brigade, and the 81st Illinois of Stevenson's brigade. The Tennessee boys are in a terrible position, and they fall back across the creek in disorder. They run up and over the ridge to the point where they began their attack.

The Yanks want to pursue Walker's retreating Tennesseans, but Colonel Farquharson's 41st Tennessee arrives in the nick of time. The 41st turns to the west at the southern base of the ridge where Colonel Walker is trying to rally and opens fire on the Federal right flank as the men begin their pursuit coming out of the woods on the north side of the creek.

Hiram Granbury of the Seventh Texas still has his men banging away at the 20th Ohio in the creek bed, but he now has his left flank uncovered by the retreat of the Third Tennessee. And, on his right flank, his companies facing the Federal cannon have pulled back and gamely begin a march to the ridgeline to fill in where the Third Tennessee retreated.

But, with both flanks now uncovered, Granbury falls back, and he rallies at Bledsoe's guns with Colms's First Tennessee Battalion as support. As Granbury's Texans approach Bledsoe's position, the rifled Whitworth bursts, which leaves the Confederates with only two 12-pounder smoothbores. Bad luck for the Rebels!

All this time, Marcellus Crocker's division has been strung back down the Utica Road due to all the dust, and Col. John B. Sanborn's brigade doesn't arrive on the field until 1:30. McPherson orders it into position to the left of Dennis's brigade, which places it on the left of the already crowded Union line. Crocker's artillery is still down the road, so the six guns of the Third Ohio Light Artillery, which belong to Logan, are sent to the far left to support Colonel Sanborn's brigade. These cannon go into battery about 350 yards west of the Illinois 24-pounders. This Ohio battery has four rifled bronze Model 1841 6-pounders, like the ones in De Golyer's battery, which they like to call 12-pounder James rifles, and two Model 1841 6-pounder smoothbores.

As the Third Ohio goes into battery, Sanborn cautiously advances his brigade and makes contact at the creek with the left flank of the 30th Illinois. With Sanborn's brigade on the battlefield, 7,000 soldiers in blue are fighting the 3,000 in gray, along with 16 Union guns against two Confederate, now that the Whitworth has burst.

Since the Texas companies on the Confederate right flank have withdrawn and moved east toward the ridge to support the Third Tennessee, McPherson thinks he can spare units from his left. He orders Sanborn to send the two regiments on his left flank, the 48th Indiana and the 59th Indiana, over to the center of the Union line. These men slowly back out of the woods along the creek, and quickstep eastward through the dust and smoke behind the lines to the center of the Union line, and there they report to Colonel Dollins of the 81st Illinois.

Dollins has his famous temper up, and he tells them, "I don't need your damn help—my men have the situation well in hand." So the two Hoosier regiments form up in the field, file to the right, and wait like reserves for something to happen. Had they stayed on the Union left, they could have been used in a flanking maneuver.

Farther out on the Union right, the two right flank regiments, the Seventh Missouri and the 32nd Ohio, have slipped eastward through the woods bordering Fourteenmile Creek and have skirmished with Beaumont's 50th Tennessee, causing Beaumont to withdraw to the Gallatin Road. The Ohioans pull to within a hundred yards of the road, fire a few parting shots at Beaumont, and take a break in a wooded ravine. But the Seventh Missouri, a regiment from St. Louis composed largely of recently arrived Irish immigrants with a sprinkling of hard rock miners, slides to the left to reestablish contact with the right of the 31st Illinois. Now that they have secured their left flank, the Irishmen, sweating profusely, swearing in Gaelic, and looking for a fight, debouch from the woods and start up the hillside to their front.

The Union Irishmen soon find a fight, because red-bearded and handsome Randy MacGavock, whose 10th and 30th Tennessee Infantry is supposed to follow Beaumont in the en echelon attack, finally realizes that Beaumont is not going to attack. Then MacGavock receives orders from Gregg to march to the right and stop the hemorrhaging in the Confederate line where the Third Tennessee has been pushed back across the creek and up the hillside. MacGavock, a Harvard law school graduate and a former mayor of Nashville, is ready to go, and he marches his Irish bullyboys back to the ridge north of Fourteenmile Creek. He then forms his lines on the left of Farquharson's 41st Tennessee, which has recently moved into position.

MacGavock can see the Irishmen of the Seventh Missouri coming up the hill. He knows he's got to do something. Despite the heat, he wears a long gray cloak with a bright red lining, and he throws it back over his shoulder. This might inspire his men, but it turns out to be a bad move, because some of the battle smoke has cleared, and the Yankee redlegs look over their cannon barrels to the hillside to their right front, and see MacGavock's men forming on the ridgetop. They see a bright red flash of color in the gray line, and they shift their fire to that spot. As the shells come in, MacGavock knows he is in a tough situation. If he falls back, the Confederate line will collapse, and if he stays where he is, the artillery will hammer his men to pieces. So the only thing left to do is to pitch into those blue uniforms of the Yankee Irish coming up the hill.

The blue Missourians, in one of those strange coincidences of war, are carrying a green flag with a golden harp, much like the one in MacGavock's Rebel Irish regiment. But the Missourians have Gaelic on the red banner of their flag, which says, "Erin Go Bragh," or Ireland Forever. The Tennesseans have English on the red banner of their flag, saying, "Go Where Glory Waits You!"

As MacGavock charges downhill at the front of his men, with Federal shells whizzing overhead, he is cut down by a Federal sharpshooter. Even with their commander shot and dying, the Confederate Irish charge downhill and smash into the Union Irish. The Yanks fight hard but soon break, and they fall back into the woods, where they are covered by the flanking fire of the 31st Illinois to the west of them. There are far too many Yanks in the woods for the Tennessee Irishmen to handle, and they slowly fall back to the crest of the ridge and hunker down. The Missouri Irish soon regroup and press back uphill, but the Tennesseans won't budge. Volley after volley is exchanged at short range on top of the ridge between the opposing Irish regiments. Then the men of the 10th and 30th look to their right and see Farquharson's men suddenly about-face, and file off to the east toward the Gallatin Road. Before the Yanks can exploit the gap in the Confederate line, it is filled with the three beaten-up companies of Texans, who still have plenty of fight left in them, and have marched over from the Confederate right flank near the Fourteenmile Creek bridge.

While this is happening, Col. Samuel Holmes's brigade of Crocker's Union division arrives on the low rise where the 16 Federal guns are blasting away. Now, the Union troop numbers rise to 9,000, and their artillery goes up to 22 cannon, because the six guns of the 11th Ohio Light Artillery of Crocker's division arrive and go into battery in the gap between De Golyer's cannon and the Illinois 24-pounders. The 11th Ohio has two 12-pounder howitzers, two 12-pounder James rifles, and two 6-pounder smoothbores.

When Holmes comes up, he is told to send the Tenth Missouri and the 80th Ohio to assist the Seventh Missouri, whose men cannot penetrate the Confederate line. The Missourians of the Tenth are placed on the right of Stevenson's brigade, and Stevenson posts the Buckeyes in reserve.

But where were Farquharson's Tennesseans going when they left the right flank of the 10th and 30th Tennessee? Gregg, not knowing that Colonel Beaumont was still out on the Gallatin Road, has ordered Farquharson out to the road, thinking a threat was developing there. It wasn't. At the same time, Beaumont, on the Gallatin Road, decides to march to the west to the sound of the firing, since there is no threat where he is. The two Tennessee regiments change places on the battlefield, and as they pass each other, nobody in either unit bothers to stop and ask where the other is going. Beaumont's 50th Tennessee ends up on the right flank of the 10/30th Tennessee, and Farquharson's 41st Tennessee ends up on the Gallatin Road.

By 4 p.m. Gregg realizes that he has bitten off a lot more than he can chew, and he seeks to get rid of that mouthful. But he has to worry about how he is going to save his command from overwhelming numbers. He sends Colms's First Tennessee Battalion down the west side of the Utica Road from its position at Bledsoe's guns, and these Tennesseans feign an attack on the Union left. The bluff works, and the Fourth Minnesota of Sanborn's brigade hunkers down in the woods at Fourteenmile Creek and doesn't advance.

Feeling good about his work, Colms shifts his men to the east side of the Utica Road so that they can cover the withdrawal of the beat-up Texans. As the Confederates start to withdraw, Beaumont, who has just marched his 50th Tennessee from the Gallatin Road and has arrived in the front of the masses of Union troops, realizes that he is in a tough spot, so he marches up a ravine in the ridge-line and then west to the Utica Road. Here he is joined by six companies of the Third Kentucky Mounted Infantry that have ridden out of Jackson to assist Gregg, and the horse soldiers cover the retreat.

Fortunately, Farquharson's Tennesseans, now way out by themselves on the Confederate left on the Gallatin Road, realize the situation is hopeless, and they fall back and go north up the Gallatin Road, through the cemetery, and into Raymond before they are cut off.

There is no pursuit by the Federals, not even by the cavalry, so Gregg's command rallies in Raymond and marches eastward toward Mississippi Springs on the Jackson Road.

When Gregg's men depart Raymond that morning the ladies of the town set up a huge picnic spread beneth the stately trees along the road for the brave, and presumably victorious, Confederates when they come back into town. But the Confederates have to conduct a fighting withdrawal to escape all those Yankees, and when they pass through Raymond, they don't have time to stop and feast. So the guys that are going to get the food prepared by the ladies of Raymond are the 20th Ohio, because they are the first ones into Raymond as the Confederates head out the Jackson Road.

The Battle of Raymond is over. It has lasted six hours. The Southerners, though decisively outnumbered, held the initiative for almost five hours. But they lose more men because many are taken prisoner. No Federals are captured. The Confederate losses are 73 dead, 252 wounded, and 190 missing, for a total of 515 casualties. Of course, many of the wounded will later die. The Federals have 66 killed, 339 wounded, and 37 missing, for a total of 442.

The Battle of Raymond shocks McPherson, but he proves himself to be a spinmaster. He sends a report to Grant, who is only six miles to the west, that he has fought a "sharp and severe contest" against 6,000 Confederates and two batteries. He doubles their size to a number which has to concern Grant, who heard the battle from six miles to the west, and his experienced ears tell him there were no 6,000 Rebs, much less 12 Confederate cannon, at Raymond.

On the evening of May 12, Grant and Sherman are headquartered at Dillon's farm with Sherman's two divisions camped all around them. Grant now reviews the situation.

McClernand has moved up to Whitaker's Ford on Fourteenmile Creek with Hovey's division in the lead, followed by the divisions of Carr and Osterhaus. They have driven the Rebels north to Mount Moriah, two miles south of Edwards on the Telegraph Road. McClernand's other division, Whiskey Smith's, has thrust up to Montgomery Bridge, three miles to the west on Fourteenmile Creek, to secure McClernand's left flank. McClernand has formed the left of the east-west line to strike the railroad, prepared to push up the Telegraph Road to gain a lodgment on the railroad at Edwards.

Sherman is in position to press up the Turkey Creek Road to hit the railroad at Midway Station. McPherson is now at Raymond and will be in position to march up the Raymond-Bolton Road and smash up the railroad at Bolton on the 13th. But the situation has suddenly changed.

Around 11 p.m. McPherson sends a message to Grant: "It is rumored, but with how much truth I have not been able to ascertain, that heavy reinforcements are coming to the enemy from Jackson tonight, and that we may expect a battle here in the morning. I shall try and be prepared for them if they come."

The Yankee intelligence is good. The first of the troops from the East Coast commanded by Shot Pouch Walker have arrived in Jackson. Walker left Jackson with a thousand men late in the morning on May 12, while the battle at Raymond was being fought, and arrived in Mississippi Springs, five miles east of Raymond, in time to meet Gregg's retreating troops.

Grant also gets word that Johnston is expected in Jackson within hours to take command of the troops there. Grant can now presume that he will have an enemy general, with a number of troops, in Jackson on his right flank. Clearly, telegraph operators and railroad employees are providing information to the Federals.

So May 12 becomes a crucial day in the Civil War. With reports of enemy forces to his left and front near Edwards, and to his right, in and near Jackson, and information of the anticipated arrival in Jackson of Johnston and more Confederates, Grant makes a key decision, which once again shows his flexibility. Instead of continuing his thrust northward toward the railroad, he says, "We are going east to Jackson."

One of the characteristics that made George S. Patton a great World War II commander was his flexibility. During the Battle of the Bulge he arrived at the commander's meeting at Verdun on December 19, 1944, and General "Ike" Eisenhower optimistically told all the commanders that the situation with the 101st Airborne at Bastogne was "to be regarded as one of opportunity for us, and not of disaster." He said, "There will only be cheerful faces at this conference table" because he knew the commanders were pessimistic about the situation.

When Patton was asked how fast he could assemble a force and attack the Germans, everyone expected him to stall for time. But Patton said, "I'm ready to go on the morning of December 22." He was ready to reverse, disengage from the Germans, and go northward because, before he went to the meeting, he told his chief of staff they had two days to get everybody ready to go.

Grant does the same thing at Dillon's on May 12. He's going to change direction, 90 degrees, but he's going to do this in just a few hours, not a few days. This decision is one of the turning points of the American Civil War, because it will lead to the withdrawal of Johnston from the campaign, the capture of Jackson, Mississippi, the defeat of Pemberton's army at Champion Hill, the capture of Vicksburg, and the opening of the Mississippi River.

On May 12, Rosecrans, in Murfreesboro, receives a telegram from Hurlbut, commanding Grant's XVI Corps in Memphis, advising him that Col. Abel Streight "is undoubtedly captured in Georgia." Hurlbut also says that he is sending Grant 16 reinforcing regiments by river but that the Confederates are expecting to receive reinforcements if Johnston shifts troops by rail to Pemberton in Vicksburg from Bragg's army in Tullahoma. Hurlbut concludes by saying, "If Johnston is permitted to throw a force on Grant, the consequences may be disastrous."

Despite Hurlbut's warning, Rosecrans remains static in Murfreesboro. His one offensive move, Streight's Raid, has ended in disaster, and Old Rosy does not intend to risk another by moving against Bragg to prevent the transfer of Confederates from Tennessee to Mississippi. There is no love lost between Rosecrans and Grant, so why should Rosecrans help Grant win the permanent rank of major general that Halleck has offered to the general "who first wins an important and decisive victory"?

Hurlbut, however, is Grant's subordinate in Memphis, and he is doing all he can to help his commander. Upon Grant's request, Hurlbut sends four Illinois regiments south, followed by the twelve regiments of Jacob Lauman's division. The four regiments of Illinoisans are soon put to work building a supply road across De Soto Point from Hecla Place Plantation to Bowers' Landing on the Mississippi River below Warrenton—an attempt to shorten Grant's supply line. Lauman's division of Illinoisans, Iowans, Indianians, and Wisconsinites will be at Grand Gulf by midmonth, protecting the supply depot there.

On May 12, 200 more heavily laden wagons depart Grand Gulf en route to Grant's army. They are guarded by Blair's third brigade, commanded by Gen.

Hugh Ewing. These men were left behind to guard the Milliken's Bend supply depot. Ewing is Sherman's brother-in-law and foster brother.

On May 13, McPherson marches eight miles northeast from Raymond to Clinton, where he destroys the railroad and cuts the telegraph line so that Pemberton can't communicate quickly with Johnston. Grant goes with Sherman to Raymond, where Grant establishes his headquarters at Maj. John Peyton's home, Waverly, north of town. Sherman continues east for five miles to Mississippi Springs, which is south of Clinton and is connected to Clinton by a good road. McPherson and Sherman are now in position to attack Jackson on two converging axes of advance.

McClernand draws the tough assignment on the 13th. From his Fourteen-mile Creek bridgehead he advances northward to feign an attack on Pemberton's advanced line south of Edwards. Hovey's division draws the fire of the Confederate troops of Bowen's, Loring's, and Stevenson's divisions. While Hovey keeps the Confederates pinned down in their defensive position, McClernand pivots his other two divisions, turns southeast and goes to Raymond. After Carr's and Osterhaus's divisions pass by in the rear of his people, Hovey breaks contact and follows. Carr and Osterhaus make it to Raymond, but Hovey has to fight a rear-guard action and only makes it as far as Dillon's that night.

At Raymond, Carr and Osterhaus are prepared to support McPherson and Sherman if needed. McClernand's fourth division, A. J. Smith's at Montgomery Bridge, marches south to Auburn to await Blair's two brigades with 200 supply wagons en route from Grand Gulf. Smith is ordered to assist Blair in getting those vital wagons safely to Raymond. On the same day Gen. Thomas E. G. Ransom, whose XVII Corps brigade remained in Louisiana to protect the supply roads, departs Grand Gulf with another large wagon train of supplies and ammunition.

Pemberton expects Grant to attack Edwards via the Telegraph Road, using a single axis of advance. He orders Bowen, who is soon to be promoted to major general for his valiant stand at Grand Gulf and at Port Gibson, to cross Big Black River to Edwards to bolster Colonel Gates's position on the ridge at Mount Moriah, two miles south of Edwards.

Bowen's soldiers leave their camps near Bovina early on May 13 and are on Mount Moriah ridge by dawn. Following Bowen's division are two brigades of Loring's division—Featherston's and Buford's. Gen. Winfield Scott Featherston digs in on Bowen's left flank, and Gen. Abraham Buford on his right. Then two brigades of Stevenson's division arrive by midmorning to strengthen the line. The Confederate line runs east and west on a commanding ridge two miles south of Edwards, parallel to the railroad, with Pemberton expecting a Union attack from the south. He has chosen good ground, but Grant will have no part of attacking it. While Pemberton is still on the defense, Grant has retained the initiative.

Gregg, after his troops retreat from Raymond, falls back east to Mississippi Springs, and on the 13th he returns to Jackson. As he falls back, his rear guard makes contact with Sherman's advance, which is moving east from Raymond toward Jackson. Gregg, knowing from his scouts that two Federal divisions have marched north from Raymond to Clinton earlier that day, assumes that the troops moving eastward are actually screening the right flank of Sherman's men as he moves to Clinton to concentrate the Federal forces. These are McPherson's divisions, but Gregg incorrectly reasons that Sherman is going to Clinton with two more divisions, and that is the information he takes to Johnston, who arrives by train in Jackson that evening.

Johnston is not a happy general. When he was ordered by Secretary of War Seddon to leave Tullahoma and to take 3,000 good troops with him from Bragg's army, he telegraphed back to Richmond that he would go, but that he was "unfit for field service." When Johnston arrives in Jackson, he gets Gregg's erroneous report of Sherman being in Clinton.

Johnston promptly telegraphs Secretary Seddon in Richmond: "I arrived this evening, finding the enemy's force between this place and General Pemberton, cutting off communication. I am too late."

Johnston may be said to be a naysayer, someone who always works to find a reason not to do something, instead of finding a way to make it happen. It is an incurable affliction, and in Johnston's mind, he has already lost. He establishes his headquarters in the Bowman House, then the skyscraper of Jackson at five stories high, located just north of the state capitol. That night, he sends a message by courier to Pemberton, announcing that he has just arrived in Jackson and has learned that Sherman is at Clinton with four divisions, repeating the faulty intelligence information from Gregg.

Johnston advises Pemberton that, "It is important to reestablish communications, that you may be reinforced. If practicable, come up on his rear at once. To beat such a detachment, would be of immense value. The troops here could cooperate. All the strength you can quickly assemble should be brought. Time is all-important."

Ironically, it is James Longstreet who comments on such timid orders in his memoirs: "It is not just to the subordinate to use [discretionary] language if orders are intended to be imperative. Men bred as soldiers have no fancy for orders that carry want of faith on their face."

To ensure that Pemberton receives the message, Johnston sends it by three different couriers. One of these men is a Union spy, and Grant will score another intelligence coup.

On May 13, General Halleck in Washington, in typical pessimistic fashion, telegraphs General Hurlbut, saying: "When you wrote, the operations of Colonel Grierson and Streight seemed most successful, but I since learned from Confederate papers that the latter has been captured with his entire force of 1,800 men and horses; possibly the former may meet the same fate. I have not heard of his reaching General Grant or General Banks."

Though Grierson has reached the safety of Baton Rouge on May 2, and Grant has sent a message to Halleck from Grand Gulf on May 3, reporting, "Grierson has knocked the heart out of the State," word has not yet reached Washington.

In Virginia, on May 13, after talking strategy with Lee, Longstreet writes to Senator Louis T. Wigfall of Texas to explain the strategy of invading the North. Senator Wigfall, like Secretary Seddon, has been a strong proponent of sending reinforcements from the East to the West, so Longstreet writes, "Grant seems to be a fighting man and seems to be determined to fight. Pemberton seems not to be a fighting man." Thus, concludes Longstreet, it would be a mistake to transfer troops from Lee to Pemberton. Longstreet continues: "When I agreed with the Secretary [Seddon] and yourself about sending troops west, I was under the impression that we would be obliged to remain on the defensive here, but the prospect of an advance changes the aspect of affairs to us entirely. . . . We can spare nothing from this army to reinforce the West."

Also on May 13, Secretary Seddon telegraphs Lee, saying: "Your letter [Lee's letter of May 10 arguing against Seddon's proposal to send troops to the West] is conclusive against the suggestion made." Thus, Lee has converted both Longstreet and Seddon that the best move is a northern offensive. Now the task at hand is to convince President Davis.

Chapter 6
CONCENTRATION OF TROOPS

May 14–16, 1863

Just after midnight on May 14, a heavy rainstorm blows into central Mississippi from the west. It is the first precipitation that either army has seen since April 28. Despite the pelting rain, at 3 a.m., Gen. Joseph E. Johnston orders the evacuation of Jackson, Mississippi, two hours before the men in the Union camps at Clinton and Mississippi Springs begin their march to Jackson, and almost eight hours before the Confederates realize that Sherman's two divisions are not in Clinton but are on the Raymond Road to the south.

WHEN JOHNSTON DECIDES TO ABANDON JACKSON, HE GIVES UP THE FORMER capital city of the state, with its railroads and manufacturing facilities, hours before he is sure that it is going to be assailed. He also believes that the enemy attack, if it comes, will be coming from only one direction, which would be much easier to defend against than the two-pronged attack that he will receive. Thus his decision to give up Jackson so quickly is curious.

Making his decision even stranger is the fact that Johnston has 6,000 troops in and around Jackson, and he also knows that a Confederate brigade, commanded by Gen. Samuel B. Maxey, should arrive in Jackson sometime that day from Port Hudson. Additionally, the remainder of Gist's and Walker's brigades should arrive soon. So Johnston should have around 9,000 men—with luck, 12,000—before day's end. He should be able to hold on to Jackson long enough for his forces and Pemberton's army to attack Grant from both sides. Johnston had to have had this in mind when he sent his "if practicable" and "could cooperate" message to Pemberton. But then, he decides not only to evacuate Jackson, but also to move away from, not toward, Pemberton's forces. The expert marksman still doesn't want to risk a shot.

To cover the Confederate withdrawal from Jackson, Johnston orders Gregg to fight a delaying action west of town on the Clinton Road, while Gen. John

Adams, commander of the troops in and around Jackson, is to remove as much public property as possible and move north to Canton, Mississippi, 22 miles north of Jackson at the terminus of the New Orleans, Jackson and Great Northern Railroad. Gregg orders Col. Peyton H. Colquitt, who is in tactical command of the 900 men and four guns of Gist's brigade that have already arrived, to march west on the Clinton Road and fight a delaying action. Gregg accompanies Colquitt in the downpour, and they pass through the partially completed and poorly placed earthworks on the western edge of town without stopping.

Gregg's Confederates continue west on the Clinton Road to a ridgeline located on the O. P. Wright farm, three miles from downtown Jackson. This ridgeline is the watershed between Town and Lynch Creeks, and here Gregg orders Colquitt to deploy his men astride the road. Five companies of Gist's 46th Georgia and a battalion of the 14th Mississippi, borrowed from Adams's command, deploy to the right of the road, and the 24th South Carolina of Gist's brigade and the four rifled guns of the Brookhaven Light Artillery, also borrowed from Adams, deploy to the left.

Lt. Col. Ellison Capers takes skirmishers from the 24th South Carolina farther west through the Wright farm, and posts them in a ravine behind a garden fence. Capt. James A. Hoskins places his guns on a slight rise to the left of the road so that they have a clear field of fire down the Clinton-Jackson Road and across the fields for a mile and one-half. Gregg's choice of ground is good. He is going to be hopelessly outnumbered, but his mission is to fight a series of delaying actions, not to become embroiled in a battle.

Behind Colquitt's men on the Clinton-Jackson Road is Shot Pouch Walker's command, which consists of the 30th Georgia, First Georgia Sharpshooter Battalion, Fourth Louisiana Battalion, Third Kentucky Mounted Infantry, and Martin's Georgia Battery. These men halt in column about two miles from downtown Jackson, within easy supporting distance of Colquitt's people.

Gregg's own brigade is now commanded by Colonel Farquharson, and Gregg orders Farquharson to remain behind in Jackson but to be prepared to march where needed at a moment's notice. Gregg also places the First Battalion, Mississippi State Troops, and some civilian volunteers in the earthworks around Jackson with 17 pieces of artillery. Gregg thinks he is ready. However, unknown to the Confederates, Sherman's men are also approaching on the Raymond-Jackson Road to the south.

As the Federals move toward Jackson, Sherman at Mississippi Springs coordinates his movement with McPherson, who is five and one-half miles to the north at Clinton. At 5 a.m. the two Union columns slog eastward on converging roads toward Jackson.

The advance guard of McPherson's XVII Corps leaves Clinton at 5 a.m. and arrives in front of Colquitt's Confederates at 9 a.m., led by Holmes's brigade of Crocker's division. As soon as Holmes sees the Confederates on a ridge about one and a quarter miles to his front, he deploys his men. The 17th Iowa moves to the left and anchors its left flank on the Southern Railroad of Mississippi, with its right flank on the Clinton-Jackson Road. The 80th Ohio deploys to the right of the road, and the Tenth Missouri goes to the right of the Ohioans.

While Holmes deploys his men, the Confederate artillery opens fire at long range with its rifled guns, and the Yanks respond by bringing up four of their rifled guns—ten-pounder Parrotts of Company M, First Missouri Light Artillery. These cannon start banging away from their position on the W. T. Mann farm. While this is happening, Crocker calls up Boomer's brigade, and Boomer goes to the left of the road. Sanborn sends two regiments of his brigade to the far right of the line, leaving two regiments in the rear as a reserve. Gregg's Confederates are clearly overmatched in numbers.

The rain, which earlier had slackened a bit and become intermittent, suddenly comes down in sheets. McPherson, in character, has moved his men slowly and cautiously, and now he is afraid to let them open their cartridge boxes for fear of ruining their ammunition. While McPherson waits for the rain to stop, the undetected southern half of the two converging Union columns is nearing Jackson.

Grant has spent the night in Raymond, and after an early start he catches up with Sherman's column. Tuttle's division is in the lead, and Tuttle places Gen. Joseph A. Mower's brigade at the front of the column. Mower has two light artillery batteries with him: the Second Iowa Battery and Company E, First Illinois Light Artillery. Behind Mower's men is the brigade of Gen. Charles Leopold Matthies, a former Prussian army officer who fled Europe to become an Iowa liquor salesman. Behind Matthies's brigade is Gen. Ralph Buckland's brigade.

As the division nears Jackson, the Yanks hear the thunder of the artillery duel between Gregg and McPherson three miles to the north, and the advance elements of Mower's men look down the hill to see that Lynch Creek is flooded bank-full because of the torrential rain. They also see Rebel artillery on the other side of the creek, covering a wooden bridge that cannot be burned in the rainstorm.

The sudden downpour has been fortunate for the Rebels, because it delayed the Union attack on the Clinton-Jackson Road. While Gregg is waiting for

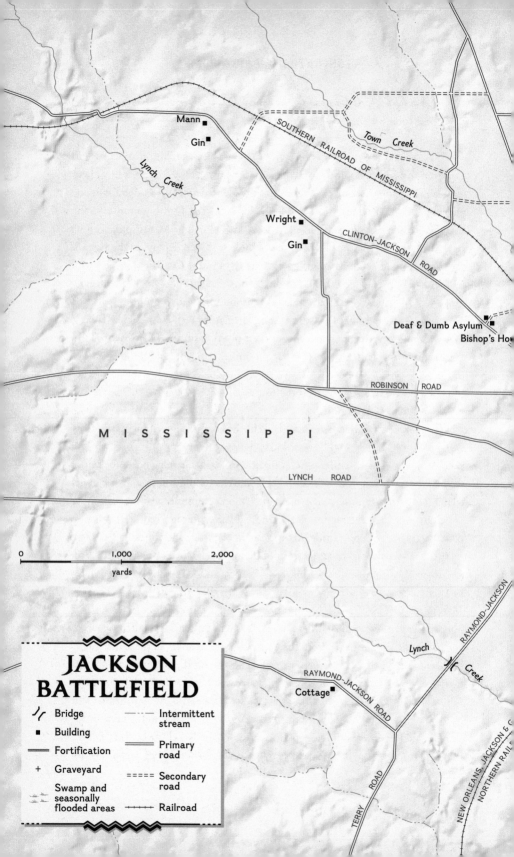

Mann

Gin

Lynch Creek

SOUTHERN RAILROAD OF MISSISSIPPI

Town Creek

Wright

Gin

CLINTON-JACKSON ROAD

Deaf & Dumb Asylum

Bishop's Ho

ROBINSON ROAD

M I S S I S S I P P I

LYNCH ROAD

0   1,000   2,000

yards

Lynch Creek

RAYMOND-JACKSON

RAYMOND-JACKSON ROAD

Cottage

NEW ORLEANS, JACKSON &

NORTHERN RAIL

TERRY ROAD

JACKSON BATTLEFIELD

⌒ Bridge

■ Building

— Fortification

+ Graveyard

Swamp and seasonally flooded areas

---- Intermittent stream

— Primary road

==== Secondary road

++++ Railroad

McPherson's attack along that road, his scouts detect Sherman's column, and race to advise him that he now has a big problem. Gregg makes a quick decision, and he orders Col. Albert P. Thompson of the Third Kentucky Mounted Infantry to assemble a task force to meet this new threat. Thompson takes his Kentuckians and borrows the First Georgia Sharpshooter Battalion and the four guns of Martin's Georgia Battery from Walker's command to form Task Force Thompson, which then moves south in the rainstorm to the Lynch Creek bridge on the Raymond-Jackson Road, and forms a blocking position. The Confederates arrive just before Sherman's men crest the ridge a mile to the southwest.

At 11 a.m. the downpour suddenly stops. Cartridges are slammed down Federal rifle barrels, and McPherson's men open fire along the Clinton-Jackson Road. Logan's division soon arrives from Clinton, and McPherson, for the second time in two days, has more men than he knows what to do with. He sends J. E. Smith's and Stevenson's brigades out to the left to extend his line, and leaves Dennis's brigade in the rear to protect the corps supply trains.

Crocker's Yankees move forward and the Rebel artillery fires down the Clinton-Jackson Road, cutting gaps in the blue line. But there are many more blue suits than there are Confederate shells, and the Yanks continue to come forward with bayonets fixed. The 24th South Carolina engages in a hand-to-hand fight with Crocker's Yanks at the Wright farm, and after a savage fight, the outnumbered but not-outfought Confederates fall back.

Gregg attempts to relieve pressure on his front with a bluff on the Union left flank by ordering Farquharson's men to the Confederate right at Town Creek. Near the creek the same Tennesseans and Texans who fought at Raymond feign an attack on the Union left flank. But even the cautious and inexperienced McPherson realizes that there are far too few Confederates to pose any real threat, and Farquharson suffers the indignity of being ignored.

Under increased pressure, Colquitt's Confederates withdraw east on the Clinton-Jackson Road toward Jackson, and McPherson, just as he failed to do at Raymond, does not pursue. Walker, behind Colquitt, realizes the situation is hopeless and falls back to Jackson. Farquharson, out on the Confederate right flank, retreats cross-country to Johnston's withdrawal route, the Canton Road leading north out of Jackson. But Gregg has done what was asked of him. He delayed the Yanks while Johnston evacuated the city.

Meanwhile, three miles south on Sherman's front, an artillery duel between the four Confederate guns near the bridge over Lynch Creek and the twelve Union guns on the high ground above the creek is decided in 20 minutes. The Rebels are pounded by the superior Union artillery, and soon withdraw a mile back toward a belt of trees in front of the earthworks, one-third of a mile northeast of modern Battlefield Park. As the Confederates withdraw, it is impossible to burn the rain-soaked bridge over Lynch Creek, especially under intense artillery fire.

Sherman's men advance, but Lynch Creek is so swollen from the rain that they have to use the narrow bridge. Of course, this takes time and prevents any kind of pursuit. Once across the creek, Tuttle redeploys his division with Mower's brigade to the left of the road, Matthies's brigade to the right, the two batteries in the mud of the road, and Buckland's brigade as a reserve behind Matthies's men. The new line advances cautiously, and soon comes under fire from the Confederate earthworks.

Ten cannon, served by the old men and boys of the Mississippi State Troops as well as civilian volunteers, are used to fire on the Yanks. When Martin's Georgia Battery is added to these ten guns, the Rebel cannon actually outnumber those of the Yankee cannon—14 to 12—and the Southerners are protected by earthworks.

The Yanks have lost the upper hand, so Tuttle commits his reserve, and Buckland moves to the right of Matthies. The Rebel guns shift fire to Buckland's men as they move forward, and the Federal attack is halted at 1:30 p.m.

Sherman has established his command post at a small cottage at the rear of Matthies's brigade, and he and Grant now have a conference. "It's time to brush these Rebs aside," Grant says.

As shells whistle overhead, Sherman sends Capt. Julius Pitzman, acting chief engineer of the XV Corps, to the Federal right to reconnoiter a route into the Rebel flank and rear. Pitzman is provided an escort of the 95th Ohio, commanded by Col. William McMillen, who is well known both as a medical doctor and as a "convivial" man, meaning he likes to tip the bottle. Pitzman finds his way to the railroad bed of the New Orleans, Jackson and Great Northern Railroad, and he and McMillen's men follow the tracks northward toward Jackson and through the Confederate earthworks. Soon they run into a black man, who tells them that the Rebels have left the city and that a few civilians have been left behind to fire the cannon and keep the Yanks at bay. He tells the bluecoats that they are now behind the cannoneers, but McMillen is still nervous about his vulnerable position inside Confederate lines. McMillen soon has his confidence bolstered by the arrival of Steele's division, sent by Sherman over to the railroad to support the 95th Ohio. So McMillen orders an attack into the unguarded enemy rear, and his effort bags six guns and 52 prisoners.

McPherson, over on the Clinton-Jackson Road, advances eastward toward town and soon finds the earthworks deserted to his front, because at 2 p.m. Gregg has ordered his troops to withdraw. General Adams has advised Gregg that the army's supply trains have left Jackson and are headed toward Canton, so Gregg has ordered Colquitt, Walker, and Task Force Thompson to withdraw up the Canton road to protect the rear of the wagons. These units skillfully fall back, leaving skeleton gun crews in the earthworks to delay the Yankees, and they move northward up the Canton Road and encamp for the night at Tougaloo, seven miles north of Jackson, where Johnston has made his camp earlier in the day.

McPherson sends Crocker's division into Jackson to take possession of the city, and the 59th Indiana of Sanborn's brigade gets the honor of raising the Stars and Stripes over the Mississippi State Capitol. Young Fred Grant ventures into the governor's office and finds a pipe lying on a table, which he confiscates for his own use.

Grant rides to the Bowman House around 4 p.m. and takes up quarters in the room that Johnston slept in the night before. He, Sherman, and McPherson tally the day's work, and determine they have suffered 41 killed, 251 wounded, and 7 missing, for a total of 299 casualties. The Confederate reports are sketchy, but it appears they suffered an estimated 845 casualties, and they lost 17 cannon to the Yankees—cannon that will later be used against Pemberton at Vicksburg.

During this conference, McPherson gives Grant some interesting information. One of Johnston's three couriers was a Union agent recently expelled from Memphis, and he had hand delivered his copy of Johnston's message to McPherson. Grant now knows that Johnston has asked Pemberton to attack the Federal forces at Clinton and that Johnston wants to reestablish communications so Pemberton can be reinforced. As Grant also has discovered, Johnston has retreated north out of Jackson, not west toward Pemberton. Grant decides to march his men west to Bolton, the nearest point on the railroad where Johnston and Pemberton could possibly meet. He will prevent them from joining their forces.

Orders are issued to McClernand, at Raymond, and McPherson, in west Jackson, to march to Bolton in the morning and concentrate their forces there. Sherman is directed to remain in Jackson and destroy the railroads and manufacturing facilities of the capital city, which, after Nashville and Baton Rouge, is the South's third state capital to fall.

Before he left Jackson on the 14th, Johnston sent messages along the railroads to the east and to the south to warn the arriving reinforcements to turn around. Gist, coming from South Carolina, has reached Brandon, 12 miles east of Jackson on the Southern Railroad, but turns around, taking his 1,500 men back east to Forest. At the same time, Maxey, who left Port Hudson and has reached Hazlehurst, gets his warning and turns around and goes back to Brookhaven. The two brigades coming from Bragg's army at Tullahoma, Ector's and McNair's, halt at Meridian.

While Johnston is evacuating Jackson, Pemberton is headquartered in Bovina, eight miles east of Vicksburg. At midmorning on the 14th, Pemberton receives Johnston's "attack" message, delivered by Capt. William S. Yerger, who has ridden all night from Jackson, veering around the Yankee troops on the Clinton-Jackson Road.

Pemberton anxiously reads the message and doesn't like the idea of moving farther away from Vicksburg.

Pemberton's reply to Johnston, written around 9:30 a.m., indicates a negative frame of mind. In his reply, he says that he has only about 16,000 men available. In fact, he has about 23,000. He goes on to say that "the men have been marching several days, are much fatigued, and I fear will straggle very much. In directing this move, I do not think you fully comprehend the position that Vicksburg will be left in, but I comply at once with your order." Pemberton wants to obey President Davis's edict to protect Vicksburg, and he is very reluctant to move farther away from the river.

After scribbling his message to Johnston, Pemberton travels six miles east to Edwards and then another two miles south to the Confederate defensive position at Mount Moriah. When he arrives, he learns from his scouts that Whiskey Smith's division has moved south from Montgomery Bridge to Auburn, presumably to protect a supply train reported to be coming up from Grand Gulf. Pemberton now has second thoughts about marching east and attacking the Yankees at Clinton, which would leave a Yankee division, maybe two, operating in his rear. So that afternoon he convenes a time-consuming council of war with his general officers to discuss the situation.

Pemberton tells his commanders at the meeting that the mission of his army is to defend Vicksburg. At least, those are his orders from President Davis. He says that, if he attacks, he will probably be defeated. Still, most of his officers are in favor of obeying Johnston and attacking. Loring offers a compromise plan. Confederate scouts have identified a large Federal supply train in the vicinity of Old Auburn, and it is being escorted by at least one division of troops, maybe more. Loring's plan is to march the army north to Edwards, then east along the Raymond-Edwards Road, then south to Dillon's, where they will capture the train and destroy its escort, which is Whiskey Smith's division and two brigades of Blair's division. If successful, the Confederate generals believe, this mission will cut Grant's supply line and destroy at least one Federal division.

Pemberton doesn't much care for Loring's idea, and says he wants to fall back to Big Black River and take up a strong defensive position in his tête de pont to await Grant's attack. In the end, however, Loring's plan is adopted by a vote of the council. Pemberton is not acting as a commander. He is serving as a board president, with motions and votes. At the conclusion of the council, orders are issued to move to Dillon's farm tomorrow morning, and a message is sent via Captain Yerger to General Johnston, advising him of the new plan. Pemberton tells Johnston in his message that he will move as early "as practicable" on the morrow for Dillon's. His plan is "to cut the enemy's communications."

In Washington, on May 14, President Lincoln writes to Joe Hooker, saying, "I shall not complain, if you do no more, for a time, than to keep the enemy at bay, and out of other mischief." Then the President drops the bombshell, saying, "I have some painful intimations that some of your corps and division commanders are not giving you their entire confidence. This would be ruinous if true; and you should therefore, first of all, ascertain the real facts beyond all possibility of doubt."

The seeds that Hooker helped plant in the cabal against Burnside have borne him bitter fruit in a short five months, and Lincoln's words to him of January 26, 1863, are prophetic: "I much fear that the spirit which you have aided to infuse into the army, of criticizing their commander, and withholding confidence from him, will now turn upon you." Joe Hooker has the support of just one of seven infantry corps commanders—Dan Sickles.

In Richmond word is received of Grant's victory at Raymond on May 12, and a clerk in Seddon's office writes, "This is a dark cloud over the hopes of patriots, for Vicksburg is seriously endangered." That afternoon Lee takes the Richmond, Fredericksburg, and Potomac train to Richmond.

On May 15, McPherson's XVII Corps gets on the road at 5 a.m. Logan's and Crocker's divisions trek westward through Clinton with Logan halting at Bolton and two of Crocker's brigades stopping three miles east of that village. Crocker's third brigade, Holmes's, camps in a field north of Clinton. Grant remains with

Sherman in Jackson during the morning and then follows McPherson westward, stopping in Clinton later in the day.

After Grant leaves town, Sherman loses control of his men, and they go on a rampage and burn much of Jackson. Late that afternoon, Grant arrives in Clinton, ten miles west of Jackson, where he spends the night. For the commanding general's security, encamped on a hillside near the smoking rubble of a railroad depot is Holmes's brigade.

McPherson's two divisions, Logan's and Crocker's, have an uneventful march west on May 15. McClernand's men, however, are spread out when they get the order to concentrate at Bolton. Carr's division is at Forest Hill Church, five miles southwest of Jackson, on the Raymond-Jackson Road, where it had marched to support Sherman at Jackson if necessary. Hovey's division, which had marched to support McPherson, is four miles southeast of Clinton on the Clinton-Raymond Road, after wallowing in the mud and rain most of the previous day trying to get the wagons and artillery across the flooded headwaters of Bakers Creek. Osterhaus's division is at Raymond with McClernand. Whiskey Smith's division is 14 miles southwest of Raymond at Old Auburn, escorting Blair's wagon train from Grand Gulf. McClernand sends orders to all of his division commanders to march toward Bolton, and, as usual, he has his cavalry scout the road network to ensure there are no glitches on the march.

Grant writes in his memoirs that "the concentration of my troops was easy." It might be easy for an experienced commander, but this is the operational art at its best. Even with the wide dispersion of his troops, by 8 p.m. on May 15, Grant has seven divisions—about 32,000 men—in camp and concentrated along three axes of advance on a north-south line from Bolton. He has Hovey's, Logan's, and Crocker's divisions immediately south of Bolton on the Jackson Road. Two miles south of the Jackson Road, McClernand is encamped with Osterhaus's and Carr's divisions on the Middle Road, which parallels the Jackson Road all the way to Champion Hill. And two miles south of the Middle Road is the Raymond-Edwards Road, where Blair and Smith arrive at 8 p.m. with the wagons and go into camp.

Blair had arrived at Auburn late the day before with two of his brigades guarding his 200-wagon train, and was dutifully met by Smith's reserve division. On the 15th Blair's two brigades and Smith's division escort the slow-moving train, hence their arriving in camp at the "late" hour of 8 p.m. At the end of the day, however, the precious 200-wagon train is positioned to distribute food and ammunition along the Raymond-Bolton Road to Grant's seven divisions.

For command and control Blair's men are temporarily attached to McClernand's XIII Corps, since Sherman's XV Corps is 15 miles away in Jackson.

On May 15, Pemberton plans to implement the vote of his council of war held the previous day. The Confederate army, however, doesn't begin the march until 8 a.m. Adams's cavalry provides the advance guard, and Loring's division is a mile behind. Bowen's divison follows Loring, trailed by Stevenson's big division with the wagon train.

Partially due to Pemberton's late start, but mostly due to his flawed scheme, the Confederate plan is already dead in the water. That's because the 200 wagons with Smith's and Blair's men have departed Auburn toward Raymond at 5 a.m. There is no way that the Confederates are going to beat the wagons to Dillon's farm, because they have a 12-mile march to that point, and the Yankees have to march half that distance. The Yanks also have a three-hour lead.

To make matters worse, the Confederates discover that they have a shortage of rations and ammunition. So Pemberton sends a train from Edwards to Vicksburg to pick up the supplies and then awaits its return to Edwards. By the time the rations are distributed, it is 1 p.m. before the march is resumed. Then the bewildered Confederate army marches two miles down the Raymond-Edwards Road, only to discover that the bridge over Bakers Creek is washed out. No one has performed a reconnaissance of the route before the 23,000 men were put on the road. In fact, the bridge has been washed out for some time, and now the creek is bank-full because of the recent rains. The army halts until 4 p.m., when finally an exasperated General Loring suggests a detour over the Upper Bakers Creek Bridge, one and one-half miles north on the Jackson Road.

After finally crossing Bakers Creek, the army marches east on the Jackson Road to the point where it meets the Middle Road, where the Jackson Road executes a sharp turn north over Champion Hill while the Middle Road continues east. This point is called the Crossroads, and at this intersection the men turn south into a farm road—the Ratliff Road—which takes them back south to the Raymond-Edwards Road.

By now it is getting dark, so Loring's men at the front of the column march for a mile to the Jackson Creek bridge. After crossing they settle in to camp in and around Sarah Ellison's modest farmhouse. Bowen's men are way behind Loring's because of the repeated stops and starts, and his soldiers don't end their march until 10 p.m. Stevenson's division, which trails the column, doesn't leave Edwards until 5 p.m., and these poor soldiers don't stop for the night until 3 a.m. Even worse, the wagon train, which is escorted by Col. Alexander W. Reynolds's

Tennessee Brigade, doesn't leave Edwards until midnight. It is dawn before these men get to the battlefield.

The Confederates have marched almost 12 miles, but they are only three and one-half miles east of Edwards and are still more than seven miles from Dillon's farm. Meantime, the target of the march—the Federal wagons and Smith's and Blair's four brigades—have advanced through Dillon's on the morning of the 15th and that night are encamped northwest of Raymond.

The contrast in commanders couldn't be greater. Grant maneuvers his army of 32,000 men in one day and has them in proper formation for battle the next day on three axes of advance, each axis within supporting distance of another. Most of his men have pitched their tents well before darkness falls, and even Smith's and Blair's men, who escorted the slow-moving wagon train, are in camp by 8 p.m. Pemberton has started his movement well after sunrise on the 15th, losing his opportunity before the march began, and has experienced delays which proper staff work would have prevented. He has aimlessly led his army of 23,000 men across the Mississippi countryside, and half of them are exhausted after marching much of the night.

When the Confederates halt, Pemberton and Loring, who do not care for each other, establish their headquarters at Mrs. Ellison's house. Why is there bad blood between Loring and Pemberton? Loring was fighting in the Second Seminole War when Pemberton was a cadet at West Point. In the old Army, Loring was wearing a colonel's eagle on his shoulder, commanding a mounted regiment, when Pemberton was an artillery captain. Loring doesn't have much use for Pemberton, because a colonel with a jealous nature doesn't like to see a West Point captain suddenly vault over him in rank. All in all, it probably was not a happy night in Sarah Ellison's house with these two men under the same roof. The situation was made worse by the long, mistake-filled day the army has endured.

Despite the delays, Pemberton still plans to move south to Dillon's on the 16th of May. Somehow, he thinks that, while he has been fumbling around all day on the 15th, the Yankees have remained static. But while Pemberton is ignoring the oncoming juggernaut of seven Union divisions less than six miles away, out in the fields next to the Ratliff Road, Bowen looks to the east and sees the glare of Union campfires in the sky. He sends out pickets and forms his men and his artillery for battle before allowing them to rest. Bowen knows there will be a fight in the morning. So does the average soldier in Pemberton's army.

Meanwhile, Johnston is in Tougaloo on the morning of May 15, and he has ordered John Gregg to start marching his men north toward Canton, which, strangely, means that Johnston is still moving away from Pemberton, not toward him. At 8:30 Captain Yerger gallops up to Johnston's headquarters, delivering Pemberton's message, which was written the previous day after the council of war south of Edwards. Pemberton advises Johnston that he is marching toward Dillon's, which is putting even more miles between the two armies. This is the reverse of concentration of forces, which Johnston always preaches. Of course, Johnston is doing the same thing by moving away from Pemberton. Still, Johnston goes apoplectic when he reads this message, and he fires off an order to Pemberton, telling him to march toward Clinton, not away from it. Then Johnston continues his march north. He continues to do the opposite of what he has told Pemberton to do.

In Virginia, Lee is summoned for a May 15 conference in Richmond with President Davis and Secretary Seddon. Lee meets with Davis and Seddon at the War Department, in the old Virginia Mechanics Institute Building, on Franklin Street. Lee finally has the opportunity to sell his idea of going north to Jefferson Davis, and he has come to Richmond prepared.

As he proposes his plan at the conference, Lee has a problem. Grant's army has crossed the Mississippi River at Bruinsburg, defeated the Confederates at the battle of Port Gibson, and then defeated Gregg at Raymond, which is only 15 miles from Jackson. The newspaper in Jackson, Mississippi, is demanding that Pemberton, who is a Pennsylvanian, be replaced by either Beauregard or Longstreet, and Governor Pettus of Mississippi (who has relocated his office several days before to Enterprise) is petitioning Davis for help. So a much concerned President Davis asks Lee's advice on how to salvage the situation in Mississippi.

Despite the fact that Davis has been quite ill, the conference goes all through the day and into the night. Lee advises Davis and Seddon that Joe Johnston, who has been sent to Mississippi, should attack Grant promptly, but that troops from the Army of Northern Virginia should not be sent to the West. His argument has several points.

First: By moving north he will transfer the theater of war from northern Virginia, which has felt the hard hand of war since 1861 and which has been foraged over by both the Confederate and the Union armies. Virtually no surplus food or fodder is left, and Lee's men and animals are hungry. Lee will go north of the Potomac River into Maryland and Pennsylvania and spend the summer campaigning in the North. By doing this he will supply the Confederate army while in Pennsylvania and also send back food and supplies to Virginia.

Second: Once Lee is in the North, the governors of Pennsylvania, New York, and New Jersey, not to mention other northern governors, will pressure Mr. Lincoln to withdraw troops from the Mississippi theater of operations to address the eastern threat.

Third: Perhaps Lee can win a major battle on northern soil. Because Lee is a soldier first and not a very good politician, he believes that a major victory on northern soil may bring British recognition. Lee believes France will then follow Britain and recognize the Confederacy.

Lee, however, does not realize the significance of the Emancipation Proclamation, signed by President Lincoln on January 1, 1863. Granted, the proclamation does not free any slaves where Mr. Lincoln has the authority to do so, but it announces the antislavery policy of the Federal government, and the British have long opposed slavery. If Viscount Palmerton, the prime minister of Great Britain, wants to recognize the Confederacy, he will undoubtedly be forced by the Liberals in Parliament to withstand a vote of confidence, and in the British form of government, that vote could send Palmerton packing. Additionally, the only members of the British Parliament who are advocating recognition of the South are a small group led by John Arthur Roebuck. Roebuck is a back-bencher in Parliament and has very little power. So recognition of the South as an independent nation is a far-fetched dream.

Although Lee is not a good politician, he is a good salesman. He knows how to handle President Davis, a gift that is completely beyond the grasp of Johnston, Beauregard, and others. In the end, Lee gets permission to invade the North.

While Lee is meeting with Davis and Seddon on May 15, word arrives in Richmond that Jackson, Mississippi, has been occupied by Federal soldiers, and a clerk in Secretary of War Seddon's office writes that the Union soldiers "cut off communication with Vicksburg, and that city may be doomed to fall at last." That night, with the lengthy conference concluded and the mission accomplished, Lee prepares to return to Fredericksburg.

At Grant's headquarters in Clinton, at 5 a.m. on May 16, two railroad men are escorted in. These men were employed on the Confederate supply train at Edwards on the previous day, and they have walked to Clinton during the night with valuable information. They tell Grant that Pemberton is at Edwards with 80 infantry regiments and 10 artillery batteries—about 25,000 men total—and that Pemberton has marched east out of Edwards. Since Pemberton has 49 regiments of infantry and 15 batteries of artillery, totaling about 23,000 men, this is not a bad estimate. It is good enough for Grant to issue orders at 5:45 a.m.

Sherman is ordered to leave Jackson immediately and bring one of his two divisions with him. McClernand is ordered to advance with two divisions, Smith's and Blair's, on the Raymond-Edwards Road. He is to advance two more divisions, Osterhaus's and Carr's, on the Middle Road. He is to advance one division, Hovey's, on the Jackson Road. Grant's orders to McClernand are to move cautiously. McPherson is to march his two divisions behind Hovey's division on the Jackson Road. After taking care of this business, Grant mounts and rides westward from Clinton to Bolton with his staff and his son.

McClernand has previously received orders from Grant instructing him to march toward Edwards early on the 16th, "so as to feel the force of the enemy." He is cautioned not to bring on an engagement, "unless you feel entirely able to contend with him."

Even before Grant issues his orders, McClernand is up and about and following his orders of the previous day. McClernand sets his men in motion on the Raymond-Edwards Road at 5 a.m. on May 16, and those on the Middle Road and Jackson Roads at six due to the differences in distance the three columns have to march. The columns are ordered to keep up communications with one another.

McClernand then rides north from the Middle Road to meet with the young McPherson, who spent the night at the William S. Jones plantation, two miles southeast of Bolton. Because Grant is in Clinton, McClernand is the senior officer on the field, so he tells McPherson that the two columns of the XIII Corps on the Raymond-Edwards Road and on the Middle Road are advancing toward the enemy, and that he would like for McPherson to follow Hovey's XIII Corps division on the Jackson Road with the divisions of Logan and Crocker. In short, McClernand plans for this to be his battle.

McPherson agrees with the senior general, and a satisfied McClernand rides back south to the Middle Road. But as soon as McClernand rides away, McPherson sends a courier to Grant at six, advising him to "come forward to the front" as soon as he can. That's all he says, but Grant can read between the lines.

Whiskey Smith's column on the Raymond-Edwards Road has Burbridge's brigade in the lead, with a detachment of the Fourth Indiana Cavalry pulling point duty. At 7 a.m. the Hoosiers run into one of Wirt Adams's mounted patrols at the M. A. Gillespie plantation on Turkey Creek, and the first shots of the Battle of Champion Hill are fired. Smith orders Burbridge to deploy his men for battle.

Adams rides back to Mrs. Ellison's to warn Pemberton that the Yankees are less than three miles east on the Raymond-Edwards Road. Amazingly, this comes as a surprise to Pemberton, but at least he has a roadblock, consisting of the 35th Alabama and 22nd Mississippi, near the junction of the Turkey Creek Road and the Raymond-Edwards Road, about one and a half miles to the east.

Pemberton is thinking about what he should do, when a courier rides up and hands him Johnston's message, written almost 24 hours earlier in Tougaloo, repeating that Pemberton should move toward Clinton. Pemberton decides it's time to obey, and he writes a quick message to Johnston, saying that he will reverse his march and go back to Edwards. Then he will take the Brownsville Road to the northeast to find Johnston.

Pemberton orders Stevenson to ensure that the trains, which are loaded with rations and ammunition, go back to Edwards, and then go northeast at least three miles on the Brownsville Road. Stevenson then directs Col. Alexander W. Reynolds to turn around 400 wagons, which are behind the army on the Jackson Road near the Crossroads. After turning the wagons, Reynolds is to have one of his regiments take them westward to Edwards, and then northeast on the Brownsville Road and out of harm's way. The rest of his brigade is to form a line of battle and protect the vital Crossroads. After the wagons are northeast of Edwards on the Brownsville Road, Reynolds is to ensure they are off to the side so that the withdrawing army can pass through the train on the march to the northeast. Remarkably, Reynolds accomplishes his task by 9:30 a.m.

Meanwhile, the three Confederate divisions form battle lines to the west of Jackson Creek. Loring, on the Confederate right, pulls back across the creek and places his artillery on the crest of the ridge to the west of the watercourse, blocking the Raymond-Edwards Road. As soon as he gets into position he sends word for the 35th Alabama and the 22nd Mississippi at the roadblock to fall back, which they do very well, delaying the advance of Burbridge's Yankees. As these regiments cross Jackson Creek, they wreck the wooden bridge over the creek to further slow the blue suits.

Bowen's division, which spent the night in line of battle on the Ratliff Road, is in the center. Bowen organizes a combat team under Lt. Col. Finlay L. Hubbell of the Third Missouri, and sends these men to man a line of outposts east of the Ratliff Road. He places Cockrell's Missouri brigade to the left and Green's brigade of Arkansans and Missourians to the right.

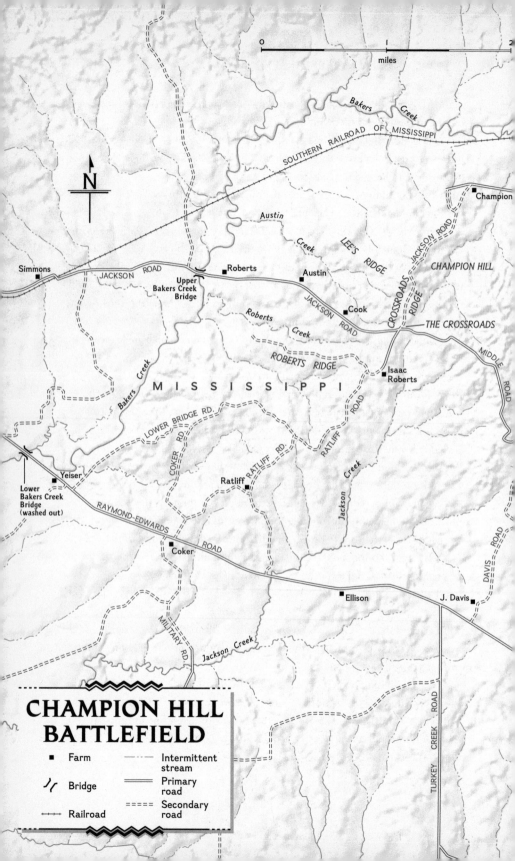

Bakers Creek

SOUTHERN RAILROAD OF MISSISSIPPI

Champion

Austin

LEE'S RIDGE

CHAMPION HILL

Creek

JACKSON ROAD

Simmons

JACKSON ROAD

Roberts

Austin

CROSSROADS RIDGE

Upper
Bakers Creek
Bridge

Cook

THE CROSSROADS

Roberts

JACKSON ROAD

Creek

MIDDLE ROAD

ROBERTS RIDGE

Isaac
Roberts

Bakers Creek

MISSISSIPPI

RATLIFF ROAD

LOWER BRIDGE RD.

COKER RD.

RATLIFF RD.

Jackson Creek

Lower
Bakers Creek
Bridge
(washed out)

Yeiser

Ratliff

RAYMOND-EDWARDS ROAD

Coker

DAVIS ROAD

MILITARY RD.

Ellison

J. Davis

Jackson Creek

TURKEY CREEK ROAD

CHAMPION HILL
BATTLEFIELD

■ Farm

)|(Bridge

┼┼┼┼ Railroad

—··— Intermittent
stream

══ Primary
road

═ ═ ═ Secondary
road

N

Stevenson's division, on the Confederate left, is blocking the Middle Road. Pickets belonging to Alexander W. Reynolds's brigade are sent to the crest of the ridge at Champion Hill, past the left flank of the Confederates. The remainder of the brigade, which has been depleted by sending a regiment to escort the wagon train, is on the Confederate left to guard the Crossroads. Reynolds is ordered to send a roadblock force eastward on the Middle Road, about one-half mile east of the Crossroads.

The Confederate line is now about three miles long, running from southwest to northeast, with the Raymond-Edwards Road running perpendicular to the right flank and the Middle Road perpendicular to the left. If the Yankees use only these two roads, the Rebels have a good chance of stopping them. But three undetected Yankee divisions are approaching on the Jackson Road, which runs east-west, then turns south to cross over Champion Hill into the Confederate right flank at the Crossroads. By 9 a.m., Pemberton has moved his headquarters to the Isaac Roberts house on the Ratliff Road, 600 yards south of the Crossroads.

While Blair is deploying his Yankees in Loring's front on the Raymond-Edwards Road, Osterhaus is rushing west on the Middle Road with his division. But to his front is a roadblock that has been hastily assembled by Alexander Reynolds's Tennesseans. As Osterhaus's men move forward, they are fired upon by the men in the roadblock, and Gen. Theophilus Garrard's brigade is rushed into line of battle. Col. Daniel Lindsey's brigade is behind Garrard's, and Carr's division, on the orders of McClernand, remains in column formation in reserve behind Osterhaus's people. The narrow road winds along the crest of a steep wooded ridge, which drops down into ravines on both sides, so there is not room enough for one division to deploy, much less two. The trees prevent the use of artillery, so the guns are parked to the side of the road. Eventually, Osterhaus finds a position for two three-inch ordnance rifles of the Seventh Michigan Battery. With the artillery supporting them, the Seventh Kentucky goes to the right of the road and the 49th Indiana to the left in an attempt to break the Tennesseans' roadblock.

The Confederates move nine companies of Georgians from Gen. Alfred Cumming's brigade to the roadblock. Lt. Col. J. F. B. Jackson commands these men, and they relieve the Tennesseans so that these men can fall back and rejoin their brigade to protect the retreating wagon train. The Georgians take their positions on the Middle Road, hunker down, and don't budge when Garrard's two regiments attack them. Osterhaus then orders Garrard to throw in his two remaining regiments, the 118th Illinois and the 69th Indiana, but the Georgia boys still won't budge.

Now that the Confederate wagon train has cleared the area, Alexander Reynolds advises Gen. Stephen D. Lee, commanding the brigade to his right on the Ratliff Road, that he is ready to withdraw to Edwards to protect the train. After his men on the roadblock have been relieved by the Georgians, Reynolds pulls his pickets off Champion Hill and marches back to a point a mile east of Edwards, where he turns into the Brownsville Road and goes two and one-half miles northeast to where the wagon train is parked beside the road. Here he deploys into line of battle and unlimbers the guns of the Third Maryland Battery to protect the trains. He is to await the arrival of the rest of the army, let it pass through the trains, and he will be the rear guard as the army marches northeast toward Johnston's men. At least, that's the plan.

Back on the Ratliff Road, Lee shifts his Alabamians to the left to protect the Crossroads and has Capt. James F. Waddell put his six guns in battery there, facing east toward Osterhaus's approaching Yankees. Lee is now on the far left of the Confederate line, and he has a very troubling avenue of approach—the Jackson Road—leading directly into his left flank. Plus, Reynolds has pulled his pickets from this road. Of course, this worries Lee, so he sends Lt. Col. Edmund W. Pettus of the 20th Alabama with a patrol to reconnoiter north, up the ridge where the Jackson Road crosses Champion Hill. Pettus is the younger brother of the governor of Mississippi, and the colonel takes his men over the crest of Champion Hill, continuing another 800 yards to a grove of trees near the Champion house.

On the Confederate right, Loring has his men fall back 600 yards to the Coker Ridge. To his front, A. J. Smith's division, spearheaded by Burbridge's brigade, moves up to Jackson Creek, only to find that the bridge has been destroyed. Federal pioneers attempt to rebuild the bridge, but soon come under fire from six guns of Wade's and Landis's Missouri Batteries of Bowen's division. But the Confederate guns are short-range smoothbores. When the Union counterbattery fire is directed against them, it comes from long-range rifled guns—six 10-pounder Parrotts of the 17th Ohio Battery. In minutes, two 12-pounder Napoleons of Landis's Battery are knocked out. Now the Federal pioneers can go to work on the bridge, and by 11 a.m. Burbridge's men are across Jackson Creek, taking the ridge formerly occupied by Loring's artillery. Here, 12 guns of the 17th Ohio and the Chicago Mercantile Batteries are brought into position. They blast away at Loring's 22 cannon for several hours, and the situation on the Raymond-Edwards Road becomes static, because Gen. A. J. Smith wants to get Landrum's brigade of his division into position, then wait for Blair's two brigades to move up. For the time being, the pressure along Loring's front is off.

On the Confederate left, however, Lee has a problem. Sometime after 9 a.m., Pettus sends a courier racing to Lee to tell him that the outpost at the Champion house has spotted a large Union column approaching on the Jackson Road. This is Hovey's division of the XIII Corps, which is followed by Logan's and Crocker's divisions of the XVII Corps. If this column is allowed to slam into the left rear of the Confederate line, it will be all over. Pemberton's army will be cut off, because the Jackson Road line of communications with Vicksburg will be cut, and with Federals on the Middle Road and the Raymond-Edwards Road, the Confederates will be virtually surrounded. The bridge over Bakers Creek on the Raymond-Edwards Road is washed out, closing that retreat route. Pemberton has ordered his engineer officer, Maj. Sam Lockett, to solve that problem, but rebuilding a bridge takes time, and time is running out.

Lee shifts his brigade left from the Crossroads for 400 yards to the crest of Champion Hill, where he places the two guns of the Virginia Botetourt Artillery—a 12-pounder Napoleon and a 6-pounder, the 12-pounder being placed on the left. This battery was badly beaten up at Port Gibson on May 1, losing all three of its lieutenant section leaders, 34 enlisted men, 53 horses, and four of its guns.

Champion Hill is the crest of a ridge, a mere 140 feet above the rest of the rolling countryside, so it doesn't stand out on the horizon like Cemetery Hill, Culp's Hill, and Big Round Top at Gettysburg. Still, it's the dominant terrain feature in the area, and the two Virginia guns are placed west of the point where the Jackson Road crests the ridge. As Lee looks to the northeast from his vantage point on the ridge crest, he realizes that he will have to turn, or refuse, his left flank and extend to the left. He will have to convert the Confederate line into something resembling the number 7.

He tells General Cumming, commanding the Georgia brigade on his right, what he is doing, and Cumming shifts his men to the left to occupy the crest of the hill at the salient angle of the 7, while Lee shifts his Alabamians to the north-west to form the top of the 7.

Lee's line stretches for almost three-quarters of a mile, with the 23rd Alabama on the far left, followed on their right by the 30th, 46th, 31st, and 20th Alabama. Forming a right angle at the crest of Champion Hill are Cumming's Georgians, with the 39th Georgia resting its left on the right of the 20th Alabama and, with the help of four companies of the 34th Georgia, extending to the two guns of the Botetourt Artillery. To help secure the vulnerable salient at the crest of the hill, two of Waddell's 12-pounder Napoleons are rushed uphill, and they go into battery next to the two Virginia guns. Cumming's line then turns south, along the Jackson Road, with the other two companies of the 34th Georgia and the entire 36th Georgia facing east. The line from the Crossroads to the crest of Champion Hill is too long, and there is a 300-yard gap between the right flank of the 36th Georgia and the Crossroads.

McClernand, down on the Middle Road, receives a message from Hovey at 9:45, telling him that he has arrived to find Rebels posted all along the ridge-line of Champion Hill, and requesting instructions. McClernand's orders from Grant are to be cautious, so McClernand, believing Grant to be in the vicin-ity of the Champion house, refers the matter to him. He asks Grant, "Shall I hold, or bring on an engagement?" This message won't get to Grant until noon, because three miles of very rough terrain separate the three parallel roads. A roundabout route of about six and one-half miles has to be taken to get from one road to another, and this route follows roads that are crowded with troops, artillery, and wagons.

Grant has ridden from Clinton at 7:30 after receiving McPherson's "come to the front" message, but he has taken the northern road—the Bridgeport Road—from Clinton to a point about three miles north of Bolton, and then he takes the Brownsville-Bolton Road south to Bolton. This is not the most direct route, but it will be quicker, thinks Grant, because he will not be behind the columns of Hovey, Logan, and Crocker on the Jackson Road. When he gets to Bolton with Holmes's brigade he finds that the bridge on the road south of Bolton over Bakers Creek leading to the Jackson Road has been destroyed by Osterhaus's men the previous day. This is because McClernand was told that Johnston and Pemberton were trying to form a junction near Bolton, so McClernand's men destroyed the bridge to cover their column moving south of Bolton in case Johnston approached from the northeast. But now Grant has to wait for his pioneers to rebuild the bridge. Then, after crossing Bakers Creek and turning west onto the Jackson Road, Grant finds Hovey's trains blocking the two divisions of McPherson's XVII Corps, and these wagons have to be moved to the side of the road.

Grant arrives at the Champion house around 10 a.m. and finds the house and grounds being converted into a Union field hospital. Hovey reports to Grant that he has sent a courier to get instructions from McClernand, but Hovey has meanwhile taken the initiative. He has already deployed his brigades in double battle lines for close combat, with Gen. George F. McGinnis's brigade across the Jackson Road and Col. James R. Slack's brigade on McGinnis's left. Hovey is ready to go, and he's tugging at the leash. He asks Grant for permission to attack, but Grant says, "Let's wait for the XVII Corps to come up; then we'll attack."

Logan's division soon tromps up the Jackson Road to the Champion house, and Grant sends Logan to McGinnis's right to extend the Union line west. Gen. Mortimer Leggett's brigade is edged up to McGinnis's right. Leggett is a New York–born Ohio lawyer and teacher, and he is also one of those teachers any student is lucky to have, because he has a lot of imagination. He is a good friend of George McClellan, and Leggett's Hill at Atlanta will be named for him after his men beat back Hood's assaults there on July 21–22, 1864. Leggett has been on leave. But as any good commander would do, when he learns his men have crossed the Mississippi, he races back south and joins his brigade in the nick of time at the Champion house, relieving Elias Dennis. Two hundred yards behind Leggett are the six guns of the hard-charging De Golyer. Extending the line to the right and rear of Leggett is J. E. Smith's brigade and the four 24-pounders of Company D, First Illinois Light Artillery, which blasted away next to De Golyer's guns at Raymond. The cannon go into battery on Smith's right. These 24-pounder howitzers are the guns of the old McAllister Battery of Shiloh fame.

After his guns were disabled at Fort Donelson, Capt. Edward McAllister was issued four bronze 24-pounders by Gen. William T. Sherman at Paducah, Kentucky, and during the Battle of Shiloh, Sherman personally took two of these guns into the final action just north of Shiloh Church on the afternoon of April 7, 1862. McAllister resigned because of illness shortly after Shiloh, and now Capt. Henry A. Rogers is the battery commander of the Illinois 24-pounders. He will be killed by a sniper while supervising the cutting of fuses in front of the Shirley house during the siege at Vicksburg on May 29, a day after De Golyer is mortally wounded by a rifle shot to the hip.

Stevenson's brigade is to be the ready reserve, so Stevenson puts his men behind De Golyer's guns in a column by battalions, and Capt. William Williams's six guns of the Third Battery, Ohio Light Artillery, go into battery on the high ground behind Logan's division. With his infantry and artillery in position at 10:25 a.m., Grant is ready to attack. Tactical command is turned over to Logan, and at 10:30 the 10,000 soldiers of Hovey's and Logan's divisions advance toward Cumming's and Lee's thin Confederate line.

Four of Lee's regiments have had to shift left to counter Logan's deployment on Hovey's right, and his men are stretched out as far as they can go. So even though the Confederate rifle fire is dropping the advancing Yanks, Logan notices that Lee's left flank is "in the air," and he orders Stevenson's brigade, his reserve, to move to Smith's right so that he can turn Lee's left flank. If Stevenson is successful, his men will soon be on the Jackson Road, between Pemberton and his trains—and between the Confederate army and Vicksburg.

Up on Champion Hill, Gen. Carter Stevenson sees John Stevenson's brigade moving to turn his left flank, and he orders Gen. Seth Barton's Georgia Brigade and the four guns of the Cherokee Georgia Artillery to double-quick the 2,000 yards from the division's right flank to extend the threatened left flank. Barton's sweating Georgians soon arrive, and he deploys the 40th, 41st, and 43rd Georgia into line just in time to confront John Stevenson's advancing ranks. The four ten-pounder Parrotts of the Georgians go into battery on the north slope of a ridge near the Roberts house, and their fire rakes through Logan's lines. Soon, these guns are joined by two sections of Capt. Samuel J. Ridley's Company A, First Mississippi Light Artillery, and Maj. Joseph W. Anderson, Carter Stevenson's chief of artillery, directs the fire of the eight pieces. Anderson, the former commander of the Virginia Botetourt Artillery, will die near the Georgia and Mississippi guns on the ridgeline west of Champion Hill.

At 11:30 the skirmishing is over, and Hovey's and Logan's divisions are in contact with the Confederate main line of resistance. McPherson gives them the go-ahead, and the Yanks attack Lee's extended line. McGinnis's brigade of Hovey's division is on the left of Logan's division, and his Hoosiers and Badgers receive fire at a range of 300 yards from the four cannon on the crest of Champion Hill. As McGinnis's men inch forward, the Rebel redlegs switch to canister, and then to double canister, which means that 54 iron balls, each of them one and one-half inches in diameter, come crashing through the woods with every shot. It sounds like a covey of quail flying at 1,485 feet per second. Fortunately for the Yanks, the ravines provide cover, and they move up close to the guns. They fix bayonets and get ready to charge across the last 75 yards in front of the four cannon.

Before McGinnis's men charge, the general has an idea, and he passes it down the line. At his signal, which will be his slashing his sword down, the men will drop face-down to the ground. If McGinnis correctly times this move, the four Confederate cannon will fire 216 iron balls harmlessly over his prone men. If he doesn't time it right, there will be dozens of grieving mothers and widows in Indiana and Wisconsin.

The Yanks charge the guns in double line of battle, bayonets fixed and screaming at the top of their lungs. McGinnis watches the Confederate gunners and chops his sword down. His men hit the dirt, the cannons fire, and the canister swooshes harmlessly overhead. Then the Yanks jump up and charge the guns before the Rebs can reload. They burst through Cumming's Georgians on the west side of the Confederate right-angle salient, and the fighting is with bayonet and rifle butt. In five minutes the Confederates of the 39th Georgia and four companies of the 34th Georgia fall back, and the two Alabama and the two Virginia guns suddenly become four Yankee guns.

Captain Johnston of the Botetourt Artillery recalled, "Under a heavy charge we were run over, our infantry breaking, and our horses being shot by the charging troops." Sergeant Obenchain wrote: "They did not kill all the horses. Some they shot and some they bayoneted. . . . I begged them not to murder the men."

The breaking of the western front of the Confederate salient on Champion Hill means that the Federals can now fire straight down the east-facing Jackson Road line, enfilading the remaining two companies of the 34th Georgia and the 36th Georgia. Col. Jesse Glenn of the 36th Georgia has no choice but to order retreat. As the Georgians race south on the Jackson Road, the 24th Indiana and 29th Wisconsin of McGinnis's brigade wheel right and push to the west, through the vacated Jackson Road line, and charge down the ridge to hit Lee's right flank.

Lee's Alabamians have held firm against Leggett's and Smith's frontal attacks. In fact, Lee has launched a limited counterattack, a sortie by Col. Franklin Beck and selected men of the 23rd Alabama to capture the four Illinois 24-pounder howitzers. Captain Rogers boldly moved these guns forward to within 400 yards of Lee's line and is firing short-range blasts. But when Beck's forlorn hope draws near the guns, they find the 45th Illinois and 23rd Indiana supporting the battery, and Beck has to withdraw. To make matters worse for the Confederates, McGinnis's flanking maneuver has forced the 20th and 31st Alabama of Lee's brigade to fall back 450 yards to the Jackson Road. Lee has no choice but to order his other three regiments to fall back to the road. There, Lee hopes to reform.

Shortly after noon, Grant finally receives McClernand's early dispatch in which he asked if he should hold or bring on an engagement. Grant scribbles a reply to McClernand, telling him "to feel and attack the enemy in force, if an opportunity occurs." Due to the road network, the courier takes two hours to ride to McClernand, who will not receive this message until around 2 p.m.

Down at the Crossroads, the 56th and 57th Georgia have protected Waddell's four remaining guns facing east down the Middle Road. But now that

Hovey's men have taken Champion Hill, these two regiments have to shift direction, so they wheel left and face north. They can do this, at least for now, because Colonel Jackson's roadblock has stymied Osterhaus's advance.

The time is now 1:30, and Carter Stevenson's new line is the Jackson Road, extending from the Crossroads on the east flank to the Upper Bakers Creek Bridge on the west. But now, up comes Slack's brigade to the left of McGinnis. While McGinnis's men initially attacked south, toward the Confederates on Champion Hill, Slack's men have had to angle to the right to attack west, against the east-facing Confederate line that extends south from Champion Hill to the Crossroads. Slack's Midwesterners, after making their way through some very rough and heavily wooded terrain, emerge into a grain field and surge forward, bayonets fixed. They capture Waddell's four cannon at the Crossroads. Waddell, in trying to withdraw his guns, has his teams ordered forward, and the unfortunate horses are quickly shot down by Slack's men. The 24th Iowa, spearheading the charge, gets the honor of capturing the Alabama guns, and the 56th and 57th Georgia run pell-mell down the Ratliff Road, where General Pemberton and his staff rally them near the Isaac Roberts house.

Out on Carter Stevenson's left flank, Barton's Georgians are in deep trouble, because Barton's right flank is uncovered when Lee's men fall back 450 yards to the Jackson Road. Barton has already committed his reserve regiment, the 52nd Georgia, on the left of his line, so he has to shift the 42nd Georgia, which is guarding the Upper Bakers Creek Bridge, to cover his right flank against John Stevenson's oncoming Yanks. It's too little, too late, and the Eighth Illinois and 32nd Ohio of Stevenson's brigade charge up the ridge into Major Anderson's eight cannon. The Georgians supporting the guns turn tail, and even though the cannoneers are blasting double canister into the Yankee lines, the guns are quickly overrun. Major Anderson is shot down and mortally wounded as he tries to keep his guns in action, and the Mississippian, Captain Ridley, is shot six times and killed as he is loading a cannon. The heroic Ridley, having lost all his gunners, was manning and firing a gun by himself—a difficult and dangerous thing to do. Despite the captain's bravery, the Federals put a hail of bullets into him to stop him from firing.

John Stevenson's men don't stop after taking the guns. They keep charging for another 450 yards to Lee's new line on the Jackson Road, and the Confederates have to retreat. Cut off, Seth Barton's Georgians on the left flank skedaddle west down the Jackson Road and across Bakers Creek, losing a number of men as prisoners to John Stevenson's Federals. Plus the Yanks have captured Anderson's eight guns, along with the four guns at the Champion Hill salient and Waddell's remaining four guns at the Crossroads—sixteen cannon in all. Pemberton has lost his Jackson Road escape route, and unless Major Lockett repairs the Raymond-Edwards Road bridge, Pemberton's army is trapped on the east side of Bakers Creek. Pemberton is in deep trouble.

Back at the Champion house, Grant rides up the Jackson Road and dismounts near the front gate. Dr. William M. Beach, assistant surgeon of the 78th Ohio, has been detailed as Logan's hospital director, and Beach is at the field hospital. He is hard at work 20 feet away from Grant when the roar of battle rolls in from Stevenson's attack, but he can hear Grant. Grant takes the stub of a cigar from his mouth, and he says to a staffer, "Go down to Logan and tell him he is making history today."

While Carter Stevenson's division is being wrecked, Pemberton is characteristically delaying making a decision, but finally, at 1 p.m. he sends Maj. C. McRae Selph with orders to Bowen and Loring. Bowen is to go to Stevenson's aid, and Loring is to shift left and help. Loring is to leave Col. T. M. Scott of the 12th Louisiana Infantry and Col. Wirt Adams's cavalry to cover the Bakers Creek crossing on the Raymond-Edwards Road.

Meanwhile, Major Lockett, with companies from both the 34th Georgia and 36th Georgia, is busy cutting through the creek bank at the washed-out bridge on the Raymond-Edwards Road to construct a ford as well as a bridge.

When Major Selph reaches Bowen with Pemberton's message, the enemy is heavily massed to Bowen's front, and Bowen says that he won't obey the order unless it is peremptory. One of Loring's staff officers tells Selph that Loring says the same thing. They have gotten used to Pemberton's democratic method of command, and they apparently want to call for a vote. When Selph takes their refusal messages back to Pemberton, he fires back a peremptory order. Bowen is told to send one of his two brigades to Stevenson's left flank immediately and to send the other brigade as soon as he can. But then an impatient and worried Pemberton decides to ride to Bowen's division and personally order Colonel Cockrell's brigade over to help Stevenson. As a Mississippi artilleryman, Pvt. William T. Moore, recalled, "Pemberton seemed to be very much excited; so much so that his aide had to assist him to mount his horse."

Cockrell's Missourians are initially ordered to help Barton's Georgians combat John Stevenson's Yankees, but when Pemberton hears that Slack's Iowans have captured Waddell's guns at the Crossroads, he directs Cockrell to go there. Cockrell's men hustle northward up the Ratliff Road and form line of battle.

Bowen, who has realized by now that his duty is to follow orders, shows up with Green's brigade, and Green forms on Cockrell's right.

Colonel Hubbell of Cockrell's brigade spent the morning with a makeshift battalion on combat outpost duty in front of Bowen's division, and Bowen recalls Hubbell's command. Hubbell's men fall back to the Ratliff Road and then double-quick north toward the Crossroads.

Cpl. Ephraim Anderson of the Second Missouri was in Hubbell's ad hoc command, and he recalled: "The colonel dashed off at the head of the column, at a gallop; the men followed in full run. Moving rapidly on for a distance of half a mile, we passed General Pemberton and his staff standing in the road, almost in the edge of the action. His manner seemed to be somewhat excited; he and his staff were vainly endeavoring to rally some stragglers, who had already left their commands in the fight."

As Hubbell's men pass the Isaac Roberts house, a group of ladies are alongside the road singing "Dixie" to encourage the soldiers. Two hundred yards north of the house, Hubbell's men pull up beside the four guns of Landis's Missouri Battery, which is pouring shot and shell into Slack's bluecoats at the Crossroads. Hubbell's men, who took off on a dead run up the Ratliff Road, finally catch up to Cockrell's brigade, their parent unit, and Hubbell disbands his command, allowing the different companies to rejoin their parent regiments. The time is 2:30 and Bowen's line is ready to charge.

Corporal Anderson, awaiting the order, later wrote, "Cockrell rode down the lines; in one hand he held the reins and a large magnolia flower, while with the other he waved his sword and gave the order to charge. With a shout of defiance and with gleaming bayonets and banners pointing to the front, the grey line leaped forward, and moving at quick time across the field, dislodged the enemy with a heavy volley from the edge of the woods, and pressed on."

The Confederate charge is led by Bowen, Cockrell, and Green, and the Missourians and Arkansans slam into McGinnis's men and drive the Yankees back in hand-to-hand fighting. Waddell's guns at the Crossroads are recaptured as the 24th Iowa gives way, and Slack's entire brigade is swept back toward Champion Hill. McGinnis, on the crest of the ridge, sees the disaster. He sends word to Hovey, and two guns of the 16th Battery, Ohio Light Artillery, are manhandled up the hill by the redlegs, placed into battery, and made to blast canister at the 4,000 charging Rebels, who seem to be immune to the iron missiles. Soon, Bowen's men recapture two of the four Confederate guns that were earlier lost on the hill's crest, as well as the two Buckeye guns.

Green's men have driven back Slack's people east of the Jackson Road in the rugged terrain, and after an hour of desperate combat, the two Confederate brigades have advanced almost three-quarters of a mile. All of the Confederates have fired their 40 rounds, and because the ammunition train has left the battlefield and is on the Brownsville Road, the desperate fighters have to rifle the cartridge boxes of the dead and wounded, both friend and foe, for ammunition. After they fire what ammunition they can find, they resort to the knife and bayonet. As they move down the north slope of the hill, they see the Federal ordnance trains parked just 600 yards to their front near the Champion house. The only ammunition on the field is the Yankee ammunition to their front, and they race toward the prize.

Bowen's men are joined in the middle of their line by the 56th and 57th Georgia, which Pemberton has managed to rally. Lee sees the success of the Missourians to his right and notices that Logan's men to his front have lost their fighting esprit when Slack's brigade falls back from the Crossroads and McGinnis's brigade retreats from Champion Hill. Logan's people see that their left flank is now uncovered. Sensing the hesitation in the Union line, Lee rides along his lines to rally the men of the 30th and 46th Alabama to launch a counterstroke. The Alabamians respond, and charge toward a rail fence, but as they attempt to clamber over it, the guns of De Golyer's Eighth Michigan Battery, which having been moved forward into an open field to the battery front, open fire and drive the Rebels back.

While the Rebels are driving Hovey's division back down the north slope of Champion Hill, the lead brigades of Crocker's division arrive at the Champion house. General McPherson sends Col. John Sanborn's brigade of Crocker's division to beef up Logan's line of Leggett's and Smith's brigades. Sanborn forms in a field to the right of De Golyer's battery, while Col. George Boomer's brigade masses in a double line of battle in a field south of the Champion house. Crocker then orders Boomer to advance several hundred yards and file to the right so that his right anchors on Leggett's left.

But while Boomer is executing this maneuver, up rides Col. Clark Lagow of Grant's staff with the bad news of Hovey's retreat down the north slope of Champion Hill, with Bowen's determined fighters in hot pursuit. Boomer races his men up the north face of Champion Hill and forms a double line of battle just as Hovey's men retreat in disorder through his lines. It doesn't take long for Bowen's hard-charging Missourians to convince Boomer's men to also turn and run, especially with Green's Confederates swinging past their left flank.

As Green's men race down the hill toward the Champion house, Hovey has had time to amass 16 cannon on a slight rise in an open field southeast of the house. These guns belong to three batteries: Company A, First Missouri Light Artillery; the 16th Ohio Battery; and the Sixth Wisconsin Battery. They are positioned to fire down the length of Green's line, enfilading his right flank. At the same time, Holmes's brigade, which spent the night in Clinton with Grant and marched to Champion Hill at the tail end of the army, arrives. They shuck their knapsacks and haversacks and race forward to protect Boomer's left flank.

Despite the arrival of Crocker's men, Grant, with Bowen's men sweeping toward him, gets nervous and orders John Stevenson's brigade back from its hard-earned position astride the Jackson Road on the Confederate left. This mistake reopens Pemberton's line of retreat. However, Grant gets away with it because Barton's mauled Georgians don't capitalize on his error. They fail to retake the road.

The arrival of Crocker's men allows Hovey to regroup, and Logan's men begin to again push forward along Lee's and Cumming's front. Cumming has rallied many of his Georgians, but they retreat a second time when the reinforced Federal line advances. The retreat of the Georgians leaves Lee's Alabamians of the 30th and 46th regiments out on a limb, since they had advanced out toward De Golyer's guns, but Col. Charles Shelley manages to get his men out. The 46th Alabama is not so fortunate, and Col. Michael Woods and most of his 46th are captured by the Fourth Minnesota and 59th Indiana of Sanborn's brigade.

Bowen's counterattack, while brilliantly executed, has reached its zenith. His men have run out of gas, whereas Crocker's arrival has refueled the Yanks. Still, Bowen's men are withdrawing grudgingly, fighting with no ammunition.

It is now four o'clock. The Yankees attack along Bowen's front, and with Cumming's retreat and the overrunning of Lee's line, they are about to turn Bowen's left flank. To make matters worse, Bowen learns from Green's officers that a strong Union column is approaching down the Middle Road, about to go through the Crossroads and get behind him.

It is after 2 p.m. when McClernand receives Grant's 12:35 message, telling him to attack "if an opportunity occurs." McClernand quickly orders Smith and Osterhaus to "attack the enemy vigorously." A. J. Smith's division is in the lead on the Raymond-Edwards Road to the south, and Osterhaus's division is in the vanguard on the Middle Road. McClernand orders Blair, who is behind A. J. Smith, and Carr, who is behind Osterhaus, to support the attacking division in their front.

On the Middle Road, Osterhaus receives McClernand's instructions immediately, and he orders Garrard's brigade to push forward. Garrard is reinforced by the 42nd Ohio of Lindsey's brigade, and this force smashes into Colonel Jackson's Confederate roadblock and pushes through it. But then Osterhaus becomes cautious when he sees Confederates at the Crossroads to his front, and he stops to wait for the rest of Lindsey's brigade to catch up. Osterhaus demands more men, so McClernand sends for Carr's division to come forward. While Carr is moving up, Osterhaus is happy to wait. But this is the powerful Federal column that Green's officers warn Bowen about.

Down on the Raymond-Edwards Road, when Bowen's division had moved north for its counterattack, Loring's men shifted to the left, or north, to fill in the gap caused by Bowen's withdrawal. Buford's brigade shifted left to Bowen's old slot, while Featherston's brigade sidled left into Buford's old slot. Abraham Buford is one of the heaviest Confederate generals. A giant who weighs in at 320 pounds, he is known for his strength and endurance. He's a cousin to Union cavalryman Gen. John Buford, and both men are from Kentucky. Abe Buford is a West Pointer, class of 1841.

Loring's far right brigade, Tilghman's, was farthest south of the Raymond-Edwards Road, so it shifted north to straddle the Raymond-Edwards Road on Cotton Ridge. With his brigade, Tilghman has two batteries of artillery: the four guns of Company C, 14th Mississippi Artillery Battalion, and the six guns of Company G, First Mississippi Light Artillery.

Loring finally decides to obey Pemberton and orders Buford's brigade north up the Ratliff Road. He decides to ride with Featherston's brigade and take a different route, but he doesn't advise Pemberton of the route he will take, which is a trace of a road that parallels the Ratliff Road.

Pemberton is desperately waiting for Loring's men while the situation on the Confederate left unravels, and, in desperation, he personally rides south to find his missing general. Soon he sees a cloud of dust—Buford's brigade moving on the double-quick. Pemberton shouts for Buford to detach two regiments and have them run to the Crossroads, where General Green is about to be overrun from the north and flanked on the east. Buford sends the 12th Louisiana and 35th Alabama. Buford is then ordered to take the remainder of his brigade and post them west of the Crossroads and help Lee along the Jackson Road. Pemberton then goes looking for Loring.

By the time Buford's men approach the Crossroads, it is too late. Hovey's and Crocker's Yankees have crested Champion Hill and recaptured the four disputed cannon there, and now they are driving Bowen's men southward. Buford's 12th Louisiana has gone east on the Middle Road to try to hold back Osterhaus's advancing soldiers, but the Louisianans are being pushed back. All that Buford can do is form a line of battle for Bowen's exhausted men to fall behind. As the Yanks overrun the Crossroads a second time, the 17th Iowa of Holmes's brigade recaptures Waddell's four guns. Buford's two detached regiments, the 12th Louisiana and 35th Alabama, follow Bowen's soldiers to the protection of Buford's line.

Pemberton is trying to find Loring, but Loring is with Featherston's brigade on the parallel road. The two generals pass one another, with half a mile of woods between them. Pemberton then rides back to his Isaac Roberts house headquarters and learns that the Confederate lines are collapsing. Feeling that he has no options, he orders a retreat across the newly repaired bridge and ford on the Raymond-Edwards Road.

Meanwhile, Loring merges into the Ratliff Road, marches north to Buford's deployed brigade, and before Pemberton's retreat order reaches him, deploys Featherston's brigade on Buford's left. Loring is waiting for Lee's brigade to reform, and he plans to attack. But Gen. Thomas Taylor on Pemberton's staff arrives and orders a retreat. Loring's mission now is to cover the retreat of the army as it heads southwest to the Raymond-Edwards Road and crosses Bakers Creek.

On the Raymond-Edwards Road, when Loring's men departed to go north, Burbridge's brigade, reinforced by the 19th Kentucky and 77th Illinois from Landrum's brigade, advanced and occupied the grounds around the Coker house. Two three-inch ordnance rifles and two six-pounders of the Chicago Mercantile Battery, plus the four ten-pounder Parrotts of the 17th Ohio Battery, move up to the ridge to do battle with Tilghman's ten cannon on Cotton Ridge. Tilghman finds himself with the responsibility of saving Pemberton's army. His task is to hold the two Union divisions to his front, keeping the retreat route open. He places himself with his gunners beside the vital roadway and orders them to hold at all costs. The artillery duel becomes ferocious at a range of 600 yards.

Capt. Patrick H. White, commanding the Chicago Mercantile Battery, recalled: "I took four guns up the road. . . . We passed the line of infantry, who were lying down on either side of the road and went into battery in front of a planter's house, which sat back from the road about 300 feet. . . . It was one of the hottest artillery fights I was ever in. I was deaf and dazed from the bursting of shells; I could hardly hear myself give an order and one of my ears bled. We used alternatively shell and canister, in order to disable them by killing their horses."

While the Union redlegs blast away at the Confederate guns, Burbridge is ordered by A. J. Smith not to advance until Blair's divison comes up for support. Burbridge's men take cover behind the Coker house. Meanwhile, the artillery exchange continues for several hours. A. J. Smith either never receives McClernand's "attack the enemy vigorously" order, or he just ignores it. He never said which, but there seemed to be a "disobedience virus" circulating among general officers, both blue and gray, at Champion Hill.

Burbridge was bitter as he wrote: "Receiving orders from General Smith through one of his staff to halt, I did so, holding the position that I had gained. It was my conviction at the time, confirmed by all that I have learned since, that, properly supported by General Blair's division, we could have captured the whole rebel force opposed to us, and reached Edwards Station before sunset."

Tilghman's guns in their blocking position are sited to allow Bowen's and Carter Stevenson's men to retreat southwestward to cross over Bakers Creek. The first to withdraw are what is left of Lee's brigade and Bowen's battered division. Pemberton and his staff ride with Bowen. To protect this withdrawal from the advance of Logan's men from the north, Featherston's and Buford's brigades form a blocking position parallel to, and south of, the Jackson Road.

Barton's Georgia Brigade of Carter Stevenson's division crosses the Upper Bakers Creek Bridge and is posted to guard the crossing. Bowen's men, after crossing Bakers Creek, are ordered by Pemberton to deploy along the west bank and hold the Raymond-Edwards Road crossing long enough for Loring's people to follow. Pemberton then rides westward to Big Black Bridge to see that the bridgehead is held open for the passage of the retreating troops.

At 5:20, at the Confederate blocking position on the Raymond-Edwards Road, Tilghman is killed by a shell fragment while he sights a 12-pounder howitzer.

Pvt. J. G. Spencer of Cowan's Battery, Company G, First Mississippi Light Artillery, described the moment: "The Federal battery opened on us, firing accurately. General Tilghman and his staff rode up to Captain Cowan and ordered him to open fire. The General dismounted and said to Captain

Cowan, 'I will take a shot at those fellows myself,' and walked up to field piece Number 2 and sighted and ordered it fired, and a shell from the Federal battery passed close to him while our gun was being loaded. Tilghman remarked, 'They are trying to spoil my new uniform.' He then sighted the gun again, and as he stepped back to order fire, a Parrott shell struck him in the side, nearly cutting him in twain. Just before he dismounted, he ordered his son, a boy about 17 years, to go with a squad & drive some sharpshooters from a gin house on our left, who were annoying our cannoneers. The son had been gone 10 or 15 minutes on this mission before his father was killed."

Col. Arthur E. Reynolds of the 26th Mississippi then assumes command of the brigade, and soon learns from the two battery commanders, Capt. John Cowan and Capt. Jacob Culbertson, that their ammunition is nearly spent. Reynolds dispatches a courier to Loring to let him know that they can't hold out much longer.

While the blocking position for the lower crossing of Bakers Creek is about to be overrun, John Stevenson's Federals along the Jackson Road and the upper crossing go into action. The Eighth Illinois moves south to harass Loring's rear guard, while Stevenson takes a strike force, made up of the 81st Illinois, the Seventh Missouri, and De Golyer's battery, west on the road toward the upper bridge.

At the same time, Grant rides southward from Champion Hill to the Crossroads, and sends a message ordering McClernand's XIII Corps to pursue, because these troops are relatively fresh. Since Osterhaus's division is still deployed in line of battle, McClernand sends Carr's division, which has remained in the road in column formation, to pursue the Rebels. Carr's men march west on the Jackson Road and meet up with Stevenson's Yanks. Carr sends Gen. Michael Kelly Lawler's brigade to the southwest in support of the Eighth Illinois, and Gen. William P. Benton's brigade goes west with Stevenson's strike force.

Loring's two blocking brigades, Buford's and Featherston's, hold their ground and force the Eighth Illinois and Lawler's regiments to deploy. The Confederates then fall back to the Raymond-Edwards Road and the lower crossing. Bravely covering this withdrawal is Company A, Pointe Coupée Louisiana Artillery. To counter these guns, the Yanks call up Company A, Second Illinois Artillery, and an artillery duel ensues. This buys time—exactly what Loring's men need. Although the Louisianans have a gun dismounted by the Federal's counterbattery fire, this economy of force mission is successful, and Col. Robert H. Sturgess of the Eighth Illinois and General Lawler realize they will not catch the

Confederates before they get across the lower Bakers Creek crossing. The Union commanders call off the pursuit and rejoin their parent units.

Stevenson's and Benton's bluecoats have better luck. They race to the upper bridge and find it unguarded, and the span falls into their hands. This is because General Barton, whose men were guarding the bridge, has learned that Pemberton's army is retreating across Bakers Creek on the Raymond-Edwards Road lower crossing. So Barton orders a withdrawal to Edwards.

Earlier that day, around 3 p.m., Col. Alexander W. Reynolds, whose brigade is guarding the Confederate wagon train north of Edwards, received a dispatch from General Barton that things are going badly. Reynolds is instructed to get the wagon train across Big Black River as soon as possible and to send some of his Tennesseans back to Barton for help. Reynolds sent two regiments and two guns of the Third Maryland Artillery to escort the train to a floating bridge over Big Black River at Bridgeport, and took his other two regiments cross-country, back toward the battlefield. As Reynolds approaches the Upper Bakers Creek Bridge, he sees that Stevenson and Benton have captured it.

McClernand is with Eugene Carr at the bridge, and he sees a chance to strike the Confederates who are retreating on the Raymond-Edwards Road one and one-half miles to the south. At the same time his scouts warn him that Alexander Reynolds's Tennesseans are approaching from the northwest. McClernand tells Stevenson to handle Reynolds, and a few rounds from De Golyer's guns convince Reynolds to turn around and go back to his trains. McClernand sends Benton's brigade southwestward to hit Bowen's division, which is guarding the lower bridge and ford. McClernand then orders Osterhaus's division, which is following Benton, westward on the Jackson Road to Edwards.

Benton's men hurry towards the lower crossing and, when in artillery range, Capt. Martin Klauss opens up with his six guns of the First Battery, Indiana Light Artillery. Bowen now knows he has been flanked, and he orders a withdrawal westward through Edwards to the Big Black Bridge. His men arrive at Big Black River about midnight.

When Benton's Hoosier guns open fire on Bowen's retreating men, only one of Loring's regiments—the 12th Louisiana—has crossed Bakers Creek. Buford's and Featherston's brigades are still on the east side of the creek, but they have reached the Raymond-Edwards Road, thanks to the delaying action of the Pointe Coupée Artillery. Col. Arthur E. Reynolds, who has taken the fallen Tilghman's place, has managed to successfully break contact with A. J. Smith's men and has fallen in behind Featherston's column. But it is now getting dark, and Loring receives a message from Bowen that the Yankees are shelling the west side of the Bakers Creek crossing. Loring's men will have to cross the bridge and head west while being enfiladed on their right flank by artillery. Although the Yankee artillerymen have been shooting too high, and the 12th Louisiana has already crossed with no casualties, Loring decides to march south and look for another crossing. He recalls the 12th Louisiana, which means these unfortunate men have to go back through the Federal artillery fire. Then he marches his division southwest on a farm road in search of another crossing. Remarkably, Loring fails to send a courier to Pemberton to tell him where he is going.

Smith's and Blair's Federals do not pursue Loring in the darkness, and go into camp. Benton's brigade of Carr's division marches south to the Raymond-Edwards Road and follows the retreating Bowen toward Edwards. Benton's men enter the town around 8 p.m., and there they find that the Confederates have set fire to Col. William T. Withers's cotton gin, as well as a dozen railroad cars packed with ammunition and rations. The Yanks quickly transform from soldiers to firefighters to save the precious cargo.

Carr's other brigade, Mike Lawler's, enters Edwards before midnight. Following Lawler is Osterhaus's division. Logan's division and two brigades of Crocker's division encamp on either side of Bakers Creek, and Holmes's brigade camps at the Crossroads.

Holmes is joined at the Crossroads by Gen. Thomas Ransom's brigade, which has been escorting a large wagon train of much needed rations and ammunition from Grand Gulf. Ransom came through Raymond at 8 a.m. and turned west toward the army with his slow-moving train. Hovey's battered division camps near the crest of Champion Hill among the dead and wounded, and details from the ambulance corps take the Federal wounded to the Champion house and outbuildings and carry the Confederate wounded to Pemberton's former headquarters at the Isaac Roberts house.

Loring's division, wandering in the darkness in the fields south of the Raymond-Edwards Road, abandons 12 cannon with their caissons and limbers, along with seven wagon loads of ammunition, which Blair's Federals find the next day. Loring's men slog their way southwestward in the night through the recently flooded Bakers Creek bottom to the Bakers Creek ford east of Mount Moriah. There, Loring sees the glowing sky from the fires in Edwards to the northwest. He knows that he can't go through Edwards. So he continues marching in the hopes that he can reach Whitaker's Ford and cross Fourteenmile Creek west of its confluence with Bakers Creek. En route, the exhausted Confederate officers hold a council of war and decide to give up trying to reach Pemberton. They march west to Auburn, then southeast to Crystal Springs, which is more than 20 miles southeast of Auburn. There, Loring can contact General Johnston and make arrangements to join his forces. After an exhausting march, much straggling, and many men lost or left behind, what's left of Loring's division reaches Crystal Springs on the evening of May 17 with no artillery or cooking gear. Two days later, Loring marches to Jackson and reports to General Johnston. Pemberton has lost Loring's division forever.

At Champion Hill, the Federals reported that they lost 410 killed, 1,844 wounded, and 187 missing. The incomplete Confederate returns list 381 killed, 1,018 wounded, and 2,441 missing. They also lost 27 cannon. Moreover, Loring, during his march to Crystal Springs, lost approximately 3,000 men due to straggling.

It begins raining that night, as it always seems to do after a battle. Grant spends the night at a house being used as a Confederate hospital, but he can't stand the screams and moans of the wounded, so he sleeps on the porch. Grant is a good soldier. Unlike George Brinton McClellan, he sleeps on the battlefield. McClellan is seldom on the battlefield. Grant doesn't like being around wounded or mutilated men, but being a great captain, he doesn't let it destroy his willpower. McClellan it unnerves.

Twelve-year-old Fred Grant recalled the night hours immediately after the battle: "About midnight I returned to the field and reached a house in which I found my father and several of his staff officers, most of whom were greatly elated over their victory. . . . The next morning we made an early start, and moved toward Big Black River."

Grant has successfully prevented the union of Johnston's and Pemberton's forces, and he has cut Pemberton's line of communications. He has defeated three of Pemberton's five divisions in battle, and while the defeated Confederate army falls back toward Vicksburg, it has lost an entire division, which will make its way to join forces with Johnston. But Vicksburg is now a trap, with Grant to the east, and Porter on the Mississippi River to the west. The Yazoo River blocks any retreat to the north, as does Big Black River to the south. There is no place for Pemberton to go.

Chapter 7
ON THE OFFENSE

May 17–29, 1863
After Grant's smashing victory, Pemberton falls back to
Big Black River, where he tries desperately to rally his beaten
and disorganized army.

AFTER ORDERING THE RETREAT FROM CHAMPION HILL, PEMBERTON dejectedly rides through Edwards to his previously constructed fortifications guarding the Big Black Bridge. Big Black River flows south-southwest, but when it reaches a point within one and one-half miles of Edwards, the river turns 90 degrees westward in a path parallel to, and a thousand yards north of, the Southern Railroad of Mississippi. The muddy waters then flow west for four and one-half miles before striking the valley wall and turning south at the point where the Southern Railroad bridge crosses the river. The Confederate tête de pont, guarding the bridge is there, east of the river.

The defenses on the railroad at Big Black River were built to protect the railroad, and Pemberton plans to use the tête de pont to hold Big Black Bridge so that his retreating army can cross the river. His defensive position, however, is on low ground on the east side of the river, and the good, defensible high ground is on the west side.

To provide an escape route across the river for the infantry, the narrow railroad bridge has been planked over. Additionally, the steamboat *Dot,* which is almost the same length as the river is wide, has been turned into a makeshift bridge by positioning her athwart the channel. *Dot* is 350 yards south of the railroad bridge, with her machinery removed and the ends of her cabins knocked out.

When Pemberton arrives at Big Black River, he orders Gen. John C. Vaughn and his East Tennesseans to take positions in rifle pits 1,500 yards east of the river. Vaughn's right rests on the railroad and his line extends northward toward Big Black River. Vaughn quickly realizes that he needs more men to man the extensive earthworks, which are more than a mile long. He sends Gen. William Baldwin a message, asking for reinforcements to help cover the bridgehead. Baldwin dispatches the Fourth Mississippi, and the Mississippians are placed on Vaughn's right flank, so that the three Tennessee regiments can extend to the left. Baldwin also sends four guns to Vaughn. The cannon are placed just north of the railroad on the right of the Fourth Mississippi, and are positioned to cover the Jackson Road, 350 yards to their front.

The majority of the Confederates retreating from Champion Hill are sent across the river to refit and rest. Bowen's men are not so lucky. They arrive at the Big Black River fortifications around 2 a.m. on May 17, and as soon as they arrive, one of Pemberton's aides, Lt. James H. Morrison, delivers Pemberton's orders to a bone-tired Bowen, instructing him to command the defenses. Bowen probably thinks he was selected for this thankless task because he is the junior division commander, but his men are the elite troops of Pemberton's army. Unlike those of Stevenson's division, they still have esprit de corps. Bowen is a firefighter, and there is a fire to be fought. He reacts promptly, and Martin E. Green's brigade files into position to the left of Vaughn's troops. On Vaughn's right flank, Cockrell's brigade filters into the trenches, south of the high railroad embankment. Cockrell's line extends 800 yards south to Gin Lake, and his right is anchored at a bend of the lake.

With Green's deployment, the line north of the railroad extends for a thousand yards north to Big Black River. On Green's left flank is a strip of woods along the riverbank that could be used by the Yankees to infiltrate and launch a surprise attack, so a detached line of rifle pits has been placed at the northern end of the line, extending outward at an angle and facing southeast to protect the flank and provide enfilading fire down the front of the entrenchments. Green, short of manpower, does not man these detached works, as Bowen does not expect an attack at that point. The anticipated attack route is south of the railroad, where the rich soil of the floodplain is cultivated, providing open ground and excellent fields of fire for more than a mile. Bowen thinks that this level, mostly dry ground is the most logical avenue of approach for Grant's pursuing army.

To cover the open ground to his front, Bowen places 18 light field guns along Cockrell's portion of the line. But for some unexplained reason, the artillery

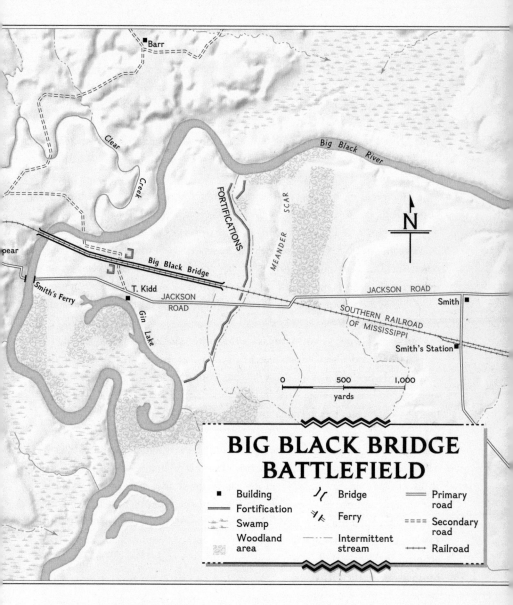

BIG BLACK BRIDGE BATTLEFIELD

■ Building	)⟋⟍ Bridge	═══ Primary road
── Fortification	⟍⟋⟍ Ferry	==== Secondary road
⸏ Swamp	─·─·─ Intermittent stream	┼┼┼┼ Railroad
Woodland area		

teams are sent to the west bank of the river. So, unless the cannon are close enough to the planked portion of the railroad trestle to be withdrawn manually, they will be almost impossible to withdraw under pressure.

After positioning his men and artillery, Bowen surveys his line, which extends for just over a mile, and realizes that it can hardly be defended by 5,000 men.

Like most of the soldiers in the trenches, he knows that his position is precarious at best. But Bowen is a good soldier, and he will do whatever he can.

The only missing troops are Loring's. Pemberton does not know that Loring has decided to march southeast toward Crystal Springs, so he plans to hold the bridgehead long enough for Loring's division to cross the river. Once across, Loring's men can provide covering fire for Bowen's men to withdraw. Then, thinks Pemberton, he will have the high ground on the west of the river with the river providing a major obstacle across his front. This will give his men the advantage of the terrain.

As the night turns to day on May 17, Pemberton worries about the missing Loring. Pemberton has to consider the hazardous position he has placed Bowen in—a position which grows more dangerous with each passing hour. If Loring does not arrive before Grant does, who will cover Bowen's withdrawal across the river? But if he gives up the bridgehead, he will be leaving Loring's division to the mercy of Grant's army. This is a Hobson's choice, and Pemberton chooses to risk Bowen's men to save Loring's. It's too bad that Loring doesn't share the same sense of loyalty.

In the meantime, Grant's army is on the move. McClernand's two lead divisions—Carr's and Osterhaus's—march west out of Edwards at 3:30 a.m. Benton's brigade of Carr's division takes the lead. Four miles from Edwards, Benton's men pass Robert Smith's plantation, and about a mile west, they spot the long line of Confederate fortifications, bristling with cannon and topped with defiant battle flags.

Carr rushes forward the six guns of the First Battery, Indiana Light Artillery. These guns go into battery east of the belt of woods on both sides of the Jackson Road so that they can fire through the gap in the timber at the road. Benton's 33rd Illinois advances as skirmishers, and Benton sends his other three regiments north of the road into the open fields, east of the timber, to support the guns. Lawler's brigade of four regiments forms in the rear of Benton's men. The troops are protected by the timber, and scouts are sent out to search for soft spots in the fortified line to their front.

Mike Lawler, a 48-year-old Irishman from County Kildare, is a huge man, weighing somewhere between 250 and 300 pounds. Charles Dana, during the Vicksburg siege, describes Lawler: "He is as brave as a lion, and has about as much brains; but his purpose is always honest, and his sense is always good."

Carr's deployment of Benton and Lawler north of the road surprises Bowen, who counted on the enemy using the open fields to the south of the railroad. Bowen orders Green to quickly cross Gates's Missourians from the west side of the river, and to send them into the detached rifle pits on the northern end of the line. If the Yanks want to crash through the woods, they will have to weave through the abatis. These are felled trees with their branches sharpened and pointed toward the enemy. Then they will have to wade across a moat in front of the Confederate works. All the while they will be subjected to enfilading fire on their right flank.

As soon as McClernand and Carr see Gates's Southerners racing to the north end of the Confederate line, they assume that the Rebs are preparing to sortie into Benton's exposed right flank, so they shift Lawler to the right and forward, extending Benton's line all the way to Big Black River. Company A, Second Illinois Artillery, moves to support Lawler, but as Lawler's infantrymen infiltrate into the belt of timber, the Illinois redlegs can't move the guns through the dense woods. So the battery remains in the fields east of the trees. Col. William M. Stone's 22nd Iowa stays with the four guns to repel any Rebel sortie that might develop.

After Carr's two brigades deploy into line, Osterhaus's division arrives, and McClernand orders Osterhaus to deploy south of the Jackson road. Col. Daniel W. Lindsey's brigade is in the lead, and he forms his men in a double line of battle, straddling the railroad on a line even with the east side of the belt of timber north of the road. Lindsey's skirmish line is composed of the 16th Ohio, and he has his men move forward 300 yards to the point where the Jackson Road makes a sharp turn south across the railroad. This point is a kill zone for the Confederate artillery.

As Lindsey moves forward, the Confederate artillery opens up and blasts gaps in his line. Because Benton's men on Lindsey's right are still 300 yards behind in the woods north of the road, Lindsey has his men go into a prone position until both brigades are ready for the assault.

Osterhaus's other brigade, Garrard's, moves forward, and just as Osterhaus is preparing to deploy Garrard's men behind Lindsey, word arrives from the right flank that the Confederates are planning a sortie. McClernand is not going to take any chances. He has Garrard send two of his four regiments—the 49th and the 69th Indiana—north to reinforce Lawler, and he sends two 20-pounder Parrott rifles of the First Wisconsin Battery to complement the four Illinois guns behind Lawler. Garrard's other two regiments—the 118th Illinois and the Seventh Kentucky—move into position on Lindsey's left.

Before any assault is made, Osterhaus wants some artillery fire to soften the Confederate earthworks, so the other four 20-pounders of the First Wisconsin Battery are brought forward. These are the big guns that virtually destroyed two sections of the Botetourt Artillery at Port Gibson, and the Confederate cannoneers know full well what 20-pounder Parrotts can do to them. The Rebs know they had better fire first.

Before Captain Foster's Parrotts can be loaded and fired, a Confederate shell screams in and hits one of his limbers. The 20-pounder shells in the ammunition box explode with a huge blast, and Foster and three of his cannoneers are wounded. Shrapnel flies in all directions, and Osterhaus's breeches are ripped off by the blast, with his back side lacerated by flying shards of iron. That will put him out of action until the next day. Now, it's not so funny when a private gets wounded in the butt, but it sure is funny to the rank and file when a general gets popped in the can and has his pants blown off. Gen. Albert Lee, a veteran of Kansas's border wars, replaces Osterhaus as division commander

While the Union and Confederate artillerymen duel, Burbridge's brigade of A. J. Smith's division arrives, and McClernand sends Burbridge south of the railroad to extend the Union left flank. Burbridge moves behind Lee's lines and beyond Garrard's left, into a belt of heavy timber. He then deploys his brigade in the woods. Everything seems to be ready for a full frontal assault, across the very ground that Bowen had predicted the Yanks would use.

Bowen, however, has not counted on Lawler's resourcefulness. Lawler's people have rustled their way through the underbrush in the trees north of the railroad, and are just inside the timber line 400 yards in front of the Confederate left. Here, the bluecoats discover an interesting feature, compliments of Col. John J. Mudd. While scouting the Union right flank, Mudd has found an old meander scar which forms a wide trough that runs through what everyone thought to be a "pool table" flat field. The northern end of this trough is about 350 yards in front of the detached Confederate works, but as it angles to the south and reaches a point about 125 yards north of the railroad, the scar is less than 90 yards in front of the trenches. It is deep and long enough to mask an entire brigade. Lawler immediately orders his regiments across the open field and into the trough. Gates's surprised Missourians, who have occupied the detached rifle pits fronting Green's brigade, are able to fire off only one round before the Yankees dash out of the trees, cross the open ground, and disappear into the depression.

Col. William Kinsman of the 23rd Iowa then makes a suggestion to Lawler. Kinsman wants to order his regiment down the meander scar to its closest point to the earthworks and have his men suddenly rush out and make a bayonet charge across the last 90 yards into the Confederate trench line. The Rebels, he believes, are so disheartened by their Champion Hill defeat that they will collapse like a house of cards. The wild idea appeals to Lawler, but he wants more artillery support, so he orders some trees near the Illinois guns to be felled to make room for one of the 20-pounder Parrotts of the First Wisconsin Battery.

Lawler forms his four regiments into two columns, two regiments deep. The hulking Lawler, freely sweating in the humidity and hot sun of late morning, wears his sword belt over his shoulder because it won't fit around his waist. When all is ready, he draws his sword and orders the charge, saying, "Boys, here's a chance to go in!" He bursts out of the hollow on horseback, and as he kicks his spurs into his horse's flanks, the heavily laden animal gives a big grunt. The sight of "Big Mike" Lawler appearing out of nowhere, followed by his brigade, astounds Gates's Missourians. They have time to fire only one or two volleys into the left flank of the Yanks, and though 221 of Lawler's men go down, the charge never loses its momentum. Lawler turns and bawls out for the 49th and 69th Indiana of Garrard's brigade to join the fight.

First Sgt. William Kendall of Company A, 49th Indiana, races forward and finds the advance of his men blocked by a ten-foot-wide ditch. He gets a running start and leaps across the ditch onto a pile of rails. Under fire, he lays the rails across the ditch so that his men can cross. For this Kendall is awarded the Medal of Honor.

The Federals punch the Confederate line like a fist in the nose. The strike point is the 61st Tennessee of Vaughn's brigade. As the Iowans burst into the Tennesseans' ranks, the Indianans come in on the Iowans' left and fire a volley before sloshing through the muck and water of the ditch.

Vaughn's East Tennesseans, many of whom are conscripts with little stomach for this kind of fight, quickly grab anything white to start waving. Handkerchiefs are converted into flags of surrender. Cotton is also a good thing to pull out of the bales in the fortification line, and handfuls of the stuff are crammed onto ramrods and lifted toward the skies. Many of the Tennesseans, however, simply throw down their rifle muskets and run for the bridge.

Lawler has led one of the Civil War's shortest charges, both in distance and time. From beginning to end the Yanks have covered 90 yards from the swale to the entrenchments, and the attack is over in less than three minutes. Most of the Confederate cannon are south of the railroad, the Union artillerists have no counterbattery fire to contend with, and they now have friendly troops to their front, so they shift their fire to the right and to Gates's detached works.

North of the collapsed Tennessee sector, Green's men see their right flank uncovered, and they cut and run, leaving Gates's men stranded in the detached work. Gates's people have the devil's choice; swim the Big Black while the Yankees shoot at them, or surrender. Some choose to swim, and as they splash and fight the current, some make it across, some are shot in the water, and some drown. Ninety men cannot swim, and they beg Colonel Gates to stay with them. He surrenders with these men, but later makes his escape into Vicksburg.

South of the railroad the rout of Vaughn's men is seen by an astonished Cockrell. He screams, "Retreat, we are flanked." He knows it will be a footrace for the railroad and the two improvised bridges, and if the Yanks win the race, his people will have no place to go. His Missouri line instantly dissolves, and as Davy Crockett said, it is "root hog or die."

On the west bank bluffs, Major Lockett sees the panorama of events, which is enough to scare anyone. Then Lee's and Baldwin's brigades arrive and help to steel Lockett's nerve. Landis's 24-pounder howitzers and the infantrymen on the west bank help keep the Yanks away from the bridges.

Lockett has to make a terrible decision, and he says to himself: "I must wait to the point when most of our men are across, but how close are the Yankees to capturing the bridge?" He'll give the signal when he thinks that most of the Confederates who can cross have done so. His people then stove in the barrels of turpentine, apply torches, and the bridge and *Dot* are soon in flames. Visible downriver are columns of smoke where the crews have set fire to three more stranded steamers: *Charm, Paul Jones,* and *Bufort.* Some of Cockrell's stalwart soldiers have formed a rear guard, and when they see the bridges on fire, they run southward along the east bank toward the burning boats. They then toss their weapons into the river, strip off their clothing, and gamely swim the 102 feet of treacherous current across to the west bank.

During the battle Grant has been stationed well behind the main Union lines near Smith's plantation house. He wrote in his memoirs that while he was watching Carr's and Osterhaus's divisions move into position, an officer arrived from General Banks's staff. Although Grant doesn't name him, that officer is Gen. William Dwight. Grant recalls that this officer delivered a message from General Halleck in Washington, dated May 11, ordering Grant to return to Grand Gulf and cooperate with Banks to capture Port Hudson. Dwight arrived in Grand Gulf on May 16, then rode hell-for-leather and reached Grant at the Big Black Bridge late in the morning of May 17. Grant wrote that he told the officer that it was too late now to turn back and that Halleck was not present to understand the situation.

Grant's almost effortless victory at Big Black River leaves only that water obstacle between his army and Vicksburg. As Pemberton gathers what is left of his shattered army and retreats into the fortifications of Vicksburg, Grant orders his three corps to bridge the river and move west to invest the city. Bridging the river takes all night.

In Tennessee, Rosecrans, who is still constructing his Fortress Rosecrans supply base near Murfreesboro, sends a telegram to Halleck, in Washington on May 17: "The Chattanooga Rebel, of the 16th, says General Grant has Jackson. Took it after a day's hard fight." That same day, Rosecrans receives confirmation from Dodge in Corinth of the capture of Streight's command by Forrest.

Robert E. Lee returns to Fredericksburg on Sunday, May 17, after winning approval in Richmond to go on the offensive into Maryland and Pennsylvania, rather than send troops from his army to Mississippi. He immediately begins planning. But with Jackson gone, Lee has lost the man who has provided discipline, daring, and swiftness to his operations.

Even before the loss of Jackson, Lee was contemplating reorganizing the Army of Northern Virginia, expanding from two to three infantry corps. It had been very difficult, if not impossible, for his two corps commanders to handle their four divisions—totaling around 30,000 men per corps—in the type of country that they had to operate.

The first problem that Lee faces is the selection of two new corps commanders. He must choose one commander to replace Jackson and another to lead the newly created corps. Unfortunately, he has lost many of his best leaders at Chancellorsville, with 12 brigade commanders killed or wounded. So his choices are limited.

Lee finally decides that the reorganized II Corps will be led by Richard Stoddert Ewell. A division commander under Jackson, Ewell has been educated in the Jackson school of command. He did as Jackson said—nothing more, nothing less. Ewell has had his lower right leg amputated from a wound received at Second Manassas. Even more unfortunate, his prosthesis does not work well and he has to use crutches. He had been for a long time madly in love with his first cousin, Lizinka Campbell Brown, now a widow, and he will soon marry her. Strangely, even after they are married, Ewell usually introduces his bride with, "Meet my wife, the Widow Brown." While some say the loss of his leg took the aggressiveness out of him, others say that Ewell's marriage was the cause.

The III Corps will be the new corps, and A. P. Hill will lead it. Hill has been a dynamic division commander who saved Lee's army at Antietam. But at Gettysburg he will be the little man who is virtually unseen. He will make only one decision at the Battle of Gettysburg and that decision prematurely opens the battle.

Stuart, who had performed admirably in Jackson's place during Chancellorsville, is passed over for an infantry corps and returned to the command of Lee's cavalry corps. This corps is increased in size by two brigades, making it the largest force Stuart will ever lead.

James Longstreet will continue to lead his reorganized I Corps. Despite his independent nature and his preference for the defense, he is the most experienced combat commander Lee has.

When Lee goes north, he will have two untested corps commanders, three new division commanders, seven new brigadier generals, and six infantry brigades commanded by the senior colonel in that brigade. Nearly one-third of his cavalry will be led by officers who have not previously served with the Army of Northern Virginia. This weakness in his command structure will be critical at Gettysburg.

Late on May 17 and early on the morning of the 18th, the soldiers of Ulysses Grant's three corps file across Big Black River on their improvised bridges. The men then march the remaining eight miles to Vicksburg. At day's end, McClernand's XIII Corps is astride the Baldwin's Ferry Road leading into Vicksburg from the southeast. McPherson's XVII Corps is blocking the Jackson Road leading into Vicksburg from the east, and Sherman's XV Corps is following the Graveyard Road leading into Vicksburg from the northeast. The only roads out of Vicksburg left uncovered are the Hall's Ferry Road and the Warrenton Road, and they lead southeast and south to Big Black River. Of course, Grant still has troops at Grand Gulf, and Porter has the Mississippi River blocked.

David Dixon Porter's movements are of interest, because after he was ordered out of Grand Gulf on May 3, he went up Red River and beat Banks to Alexandria on May 7. Porter has a big ego, so he delighted in one-upping the army, particularly a force led by a political general. Porter then headed back down Red River on his ponderous flagship, *Benton,* to the Mississippi on May 11. He had a sense of urgency, so he transferred his flag to the much faster *General Price* and steamed up the Mississippi to Grand Gulf, arriving there on May 13, beating *Benton* there by three days. He spent two days at Grand Gulf, obviously sizing up Grant's situation.

By May 15, Porter has fathomed Grant's plan, so he steams upriver to Bowers Landing, on the Louisiana side below Vicksburg. There he obtains a horse and rides across the De Soto Peninsula to Young's Point, where he makes contact with Lt. Cmdr. K. Randolph Breese, who has been left in command of the vessels operating upstream from Vicksburg. Porter establishes the large, comfortable *Black Hawk* as his flagship, and quickly organizes a massive supply depot at Johnson's plantation on the Yazoo River. He knows Grant's army will soon arrive at Vicksburg, and he knows the army will need rations and ammunition.

When Grant arrives at Vicksburg late on May 18, food and ammunition are running short, and he needs to reestablish his line of communications. About 8:30 a.m. on May 19, he and Sherman arrive at the ridge that gives them a view of the Yazoo River and Johnson's plantation, almost five miles to the northeast. Porter is waiting for them on the Yazoo River in his flagship, *Black Hawk,* and the plumes of black smoke from his boats can be seen from the bluff.

When Sherman sees that Porter has amassed a huge supply dump at Johnson's plantation in anticipation of Grant's arrival, he has an epiphany. He turns to Grant and tells him that he never believed that this risky campaign would succeed. But now he realizes that this is one of the great campaigns of military history. Grant, he says, needs to report it to Washington immediately.

> Grant wrote in his memoirs: *"The enemy had been much demoralized by his defeats at Champion's Hill and the Big Black, and I believed that he would not make much effort to hold Vicksburg." He believes the time is right to end the campaign, and he orders his corps to attack the Confederates in their trenches.*

The soldiers also want to end it fast. They dread what a long, hot Mississippi summer might do to their army. Yellow Jack—another name for yellow fever—or some other disease just as atrocious might break out. So with little preparation at all, Grant orders an attack on the Confederates that afternoon.

The earthworks around Vicksburg were surveyed by Major Lockett in late July and in August 1862. The earthen lines form a rude crescent, almost nine miles long, that extends a mile or more outside of Civil War Vicksburg. Along the ridges Lockett laid out redoubts, redans, lunettes, and fieldworks to guard the major avenues of approach into the city, and these works have been connected by rifle pits. A redoubt is a fortification with right angles, a redan is a triangular fortification, and a lunette is crescent-shaped fortification. Work started on these fortifications in September 1862, but until now the works have not been occupied. Winter rains eroded them in many places, and some portions were never completed. When Lockett arrives back in Vicksburg after the disaster at Big Black Bridge, he has his work cut out for him. Not more than 500 entrenching tools are available for the fatigue parties.

Against these defenses, Grant orders an attack by all three of his corps for 2 p.m. The artillery will fire three salvos to signal the attack, and Grant expects only feeble resistance from the Confederates.

Sherman's XV Corps occupies the northern Union sector, and Sherman assigns to Blair's division the mission of carrying the Stockade Redan. Blair plans to attack from the north and east. Unfortunately for Blair's people, Pemberton orders four of Cockrell's five feisty Missouri regiments to help the 36th Mississippi and 27th Louisiana defend the Stockade Redan complex on Graveyard Road. Cockrell's fifth regiment, the Third Missouri, remains in reserve.

When the cannon salvo signals the attack, Col. T. Kilby Smith's brigade of Blair's division moves forward from a ridge about 500 yards northeast of the Stockade Redan. His regiments guide on and advance on either side of the Graveyard Road, but the terrain, obstacles, and enemy fire force most of them to take cover behind the brow of a ridge 100 yards to the east of the Stockade Redan. One regiment has no ridge to duck behind and has to go forward into the ditch of the redan to find cover. During the fighting, a 14-year-old musician, Orion P. Howe of the 55th Illinois, volunteers to race to the rear to order up ammunition for the infantrymen. He is hit in the leg by a bullet, but manages to reach Sherman with the request. Sherman is impressed by Howe's determination, and the youth is awarded the Medal of Honor.

Col. Giles Smith's brigade is to the right of Kilby Smith's people, behind the crest of a ridge. As the men move forward into a deep ravine, Giles Smith sees the confusion caused by the punch-bowl effect as the terrain drops downward and inward, forcing the descending troops to converge into a mass. A rail fence has to be kicked down before they can even attempt to fight their way through the abatis. Smith yells for the commander of the Eighth Missouri to halt his regiment to help alleviate the traffic jam as the men bunch together in the hollow, and then he has them fall back to behind the ridge crest and provide covering fire for the other attacking units.

Smith's regulars in the First Battalion, 13th U.S. Infantry, are on the left flank of the brigade, and they have to pass through an area swept by enemy fire. As they drop down into the hollow they are caught in the crossfire of the Stockade Redan and the 27th Louisiana Lunette. In the hail of bullets the

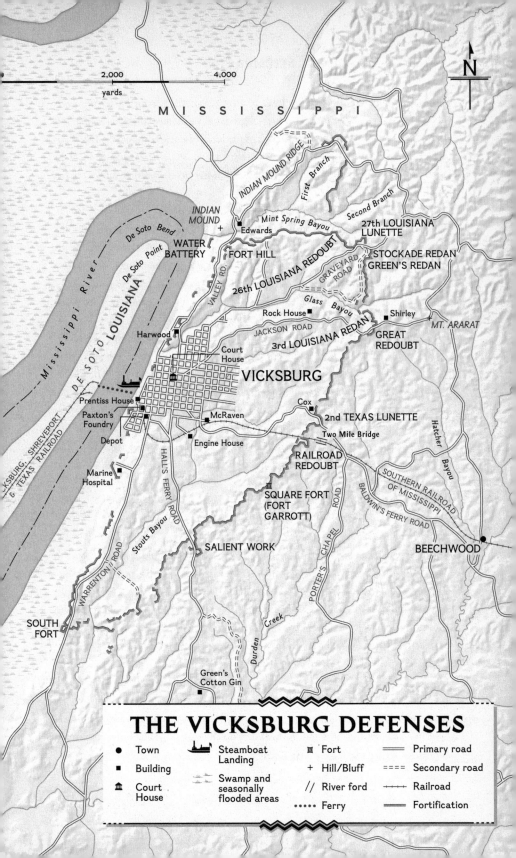

MISSISSIPPI

INDIAN MOUND RIDGE

First Branch

Second Branch

INDIAN MOUND

Mint Spring Bayou

Edwards

27th LOUISIANA LUNETTE

WATER BATTERY

FORT HILL

VALLEY RD.

26th LOUISIANA REDOUBT

GRAVEYARD ROAD

STOCKADE REDAN

GREEN'S REDAN

De Soto Bend

De Soto Point

Mississippi River

DE SOTO LOUISIANA

Harwood

Glass Bayou

Rock House

JACKSON ROAD

Shirley

MT. ARARAT

GREAT REDOUBT

3rd LOUISIANA REDAN

Court House

VICKSBURG

Prentiss House

Paxton's Foundry

Cox

McRaven

2nd TEXAS LUNETTE

Two Mile Bridge

Depot

Engine House

RAILROAD REDOUBT

VICKSBURG, SHREVEPORT & TEXAS RAILROAD

Marine Hospital

SQUARE FORT (FORT GARROTT)

PORTER'S CHAPEL ROAD

BALDWIN'S FERRY ROAD

SOUTHERN RAILROAD OF MISSISSIPPI

Hatcher Bayou

BEECHWOOD

HALL'S FERRY ROAD

Stouts Bayou

SALIENT WORK

WARRENTON ROAD

SOUTH FORT

Durden Creek

Green's Cotton Gin

THE VICKSBURG DEFENSES

- ● Town
- ■ Building
- ⛪ Court House

- 🚢 Steamboat Landing
- 🌿 Swamp and seasonally flooded areas
- • • • • Ferry

- ▣ Fort
- + Hill/Bluff
- // River ford

- ═══ Primary road
- ════ Secondary road
- ┼┼┼┼ Railroad
- ▬▬ Fortification

N

commander, Capt. Edward C. Washington, the grandnephew of George Washington, is mortally wounded. Capt. Charles Ewing, Sherman's brother-in-law, picks up the colors and leads ten men into the ditch of the Stockade Redan. A bullet hits the flagstaff and takes away part of one of Ewing's fingers, so Sherman writes to his wife that night to tell her that her brother was wounded in the hand but saved the colors.

The Confederates don't care much for the Yankees taking up residence in their ditches, so they begin to light 6-pounder and 12-pounder shells and roll them over the parapets into the ditch. The explosions wreak havoc among the soldiers below, but occasionally a brave Yank succeeds in throwing a shell with a sputtering fuse back over the parapet and into the fort. This teaches the Confederates to hold the shells and let the fuses burn until the last moment before tossing them over the parapet. Today that's known as cook-off time.

Hugh Ewing's brigade is on Giles Smith's right. Ewing, who dropped out of West Point because of bad engineering grades, is a convivial man. He and Frank Blair, who also worships in the temple of John Barleycorn, must have had some good times together. Ewing's men have transferred from the East in January, and they are known as bandbox soldiers. They wear kepis, while the Westerners prefer the beat-up, dusty, sweat-stained, black Hardee hats with the cylindrical crowns crushed down and the straight, plate-like brims turned floppy from the rain. Also, the Easterners wear those damned celluloid collars that no Westerner would be caught dead in.

Ewing's newcomers have taken a lot of ribbing, and they want to make an impression on the rough-shod Westerners. The 47th Ohio and Fourth West Virginia charge recklessly down into the hollow, fight their way through the abatis, and scale the almost vertical southern wall of the ravine. Soldiers of the Fourth West Virginia make this tough climb in full gear. They manage to scale the cliff-like slope to a plateau, which is crowned with the farm buildings of Adam Lynd. In these buildings they place sharpshooters to cover some of their comrades who move to within a few yards of the ditch fronting the lunette. But here the point-blank fire of the Confederate defenders brings the attack to a halt.

To the left of Sherman's sector and three-quarters of a mile south of the Graveyard Road is the Jackson Road. McPherson's XVII Corps in the central sector is strung out in a north-south line perpendicular to the road. McPherson has only one brigade in position to attack—Gen. Thomas Ransom's—and these men are 600 yards south of the Stockade Redan on the east ridge bordering the north fork of Glass Bayou.

Although the attack is scheduled for 2 p.m., the 17th Wisconsin advances 17 minutes ahead of schedule. Col. Thomas W. Humphrey of the 95th Illinois, on the right of the 17th Wisconsin, sees the Badgers move and decides to move forward to cover the right flank of his comrades, although he knows the other three regiments of the brigade are not in position. A member of the 95th Illinois is everybody's favorite Yankee, Pvt. Albert D. J. Cashire, whose real name is Jennie Hodges—the frail young female soldier who poses as a man until 1911, when she is struck by a hit-and-run driver, taken to the hospital, examined, and found to be a Jennie instead of an Albert.

As the two regiments drop into the ravine, the Irishmen of the 17th Wisconsin become entangled in the obstacles of the deep bayou of the north fork, and they give up the attack. But Humphrey's Illinoisans climb their way out of the abatis and ascend the steep west face of the hollow. They manage to scramble to within 100 yards of the rifle pits before the fire of the 37th and 38th Mississippi brings them to a halt. The Illinois soldiers also receive long-range enfilading fire on their left flank from the Third Louisiana Redan on the Jackson Road ridgeline, 750 yards to the south, which at first is annoying but not particularly harmful. Then a puff of smoke is seen on the crest of the ridgeline, and a second later a cannon bark is heard. A shell screeches in from the left and sweeps away an entire file of Humphrey's men. This catastrophe convinces the survivors to dig in. Using canteens, bayonets, mess kits, and bare hands, they scrape away Mother Earth as quickly as they can and remain hunkered down until 4 a.m. the next day.

Down in the southern sector, McClernand opens fire with 18 rifled guns. The infantry, 800 yards away from the Confederate line, charges down into Two Mile Bridge branch under a terrible crossfire. As the men climb upward, the terrain and the rifle and cannon fire break the lines apart. Gen. Albert Lee's brigade on the left flank becomes disordered. Lee, an abolitionist and Kansas border warrior, is hit by a bullet in the right cheek as he issues his orders. Although the bullet exits through his neck, Lee is down, and Col. James Keigwin of the 49th Indiana assumes command. The attack fails to reach the Confederate line, but by dark McClernand's men occupy the ridge 400 yards east of the Confederate fortifications, with their right flank resting on the railroad and their left flank opposite the Confederates' Square Fort.

Grant and his men have underestimated the will of Pemberton's army, and the first attack is a failure, costing more than 900 Union casualties. The Confederates lose around 200.

On Tuesday, May 19, word reaches the Confederate capital in Richmond that a major battle has been fought in Mississippi on May 16 and that Pemberton was driven from the field.

On May 20, Grant, undaunted, meets with his three corps commanders to compare notes and glean the lessons learned from the failed attack of the previous day. The meeting results in orders for another attack at 10 a.m. on May 22.

In Richmond, Jefferson Davis learns on May 20 that Pemberton's beaten army has fallen back across Big Black River. Secretary of War Seddon still hopes to reinforce Bragg or Pemberton from eastern troops, but on that same day, Lee writes Seddon that "the services of General Longstreet will be required with this army." Lee will go north into Pennsylvania, and Longstreet will march with Lee.

On the afternoon of May 21, Grant rides along the lines, and one private says quietly but loud enough for Grant to hear him, "Hardtack!" Then all the other hungry soldiers chant, "Hardtack! Hardtack!" Grant explains to the men that rations are on the way, and he writes in his memoirs, "The cry was instantly changed to cheers." Sure enough, that night the men are fed when the first road to Porter's supply dump at Johnson's plantation is completed. Grant said that "the bread and coffee were highly appreciated." Now, some romanticists claim that the men were tired of eating meat and wanted hard bread, and that's why they're chanting for hardtack. Those who say that have never eaten either hardtack or C-ration crackers. No, these men were hungry, and for almost two days they have been surviving on ground cornmeal that they have foraged from the abandoned Confederate knapsacks, because the last three days of rations had arrived with Hugh Ewing's wagon train at Champion Hill on the night of May 17.

Grant now has food and ammunition, and he has decided to attack the Vicksburg defenses again. But he decides the next attack is going to be different. This time he is going to use all his available men. Grant is also going to ask for the cooperation of the Navy. He wants Porter to bombard Vicksburg with his six XIII-inch mortars during the attack, and he wants the ironclads to shell South Fort and the lower river batteries to provide covering fire for a supporting attack up the Warrenton Road.

Grant issues his field order for the attack, which "will be made tomorrow [May 22] at 10:00 a.m. by all the army corps of this army." He orders a preparatory

artillery barrage to begin at 6 a.m. At the conclusion of the barrage, "Promptly,
at the hour designated all will start at quick time, with bayonets fixed, and
march immediately upon the enemy without firing a gun until the outer works
are carried. . . . Every day's delay enables the enemy to strengthen his defenses
and increases his chance for receiving aid from the outside."

In Richmond, rumors that Vicksburg will have to be evacuated begin
to circulate on May 21, and the next day, the word that Vicksburg has been
"closely invested" spreads throughout the city.

On May 21, Sherman ponders the failed attack of two days earlier, which
went through the ravines to the north and south of the Graveyard Road. He
decides that the terrain and the abatis are what beat him. So he comes up with a
new plan, to use his men like a battering ram to punch a hole in the Confederate
defenses. He plans to send Blair's and Tuttle's divisions down the Graveyard Road
in column by regiments. Steele's division, farther to the west, is to attack in the
same column formation, and since no road leads into the fortifications in Steele's
sector, Sherman suggests the area of the Mint Spring bottom to the north of the
26th Louisiana Redoubt, although the south face of the Mint Spring hollow, up
which the attackers will have to climb, is menacingly high and steep at that point.

Blair's column will be preceded by a storming party of 150 volunteers,
dubbed the forlorn hope, and these men will carry planks and logs to fill and to
cross the ditch. They will also carry ladders to scale the loose dirt parapet of the
Stockade Redan. The men will be led by Capt. John H. Gorce of the 30th Ohio,
and each of Blair's three brigades will provide 50 men for the forlorn hope.

On the morning of May 22, all of the Union officers nervously glance at their
pocket watches, and Grant has had every watch synchronized to his time. No
standard time system exists in North America in 1863—standard time does not
come into effect until the railroads introduce it in 1883—and everyone uses local
mean time. So Grant has to get everyone on the same time.

At 10 a.m. Sherman gives the word, and the forlorn hope dashes westward on
the Graveyard Road. The officers wave their swords and the men follow with rifle
muskets slung so that they can carry the ladders, logs, and boards. As they near
the fortified line, the artillery shifts to the left and right of the works, and the forlorn hope reaches a curve in the Graveyard Road that cuts through the northern
end of a ridge, a hundred yards east of the Stockade Redan. As Gorce's brave volunteers debouch from the road cut in the ridgeline, they enter the point at which
the Confederates fire converges, known as the beaten zone.

To the front of the forlorn hope, up pop the heads of the Confederate soldiers over the parapets like scores of gophers, and then come the flash and report of the rifle muskets. The fort's parapet becomes a wall of flame from the muzzle blasts of the cannon and musketry. The head of the Federal column goes down like it was cut by a giant scythe. The men trailing see the bodies collapse in their front, and they pause in horror and scatter for cover. Those who miraculously survive the volley run pell-mell into the ditch of the Stockade Redan, dodging the sharpened stakes protruding from the depths of the ditch.

General Ewing has placed a new flag in the hands of Pvt. Howell G. Trogden of the Eighth Missouri and told him to place it on the enemy's ramparts. Trogden promises to "do so or die." True to his word, the private races along the road while bullets fill the air and skip over the ground around him. Reaching the ditch, he maneuvers through the stakes to firmly plant Ewing's headquarters flag in the loose dirt, partially up the exterior slope of the redan. The flag provides both a source of inspiration to the Yanks and irritation to the Rebs.

The other men who make it to the ditch burrow in like moles, then unsling their rifles and shoot any Confederate brave or foolish enough to climb over the parapet and reach down the slope to capture the coveted ensign. The banner defiantly remains on the slope into the afternoon, flapping in the almost constant breeze.

The 150 volunteers of the forlorn hope suffer 19 killed and 34 wounded, including two officers. Seventy-eight of the men will receive the Medal of Honor for their bravery at Stockade Redan.

Behind the forlorn hope is Hugh Ewing's brigade. The soldiers double-time down the road, four abreast, with arms at the trail, cheering as loudly as they can. The front of the cut is blocked with the bodies of men who have tried to breach the wall of lead, and Ewing's men have little choice but to either leap over the bodies and run forward into the ditch, or retreat a few yards to the rear to take refuge in the curve of the cut or in depressions in the cut, north and south of the road.

In McPherson's central sector, the artillery barrage has been pounding away at the Third Louisiana Redan to the north of Jackson Road and at the Great Redoubt to the south of the road. Logan's plan is to have John E. Smith's brigade attack the redan, while Gen. John Stevenson's brigade assaults the Great Redoubt. Mortimer Leggett's brigade is held in reserve. Smith will send sharpshooters forward to keep the Confederates' heads down in the Third Louisiana Redan while he forms an assault column in the hollow. At 10 a.m. the blue column surges forward and races westward on the Jackson Road. When the men get to within a hundred yards of the Third Louisiana Redan, they are hit by heavy fire and they go to the dirt. The 20th Illinois makes it all the way to the exterior slope of the redan, but the slope is too steep to climb, so the men file to the left and hunker down. Smith, realizing the futility of his efforts, calls off the attack.

About 300 yards south of the Jackson Road, John Stevenson assembles his troops in a deep ravine fronting the Great Redoubt, which is perched on the highest point in the area. The Yanks have only 200 yards of ground to traverse, but the grade is steep and there is little cover. Stevenson organizes his men into two assault columns. Some of the men—the Irishmen of the Seventh Missouri— are burdened with scaling ladders, which will make the exhausting uphill climb even more arduous.

When the artillery barrage ceases, Stevenson orders his men forward. The Seventh Missouri on the right begins to enter a deep, narrow depression in the ridge, which eventually places them in defilade, or protected from fire, for most of the hundred-foot uphill climb. But the other regiment in the column—the 81st Illinois—moves onto the narrow plateau on the crest of a watershed spur south of the Seventh and takes fire from three directions. As the bullets exact a heavy toll, Stevenson bawls out for his brigade to deploy from column into line formation. The 81st forms its battle line with its commander, the belligerent Colonel Dollins, in front, screaming orders. In seconds, Dollins is dead.

Just north of the 81st Illinois, Capt. Robert Buchanan, leading the Irishmen of the Seventh Missouri, cannot deploy because of the constricting nature of the hollow. Then, as the plunging fire from uphill inflicts heavy casualties, Stevenson yells at the top of his lungs for his entire brigade to lie down. The two left regiments, the Eighth Illinois and 32nd Ohio, go to ground at the protective edge of the hollow, 200 yards in front of the rifle pits to the south of the Great Redoubt. From here they provide covering fire, while the 81st Illinois on their right faces open, exposed ground, and the Seventh Missouri is trying to get deeper into the hollow to their front for cover.

Stevenson then orders the Federal artillery in the rear to resume fire. This second barrage seems to silence the Confederate cannon in the fort, but that turns out to be only an illusion. When the barrage ends, the Yanks are ordered to stand and charge. As they do, two Confederate guns in the redoubt that have survived the storm of shot and shell blast the Federals with canister. The 81st Illinois moves forward a few more yards, but the fire is pouring into their ranks from the redoubt to their front and, because of an undulation in the terrain, the men on their left flank are receiving fire from the rifle pits to the south of the redoubt.

The 81st loses two-thirds of its officers, with 98 total casualties, and the regiment withdraws in confusion.

Soldiers of the Seventh Missouri move forward, and as they do, the protection of the hollow allows them to reach the ditch fronting the redoubt before they become visible to the Confederates. Despite having a volley fired into their faces, the Irishmen leap into the ditch and plant their emerald-green flag on the exterior slope of the fort. They have lost six color bearers in the uphill charge. The scaling ladders are then thrown up the exterior slope of the Great Redoubt, but the hastily built ladders are too short. After all the work of toting the ladders to the highest ground in the area, the ladders are too short. The Louisianans inside the redoubt hear what they believe to be cursing, but it is in Gaelic.

From the multitude of blue forms littering the ground to the front, Stevenson knows the attack on the Great Redoubt has failed. He has no choice but to order the 81st Illinois and Seventh Missouri to withdraw while the Eighth Illinois and 32nd Ohio provide covering fire. In less than half an hour, his casualties are 272 officers and men.

South of Logan's division, Isaac Quinby's division advances, but after the loss of less than a dozen men, the attack is suspended. Quinby, a classmate of Grant's who has been sick since the Yazoo Pass Expedition, is unsure of what to do next and discusses the situation with his officers. Col. George Boomer says he is doubtful of the ability of his brigade to get to the enemy works in his front, so Quinby gives him one of Col. John Sanborn's regiments, the 59th Indiana, as reinforcement. The order now is for the attack to proceed en echelon from Boomer on the right to Sanborn on the left, but for some reason Boomer never initiates the attack. The men lie behind the ridge until 3 p.m. awaiting orders.

McClernand's XIII Corps is the farthest south, and to his front are three major fortifications—the Second Texas Lunette, the Railroad Redoubt, and the Square Fort. McClernand's right flank is anchored on Quinby's division of McPherson's XVII Corps, but his left flank is exposed because he does not have enough men to extend all the way to the Mississippi River. A three-mile gap lies between McClernand's left and the river. This portion of the Confederate line is manned by the men of Carter Stevenson's division, and Stevenson's men, though battered at Champion Hill, cannot be ignored.

For the 6 a.m. artillery cannonade McClernand, unlike the other corps commanders, decides to mass his artillery as much as the terrain will allow. He has 45 guns, ranging from 30-pounder Parrott siege guns to 6-pounder smoothbore field guns. But McClernand does something different. He wisely places a general officer—Alvin Hovey—in charge of the guns.

McClernand has seven brigades available, and he assigns to Carr the control of four of these brigades on his right. Carr is to conduct the attack on the Second Texas Lunette and the Railroad Redoubt. Osterhaus is the other attack force commander, commanding the other three brigades, and his mission is the assault on the Square Fort defenses.

Both Carr and Osterhaus report to McClernand, who takes position in Battery Maloney, 600 yards to the east of the Railroad Redoubt and about the same distance southeast of the Second Texas Lunette. From here McClernand can oversee the attacks.

Carr designates two brigades apiece to assail the Second Texas Lunette and the Railroad Redoubt. He uses one brigade of his own and one brigade of A. J. Smith's division in each attack force. Carr doesn't reveal his reasoning for his selection of which units attack which fort, but the two *B's*—Benton and Burbridge—will attack the Second Texas Lunette, and the two *L's*,—Lawler and Landrum—will assault the Railroad Redoubt.

During the four-hour artillery barrage, Hovey's massed and well-directed fire punches holes in a number of places, permanently silencing four Confederate guns—three in the Railroad Redoubt and one in the Second Texas Lunette—and temporarily disabling a 24-pounder siege gun emplaced about 400 yards west of the lunette.

When Hovey's 22 guns go silent at 10 a.m., Benton moves toward the lunette, with Col. George Bailey's 99th Illinois in the lead. Bailey, like Lawler at Big Black Bridge, is in his shirt sleeves. As they come out of the hollow, the 99th deploys to the left into line of battle, followed by the 33rd Illinois and the Eighth Indiana. The men have scaling ladders, and they race forward shouting, "Vicksburg or hell!"

After the pounding of the artillery barrage, the Confederates have only one 12-pounder operational in the Second Texas Lunette—manned by Mississippi redlegs—and it spews canister at the oncoming blue lines. The Texas riflemen then pour murderous fire into Benton's oncoming ranks, and soon the ground is carpeted in blue. Actually, many of these Yankee attackers, intimidated by the Rebel fire, are not hit, but simply drop to hug the loess soil.

Capt. A. C. Matthews, commanding the color company of the 99th Illinois, hands the flag to Cpl. Thomas Jefferson Higgins, a strong, athletic Irishman. Matthews tells Higgins not to stop until he gets to the Confederate works.

As the 99th Illinois charges, the Texans wait until the blue line is 50 paces away, and at that range the Texas boys open fire. Each man fires his weapon as fast as he can draw a bead, and when the smoke clears no one is left standing except one man carrying the U.S. flag. Incredibly, this most visible target on the field is stubbornly stepping over the bodies of his fallen comrades while advancing toward the rifle pits. The Texans fire again, and bullets rip through the color-bearer's uniform and the red, white, and blue flag. Still, the flag bearer is unharmed and steadily advancing. Many of the Texans suddenly drop their weapons and shout at those who are still taking aim, "Don't shoot at that man again. He is too brave to be killed that way!" Weapons are tossed aside, and the Texans scream in unison, "Come on, you brave Yank, come on!" Higgins reaches the parapet and is taken by the hand and pulled to safety within the Confederate lines. Higgins will later be awarded the Medal of Honor.

Burbridge's brigade follows, and as they reach the ditch of the lunette, the left flank of the 16th Indiana rests on what is left of the right flank of the 18th Indiana. Lt. Col. Theodore E. Buehler's 67th Indiana, on the right of Burbridge's line, finds itself on a knoll northeast of the lunette, and from this small but commanding eminence, the Yanks fire into the lunette. Burbridge soon receives orders to send two of his four regiments to Benton's aid, because Benton's men are pinned down between the Railroad Redoubt and the Second Texas Lunette. Burbridge's situation, however, is just as desperate, and he needs these men. He vigorously protests the order, taking the matter all the way to McClernand, who refers it to the attack commander, General Carr. Burbridge loses the argument and reluctantly sends the 67th Indiana and the four companies of the 23rd Wisconsin from the knoll to Benton.

Because many of Burbridge's troops are still in the ditch fronting the lunette, Col. Ashbel Smith, commanding the Second Texas, orders the ditch to be cleared with the fire of his remaining 12-pounder cannon. The Mississippi artillerymen come forward. The cannoneers take their 12-pounder and attempt to sweep the ditch by depressing the muzzle. But the Federals are like fire ants on the exterior slope, and the hapless Mississippi gunners are shot down so rapidly that they can't get their cannon into action.

In the lunette, bales of cotton have been put in place to reinforce the traverse between the two gun positions. The cotton is set afire by muzzle and shell blasts, and now the acrid, choking smoke nearly blinds the men in the angle of the lunette. The Federals take advantage of this confusion. They fire their rifle muskets into the lunette by pointing them through an embrasure and blasting wildly into the smoke. A desperate Ashbel Smith roars, "Volunteers to clear that embrasure!" He immediately gets four volunteers, and they run into the smoke and fire their weapons into their tormenters. The Yanks roll back into the ditch, but two of the four Texans pay for their courage with their lives. Other Texans then throw and roll 6-, 12-, and 18-pounder shells with five-second fuses into the ditch, which is packed with Union soldiers. The exploding shells are more deadly than hand grenades, and the carnage is terrible. Yanks literally burrow into the dirt walls, desperately seeking refuge.

Burbridge races over to see Benton and, despite Benton's protests, retrieves his two regiments. He then decides that his men will take the Second Texas Lunette. He calls for artillery support. Responding to Burbridge's request, the Chicago Mercantile Battery sends a detachment of gunners and a bronze six-pounder forward into the deep, steep-walled gully fronting the lunette. Infantrymen of the 23rd Wisconsin assist the cannoneers with a long rope and a lot of brawn, and the gun is somehow manhandled out of the deep cut and onto the narrow plain of the Baldwin's Ferry Road. It is quickly hand-rolled to a point where it can fire through one of the lunette's embrasures.

Captain White, commanding the battery, wrote: "The infantry carried the ammunition in their arms. We used shrapnel, the fuse cut so close the shell exploded almost as soon as it left the gun. The first discharge was simultaneous with the rebels' and struck their gun in the muzzle, scattering death among their cannoneers. I never saw a gun loaded and fired so quickly, as every man was at his best."

The range is 30 feet—point-blank—and the Union redlegs blast into the embrasure as fast as they can without even bothering to sponge the bore. Each blast of the cannon is like a hive of deadly bees flying into the fort. It looks as though the lunette will be overrun.

Posted less than a half mile west of the Second Texas Lunette, Gen. Martin Green's reserve Confederate brigade shifts south in support. Green places two regiments, the 19th and 20th Arkansas, to fight beside Smith's Texans. The appearance of Green's men stabilizes the situation in the lunette, and Burbridge fails to gain the position.

Burbridge would later report: "Had we been reinforced at 12 noon, or the demonstration kept up along the line to our right, thus preventing the enemy from massing directly in our front, we could have gained a lodgment in the enemy's works."

Three hundred yards southwest of the Second Texas Lunette is Railroad Redoubt, and for the attack on those works Carr has designated the fighting Irishman, Mike Lawler, as the spearhead. As at Big Black Bridge, Lawler uses the column formation and, in the darkness before the dawn of May 22, he manages to infiltrate his men to within 150 yards of the Railroad Redoubt. The bluecoats are posted in a ravine, the bottom of which is a marshy creek bottom.

At 10 a.m., Lawler's men surge forward out of the creek bottom. Col. William M. Stone and the 22nd Iowa advance out of the marshy area and charge uphill to Railroad Redoubt. A shallow saddle on the ridge makes their going a bit easier, but when they come out of its protection, all hell breaks loose. The 11th Wisconsin, commanded by Col. Charles L. Harris, is on the left. This regiment veers to the southwest to strike the rifle pits south of the redoubt, and the men move around a slight spur jutting east from the redoubt, which provides cover for a short distance. But when they turn west and proceed uphill to the rifle pits, they catch fire from three sides. The toll from the small-arms fire is punishing, but the men press forward.

The 21st and 22nd Iowa scramble up the steep hillside fronting the redoubt and get to the fort's ditch, and there the gasping soldiers halt. Then they see that Hovey's massed artillery has blasted a gaping breech in the parapet. Two sergeants, Nicholas C. Messenger and Joseph E. Griffith, lead a dozen men into the ditch, up the steep exterior slope, through the breech, and into the fort. Inside the redoubt they fight hand to hand with a small group of Alabamians and drive out most of them. The flag of the 22nd Iowa is placed on the superior slope of Railroad Redoubt, and McClernand, watching from Battery Maloney, sees that his men are inside one of the nine major Confederate works. Vicksburg, he thinks, is ours.

The Railroad Redoubt is initially defended by a detachment of Col. Charles M. Shelley's 30th Alabama. But the fort has only limited space, and the remainder of the regiment is posted in a line of rifle pits extending across the gorge, or open space, to the rear of the redoubt.

Landrum's Union brigade now arrives in front of the redoubt, and some brave souls from the 77th Illinois cross the ditch fronting the work and spear their colors into the ground near to those of the 22nd Iowa. Soldiers of the 130th Illinois and the 48th Ohio follow and leap into the ditch.

Early in the afternoon, the Confederates seek to retake Railroad Redoubt. Colonel Shelley asks for volunteers to clear the Yankees from the ditch in front, and Capt. H. P. Oden and Lt. William Wallis and around 15 men of Company A, 30th Alabama, answer the call. As they charge into the fort, they see a Confederate officer, Lt. J. M. Pearson, and a number of his men hiding behind a traverse. Oden yells, "Why in the hell are you not fighting?" Pearson replies to Oden that if he doesn't get down, he won't be fighting for long. No sooner than the words are uttered, Oden and Wallis are shot down along with several other men. The survivors run back to the gorge, and that is enough to convince Pearson. He and his men ground their arms and surrender, and the redoubt remains a no-man's-land.

Farther south, Osterhaus's two-brigade attack is launched at 10 a.m. toward Square Fort. Osterhaus attacks in three columns, with the 16th Ohio in front as skirmishers. He has a brigade of Hovey's division, Col. William Spicely's, as a reserve in case an opportunity presents itself.

Osterhaus's columns move across a ridge toward the rifle pits, situated north of Square Fort, and are soon hit by scathing small-arms fire. The right two columns close to within 200 yards of the rifle pits and go to ground. The left column, spearheaded by the Seventh Kentucky, crosses a naked brow 250 yards east of South Fort and is hit by ferocious fire from the 20th Alabama. The Yanks go downhill as fast as they can into a ravine and take shelter behind the 25-foot rise of a spur that bisects the head of the ravine. They go no farther.

The Confederates, despite difficulties containing McClernand's men, have stabilized the situation through the use of interior lines to shift their troops and employ their reserves. Flags have been planted on the exterior slopes of Stockade Redan, Great Redoubt, Second Texas Lunette, and on the superior slope of the Railroad Redoubt, but only this last fortification has been penetrated.

McClernand is only 600 yards away from Second Texas Lunette and Railroad Redoubt, watching his men plant flags on their parapets. He also sees Confederate reserves being shifted to negate his successes. To prevent this, he wants pressure to be placed on the Confederate lines to his right.

At 11:15, McClernand has a message signaled to Grant: "I am hotly engaged. The enemy are pressing me on the right and left. If McPherson would attack, it would make a diversion."

General Grant has established his command post near Battery McPherson, located just south of the Jackson Road. Grant is now almost two miles north of

McClernand, and he soon receives McClernand's message from his signal people.

Grant wrote in his official report: "I had taken a commanding position near McPherson's front, and from which I could see all the advancing columns from his corps, and a part of each of Sherman's and McClernand's. . . . I believed I could see as well as he [McClernand] what took place in his front, and I did not see the success he reported."

Could Grant, on the high ground of the Jackson Road, see the action at Second Texas Lunette and Railroad Redoubt as well as McClernand? Grant did have a view of McClernand's sector, because the Jackson Road ridge is the highest in the area at 375 feet. But McClernand is one-third of a mile away from his objectives, while Grant is about one and one-half miles away.

Grant could easily turn to McPherson and tell him to get Quinby's division, which has barely inched forward, moving. That would create the diversion that McClernand wanted. After all, Quinby is about one-half mile south of Grant, and his division is on McClernand's immediate right flank. Grant, however, chooses not to help but to send a message that provides superfluous advice. He instructs McClernand to use his reserves.

Grant's message is signaled to McClernand at 11:50 a.m.: "If your advance is weak, strengthen it by drawing from your reserves or other parts of the lines." Receiving Grant's message, McClernand sends a more lengthy explanatory reply by courier rather than signal it, saying: "We have gained the enemy's entrenchments at several points, but are brought to a stand. I have sent word to [John] McArthur to reinforce me if he can. Would it not be best to concentrate the whole or part of his command at this point? P.S. I have received your dispatch. My troops are all engaged, and I cannot withdraw any to reinforce others."

Grant's actions are curious. Before he receives McClernand's "my troops are all engaged" written message, he rides north to see Sherman on the Graveyard Road near Stockade Redan, not south to see McClernand at Battery Maloney. When Grant gets to Sherman's position, he is unable to see what McClernand's men are doing, unless, that is, Grant is from the planet Krypton and has x-ray vision, because the Jackson Road ridgeline to the south is higher than the Graveyard Road ridge.

At noon, McClernand pens another message to be delivered to Grant by courier. This courier rides up on a lathered horse to hand it to Grant on the Graveyard Road just as Grant reaches Sherman. It gets to Grant before McClernand's previous "my troops are all engaged" message, which is first routed to Grant's Jackson Road command post and then sent in the direction of the Graveyard Road.

McClernand's noon message is read by Grant in front of Sherman: "We are hotly engaged with the enemy. We have part possession of two forts, and the Stars and Stripes are floating over them. A vigorous push ought to be made all along the line."

Grant recalled the contents of McClernand's message a bit differently in his official report: "I . . . rode around to Sherman, and had just reached there when I received a second dispatch from McClernand, stating positively and unequivocally that he was in possession of and still held two of the enemy's forts; that the American flag waved over them, and asking me to have Sherman and McPherson make a diversion in his favor. This dispatch I showed to Sherman, who immediately ordered a renewal of the assault on his front."

Around 2:15 Grant finally decides to do what he should have done when he received McClernand's first message three hours earlier. He rides south to McPherson on the Jackson Road and orders him to get some action out of Quinby's division. McClernand's request, however, has now changed from needing a diversion to needing reinforcements.

Grant sends a message to McClernand by courier at 2:30: "McPherson is directed to send Quinby's division to you if he cannot effect a lodgment where he is. Quinby is next to your right, and you will be aided as much by his penetrating into the enemy's lines as by having him support the columns you have already got. Sherman is getting on well." Grant also tells McClernand that he has ordered McArthur's men, who are near Warrenton, to assist. McArthur, however, is miles away and is unavailable.

McClernand wrote back, "I have received your dispatches in regard to General Quinby's division and General McArthur's. As soon as they arrive, I will press the enemy with all possible dispatch, and doubt not that I will force my way through. I have lost no ground. My men are in two of the enemy's forts, but they are commanded by rifle-pits in the rear. Several prisoners have been taken, who intimate that the rear is strong. At this moment I am hard pressed."

Grant also shared McClernand's messages with McPherson and ordered his young protégé to create a feint. McClernand, the politician turned soldier, is conducting the principal effort, while Grant—a West Pointer—orders the other two corps commanders—both West Pointers—to undertake feints to support the main attack. This state of affairs certainly has to rub Grant, Sherman, and McPherson the wrong way. After all, the professional soldiers will be playing second fiddle to a volunteer soldier.

But this has happened because that volunteer soldier is the only one of the three commanders who carried out the commanding general's intent. Sherman committed only 150 soldiers of the forlorn hope to the attack, and essentially only two regiments—the 30th and 37th Ohio—out of 40 infantry units available to him. McPherson engaged only 7 of his 32 regiments. In contrast, McClernand massed his artillery under a general officer, appointed two attack commanders, made plans for a demonstration to protect his left flank, and sent 30 of his 35 infantry regiments into battle. After all the dust and smoke settles, McClernand has reason to complain about the half-hearted attempts of McPherson and Sherman on May 22.

Sherman is not about to have McClernand, or anyone else, accuse him of not conducting an active diversion. So at 3 p.m. he sends Tuttle's division forward. Tuttle's people did not engage in the morning fight, and Sherman asks Tuttle to have his best combat commander, Gen. Joseph A. Mower, report to him. Mower is from Woodstock, Vermont, was a carpenter before enlisting for service in the Mexican War, and reentered the Regular Army in 1855 as a lieutenant.

Mower reports to Sherman and is immediately asked, "General Mower, can you carry those works?" Mower nods his head in his "peculiar manner" and answers, "I can try." Sherman says, "Then do it." Joe Mower's Eagle Brigade will spearhead the attack.

After the artillery pounds the Rebel defenses with near–point blank preparatory fire, General Mower and Col. Andrew J. Weber of Mower's old regiment, the 11th Missouri, lead the charge westward on the Graveyard Road. The soldiers are four abreast, their arms at the trail. Screeching in the middle of the column behind the 47th Illinois is the Eighth Wisconsin's eagle mascot, "Old Abe," who is mounted on a perch and is carried next to the colors. Like the morning attack when the forlorn hope debouched from the cut, the Federals are cut to pieces. Sherman's three afternoon attacks, first by Giles Smith's and Ransom's brigades at 2:15, then Tuttle's division at three, and finally Steele's division at four, were not coordinated. This allows the Confederates time to shift their reserves via their interior lines to the point of attack. As a corps commander, Sherman has attacked piecemeal and failed to synchronize his fire and maneuver.

McPherson's response to the diversion can be characterized as feeble, at best. At 2 p.m. John Logan plans to send two regiments, the 45th Illinois and the 20th Ohio, to support the 20th Illinois. The 45th Illinois charges westward in regimental column on Jackson Road and encounters a hailstorm of musketry. Logan takes one look at the slaughter and calls off the attack of the 20th Ohio.

> *About 3 p.m. Isaac Quinby receives the order from McPherson to move south to support McClernand's principal attack. Col. Holden Putnam, commanding the 93rd Illinois of Boomer's brigade, later wrote: "Receiving renewed orders to charge, preparations were immediately made and the charge ordered, when an aide from the divisional commander arrived, countermanded former orders, and ordered us to the support of General McClernand's corps on the left."*

When Quinby moves south to support McClernand, soldiers of the 18th Wisconsin of Col. John Sanborn's brigade, already deployed forward in a skirmish line, are left in place to keep the Confederates to their front occupied. The rest of Quinby's men fall back to the east side of a ridge to their rear, using the ridge to screen the march south. Quinby's three brigades—Sanborn's, Holmes's, and Boomer's—make a circuitous two-mile trek to the vicinity of McClernand's command post at Battery Maloney, arriving at four o'clock.

McClernand then makes a tactical error. He divides Quinby's division, sending Sanborn's and Boomer's brigades to report to General Carr and Holmes's brigade to report to General Osterhaus. McClernand wants to treat both attack commanders fairly, but by splitting the troops, he dilutes the strength.

McClernand does not make clear his intentions, and Burbridge believes that his hard-fought brigade is being relieved, rather than reinforced. When General Call sends Sanborn's brigade to support him, Burbridge rapidly withdraws, leaving a bewildered Sanborn in front of the Second Texas Lunette.

In front of Railroad Redoubt, Carr assigns Boomer's brigade the mission of carrying the Confederate rifle pits between Second Texas Lunette and Railroad Redoubt. Around 4:30 Carr assembles Boomer and his commanders. The nature of the assault is explained, and the officers are told to briefly rest the men behind the ridge between them and the enemy rifle pits, take a few breaths, and charge down into the ravine and uphill to the trenches. Adjutant Henry G. Hicks of the

93rd Illinois recalled that the officers knew how desperate this charge would be, but that "they were soldiers, and it was their duty to obey." Boomer shouts, "Attention, Third Brigade! Shoulder arms! Right shoulder shift arms! Forward, common time, march!" The men shout and cross over the brow of the ridge in perfect formation, only to face a scalding fire from the front and flanks. Some of the men take a quick glance to the southwest and see the colors of the 22nd Iowa and 77th Illinois waving in the breeze over the parapet of Railroad Redoubt. Boomer's men charge down the ridge and into the abatis-filled hollow. Then, in the confusion caused by the felled trees, Boomer calls a halt to realign his command.

Lee sees the threat posed by Boomer's approaching brigade because this part of the Confederate line is still a no-man's-land. Colonel Shelley of the 30th Alabama has been unsuccessful in his attempt to find volunteers to clear the invaders out of the Railroad Redoubt. Lee has been offering the two stands of Federal colors to the unit that recaptures the fort. Then a third stand of Federal colors— those of the 48th Ohio—is thrust into the earthen parapet near those of the 22nd Iowa and 77th Illinois.

Coolly watching near Lee is 48-year-old Col. Thomas Neville Waul, a South Carolina–born lawyer who studied law in Vicksburg under the renowned Sargeant Prentiss. After practicing law and becoming a judge in Mississippi, Waul went to Texas, and he is now more a Texan than a South Carolinian. At the beginning of the Civil War he was elected as a member of the Confederate Congress from Texas. But Waul wanted action, so he resigned and recruited Waul's Texas Legion.

When Lee's offer of the Federal colors to the unit that recaptures the fort is turned down by the Alabamians, he swallows his pride and turns to Waul, the Texan, and asks him if his men can retake the redoubt. Waul's answer is a resounding "Yes!"

Waul goes to the rifle pits west of the gorge of the redoubt and explains to two company commanders, Capt. L. D. Bradley and Lt. James Hogue, the critical nature of their mission. Due to the limited area of the approach route through the gorge and into the narrow fort, Bradley is told to select only 20 men and Hogue only 15 men for this hazardous mission. Colonel Pettus, who knows the ground, volunteers to lead the detail, and three soldiers of the 30th Alabama volunteer to go with Pettus and the Texans. It will be up to 38 men and three officers to save the day at Railroad Redoubt.

At 5:30 the small band of Texans and Alabamians bursts forth from the gorge, shrieking the Rebel yell—the shrill cry used by generations of the South's fox and coon hunters to bring in their dogs from the swamps—and the rush is on. Anyone in front of these madmen falls back, and the soldiers of the 48th Ohio and 22nd Iowa are fortunate to remove their colors, as well as their hides. The 77th Illinois is not so lucky, however, as their flag is lassoed by the Texans and becomes a trophy for Colonel Waul.

The Texans, now ensconced back in Railroad Redoubt, have a perfect view of Boomer's approaching brigade to the northeast, and they pour a devastating enfilading fire into his command as he tries to realign his regiments in the abatis and then ascend the slope. As the bullets whiz past, Boomer forms his men into regimental columns. Just as he is about to give the command to go forward, a minié ball is fired from Railroad Redoubt 200 yards away, and it smashes into his skull. Boomer's last words are, "Let the rifle pits alone."

Two more companies of Texans are called into the redoubt to remove the Yanks in the fort's ditch. The bluecoats have dug into the parapet with their bare hands and bayonets and are hanging on like ticks in a dog's ear. Lee accompanies these Texans, and soon 6- and 12-pounder shells are thrown over the parapet as tenant-removal devices. For the coup de grâce, Lee and some soldiers roll 18-pounder shells into the ditch, and the huge explosions persuade Lt. Col. Harvey Graham of the 22nd Iowa and 58 of his men to surrender. A battalion of Waul's legionnaires move out on a mopping-up mission into the ravine fronting the redoubt. There they capture additional Federals as well as the colors of the 22nd Iowa. Carr's attack is over.

Down at Square Fort, Holmes's brigade, sent by McClernand to reinforce Osterhaus, is saved by the bell. The men reach the ridges east of the fort late in the afternoon, and Osterhaus orders them to be formed in line of battle behind the ridge. But Osterhaus never issues the attack order, giving the lateness of the day as his reason. The next morning, McClernand, concerned about the gap between his corps and McPherson's, sends Quinby's division back north to the position they previously held.

Grant's second assault on Vicksburg has failed, at almost ruinous cost. But during the last several weeks, he has been reinforced from Memphis and Helena, and now has about 49,500 effectives, committing about 42,000 men to the May 22 assault. The other 7,500 are at Grand Gulf, Big Black Bridge, and Snyder's Bluff. Pemberton has about 28,000 men in Vicksburg, but since the Federal onslaught was directed against about three and one-half miles of the nine-mile Vicksburg perimeter, only half of these men were involved in repelling the assaults. Detailed Confederate casualty reports are nonexistent, but their casualties were probably around 500—no more. The Federals reported 502 killed, 2,550 wounded, and 147 missing, for a total of 3,199.

In Grant's headquarters on the night of May 22, Capt. William L. B. Jenney, chief engineer of the XV Corps, recalled "there were some stirring times." He said that "most of the corps and division commanders assembled" there and that "McClernand was spoken of in no complimentary terms."

Grant, although a superb commander, is always prepared to shift blame when things go awry. This time he places it on McClernand.

On May 24, Grant writes to General in Chief Halleck: "The assault was made simultaneously by the three army corps at 10 a.m. The loss on our side was not very heavy at first but receiving repeated dispatches from General McClernand, saying that he was hard pressed on his right and left and calling for re-enforcements, I gave him all of McPherson's corps but four brigades and caused Sherman to press the enemy on our right, which caused us to double our losses for the day. The whole loss for the day will probably reach 1,500 killed and wounded. General McClernand's dispatches misled me as to the real state of facts, and caused much of this loss."

Charles A. Dana writes to Secretary of War Stanton on May 24: "Yesterday morning he [Grant] had determined to relieve General McClernand, on account of his false dispatch of the day before stating he held two of the enemy's forts, but he changed his mind."

An army is a family in which the members talk freely—often too freely—among themselves, and the disparaging words spoken about McClernand spread rapidly. McClernand is Grant's senior corps commander, and such talk should never have been tolerated, especially in the commanding general's headquarters.

On May 24, Gen. Joe Johnston, in Canton, advises Richmond that he has received a message from Pemberton, reporting that the "enemy assaulted our entrenchments" and were "repulsed with heavy loss."

On May 25, after two failed attempts to storm the Vicksburg fortifications, Grant is satisfied that the place is too strong for frontal assaults. He decides he will have to take Vicksburg by siege.

Grant issues Special Order Number 140: "Corps commanders will immediately commence the work of reducing the enemy by regular approaches. It is desirable that no more loss of life shall be sustained in the reduction of Vicksburg and the capture of the garrison."

That same day, the news that Grant has reached Vicksburg extends all the way to the Army of the Potomac. Gen. George Meade writes to his wife, "We have today the glorious news from Grant. It is in sad contrast with our miserable fiasco."

On May 26, after the issuance of Grant's siege order, the construction of approaches to the Confederate earthworks begins. Of the 13 approaches, the most important one is Logan's Approach in McPherson's XVII Corps sector. This approach is directed toward the Third Louisiana Redan, and is driven along the Jackson Road ridge.

On May 26, President Davis meets all day with his cabinet to discuss the situation in Mississippi, as well as Lee's strategy for invading the North.

The sole holdout in Davis's Cabinet still wanting to send troops from Lee's army to Mississippi is Postmaster General John H. Reagan. A Texan, Reagan views the Trans-Mississippi as vital to the Confederacy, and he is very concerned that Grant's forces will seal off any contact with Texas, Arkansas, Missouri, most of Louisiana, and of course, the Matamoros connection from Mexico, which allows goods to be brought around the Union naval blockade through Texas and Louisiana and into the Mississippi River by the Red River, just above Port Hudson. In the end, even though Lee is with his army in Fredericksburg and not at the Cabinet meeting in Richmond, Reagan loses and Lee wins.

President Davis, possibly "whistling past the graveyard," writes to Lee, saying, "Pemberton is stoutly defending the entrenchments at Vicksburg, and Johnston has an army outside, which I suppose will be able to raise the siege."

On May 28, President Lincoln telegraphs Rosecrans in Tennessee and asks that he send help to Mississippi. Lincoln writes very diplomatically: "I would not push you to any rashness, but I am very anxious that you do your utmost, short of rashness, to keep Bragg from getting on to help Johnston against Grant."

On May 29, a clearly irritated Rosecrans tersely answers the President: "Dispatch received. I will attend to it." Then Rosecrans does nothing.

Chapter 8
COMMIT NO BLUNDER

May 30–June 30, 1863
At Vicksburg, General Grant consolidates the limited gains he
made from his two frontal assaults, and settles in for the siege.
His entrapment of Pemberton's army, coupled with the threat
of Joe Johnston's concentrating forces, stirs activity in both
Richmond and Washington. For the Confederacy, the threat to
Vicksburg means that Lee's planned offensive assumes even more
importance. For the Union, the prize of Vicksburg means that
Grant must be reinforced.

IN EARLY MAY, WHILE GRANT WAS MOVING INLAND, JOHN PEMBERTON
sent a letter to Gen. Edmund Kirby Smith, commanding the Department of the
Trans-Mississippi, asking Smith to help with the defense of Vicksburg by attacking
Grant's line of communications on the west side of the river. However, at that time
Smith was concerned about Gen. Nathaniel Banks's Federal troops in Alexandria,
Louisiana. But by the third week of May, Smith realized that Banks was withdrawing southeast from Alexandria to attack Port Hudson, so he talked to his subordinate, Gen. Richard Taylor, about attacking Grant's Louisiana supply line. Smith
believed he could spare the 5,000 men of Gen. John G. Walker's Texas division for
the task. Taylor had wanted to go south to New Orleans to liberate that city now
that Banks had become preoccupied with Port Hudson, but he lost the argument.

In 1879, Taylor recalled: "Remonstrances were of no avail. I was informed
that all the Confederate authorities in the east were urgent for some effort on
our part in behalf of Vicksburg, and that public opinion would condemn us
if we did not try to do something."

It is often assumed that Jefferson Davis sent his weak generals out west, but
that was not always the case. In 1862 two men were sent west: Richard Taylor

and John G. Walker. Richard Taylor was the son of President Zachary Taylor and the brother-in-law of Jefferson Davis, from Davis's first wife. Dick Taylor was a Yale man, having graduated from that school in 1845, and he was a brilliant, if not a bit eccentric, man and a good soldier. He had commanded the Louisiana Tigers, a brigade under Richard Ewell. Ewell admired Taylor for his military genius but did think he was a bit strange, and worried that he might go off the deep end someday.

John Walker was a former Regular Army officer who was directly commissioned in 1846. He had served under Stonewall Jackson, and when he was transferred to the Trans-Mississippi, he commanded a division of Texas regiments, which became known as Walker's Greyhounds for their marching ability.

Taylor is the overall commander of Walker's three brigades and three batteries, all Texans, when they arrive on May 31 at Judge John Perkins's Somerset Plantation south of Vicksburg on the Mississippi River. During Grant's march south, Somerset Plantation had been a huge forward supply depot, but the Rebels now find Somerset deserted. Taylor is told by locals that Grant is outside of Vicksburg and that his supply line from Milliken's Bend to Hard Times has been abandoned. They do say, however, that the supplies coming downriver from Memphis are being stockpiled at three lightly manned Yankee depots at Lake Providence, Milliken's Bend, and Young's Point. And because the Emancipation Proclamation has been issued, black soldiers can now be recruited and trained to serve in the U.S. Army. Consequently, in Louisiana there are training bases for black soldiers.

Milliken's Bend, the huge supply depot that was the stepping-off point for Grant's march south through Louisiana, is a supply and training base garrisoned by the Ninth, 11th, and 13th Louisiana, and the First Mississippi, African Descent—all black regiments. Farther north on the river is Goodrich's Landing, another training base with the First Arkansas and 10th Louisiana regiments of African Descent. At Lake Providence there is a supply base with the First Kansas Mounted Infantry and the 16th Wisconsin, and the Young's Point supply base is garrisoned by the 108th, 120th, and 131st Illinois.

The siege of Vicksburg, while getting the attention of Kirby Smith, has also generated activity in Washington, and Halleck looks for help from commanders in other theaters. On June 2, he telegraphs Rosecrans in Tennessee telling him that Johnston is "collecting a large force against General Grant, a part of which comes from Bragg's army. If you can do nothing yourself, a portion of your troops must be sent to Grant's relief." Virtually the same message goes to General Burnside, commanding the Department of the Ohio in Cincinnati, and to General Schofield, commanding the Department of the Missouri in St. Louis.

Halleck then sends a message to Grant, saying, "I will do all I can to assist you." Grant later remembered this in his memoirs, saying: "General Halleck appreciated the situation and, without being asked, forwarded reinforcements with all possible dispatch."

Rosecrans defiantly answers Halleck on the same day: "My anxiety about General Grant equals your own. The course I have pursued has been, in my judgment, the best to hold the rebel army in Middle Tennessee, without committing too much to hazard. . . . Up to this date there is not a general officer of my command who does not concur in these views as expressed. They have expressed them in council and private conversation."

Late on June 3, Halleck testily responds to Rosecrans's defiance: "Accounts received here indicate that Johnston is being heavily re-enforced from Bragg's army. If you cannot hurt the enemy now, he will soon hurt you." Once again, this falls on deaf ears. Rosecrans will not move, nor will he send men to help his old nemesis Grant.

In contrast, General Schofield offers help, citing "the vast importance of Grant's success." He replies that he can send eight regiments and three batteries of artillery. Halleck instructs him to send six regiments, which join Grant's army in nine days.

Burnside replies to Halleck on June 3 that he is supposed to advance into East Tennessee in concert with Rosecrans, so that he can guard Rosecrans's left flank while Rosecrans moves against Bragg. If Halleck, however, is willing to accept a delay in that movement, Burnside says he can spare 8,000 to 10,000 men for Grant. Since Rosecrans shows no sign of moving, by 11 a.m. that day Halleck responds to Burnside with a peremptory order to send 8,000 men to Grant. These men arrive in the Vicksburg area in 11 days.

Although Gen. Joe Johnston in Mississippi is receiving reinforcements, he remains the pessimist and continually underreports his strength to Richmond. In actuality, for a short period of time Johnston and Pemberton outnumber Grant. Bragg sent Gen. John Breckinridge's division of 5,500 combat-tested troops to Mississippi, and they arrived in Jackson on June 1. This brought the strength of Johnston's Army of the Relief up to 28,000, and when added to Pemberton's strength, the two had between them around 58,000 soldiers. At this time, Grant had 51,000. Then, on June 3, Gen. William "Red" Jackson's division of 3,000 troopers of Bragg's army rode into Canton, Mississippi, giving Johnston 31,000.

Despite these reinforcements, Johnston telegraphs Richmond in early June: "My only plan is to relieve Vicksburg. My force is too small for the purpose; tell me if you can increase it, and how much. Grant is receiving reinforcements." Secretary of War Seddon replies that he regrets his "inability to promise more troops, as we have drained resources even to the danger of several points. You know best concerning Bragg's army, but I fear to withdraw more. We are too far outnumbered in Virginia to spare any. You must rely on what you have and the irregular forces Mississippi can afford. Your judgment and skill are relied on, but I venture the suggestion that to relieve Vicksburg speedy action is essential."

At Vicksburg, by June 3, Grant's soldiers working on Logan's Approach along the Jackson Road ridgeline have reached a commanding knoll, 130 yards east of the Third Louisiana Redan. Here, Capt. Andrew Hickenlooper spends the next 48 hours building a forward artillery battery. The soldiers dub this position Battery Hickenlooper.

That same day in Virginia, June 3, Robert E. Lee begins his offensive. He sends two divisions of Longstreet's I Corps to Culpeper Court House. Artillerist Col. Edward Porter Alexander wrote: "I recall the morning vividly. A beautiful bright June day, and about 11:00 a.m. a courier from Longstreet's headquarters brought the order. Although it was only to march to Culpeper Court House, we knew it meant another great battle with the enemy's army, which still confronted ours at Fredericksburg."

Gen. Lafayette McLaws's division is the vanguard of Lee's march to Culpeper, and Gen. John B. Hood's division follows. Gen. George E. Pickett's division remains south of the Rappahannock at Hanover Junction. To keep Hooker's attention focused on Fredericksburg, A. P. Hill's III Corps remains behind.

On June 4, although the fighting in front of Vicksburg has subsided, the infighting within the Union command structure continues. McClernand has heard that Grant is blaming him for the additional losses suffered during the attacks on the afternoon of May 22. He sends a letter to Grant, demanding an end to these rumors. "My attack was prompt and in a larger measure more successful than any other. . . . It remains for you to determine whether truth, justice, and generosity do not call on you" to stop these rumors. The letter goes unanswered, and both men fume in anger.

On June 4, Richard Taylor, when he learns that Grant has abandoned his forward supply base at Perkins's plantation on the Mississippi River, makes plans to attack Grant's supply bases at Young's Point, Milliken's Bend, and Lake Providence. He travels ahead of Walker's Greyhounds and arrives with his staff in Richmond, Louisiana. He makes plans to destroy the three Union bases.

In Virginia on June 4, Gen. Robert E. Rodes's division of Ewell's II Corps departs for Culpeper. Rodes is followed the next day by the divisions of Jubal Early and Edward "Allegheny" Johnson.

In Falmouth, Virginia, at 11:30 a.m., General Hooker knows the Confederates are moving, and he telegraphs President Lincoln to advise him that "this could be for no other purpose but to enable the enemy to move up the river, with a view to the execution of a movement similar to that of Lee's last year. He must have it in mind to cross the Upper Potomac, or to throw his army between mine and Washington. . . . I am of the opinion that it is my duty to pitch into his rear. . . . Will it be in the spirit of my instructions to do so?"

Lincoln responds to Joe Hooker at 4 p.m.: "I have but one idea which I think worth suggesting to you. In case you find Lee coming to the north of the Rappahannock, I would by no means cross to the south of it. If he should leave a rear force at Fredericksburg, tempting you to fall upon it, it would fight in entrenchments and have you at disadvantage, and so, man for man, worst you at that point, while his main force would in some way be getting an advantage of you northward. In one word, I would not take any risk of being entangled upon the river, like an ox jumped half over a fence and liable to be torn by dogs front and rear, without a fair chance to gore one way or kick the other. If Lee would come to my side of the river, I would keep on the same side."

Robert E. Lee does, indeed, want Hooker to believe that the Confederate army is planning to march toward Washington; thus, he makes no effort to conceal his concentration of cavalry in Culpeper County. In fact, Jeb Stuart announces his presence with three highly visible reviews. He has already had one in May, but the second review, conducted on June 5, is the famous one—the one for which Stuart's staff invites large numbers of women and their families from Culpeper and surrounding counties to come up by special trains and see the cavalry pass in review. They especially invite women with eligible daughters, and the night before the review a grand ball is held at the Culpeper Court House.

The review formation is impressive. It is one and one-half miles long with the troopers of Wade Hampton, Fitz Lee, Rooney Lee, William E. "Grumble" Jones, and Beverly Robertson. The troopers make two passes in front of the reviewing stand, and during the second pass they start off at a trot, and then they put the spurs to the steeds and go by at a gallop, screeching the Rebel yell with drawn sabers. All the while the horse artillery battalion on a nearby hill blasts away with blank charges. The event is glorious, and ladies swoon into the arms of their escorts. The dramatic spectacle is a huge success, and this is probably one of the greatest days of Stuart's life, because he lives for this sort of pageantry.

At Vicksburg, General Grant, always with his ear to the ground, has heard rumors of a planned Confederate attack on Milliken's Bend. He has appointed a new commander for the area, Gen. Elias Dennis, and on June 5 Dennis hears reports that Confederate cavalry is in Richmond. He quickly warns Col. Hermann Lieb, commanding at Milliken's Bend.

Early on June 6, Lieb confirms that the Confederates are approaching, sounds the alarm, and sends a message to General Dennis, who immediately has the combat-hardened veterans of the 23rd Iowa rushed to Milliken's Bend by steamboat. Dennis also asks Admiral Porter for help, and a giant ironclad, *Choctaw*, steams up from her anchorage at the mouth of the Yazoo River. Lieb doubles the guard at Milliken's Bend, adds cotton bales and abatis to his fortified line, and instructs the regimental commanders to have the troops posted behind the breastworks. The Federal actions are timely, because that night Walker's Texans march out of Richmond with Gen. Henry E. McCulloch's brigade headed to Milliken's Bend.

At Falmouth, Virginia, Joe Hooker is not prepared to sit idly by and let Lee take his army north. He telegraphs Halleck on June 6: "As the accumulation of the heavy rebel force of cavalry about Culpeper may mean mischief. . . . I shall send all my cavalry against them, stiffened by about 3,000 infantry. It will require until the morning of the 9th for my forces to gain their positions, and at daylight on that day it is my intention to attack them in their camps."

At 3 a.m. on June 7 in Louisiana, Gen. Henry McCulloch's men are one and one-half miles from Milliken's Bend. Even at this early hour it's muggy and hot. At the same time Colonel Lieb's Federals file into position behind their breastworks on the outer levee. Just over a thousand men answer the roll. Lieb also has a line of skirmishers posted in the series of parallel hedgerows in front of the levee, and he has pickets posted on the road to Richmond. The Confederate cavalry soon trots up and is fired upon by the pickets. The horsemen withdraw, and some of them are fired upon by their own infantry as they race toward the Confederate lines in the darkness.

General McCulloch sees his cavalry fall back, and roars out the command, "McCulloch's brigade advance!" As they move forward in the predawn darkness, the first hedgerow to their front seems to come afire from the musket blasts, and McCulloch's skirmishers begin to fall. He halts and forms his 1,500 men into line of battle. The advancing Texans then move forward and break through the first hedgerow, pushing the Federals back 600 yards to a second. The Confederates then push through the second hedgerow, and the Federals fall back to succeeding hedgerow barriers.

The first streaks of daylight of June 7 peak through the misty fields near the Mississippi River as the Texans approach to within 25 yards of the main Federal line on the levee. Here, there is an impenetrable hedge, except for the occasional openings used as gates. The Texas battle line loses all cohesion, and the men have to go through the hedge gates a half company at a time.

Colonel Lieb has ordered his men to hold their fire until the last minute. He wants the targets to be as close as possible, because the black troops are inadequately trained, and they have been issued obsolete Austrian smoothbore muskets, which have an effective range of 65 to 70 yards.

Once through the last thick hedge, the Texans form for the charge with fixed bayonets. Firing one volley, they surge up the levee. Lieb gives the command, and his Federals fire a volley into the Confederate line at point-blank range. The gray and butternut line shudders, and men fall, with some retreating. But the line doesn't dissolve, and most of the Texans grimly continue forward. After their initial volley, many of the black soldiers are unable to reload before the Texans are upon them, and several of the Federal white officers shamefully abandon the field, including Col. Edwin W. Chamberlain of the 11th Louisiana. General McCulloch later wrote that the blacks fought with "considerable obstinacy" while some of the white officers "ran like whipped curs." The Federals are left to fight it out in a desperate, hand-to-hand struggle, and Colonel Lieb, who stayed to fight with his men, is seriously wounded. The fighting is brutal as bayonets stab into torsos and rifle butts smash into faces before the defenders give way.

The Texans now believe they have won the fight, but their elation is dampened when they see a second levee to their front, next to the river. As they ascend that levee, they spot the black smoke of the ironclad *Choctaw*'s smokestacks rising from behind. Suddenly the gunboat's 100-pounder rifled Parrott and IX-inch Dahlgren guns open fire. The gunners on the boat can't see over the levee, so they use soldiers on the top of the second levee as gun spotters, and they take a stab at indirect fire. The plunging fire dropping behind the levee is remarkably accurate.

Despite the explosions in their ranks, the Texans attempt to storm the second levee, but the guns of *Choctaw* then sweep the top of the levee in direct fire, and it is certain death to be silhouetted on the crest. The Texans have to be content to fall back and take as many prisoners as they can while looting the Federal tents. But the indirect fire of *Choctaw* soon drives them back to shelter behind the first levee. Then, around 9 a.m., the reliable old timberclad *Lexington* steams upriver with its eight-inch guns, and McCulloch orders a withdrawal. The Confederates are also unsuccessful at Young's Point and Lake Providence, and Taylor's expedition is over.

In Richmond, on June 8, Secretary of War Seddon telegraphs Gen. Joe Johnston in Mississippi: "Do you advise more reinforcements from General Bragg?" Johnston petulantly does not send an answer until four days later. Then his answer is full of defeatism and abrogation of responsibility, saying, "To take from Bragg a force which would make this army fit to oppose Grant, would involve yielding Tennessee. It is for the Government to decide between this State and Tennessee."

That day, Gen. Robert E. Lee, who could not attend either of Stuart's previous cavalry reviews, attends a third review to evaluate the condition of the men, horses, and equipment. Lee doesn't want a showy review as before; he just wants to see the men and the horses, not burning gunpowder and swooning ladies.

Afterward, Lee writes his wife: "I reviewed the cavalry. . . . It was a splendid sight. The men and the horses looked well. They had recuperated since last fall. Stuart was in all his glory. Your sons and nephews well and flourishing. . . ."

As Lee moves north, President Lincoln decides to keep Joe Hooker in command of the Army of the Potomac. However, Hooker knows that the defeat at

Chancellorsville must be placed at someone's feet, so he makes some personnel changes in the army leadership, and Gen. George Stoneman gets the axe.

The Cavalry Corps gets a new commander, Gen. Alfred Pleasonton. A bachelor, born in the District of Columbia, he is a West Pointer, class of 1844. Pleasonton is an excellent bureaucrat, but he handles the truth recklessly. He is slick looking, resembling a fairgrounds carny with his waxed mustache and fancy straw hat. He is also a shameless self-promoter. But his major weakness is in intelligence gathering, which is a key function of the cavalry.

Command of the I Corps of the Army of the Potomac remains with John Fulton Reynolds, who was born in Lancaster, Pennsylvania, is 42 years old, is a former artilleryman, and is a West Point graduate, class of 1841. Reynolds is one of the more well-considered commanders in the Army of the Potomac.

The II Corps goes to Maj. Gen. Winfield Scott Hancock. He has gained the nom de guerre—from French, meaning "war name"—Hancock the Superb for his performance at the Battle of Williamsburg during the Peninsula Campaign. Hancock is six feet two, a resident of Norristown, Pennsylvania, and a West Pointer, class of 1844. He graduated 18th in his class and was commissioned in the infantry. Hancock uses profanity like an artist uses oils. Despite these outbursts, it's said that men feel confident when they are around him. At the age of 39, Hancock is losing the battle of the bulge, so he wears a long frock coat. His other trademark is his ever-present clean, starched white shirt, furnished by an English valet named Shaw, who is described as the epitome of the British army manservant.

Still commanding the III Corps is Gen. Daniel Edgar Sickles, a New York politician who killed his beautiful young wife's lover, Philip Barton Key, son of Francis Scott Key, on a cold Sunday, February 27, 1859, in Washington, D.C. Sickles was a U.S. congressman at the time, and Key was the United States Attorney for the District of Columbia, so Sickles's trial was the murder trial of the 19th century. Sickles is closely associated with Gen. Joe Hooker and Gen. Dan Butterfield, and many officers feel that this trio has turned the army headquarters into a bar and brothel.

Gen. George Meade is commander of the V Corps. Meade was born in Cadiz, Spain, in 1815, although his parents were American. He is a 47-year-old West Pointer, class of 1835, and graduated 19th in a class of 56. He was commissioned in the artillery, served in the Second Seminole War in 1835 and 1836, and left the Army to become a civil engineer. He re-entered the Army in 1842 as a topographical engineer and served on the staff of Gen. Zachary Taylor in the Mexican War.

"Uncle John" Sedgwick still commands the huge VI Corps, numerically the strongest corps in the army. He is from Connecticut and graduated from West Point in 1837. Sedgwick will lose his life on May 9, 1864, at Spotsylvania Court House, uttering the famous last words, "They can't hit an elephant at this distance." Maybe those Rebels couldn't hit an elephant, but they sure could hit a Union major general.

Gen. Oliver Otis Howard remains as commander of the XI Corps. Howard is sometimes called the conscience of the army, due to his strong religious beliefs. When Howard lost his right arm at Seven Pines, Phil Kearny, missing his left arm due to a round of canister at Churubusco in the Mexican War, went to see him. Howard, who was feeling sorry for himself, mentioned that he and Kearny had both lost an arm, and Kearny, with tongue in cheek, replied, "Howard, the ladies won't think any less of us now that you have an arm off. Besides, we will only have to buy one pair of gloves between us."

Still commanding the XII Corps is Henry W. Slocum, a West Pointer, class of 1852. Next to Meade and Reynolds, Slocum is the highest-ranking major general in the Army of the Potomac. He has a reputation for being more deliberate than a commander should be. Because of his upcoming role at Gettysburg, his nom de guerre in certain circles will be Slow Come.

In the Vicksburg defenses on June 8, Grant's siege order is producing action along Logan's Approach on the Jackson Road.

Confederate Gen. Louis Hébert at the Third Louisiana Redan on the Jackson Road can see that the Yankees are coming closer with Logan's Approach. Hébert is a convivial man, a West Pointer, class of 1845. He sees a railroad flatcar loaded with cotton bales, protecting the Yankee sappers, and it is being inexorably rolled toward his works. He wonders, "How are we going to get rid of this thing?" He says to Lt. Col. Samuel D. Russell of the Third Louisiana, "Do something about that flatcar." Russell says to one of his men, "Get me a smoothbore musket!" Russell then gets some tow—which is refuse cotton—and soaks it in turpentine. He wraps the soaked tow around a small rifle ball, rams it into the musket, and fires his contraption into a cotton bale on the sap roller. Within a few minutes the cotton bale starts smoldering; the sap roller catches fire, and the flatcar is no more.

The Yankees make a new sap roller by weaving a wicker casing out of strips of cane. This roller is five feet in diameter and ten feet long, and the Yanks pack it with cotton. Then they get careless and leave a cotton bale next to this second sap roller, and soon the Confederates torch this cotton bale with their fireball bullets. The fire spreads to the cotton in the sap roller and burns it. For the third sap roller the Yankees get 55-gallon wooden barrels, nail two of them together, fill them with dirt, and then wrap the whole contraption with cane. This gives them a reasonably nonflammable portable barrier, albeit of smaller dimensions, and it is put in operation.

On June 9, thanks to Joe Hooker, the first fighting of the Gettysburg Campaign begins, but not the way that Gen. Jeb Stuart wants. Stuart's mission is to cross the Rappahannock to screen the march of Lee's army northward. But, with Lee's compliments about the grand review of June 8 ringing in his ears, Stuart is not thinking about the Yankees when he goes to bed after the review. He has ordered his command to split up so that the divisions can cross the river in parallel columns on the following morning. He has his staff pitch his headquarters tents next to a white two-story board house on Fleetwood Hill, a mile northeast of Brandy Station. Little does Stuart know that in a few hours his troopers will be fighting Federal cavalry.

Hooker orders Pleasonton to conduct a two-pronged attack on Tuesday, June 9, with 7,900 cavalrymen and 3,000 infantrymen. Gen. John Buford takes the right wing and crosses at Beverly Ford, four miles northeast of Brandy Station, and Pleasonton rides with him. The left wing is commanded by Gen. David McMurtrie Gregg. Gregg is a good fighter—a Pennsylvanian, a cousin of the state's governor, Andrew G. Curtin, and a West Pointer, class of 1855. Gregg is to cross the Rappahannock six miles downstream at Kelly's Ford, six and one-quarter miles southeast of Brandy Station. The river crossings are to commence at 4:30 a.m. and the two columns are to converge at Culpeper Court House. However, it doesn't happen that way, because part of Gregg's column takes a wrong road, with the delay causing Gregg to arrive on the battlefield nearly four hours behind Buford.

Buford's first brigade across the river belongs to Col. Benjamin F. "Grimes" Davis, a very good cavalryman, West Point, class of 1854, who was born in Alabama, was raised in Mississippi, and has two brothers fighting in the 11th Mississippi. Davis's men splash across the river and exchange shots with Confederate pickets before stumbling into 16 Confederate cannon, which have carelessly been left unsupported near the stream.

The Confederates are surprised, but Capt. James Hart of the South Carolina Washington Artillery manages to get one of his Blakely 12-pounder rifled guns into the road and starts blasting canister into the charging Yanks, allowing the other batteries to withdraw. As they do, Gen. Grumble Jones's Confederates

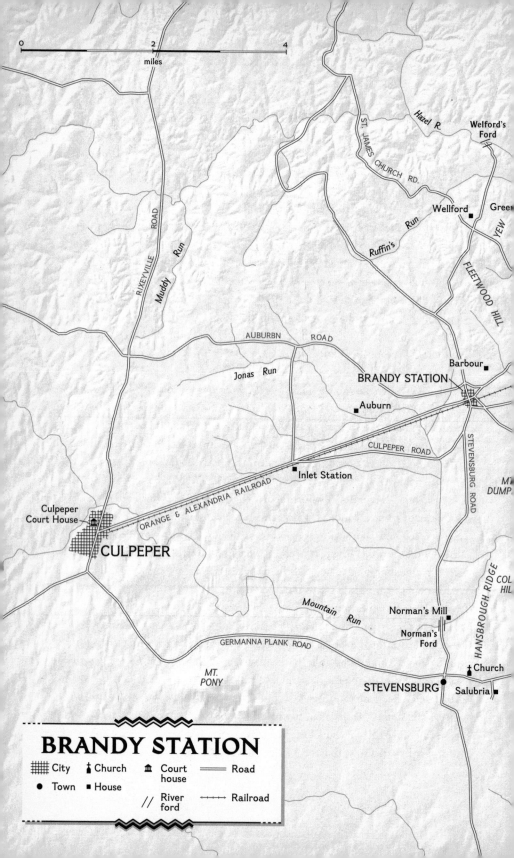

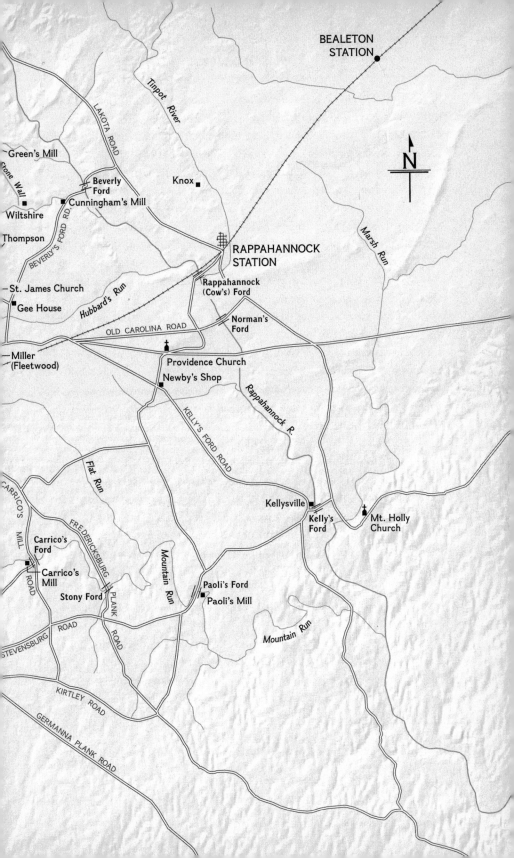

charge into the fight. When the cavalrymen of both sides clash, Grimes Davis slashes at Lt. R. O. Allen of the Sixth Virginia Cavalry. The lieutenant ducks the saber cut by deftly dropping down under his mount's neck and firing a pistol ball into Davis's brain. Grimes Davis is hors de combat, or out of combat.

At Fleetwood Hill, Jeb Stuart hears the firing and sounds the alarm. Gen. Beverly Robertson is ordered to cover the lower fords on the Rappahannock with his Confederate cavalry. Eight miles to the northwest Gen. Fitz Lee's brigade, which is led today by Col. Thomas Munford, an able Virginia Military Institute man who has little respect for the Lees, is ordered forward. Gen. "Rooney" Lee, one of Robert E. Lee's sons, is called up to support Grumble Jones on the left, and Gen. Wade Hampton, camped on the Stevensburg Road south of Brandy Station, is ordered up to Jones's right.

Stuart arrives at St. James Church to pitch into the fight, and some of his young staff officers climb up into a big cherry tree to pitch down the ripe fruit to the general. Suddenly, a Federal shell screeches through the tree, and splintered branches fly in all directions. Stuart thinks this is hilarious and yells, "What's the matter, boys, cherries getting sour?" But his fun is soon over when he learns that Union cavalry is approaching Brandy Station in his rear. Gregg's delayed left wing is finally showing up.

Gregg sends Col. Alfred Duffié's division west to Stevensburg to prevent any Confederate reinforcements from coming up from the south. Gregg then takes his own division northwest to Brandy Station. As Gregg approaches, Maj. Henry McClellan, Stuart's assistant adjutant general, manages to get one six-pounder on Fleetwood Hill to fire at the approaching Federal column, led by Col. Sir Percy Wyndham's brigade. Wyndham, a British soldier of fortune and the son of a Royal Navy captain, has served in the French navy and marines, the British Royal Artillery, and the Austrian Eighth Lancers. While with Garibaldi in Sicily, he was knighted in Italy. With his fancy ten-inch waxed mustache, his high boots with ornate spurs, his plumed slouch hat, and his array of medals, Sir Percy poses quite a picture.

Despite having just a few rounds to fire, the six-pounder shells that Major McClellan places downrange cause the Federals to halt and call up their artillery. This buys enough time for Stuart to get some troopers from Grumble Jones and Wade Hampton, who are engaged at St. James Church, back to Fleetwood Hill.

Soon, Sir Percy leads an advance, and a wild fight for the hill begins. Sir Percy eventually has to leave the field due to loss of blood from a leg wound. The normally phlegmatic David Gregg gets excited and leads a charge, swinging his gauntlets over his head and giving the Yankee "huzzah." Gregg leads his second brigade, which is commanded by Col. H. Judson Kilpatrick, known as Kil-Cavalry by many of the enlisted men due to his reckless tactics. The horse soldiers of the First Maine go over Fleetwood Hill and keep going for almost a mile, nearing the Barbour house. The troopers then run out of steam and turn back to the Federal lines. Back at St. James Church, John Buford has been unable to break through to assist Gregg. Rooney Lee leads a late charge and drives back the Yankees, but at 4:30 Rooney receives a severe wound in his thigh. Robert E. Lee briefly sees his son as they are bringing the wounded off the field.

South of Brandy Station, near Stevensburg, Col. Matthew Calbraith Butler, commanding the 200-man-strong Second South Carolina Cavalry, manages to hold off Colonel Duffié's 1,900 Yankees and prevent them from getting to Fleetwood Hill. In the fight Butler loses his right foot to a ricocheting cannonball. The ball goes through his foot and horse, then through the horse of Captain W. D. Farley, and takes off Farley's leg, mortally wounding him.

Pleasonton eventually realizes his two wings cannot unite, and he orders a withdrawal. Stuart does not pursue, and by 9 p.m. the Federals have recrossed the Rappahannock, unmolested. One of the largest cavalry battles of the Civil War, though technically a Confederate victory, has embarrassed Jeb Stuart, because he was taken by surprise. He did not post sufficient pickets, and he came very close to losing his horse artillery. Stuart was saved from defeat by the delay of Gregg's column in crossing the Rappahannock. This allowed him to fight the Union cavalry piecemeal, and once the fight began, Stuart did handle his people well. But Brandy Station has tarnished Jeb Stuart's reputation, and for the first time "Beauty" Stuart suffers harsh criticism.

The Richmond Examiner *charges Stuart with "negligence and bad management" at Brandy Station, and calls his cavalry "puffed up," while labeling Stuart and his officers as "vain and weak-headed." After reading the article, Stuart writes to his wife saying "the papers are in great error, as usual," but that he will "take no notice of such base falsehood." But the criticism spreads, and an article in the* Richmond Enquirer *states: "General Stuart has suffered no little in public estimation by the late surprises of the enemy." News of the fight reaches Charleston, and the* Charleston Mercury *terms Brandy Station an "ugly surprise." Even the* Daily Mississippian *in Jackson reports, "That our forces were surprised there seems no longer any reason to doubt."*

Unfortunately for the Confederates, the Battle of Brandy Station forces Stuart to take six days to refit. Stuart will spend the rest of the campaign trying to regain lost time.

At 2:30 p.m. on June 10, Hooker telegraphs Lincoln: "General Pleasonton . . . reports that he had an affair with the rebel cavalry yesterday near Brandy Station, which resulted in crippling him so much that he will have to abandon his contemplated raid into Maryland, which was to have started this morning. . . . Will it not promote the true interest of the cause for me to march to Richmond at once?"

Hooker's telegram is received in Washington at 5:10 p.m., and Lincoln responds at 6:40 p.m.: "I think Lee's army, and not Richmond, is your sure objective point. If he comes toward the Upper Potomac, follow on his flank and on his inside track, shortening your lines while he lengthens his. Fight him, too, when opportunity offers. If he stays where he is, fret him and fret him."

On June 10, Robert E. Lee resumes his march northward. The Confederate vanguard is Dick Ewell's II Corps, which two days later passes through Chester Gap and marches west of the Blue Ridge Mountains. Ewell is chosen for this route because of his familiarity with the Shenandoah Valley.

Lee sends a letter to President Jefferson Davis, saying that his "ranks are growing weaker and that its losses are not supplied by recruits." He says the Federals have superiority in "numbers, resources, and all the means and appliances for carrying on the war." Lee then says the Confederate government should "give all the encouragement we can . . . to the rising peace party of the North," and confidently predicts, "When peace is proposed to us, it will be time enough to discuss its terms, and it is not the part of prudence to spurn the proposition in advance."

In the Union siege lines on the Jackson Road near Vicksburg on June 11, two mammoth nine-inch Dahlgren naval guns are manhandled into position next to two of the army's 30-pounder Parrotts. This formidable firepower is on a hillock, dubbed Battery McPherson, located 800 yards east of the Third Louisiana Redan, and the guns can fire the length of Logan's Approach.

In Tennessee, Rosecrans telegraphs Halleck: "I called on my corps and division commanders and generals of cavalry for answers, in writing. . . . Not one thinks an advance advisable until Vicksburg's fate is determined. I therefore counsel caution and patience at headquarters. Better wait a little to get all we can ready to insure the best results."

On June 12, Halleck angrily replies to Rosecrans: "There is a military maxim that 'councils of war never fight.' If you say that you are not prepared to fight Bragg, I shall not order you to do so, for the responsibility of fighting or refusing to fight at a particular time or place must rest upon the general in immediate command. It cannot be shared by a council of war, nor will the authorities here make you fight against your will. You ask me to counsel them 'caution and patience.' I have done so very often; but after five or six months of inactivity, with your force all the time diminishing, and no hope of any immediate increase, you must not be surprised that their patience is pretty well exhausted."

While Halleck prods Rosecrans in Murfreesboro, Jefferson Davis is prodding Bragg at Tullahoma. On June 13, Joe Johnston in Mississippi reports an estimated 30,000 reinforcements coming down the Mississippi River for Grant. That same day Davis telegraphs to Bragg, asking if he can do one of two things: advance on Rosecrans or send more troops to Johnston.

In Virginia, on June 13, General Ewell reaches Winchester, where Union Gen. Robert H. Milroy's division is garrisoned. Milroy, who is warned of the Confederate approach, says, in effect, "Let them come." Milroy is an 1843 graduate of the military academy in Norwich, Vermont, a Mexican War veteran, and an Indiana lawyer and judge. But he has a deaf ear to any opinions other than his own, and he chooses to ignore suggestions that he fall back to Harpers Ferry. Milroy believes that his fortified position at Winchester, Virginia, can be held against any attack. He has little idea that Ewell's 23,000-man corps is about to strike his 6,900-man force. Dick Ewell, happily finding Milroy still at Winchester, promptly moves Gen. Jubal Early's and Gen. Edward "Allegheny" Johnson's divisions toward the town.

That same night, Hooker reluctantly obeys Lincoln and orders his army to follow Lee north. Hooker has wanted to go south to Richmond, but Lincoln has repeatedly said that Lee's army, not Richmond, is the objective.

Joe Hooker will march north in two columns. The left, or western, wing includes four corps—I, III, V, and XI Corps—as well as Pleasonton's cavalry, and is commanded by Gen. John Reynolds. The right, or eastern, wing has Hooker with the Army of the Potomac's headquarters and the II, VI, and XII Corps, as well as the reserve artillery.

On Sunday, June 14, Jubal Early spends most of the day maneuvering to the west of Winchester and places 20 cannon on a ridge that overlooks West Fort, one of three forts northwest and north of Winchester. At 5 p.m. Early's artillery opens with a suppressing fire that forces the Union defenders in West Fort to seek cover. Then, Harry Hays's brigade of Louisiana Tigers overruns the position. Soon, darkness ends the fight.

At 1 a.m. on June 15, Robert Milroy belatedly decides to withdraw from Winchester. Ewell anticipates Milroy's move and sends Allegheny Johnson's division to the northeast to cut off his retreat route. At 4 a.m. there is another of those rare Civil War night fights, as Milroy's retreat column runs into Johnson's ambush on the Martinsburg Road. By dawn, every Federal soldier is left to his own devices. Milroy is one of the first out of town, but he suffers 4,443 men lost, of which 3,856 are captured. He also loses 300 wagons, loaded with supplies, 300 horses, tons of quartermaster and commissary stores, and 23 cannon. General Ewell suffers only 269 casualties—47 killed, 219 wounded, and 3 missing, and it looks like the "second coming of Jackson."

On that day Gen. A. P. Hill begins to move his III Corps from the Fredericksburg area to Culpeper. That afternoon, Lee gives Longstreet his marching orders. He is to march north along the east side of the Blue Ridge Mountains, while Hill follows the route pioneered by Ewell through Culpeper and Chester Gap and into the Shenandoah Valley on the west side. Longstreet's movement is intended to confuse the Federals as to Lee's true intent and to screen both Ewell's and Hill's march. Stuart's cavalry is to ride east of Longstreet and screen his corps. Then, as Hill begins to catch up to Ewell at the Potomac River, Longstreet will cross over the Blue Ridge through Snicker's and Ashby's Gaps into the valley to protect the rear of the army. The Army of Northern Virginia—with Ewell in the lead, Hill in the center, and Longstreet in the rear—will then be poised to cross Maryland's wasp waist and press on into Pennsylvania.

That same day in Mississippi, Joe Johnston has given up. He telegraphs Secretary Seddon: "I consider saving Vicksburg hopeless." Seddon disagrees, and replies on the 16th that "Vicksburg must not be lost without a desperate struggle. The interest and honor of the Confederacy forbid it. I rely on you to avert the loss."

At Vicksburg, William Tecumseh Sherman has been out all day on a hot 16th day of June, and he returns to his headquarters to find Frank Blair waiting for him with a copy of the *Memphis Evening Bulletin,* printed three days earlier. In the newspaper is a congratulatory order from John McClernand, and when Sherman reads it, he explodes. McPherson has likewise seen a recent copy of the *Missouri Democrat* with an identical article, and his reaction mirrors Sherman's.

McClernand's lengthy General Orders Number 72 of May 30 congratulates the soldiers of the XIII Corps by recounting their exploits from the beginning of the march in Louisiana all the way through the attacks of May 22. Infuriating Sherman, however, is the portion of the order that begins with, "How and why the general assault failed, it would be useless now to explain. If, while the enemy was massing to crush it [McClernand's XIII Corps], assistance was asked for by a diversion at other points, or by re-enforcement, it only asked what in one case Major General Grant had specifically and peremptorily ordered, namely simultaneous and persistent attack all along our lines until the enemy's outer works should be carried, and what, in the other, by massing a strong force in time upon a weakened point, would have probably ensured success."

Sherman and McPherson send a formal letter of protest to Grant, quoting an army regulation that requires all press releases to be approved by the army commander.

In Washington, on June 16, Halleck impatiently wires Rosecrans, asking, "Is it your intention to make an immediate movement forward? A definite answer, yes or no, is required." Rosecrans snaps back at 6:30 p.m. that day: "In reply to your inquiry, if immediate means to-night or to-morrow, no. If it means as soon as all things are ready, say five days, yes."

At 10:15 p.m., Halleck telegraphs Hooker: "I want you to push out your cavalry, to ascertain something definite about the enemy." Joe Hooker's Army of the Potomac has been moving north to protect Washington and Baltimore. Hooker sends Pleasonton's cavalry out to find Lee, and Pleasonton runs into Stuart's cavalry on June 17.

On June 17, at Vicksburg, Grant receives the protest letters from Sherman and McPherson about McClernand's press release. Grant doesn't call McClernand in for an explanation, but immediately sends a message to him, asking if the order, as printed, is a "true copy." McClernand responds, defiantly saying the order is true and that he is ready to stand behind its contents.

In Virginia on June 17, Jeb Stuart moves into Loudoun Valley. The Bull Run Mountains border the east side of Loudoun Valley, and Stuart has to protect two gaps in these mountains—Aldie's Gap and Thoroughfare Gap. Crossing Loudoun Valley from these gaps are two turnpikes that run west across the valley to the Blue Ridge Mountains, where Ashby's and Snicker's gaps are located. Ashby's and Snicker's are the gaps that Longstreet plans to use to rejoin the rear of Lee's army. If the Federals cross Loudoun Valley and get to either of these two gaps in the Blue Ridge, they will be able to spot Lee's army moving northward on the west side of those mountains. So Stuart sends Fitz Lee's brigade to Aldie's Gap to prevent any Federal incursion through that gap into Loudoun Valley. The brigade is led by Col. Tom Munford because Fitz is off duty, suffering with inflammatory rheumatism. Rooney Lee's brigade is sent to Thoroughfare Gap. Because Rooney Lee was wounded at Brandy Station, his men are commanded by Col. John R. Chambliss.

En route to Aldie's Gap, Munford's troopers ride east to Dover, about two miles west of Aldie, and stop at Little River to rest their jaded horses. Rebel pickets are sent forward to Aldie's Gap, where they are soon attacked by Pleasonton's cavalry. General Kilpatrick—he was promoted from colonel to brigadier general on June 13—decides to attack Munford with his four regiments. But Kilpatrick makes the same mistake he made at Brandy Station—he sends the regiments into action piecemeal. Munford's pickets have to fall back, and their fellow horse soldiers quickly ride eastward toward the community of Aldie, where they form on a commanding hill near the fork of the two turnpikes, west of the gap and the village. From here they repel four separate Union attacks in a bloody fight. Kilpatrick's first fight as a general has not been a good one.

Twelve miles south of Aldie's Gap, at Thoroughfare Gap, are the 275 troopers of the First Rhode Island Cavalry, with Colonel Duffié in command. Duffié has been demoted because of his poor performance at Brandy Station. After brushing aside Chambliss's pickets at Thoroughfare Gap, Duffié enters Loudoun Valley and comes close to capturing Jeb Stuart and his staff at Middleburg. A startled Stuart races out of town, but he returns at dark with Beverly Robertson's reserve brigade, which Stuart has wisely posted about seven miles south of Middleburg to support either brigade at the two gaps. They quickly drive Duffié out of Middleburg.

June 18 is a busy day at Vicksburg. The two 30-pounders at Battery McPherson are moved forward through the ditch of Logan's Approach for 470 yards to

Battery Hickenlooper, and they are placed next to two 24-pounder howitzers. This places incredible firepower only 130 yards from the Third Louisiana Redan.

Late that day Grant tells John Rawlins to draw up a relief of command order for the XIII Corps commander. For all intents and purposes, John McClernand's active military career is ended.

In Virginia on June 18, Jeb Stuart meets with Robert E. Lee and James Longstreet, at Paris, a hamlet on the turnpike in the Loudoun Valley a mile east of Ashby's Gap, to discuss the role of the cavalry in the campaign. Lee is concerned that the cavalry was detached, and he wants Stuart to keep the enemy to the east as far as possible, protect Lee's lines of communication, and watch the enemy's movements. This means that the cavalry should operate on the right flank of the army. Lee also wants two cavalry brigades to hold the passes of the Blue Ridge until all of his infantry has crossed the Potomac. By now the fourth estate criticism is bothering Stuart, and he wants redemption. He comes up with the suggestion that he be allowed the option of taking three brigades and crossing the Potomac River to the east of the Union Army, passing it and Washington. Nothing definite is decided, and the next day Lee crosses over the Blue Ridge and into the Shenandoah Valley.

Grant's order relieving McClernand of command of the XIII Corps and sending him home to Illinois is to be delivered to McClernand on the morning of June 19, but Lt. Col. Harry Wilson and Lt. Col. John Rawlins, both of whom detest McClernand, decide to deliver the order before Grant might change his mind.

Harry Wilson delivers the relief of command order to John McClernand at 2 a.m. on the 19th. Wilson and McClernand at one time had an amiable relationship, but that time has long passed. McClernand reads the order and says to Wilson, "Well, sir! I am relieved!" Then he adds, "By God sir, we are both relieved." Wilson has to hide his smirk, and McClernand is sent home to Illinois. Gen. E. O. C. Ord, a West Pointer who graduated with Halleck in 1839 and who has recovered from a wound received at Davis Bridge the previous October, happens to have conveniently arrived at Vicksburg the previous day. He is given command of the XIII Corps.

In the Loudoun Valley in Virginia, Federal and Confederate cavalry clash at Middleburg on June 19, and at Upperville on the 21st, but Stuart successfully

GETTYSBURG CAMPAIGN

Symbol	Meaning	Symbol	Meaning
City		Road	
Town	Bridge	Railroad	
Gap	River ford		

N

PENNSYLVANIA

Carlis
Creek
Papertowr
Yellow
Mount Hol
CUMBERLAND VALLEY RAILROAD
Conodoguinet
SOUTH MOUN
Shippensburg
Scotland
Chambersburg
Conococheague
Greenwood
Middletown
Creek
Mummasburg
McConnellsburg
Fayetteville
Cashtown
Marsh
New Guilford
Cashtown
Gap
Gettysbur
Altodale
Mercersburg
Quincy
Run
Fairfield
Greencastle
Monterey
Horners Mills
Waynesboro
Middleburg
Fountaindale
PA.
Ringgold
Emmitsburg
MD.
Bridgeport
Mechanicstown
Brucevi
Middlebur
Hagerstown
Cavetown
Creagerstown
BALTIMORE & OHIO RAILROAD
Williamsport
Lewistown
Johnsville
Falling Waters
Monocacy R.
Woodsbor
Boonsborough
Utica
WEST
Turner's Gap
Walkersville
Libert
VIRGINIA
Antietam Cr.
Middletown
Creek
Martinsburg
Ceresville
Shepherdstown
Sharpsburg
New
MD.
Mark
W. VA.
Antietam
FREDERICK
Bunker
Furnace
Hill
Opequon
Monrovia
Sandy
Monocacy Junction
W. VA.
Hook
VA.
Knoxville
Hyattstown
WINCHESTER &
POTOMAC RAILROAD
Harpers
Ferry
Point of Rocks
MD.
Stephenson's
Charlestown
VA.
Depot
VIRGINIA
Barnesville
Winchester
Shenandoah R.
Berryville
Potomac R.
Poolesville
Kernstown
Leesburg
Edwards Ferry
VALLEY
Snicker's Gap
Seneca
ALEXANDRIA, LOUDOUN &
HAMPSHIRE RAILROAD
Rowser's
Ford
MD.
VA.
SHENANDOAH
BLUE
RIDGE
MOUNTAINS
Dranesville
Ashby's
Paris
Strasburg
Gap
Upperville
Goose Creek
MANASSAS GAP
RAILROAD
Aldie
Aldie's
Gap
Front Royal
LOUDOUN VALLEY
Middleburg
Gum Springs

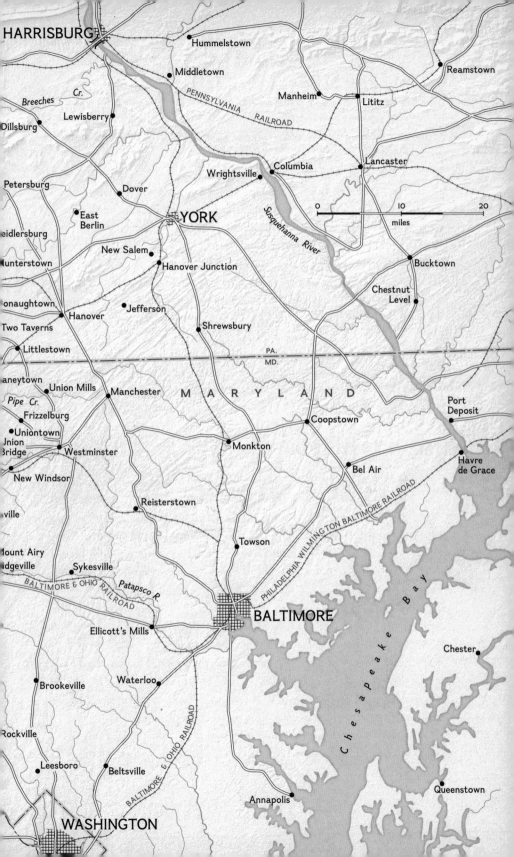

screens Lee's movement. Now it is time for Stuart to move northward and rejoin Lee's army.

At Vicksburg, Union soldiers digging Logan's Approach continue to inch their way toward the Third Louisiana Redan.

By the evening of June 21, the head of the Logan's Approach sap is only a few yards from the exterior slope of the Third Louisiana Redan, and volunteers are sought to dig a mine. The Rebels can hear the Yanks as they dig, so they do two things. They build a traverse across the rear of the redan so that they can fall back. Then six volunteers from the 43rd Mississippi start to dig a countermine. They want either to tap into the Union gallery or to get close enough to it to light a barrel of powder. If successful, that would be the end of the Yanks working in the mine's gallery.

In Virginia, Lee issues General Orders Number 72 to provide for the protection of private property in "the enemy's country," and to ensure that requisitions by the army "upon the local authorities or inhabitants for the necessary supplies" will be paid using the market price. Any violation of the policy will be "promptly and rigorously punished." Of course, payments are made in Confederate money or military vouchers.

On the morning of June 22, the Confederate invasion of Pennsylvania begins when Rodes's division crosses the Potomac River at Williamsport, Maryland, and then crosses the Mason-Dixon Line. As Rodes approaches Greencastle, Pennsylvania, his cavalry escort sends a scouting party north toward Chambersburg. One mile north of Greencastle, they see Union cavalry coming south toward them. The Confederate troopers quickly race back to a wheat field, dismount, take cover behind a wooden fence bordering the road, and pour a volley into the oncoming Yanks, hitting two of them and scattering the rest. As they move up, they find the body of Cpl. William Rihl, a Pennsylvanian. Rihl is the first Union soldier killed in Pennsylvania in the Gettysburg Campaign. Jubal Early's division is guarding the east flank of the army while threatening Harpers Ferry. Early takes a route ten miles to the east of Rodes and Johnson on June 22, crossing the Potomac River at Shepherdstown, West Virginia. He then turns northeast, moves into Pennsylvania, and encamps at Waynesboro the next night.

On June 22, Lee is just past Berryville, Virginia, on the Charlestown Road, and he sends his orders to Stuart. First, however, he sends them through Longstreet and asks his opinion. The orders read that, if Hooker moves north, Stuart is to move into Maryland and form on Ewell's right. He is to gather intelligence while guarding Ewell's column, and collect all the supplies he can for the army. Lee adds a note addressed to Longstreet and, according to Longstreet's recollection of this lost note, the option of riding around Hooker's army is left open. So Longstreet adds his own note to the order and sends it to Stuart, suggesting that a move around the enemy's rear would be less likely to disclose the Confederate plans.

> *The next day, June 23, Lee sends another order to Stuart, apparently intended to clarify the first order. But this second order still gives Stuart the option he wants. Lee says, "You will, however, be able to judge whether you can pass around their army without hindrance, doing them all the damage you can, and cross the river east of the mountains. . . . After crossing the river, you must move on and feel the right of Ewell's troops, collecting information, provisions, etc."*
>
> *On June 24, Rosecrans telegraphs Halleck with the long-awaited news, "The army begins to move at 3 o'clock this morning." The Tullahoma Campaign begins, and Joe Johnston will get no more troops from Bragg in Tennessee. Rosecrans's goal is to get into the Confederate rear and threaten the Nashville and Chattanooga Railroad bridge over the Elk River, which would sever Bragg's line of communications.*

On June 24, the lead division of A. P. Hill's III Corps, Richard Anderson's, splashes across the Potomac River near Shepherdstown and marches through Sharpsburg, while Dorsey Pender's and Harry Heth's divisions remain in camp. Robert Rodes moves into Chambersburg that day, and Jubal Early leaves Waynesboro and marches north through Quincy and Altodale, today's Mont Alto, and encamps that night at Greenwood.

> *Hooker is flooded with information on Lee's movements, but he is unable to make a decision. Finally, at 3:15 p.m. on June 24, Hooker receives the confirmation he needs. John C. Babcock, Bureau of Military Information, in Frederick, Maryland, supplies the "trigger" for the Army of the Potomac's crossing of the Potomac. Babcock writes: "I learn beyond a doubt that the last of Lee's entire army has passed through Martinsburg toward the Potomac. The last of them passed Monday night [June 22]. The main body are crossing at Shepherdstown . . . can see them from the mountain. Nine thousand men*

and sixteen pieces of artillery passed through Greencastle yesterday p.m. . . . Large bodies of troops can be seen from South Mountain, at Antietam Furnace, by aid of glasses. . . . All of which may be considered as reliable." At 11:35 p.m., Hooker orders his army to cross the Potomac at Edwards Ferry, twenty seven and one-half miles northwest of Washington.

At Vicksburg, on June 25, the Federals complete the digging of the mine under the Third Louisiana Redan and pack three galleries at the head of the mine with 2,200 pounds of black powder. Captain Hickenlooper tells General McPherson he is ready, and McPherson relays this information to Grant, who comes to Battery Hickenlooper to watch the assault with McPherson.

The fuse is lit at 3:30 p.m. and the ground opens, a great geyser of dirt shoots skyward, and the six Mississippians working in the Confederate countermine are blown to pieces or buried alive. The resulting crater is about 12 feet deep and 40 feet wide. Before the dust settles, the 45th Illinois charges into the crater. The men from the Third Louisiana pour a volley into the "lead miners" of the 45th, and the Yanks can't get out of the crater. The counterattacking force, the Sixth Missouri, is led by Col. Eugene Irwin. He sees the Yanks in the crater, and yells, "Forward, boys, don't let the Louisianans go farther than you do!" He is killed by two minié balls.

Throughout the night, the Yankees use the crater to stage attacks against the Third Louisiana Redan, rotating units in two-hour intervals. All during the fight, which will last for 20 hours, the Union engineers build a timbered casemate in the crater for the emplacement of two guns, but the Confederates use hand grenades against the Yanks. The best the Yankee engineers can do is to construct a covered gallery with a traverse thrown across its front.

Early on Thursday, the 25th of June, the Union Army begins to cross the Potomac River. The soldiers cross over the bridges at Edwards Ferry and move into the Frederick, Maryland, area. Oliver Howard's XI Corps is the first to cross the bridges at 3:45 a.m.

The day that the Federals begin their crossing of the Potomac, A. P. Hill's III Corps, which was the last corps of Lee's army to leave Fredericksburg, reaches its assigned staging area. This is accomplished when Anderson marches his division through Hagerstown, Maryland, and crosses into Pennsylvania at Middleburg, today's community of State Line, and when Pender's and Heth's divisions march from Shepherdstown and cross the Potomac into Maryland, camping within ten miles of Hagerstown.

That same rainy day, Robert E. Lee rides through Falling Waters, West Virginia, and crosses the Potomac River with Pickett's division of Longstreet's I Corps. While Pickett's men march another mile and encamp, Lee proceeds through Williamsport on the road to Hagerstown and goes into camp in a hickory grove on a hill, three miles past Williamsport. Here he receives correspondence from Richmond. He writes back to President Davis and suggests a redeployment of units from Gen. P. G. T. Beauregard's Department of South Carolina, Georgia, and Florida, to the vicinity of Culpeper to keep Lincoln worried about the security of Washington.

> *Lee knows that Davis is concerned about Vicksburg, so he optimistically concludes his message with the following: "I still hope that all things will end well for us at Vicksburg. At any rate, every effort should be made to bring about that result."*

At 1 a.m. that day, Jeb Stuart has departed from Salem, Virginia, which is today's Marshall, with three brigades, led by Wade Hampton; Fitz Lee, who has returned from sick leave; and John Chambliss, commanding the wounded Rooney Lee's brigade—a total of 5,000 horse soldiers and six pieces of artillery. Later that morning, east of the Bull Run Mountains at Haymarket, Stuart discovers that the road is jammed with Hancock's II Corps, marching north.

Now, this is the news that Lee has been looking for—that Hooker is marching north—but he won't get it, because Stuart sends a courier to Lee and the courier never gets through. Meanwhile, to deceive the enemy as to the direction he plans to travel, which is north, Stuart has his horse artillery fire upon Hancock's infantry columns, and he then drops back to the village of Buckland, three miles southwest of Haymarket.

Stuart can't get through Hancock's men, so he halts for the night near Buckland Mills to graze his horses. The next morning he heads southeast by way of Brentsville, and stops for the night near Wolf Run Shoals on the Occoquan River. Here the troopers spend the night grazing their horses, which are starting to show signs of breaking down due to a lack of grain.

On June 26, Longstreet's other two divisions—Hood's and McLaws's—cross the Potomac at Williamsport, completing the crossing of that water obstacle by the Army of Northern Virginia. Pickett's division marches to within a mile of Greencastle and encamps. Hood's division camps near Greencastle, while McLaws goes into camp just beyond Williamsport.

On June 26, Dick Ewell has been issued his orders from Robert E. Lee. Ewell, with two divisions—Rodes's, followed by Johnson's—will continue to travel northeast in the Cumberland Valley, through Shippensburg to Carlisle, then toward Harrisburg and the Susquehanna River. They will be screened by the Buttermilk Rangers of Albert "Galloping" Jenkins's cavalry brigade. Jubal Early will leave Greenwood, go through South Mountain at Cashtown Gap, then on to Gettysburg and continue east through York to Wrightsville on the Susquehanna River, 25 miles downstream from Harrisburg.

Early is to cut the North Central Railroad at York, and then move east to burn the Columbia Bridge over the Susquehanna at Wrightsville. By doing this he will cut the rail links to Harrisburg, so that Hooker cannot shift troops there by rail. Early is then to strike northwest through Dillsburg to Carlisle to reunite with Ewell for the next objective, which is to be Harrisburg.

As soon as the rain allows, Early marches east on the Chambersburg Pike. After three miles he reaches South Mountain and the Caledonia Iron Works, which belong to an ardent abolitionist, Congressman Thaddeus Stevens. Early, despite Lee's order, has the Caledonia Iron Works burned because, as he later writes, Stevens was an advocate of "vindictive measures" against the South.

As Early continues over South Mountain, his men come to a rise in the road known as Gallagher's Knob, and it was here, three days earlier, that Pvt. Eli Amick of Jenkins's 14th Virginia Cavalry was ambushed and killed by four locals, Henry Hahn, Henry Shultz, David Powell, and Uriah Powell. These men are probably full of John Barleycorn from the nearby Willow Springs Hotel. So they decide to ambush—the term is "bushwhack," because these men are civilians—the oncoming Confederates. Hahn is the only one who is armed, and he has a shotgun loaded with buckshot. He has drawn a line in the pike with the butt of his gun, and he has sworn to kill the first Reb that crosses it. When the Confederates trot past, Hahn jumps up and blasts the unsuspecting Amick as the Virginian unknowingly crosses the line. The four bushwhackers scamper into the woods at Gallagher's Knob and hide there for ten days.

After passing Gallagher's Knob, Jubal Early turns left on the Hilltown Road, rides almost a mile, and stops at a tavern on the north side of the road, owned by John Harding. He dismounts and goes inside, where he sees several ladies drinking tea. He notices a "vanity map" of Adams County on the wall and cuts it down, saying that he needs the map more than the locals do. That afternoon,

Gordon's brigade of Early's division clashes with a regiment of Pennsylvania militia near the Marsh Creek bridge west of town. The old men and boys are routed and Gordon's men spend the night of June 26 in Gettysburg.

> *Lee, with Longstreet, leaves his camp in the hickory grove north of Williamsport around 11 a.m. on June 26, and rides through Hagerstown to a point near Greencastle, where Lee goes into camp near the road. He unfolds a map of Pennsylvania and says to Gen. Isaac Trimble, "I have not yet heard that the enemy have crossed the Potomac, and am waiting to hear from General Stuart." After more discussion, Trimble recalls that Lee "laid his hand on the map over Gettysburg and said: 'Hereabout we shall probably meet the enemy and fight a great battle; and if God gives us the victory, the war will be over, and we shall receive the recognition of our independence.' "*

In Vicksburg, on June 27, a second mine is started at the crater fronting the Third Louisiana Redan. The Confederates start work on a countermine, and both sides dig frantically.

> *In Pennsylvania that day, the march of Rodes's and Johnson's divisions into Carlisle is without incident, and Dick Ewell makes his headquarters at Carlisle Barracks, where he had been stationed as a lieutenant of dragoons 20 years earlier.*

Jeb Stuart crosses the Occoquan at Wolf Run Shoals on the 27th and rides almost ten miles north to Fairfax Station. His men and horses pause there, and they then travel north for 12 miles to Dranesville. Here Stuart learns that Sedgwick's VI Corps has just left the area that morning. The Confederates ride an additional four miles northeast to Rowser's Ford and begin crossing the Potomac that night. At Rowser's Ford, Stuart's troopers destroy a lock-gate on the Chesapeake & Ohio Canal. Stuart has passed by the rear of Hooker's army, but his detour has taken 74 hours, and he is still 110 miles from Ewell's II Corps in Carlisle, Pennsylvania.

Joe Hooker has now convinced himself that Robert E. Lee has 91,000 men—80,000 is a much closer figure—and Fighting Joe is down to about 90,000. He decides he needs more men. Halleck gives him reinforcements from the Department of Washington, to include infantry divisions led by Gen. Samuel W. Crawford and Gen. John J. Abercrombie plus Gen. Julius Stahel's cavalry division—a total of about 8,400 infantry and 3,600 cavalry.

But Joe Hooker knows that 10,000 additional Federals are at Harpers Ferry under the command of Gen. William H. French, and he knows that French reports directly to Washington. Still, Hooker makes plans to take these men, and when Halleck learns this, he sends a message to French, telling him to "pay no attention to General Hooker's orders." Halleck knows that French will have to show this message to Hooker. Worse still, there is no good reason not to let Hooker have the men.

On June 27, Hooker, because his army is north of the Potomac and in proximity to Lee, now lets Halleck's insult goad him into making a mistake. He doesn't think the Lincoln Administration can replace him at such a critical moment, and at 1 p.m. from Sandy Hook, Maryland, he telegraphs—"I request to be relieved."

Lincoln and Halleck quickly decide to grant Hooker's request, and they call in Secretary of War Edwin Stanton to make sure that the relief is handled properly. Stanton brings in Lt. Col. James Allen Hardie, an 1843 West Pointer who has served on the staffs of McClellan and Burnside and is now Stanton's chief of staff. Stanton instructs Hardie to deliver the orders from the President, in secret, directly to Gen. George G. Meade. Hardie is to then accompany Meade to Hooker's headquarters and ensure that the order is executed. Now, this is a delicate matter, and Hardie is reluctant to accept so sensitive an assignment, which could earn him the everlasting enmity of one, or even two, general officers.

Hardie is assured by Mr. Lincoln "that he would take the responsibility upon himself for any wound to the feelings of the two generals, or of the bearer of the order."

Hardie travels in civilian clothes and arrives at Monocacy Junction late on June 27. Around midnight he hires a buggy and driver to take him to Meade's headquarters tent at Arcadia mansion on Ballenger Creek, three and one-half miles south of Frederick.

While A. P. Hill's III Corps marches to Chambersburg on the 27th, Robert E. Lee leaves Greencastle and rides into the Chambersburg town square shortly after 9 a.m. Two local spies see Lee arrive, and leave Chambersburg for Harrisburg at 11 a.m. to report Lee's and Hill's arrival in Chambersburg to Gen. Darius Couch. After Chancellorsville, Couch was so disgusted with Hooker's performance that he applied for relief of duty with the Army of the Potomac, and was given command of the Pennyslvania militia. Couch receives this information from these spies two days later and telegraphs it to Joe Hooker.

After talking to A. P. Hill in the Chambersburg town square or "diamond," Lee rides east on the pike to Gettysburg for a mile and establishes his tent headquarters in a grove on the eastern edge of town, known as Shetter's Woods or Messersmith's Woods.

That afternoon, Heth's and Pender's divisions of Hill's III Corps, marching from south of Hagerstown, arrive at Chambersburg. They also turn east at the diamond, and then march east to Fayetteville.

Pickett's and Hood's divisions of Longstreet's I Corps remain in camp on the morning of the 27th to allow all of Hill's men to pass to the front, while McLaws's men get an early start from Williamsport. Late that afternoon, Pickett's and Hood's men march through Greencastle and Chambersburg and continue north up the Harrisburg Pike to encamp along the east bank of Conococheague Creek north of Chambersburg, while McLaw's men go into camp about six miles south of Chambersburg.

Early on June 28, George Meade is awakened by Colonel Hardie, and he thinks he's being arrested. At least, that's what he writes to his wife. Hardie informs Meade that he has orders from the War Department for Meade to take command of the Army of the Potomac. Meade tries to argue, but Hardie says that the President will not hear otherwise and that the order is peremptory. George Meade is to command the army, and Meade and Hardie are both to deliver the news to Hooker. Hardie later says that Meade finally mutters, in a somewhat light-hearted manner, "Well, I've been tried and condemned without a hearing, and I suppose I shall have to go to the execution."

Meade's appointment as the commander of the Army of the Potomac is certainly not a surprise to anyone in the army, and it is not an unwelcome burden for Meade. Just three days earlier, he had written to his wife: "I see you are still troubled with visions of my being placed in command. I thought that had all blown over, and I think it has, except in your imagination, and that of some others of my kind friends. . . . I do not stand, however, any chance, because I have no friends, political or others, who press or advance my claims or pretensions, and there are so many others who are pressed by influential politicians that it is folly to think I stand any chance upon mere merit alone. . . . But do you know, I think your ambition is being roused and that you are beginning to be bitten with the dazzling prospect of having for a husband a commanding general of an army. How is this?"

Meade dresses and goes with Hardie to Hooker's headquarters tent at Prospect Hall on Red Hill, the highest elevation in Frederick, arriving there just after daylight. Hooker, in full uniform, has already heard of the arrival of Hardie, and he has almost certainly divined the intent of this visit. Hardie then informs Hooker that his request to be relieved has been accepted, and that George Meade is in command of the Army of the Potomac. Meade and Hooker talk for a while and then Dan Butterfield, Hooker's chief of staff, is summoned.

Meade's orders are explicit. He must remember that the Army of the Potomac has two missions: It has to cover Washington and Baltimore, and it must oppose the invading Confederate Army. Meade posts himself up and learns that the Army of the Potomac is widely scattered. The I Corps of 10,000 men is at Middletown, 8 miles northwest of Frederick. The 13,000 men of the II Corps are en route to Frederick from Barnesville, 15 miles south. The III Corps of 12,000 soldiers is at Middletown. The V Corps, which has 12,500 soldiers, is encamped at Ballenger Creek, just south of Frederick. The VI Corps of 15,700 men is at Hyattstown, 11 miles southeast of Frederick. The XI Corps of 9,900 soldiers is with I and III Corps at Middletown, watching the gaps in South Mountain. The XII Corps of 8,600 soldiers is en route to Frederick from Knoxville, 20 miles southwest on the Potomac River.

The scattered army is a concern for Meade, so he orders the three corps at Middletown to march east and concentrate around Frederick. The I Corps is to camp in Frederick, the III Corps at Walkersville, six miles northeast of Frederick, and the XI Corps at Worman's Mill on the northern fringe of Frederick. He also orders the II Corps, already en route from Barnesville, to encamp at Monocacy Junction, three miles south of Frederick.

Meade then agrees to Alfred Pleasonton's reorganization of the cavalry corps, which involves three unusual promotions. It will create some new brigade command slots, and Pleasonton wants to "jump promote" two captains and one first lieutenant to brigadier general. The two captains are Elon Farnsworth and Wesley Merritt, and the first lieutenant is George Armstrong Custer. Farnsworth is not a Regular Army officer, but his uncle, John Farnsworth, was the original colonel of the Eighth Illinois Cavalry and is now a U.S. congressman from Illinois. Merritt is a West Pointer who was commended for "gallant and meritorious service" at Brandy Station and Upperville. Custer is a West Pointer who has been a good staff officer and has served on the staffs of McClellan and Pleasonton. Farnsworth and Custer get the First and Second Brigades, respectively, under Judson Kilpatrick, while Merritt gets the reserve brigade under John Buford.

Meade believes from his intelligence sources that Ewell's II Corps is on the Susquehanna River at Harrisburg and Columbia, that Longsteet's I Corps is at Chambersburg, and that Hill's III Corps is between Chambersburg and Cashtown. He decides to move his army north and northeast in Maryland, forming an east-west line, with the western end at Emmitsburg and the eastern flank at Westminster. Before the end of his first day in command, Meade advises Halleck that he will move the army northeast toward the Baltimore and Harrisburg Road, so that he can cover that road and draw supplies from it. He says that he is convinced that Lee has passed through Hagerstown and is en route to Chambersburg. He orders Butterfield and the staff to prepare marching orders for 4 a.m. on June 29. The seven army corps will move out, each in supporting distance of one another.

Per Meade's orders, on June 29, the I Corps under John Reynolds and the XI Corps under Oliver Howard are to march to Emmitsburg, Maryland. The I Corps is to march north from Frederick, through Lewistown and Mechanicstown—today's Thurmont—to Emmitsburg. The XI Corps is also to march at 4 a.m. from Frederick to Emmitsburg, but by a road to the east of the I Corps, through Utica and Creagerstown.

Covering the left flank of the army as it moves north will be two brigades of John Buford's cavalry division, commanded by Col. William Gamble and Col. Thomas C. Devin. They have with them six three-inch rifles of Company A, Second U.S. Artillery, commanded by Lt. John H. Calef. This force totals just over 3,000 men. Buford's third brigade is Gen. Wesley Merritt's reserve brigade, and it is to be sent to Mechanicstown to guard the army's rear as it heads north, as well as to pick up stragglers.

Gen. Dan Sickles's III Corps is to march from Walkersville, through Woodsboro and Middleburg, to Taneytown. The XII Corps is to march from Frederick, through Ceresville to Walkersville, and then follow the III Corps to Taneytown.

The II Corps, commanded by Winfield Scott Hancock, is to move at 4 a.m. from Monocacy Junction through Frederick, Liberty, Johnsville, and Uniontown to Frizzellburg, a community about four miles northwest of Westminster on the Taneytown Pike. Marching immediately behind the II Corps will be the V Corps, so the V Corps will not start until 8 a.m.

Replacing Meade as the V Corps commander is Gen. George Sykes, an 1842 West Point graduate from Delaware, who is known in the Regular Army as "Tardy George." His corps is to march from Ballenger Creek to Frederick and then follow the II Corps route to Uniontown, a town two and one-half miles southwest of Frizzellburg.

Marching at the designated hour from Hyattstown to New Windsor, a village six miles southwest of Westminster, will be the big VI Corps—the army's right—commanded by John Sedgwick and accompanied by the cavalry, led by Gen. David Gregg. The men are to ride through Monrovia and New Market to Ridgeville, just northwest of modern Parrsville, and follow the Ridge Road on Parrs Ridge through Mount Airy to New Windsor.

Meade is to move his headquarters from Frederick to Middleburg, five miles southwest of Taneytown. The headquarters train will roll at the same time, and will go through Ceresville and Woodsboro to Middleburg.

Meade's immediate actions impress Col. Charles S. Wainwright, commanding the artillery brigade of the First Corps, who writes in his diary for the 29th that their "new commander is determined not to let the grass grow under his feet."

By the end of the day's march, Meade plans to have his army extended along a 21-mile front from Emmitsburg through Taneytown to Westminster. This will protect Washington and Baltimore, Meade believes, from any thrust the Confederates might make from their positions in Pennsylvania.

Sunday, June 28, is a day of rest for Longstreet's and Hill's men at Chambersburg and for Ewell's men at Carlisle. But the day will not end restfully for Lee. At 10 p.m. Longstreet's spy, Henry Thomas Harrison, is brought to Lt. Col. G. Moxley Sorrel, Longstreet's chief of staff.

Before leaving Culpeper, Longstreet gave Harrison "all the gold he thought he would need" and sent the scout to Washington to find out whatever news he could. Harrison spent his time in the saloons of Washington talking to loose-lipped army officers, and as soon as he learned that Hooker had crossed the Potomac, he went in search of Longstreet, passing through Frederick along the way. Harrison has such incredible news that Sorrel feels he must wake Longstreet, who is impressed with the report. He sends Harrison, accompanied by Maj. John W. Fairfax, an aide, to see Lee at Messersmith's Woods, where the general listens to Harrison "with great composure and minuteness." Harrison tells Lee that Hooker has crossed the Potomac and that he has seen Union infantry as far west as Middletown Valley.

Lee, after hearing Harrison's report, does not know the enemy's intent, but he becomes concerned about his own line of communications. He wants to prevent the Army of the Potomac from advancing farther west and interdicting the Army of Northern Virginia's connection with Virginia. That, however, is not Meade's intent.

Lee desperately needs reliable intelligence, but Stuart is 80 miles southeast of Chambersburg, with the Union Army of the Potomac now between him and Lee. That afternoon Stuart captures 125 new wagons at Rockville, Maryland, with "splendid teams" heading to the Federal Army out of Washington. Stuart sends another messenger to Lee to advise him of the location of the Army of the Potomac, but again the messenger does not get through.

Stuart starts north to join Ewell with the captured wagons, meaning he isn't going to move with much celerity. While Harrison is talking to Lee in Chambersburg, Stuart is slowly moving north out of Rockville with the long wagon train and 400 Yankee prisoners.

After raising the Confederate flag on the post flagstaff at Carlisle Barracks, Pennsylvania, Rodes's and Johnson's II Corps divisions rest on Sunday. But Early's Sabbath is more interesting, because when his men march into York, Gen. William "Extra Billy" Smith's brigade is in the lead. Smith is almost 66 years old, one of the oldest Confederate generals. He has been called Extra Billy since 1831, when he was awarded the postal contract to deliver mail between Washington, D.C., and Milledgeville, Georgia. Smith created spur routes to increase his fees. So, when the postal system was investigated and his fees were uncovered, he became known as "Extra Billy." Now, when Jubal Early approaches York he finds the town square blocked with a crowd of townspeople listening to a band playing "Yankee Doodle," after which Smith, in his customary civilian clothes, gives the folks a speech. Smith is also a former governor of Virginia, so his politician blood requires him to make a speech. Just about everyone in the Army of Northern Virginia knows that if Smith's brigade is in the vanguard, "there will be a breeze blowing at the head of the column."

Jubal Early has requisitions he wants the town to fill, and after the square is cleared, the citizens don't do a bad job of filling them. Although they come up short of Early's demands, he places guards at the stores, hotels, and businesses to protect private property.

Robert E. Lee has some decisions to make. He makes them quickly. He calls off his move against Harrisburg and orders a concentration of his army east of South Mountain. He sends an order to Ewell at Carlisle on the night of the 28th, ordering him to march back to Chambersburg to unite with Longstreet and Hill. But as the hours pass, Lee thinks more about this, and about 7:30 the next morning, he sends a second message to Ewell, changing his route of march. Instead of returning to Chambersburg, Lee orders Ewell's II Corps to stay east of South Mountain and march south to Heidlersburg. Lee gives Ewell the option of sending the II Corps trains to Chambersburg, but says, "If the roads which your troops take are good," it would be better for the trains to follow the troops. This message doesn't get to Ewell until late on the following afternoon—too late to stop Johnson's division, which is en route to Chambersburg, escorting the 14-mile-long II Corps wagon train and two battalions of the artillery reserve. This will prove to be critical in the upcoming battle.

In Tennessee on that Sunday, Rosecrans is successful in slipping Col. John T. Wilder's Lightning Brigade across the rain-swollen Elk River and into Bragg's rear. The mounted soldiers then race into Decherd, five miles south of Elk River, on the Nashville and Chattanooga Railroad. Here they tear up 300 yards of track and burn the depot, which is filled with Confederate rations. Rosecrans has shown he can get into the rear of Bragg's new line at Tullahoma.

On June 29, Longstreet's I Corps stays at Chambersburg, along with Lee. In Ewell's II Corps, Rodes's division remains at Carlisle and Early's stays at York. It is raining, and Lee is uneasy, still wondering where Stuart might be.

Hill's III Corps is at Fayetteville. At 4:30 a.m. Hill sends Harry Heth's division east to Cashtown, seven and three-quarters miles west of Gettysburg, and Heth arrives there late that day, while Pender's and Anderson's divisions remain at Fayetteville.

That same day, Fitz Lee's brigade races ahead of Stuart's main body and tears up the tracks of the main line of the Baltimore and Ohio Railroad at Hood's Mill on the South Branch of the Patapsco River. They burn the bridge at Sykesville three miles to the east, and cut all the telegraph lines in the area.

When Stuart's other two brigades finally arrive at the Patapsco River, the entire command rides on 15 miles farther north to Westminster, arriving at 5 p.m. As Stuart's vanguard rides into town, it is attacked near the intersection of Washington and Main Streets by horse soldiers of the First Delaware Cavalry, but despite the surprise of this charge, the bluecoats are routed.

Stuart has learned that Meade is moving north through Frederick, and his scouts have advised him that Kilpatrick's two brigades of cavalry are in Littlestown, Pennsylvania, a scant 13 miles to the northwest. Stuart rides six miles northwest and halts at Union Mills, Maryland, before daybreak on June 30.

The Army of the Potomac's march begins as planned on June 29. Reynolds's I Corps and Howard's XI Corps reach Emmitsburg, and Sickles's III Corps arrives at Taneytown. Buford's cavalry rides north out of Middletown at 9 a.m. and passes west through Turner's Gap in South Mountain to Boonsboro. The horsemen turn north and pass through Cavetown, Maryland, cross into Pennsylvania, and ride back over South Mountain through the pass at Monterey to encamp at 10 p.m. at Fountaindale, six miles southwest of Fairfield. The officers eat an ample supper of local food at the Monterey Inn, and Buford plans to ride through Fairfield to Gettysburg the next morning.

On the road from Frederick to Taneytown Slocum's XII Corps, which is following Sickles's III Corps, is held up by the III Corps trains at a road junction one mile west of Middleburg. Only the lead elements of the XII Corps make it to Taneytown. The remainder of Slocum's XII Corps crosses Big Pipe Creek and halts near Bruceville, five miles to the southeast of Taneytown.

Hancock's II Corps receives its marching orders two hours late due to a clerical error, and the departure is delayed from 4 a.m. until 8 a.m. This holds up the V Corps, which is to follow the II Corps. The tardy II Corps does not reach Frizzellburg as planned, but finally halts at two o'clock the next morning, two miles southwest of Frizzellburg on the Babylon farm a mile east of Uniontown. Uniontown was supposed to be the V Corps' objective, but that corps gets only as far as Liberty, which is more than ten miles away, and is only about half the distance the corps was to march.

When Hancock arrives at the head of his corps in Uniontown, he meets with his staff in the Segafoose Hotel and hears from the locals that Jeb Stuart is in Westminster, about seven miles due east. At 9:30 p.m. Hancock sends a special messenger to Meade at Middleburg, and Meade refers the matter to his cavalry commander, Alfred Pleasonton. At 12:15 a.m. on June 30, Hancock is sent a reply: "The country people must have mistaken our own cavalry for that of the enemy, as the commanding general has been officially informed by General Pleasonton that he has two brigades under General Gregg at Westminster." Stuart's command was, in fact, encamped both at Westminster and at Union Mills, which is six miles north of Westminster. Kilpatrick's division was about seven miles northwest of Union Mills at Littlestown and, had Pleasonton acted on this information and sent Kilpatrick's cavalry and Hancock's infantry to Westminster, Stuart's campsites at Westminister and Union Mills could well have been his last ones.

Sedgwick pushes his VI Corps well into the night to reach New Windsor, and as if to show Meade he shares the commanding general's sense of urgency, he has his men go a bit farther and camps about five miles southwest of Westminster.

On the night of the 29th, "Old Snapping Turtle" Meade is furious about the problems on the marches that day. At 7 p.m. he sends a message from Middleburg to Dan Sickles at Taneytown, saying that Sickles's trains at Middleburg have delayed the movements behind him.

The next morning Meade sends Sickles a message pouring salt into the wound by saying, "The II Corps in the same space of time made a march nearly double your own." As the only non–West Point corps commander, Sickles feels he is being singled out. Meade does not like Sickles, and Sickles knows it.

On the 30th Lee breaks camp at Messersmith's Woods, and rides east from Chambersburg to Greenwood with McLaw's and Hood's divisions of the I Corps. McLaws leaves Gen. Joseph B. Kershaw's brigade at Fayetteville, and Hood sends Gen. Evander M. Law's brigade and a battery of artillery to New Guilford, about three and one-half miles southwest of Greenwood, to guard the mountain road leading south to Waynesboro and Emmitsburg. Pickett's division of the I Corps remains in Chambersburg to guard the rear of the army until Gen. John D. Imboden's cavalry brigade can arrive. Imboden has been operating in the mountains well to the west of the army invasion corridor and foraging liberally on the Pennsylvania countryside on the march north.

In the II Corps, Rodes marches from Carlisle through Papertown and Petersburg to Heidlersburg, while Early moves west from York through East Berlin to Heidlersburg.

Back at Fayetteville, the III Corps soldiers of Pender's division, accompanied by Hill and his staff, follow Heth's previous day's route from Fayetteville, over South Mountain, to Cashtown. When Hill arrives at Cashtown, he sends a message to Ewell at Heidlersburg, advising him of his location. Hill's third division, Richard Anderson's, remains at Fayetteville.

Early that morning at Cashtown, Harry Heth sends Gen. J. Johnston Pettigrew's brigade to Gettysburg. Pettigrew starts at 6:30 a.m., with three guns and several empty wagons to transport the goods they hope to find. Pettigrew is warned by Heth not to bring on a fight, but that he can sweep aside any home guard he might find. As they march toward Gettysburg, Pettigrew's aide recalls that Longstreet's scout, Harrison, passes them, rides into Gettysburg, and returns with the report that Buford's cavalry division of 3,000 troopers is en route to that borough. Pettigrew takes heed of this warning and sends a courier back to Heth for instructions. Heth sends word back for Pettigrew to keep going—that the Army of the Potomac is nowhere near Gettysburg. At Herr Ridge, Pettigrew meets Dr. John C. O'Neal, a native Virginian as well as a doctor in Gettysburg, and O'Neal is asked if any Yankees are in Gettysburg. O'Neal truthfully says that when he left town early that morning, there were no Union soldiers around. That's because Buford's cavalry didn't arrive in Gettysburg until after O'Neal left town.

Pettigrew continues toward Gettysburg and arrives at McPherson Ridge about 10:30 a.m., where he can see the vanguard of John Buford's cavalry riding into town from the south. Pettigrew's orders are peremptory—not to bring on a fight—so he withdraws and marches back to Cashtown, arriving late that afternoon. He tells Heth that Union cavalry is in Gettysburg, but Heth doesn't believe him. Then A. P. Hill rides up and is given Pettigrew's report. Like Heth, Hill doesn't believe Pettigrew. Hill is stubborn, and he cannot make himself believe that the enemy is this far north.

Heth then asks Hill if he has any objection to his taking a division into Gettysburg in the morning. Hill responds: "None in the world." This is the only command decision Hill is going to make at Gettysburg, and instead of sending one regiment to feel out what is in Gettysburg, he sends two divisions. One can argue that this is the worst decision any Confederate commander is going to make at Gettysburg, because Lee does not want to fight until his army is concentrated. But it is not, because Hill still has Anderson's division in Fayetteville. McLaws's and Hood's divisions of Longstreet's corps are at Greenwood, and Pickett's division is in Chambersburg. Early's and Rodes's divisions of Ewell's II Corps are in or near Heidlersburg, and Johnson's division and the II Corps trains are in Scotland, north of Chambersburg.

Meanwhile, Jeb Stuart is attempting to avoid Kilpatrick's cavalry at Littlestown, so he rides north from Union Mills to Hanover, 11 miles distant, arriving at 10 a.m. Here he has bad luck, running into the rear of Kilpatrick's division at Hanover, which has just ridden over from Littlestown. A spirited fight ensues with the brigades of the newly minted generals, Elon Farnsworth and George A. Custer. This fight burns up precious time. Late that afternoon Stuart successfully breaks contact, but he cannot resume his march until nightfall for fear of being attacked.

Stuart has heard that Early is in York, fifteen miles to the northeast, but his cavalry column has to ride seven miles east to Jefferson, and then turn north to

York. After seven more miles on the road from Jefferson to York, Stuart passes through New Salem, and learns that Early has left York, and is marching west through Dover. Stuart shifts his course to the northwest and travels eight more miles, thoroughly exhausting his men and animals before he reaches Dover at two o'clock the next morning.

On June 30 Meade shifts his army to the right to better cover the road from Harrisburg to Baltimore. He places John Reynolds in command of the left wing of the army, which now includes the I, III, and XI Corps. Meade realizes that the marches of the 29th were exhausting to his troops, so he has ordered shorter marches for the 30th. The I Corps trudges north some six miles beyond Emmitsburg and encamps halfway to Gettysburg at Marsh Creek, while the XI Corps marches only a mile or so from its camps near Mount St. Mary's College into Emmitsburg and bivouacs at St. Joseph's Academy. The II Corps rests in its camps near Uniontown, and the III Corps remains at Taneytown until 2:45 p.m., when Meade decides he wants Sickles's men to move closer to Reynolds, so he orders the III Corps to march five miles toward Emmitsburg from Taneytown, and Sickles's people encamp near Bridgeport on the Monocacy River.

Meade's Middleburg headquarters moves 5 miles northeast to Taneytown. The XII Corps marches 13 miles from Bruceville, through Taneytown and continues another 8 miles northeast to Littlestown. At Littlestown they receive reports of the fight with Jeb Stuart's cavalry at Hanover, so they pass through town on the road to Hanover and prepare to receive the enemy troopers. Receiving no attack, they go into camp. The V Corps, which is behind the rest of the army at Liberty, has a 16-mile march to Union Mills. The VI Corps moves to form the army's new right flank by marching to Manchester from its camps east of New Windsor, which is a rugged, 22-mile march.

At 4:30 p.m., Meade telegraphs Halleck, saying that "the information seems to place Longstreet at Chambersburg, and A. P. Hill moving between Chambersburg and York." He believes that Ewell is "in the vicinity of York and Harrisburg," so he plans to march toward Hanover and Hanover Junction.

Meade issues orders for the next day's march: I Corps to Gettysburg, II Corps to Taneytown, III Corps to Emmitsburg, V Corps to Hanover, VI Corps remains in Manchester, XI Corps to Gettysburg or within supporting distance, and XII Corps to Two Taverns. Thus Meade will continue to have the major roads to Baltimore and Washington covered.

Meade does something else—something that he will later be highly criticized for doing. But like any good commander, he has a backup plan in case the situation changes. He tasks his chief engineer, Gen. Gouverneur Warren, to perform a reconnaissance to identify a defensive position from which he can fight Lee. Meade's engineers recommend the heights of the ridge on the south of Big Pipe Creek in northern Maryland. Here he could establish a 20-mile-long "fall back" line ranging from Manchester east to Middleburg. Meade knows that this defensive line would accomplish his mission of covering Baltimore and Washington, and he knows that Lee cannot remain north indefinitely.

Meade states in the "Pipe Creek Circular" that "the time for falling back can only be developed by circumstances," and that developments may cause him "to assume the offensive from his present positions."

Meade wants to issue the circular on June 30, but Butterfield cannot get it ready in time, so, much to Meade's dissatisfaction, it is not distributed until the next day.

At dawn on the foggy morning of June 30, Buford's Union cavalry rides down the east slope of the South Mountain range to within a half mile of Fairfield, Pennsylvania, and comes under fire from Confederates of a detachment of Heth's division of Hill's III Corps, which was posted at Fairfield to protect the road from Emmitsburg to Cashtown. Buford does not want a pitched fight here, so he disengages and rides south, and then southeast, to reach Emmitsburg around 9 a.m. Here, Buford meets briefly with John Reynolds before riding north to Gettysburg.

Buford arrives at Gettysburg around noon, and establishes his headquarters at the Eagle Hotel. He sends Gamble's brigade west of Gettysburg to encamp near the Lutheran Theological Seminary on the west side of Seminary Ridge, south of the Chambersburg Pike, while Devin's men encamp north of the road. Gamble sends scouts to the west on the Chambersburg Road, and they see the soldiers of Pettigrew's brigade withdraw back toward Cashtown.

That night, Buford talks with Devin in his camp north of the turnpike, and Buford tells Devin that a battle is certain for tomorrow. Buford says he is worried that it will begin before the Federal infantry can arrive. Devin tells Buford he can hold his position for 24 hours, and Buford says, "No, you won't. They will attack you in the morning and will come 'booming,' skirmishers three deep. You will have to fight like the devil to hold your own until supports arrive. The enemy must know the importance of this position, and will strain every nerve to secure it, and if we are able to hold it, we shall do well."

John Reynolds and Oliver Howard have supper together on the 30th in Moritz Tavern, three miles north of Emmitsburg. Here they go over the day's messages and intelligence. They, too, are convinced that a fight is coming. By 11 p.m. they have not received orders from Meade, so Howard rides back to his quarters at St. Joseph's Academy in Emmitsburg. At midnight, a message from Buford specifying the location of Lee's divisions arrives, and Reynolds reads it and forwards it to Meade at Taneytown. Reynolds then lines up four kitchen chairs to use for a makeshift bed, and falls asleep for his last night on earth.

During the day of June 30, Lee and Longstreet learn that George Meade has taken command of the Army of the Potomac.

Lee says, "General Meade will commit no blunder in my front, and if I make one he will make haste to take advantage of it."

Chapter 9
THE DEVIL'S TO PAY

July 1, 1863

At Vicksburg, Grant's pioneers and engineers explode another mine under the Third Louisiana Redan at 3 p.m. on July 1. This time they do not attack, but the message is clear. Grant's army has dug 60,000 feet of trenches, constructed 89 artillery battery positions, and emplaced 220 guns, and it has been reinforced to almost 80,000 men. After almost seven weeks of siege operations, Grant has the means and the will. He is preparing to blow 13 mines under the major Confederate fortifications, followed by an all-out assault, and he makes no secret that he will do this within a few days.

ON A BREEZY PENNSYLVANIA MORNING, ROBERT E. LEE BREAKS CAMP ON July 1 at a deserted saw mill near Greenwood. The day is sun-filled, accentuated by an occasional isolated cloud that drops a hint of a shower. Lee is in a good mood as he rides east toward South Mountain on his iron gray gelding, Traveller. He calls to Longstreet, who is mounted on his favorite horse, Hero, to ride with him.

Two and one-half miles behind Lee and Longstreet, Anderson's division of Hill's corps leaves its Fayetteville camp at first light and marches east through Greenwood. McLaws's and Hood's divisions of Longstreet's corps are breaking camp at Greenwood as Anderson's men march through. Anderson then goes past the burned-out Caledonia Iron Furnace and over South Mountain and reaches Cashtown early that afternoon.

McLaws has his men ready to follow Anderson at 8 a.m. but is told to wait for Johnson's division to cut in to his front. Johnson is marching southeast from Scotland, which is five and one-quarter miles northeast of Greenwood, down the Black Gap Road to the Chambersburg Pike just east of Greenwood to rejoin Ewell's other two divisions east of South Mountain. Unfortunately, behind Johnson is the 14-mile-long train of the II Corps. McLaws is told to let those wagons pass, so he won't clear Greenwood until 4 p.m. Hood's men follow McLaws, and both divisions march into the night of July 1, halting several miles west of Gettysburg and missing the first day's fight.

Lee and Longstreet watch the slow-moving wagons pass for a few minutes, and Lee says, "Let's ride on ahead." Their staffs accompany them as they climb the western slope of South Mountain. Before they get to the crest of Cashtown Gap, they hear the long-distance rumble of cannon, and when they reach the gap, the sounds of battle are clear. A concerned Lee leaves Longstreet and rides ahead to Cashtown to see what he can learn from A. P. Hill.

At 5 a.m. Hill watches Harry Heth's division, accompanied by Maj. William "Willie" J. Pegram's Artillery Battalion of five batteries, depart Cashtown for Gettysburg. At 8 a.m. Heth is followed by Pender's division and more artillery under Maj. David G. McIntosh's command. So Hill, without any cavalry to see what is in Gettysburg, decides to send 13,500 infantry and 36 cannon on a reconnaissance mission, when one brigade would suffice. Even worse, Hill is not feeling well, so he doesn't go with them. He does, at least, send a courier to Ewell at Heidlersburg, advising that he is moving toward Gettysburg.

Heth has Pegram's artillery as the vanguard of his march, because he thinks he will see more Pennsylvania home guard troops. If so, he will fire a shell or two to scatter them quickly. It is dangerous to lead a road march with artillery, but Heth is not expecting any problems.

In Gettysburg, John Buford knows that Reynolds's I Corps will march toward him from north of Emmitsburg, so all he has to do is to keep the Confederates at bay until Reynolds arrives. At 7:30 a shot rings out from Buford's outpost at Knoxlyn Ridge. Lt. Marcellus E. Jones has borrowed a carbine and propped it in a crotch of a wooden rail fence just west of blacksmith Ephraim Wisler's brick home on the north side of the Chambersburg Road, and he fires a round at a mounted Confederate at the lead of Heth's column. The range is several hundred yards and the shot falls harmlessly, but the Battle of Gettysburg has begun.

Heth, hearing firing to his front, deploys skirmishers north and south of the road. This takes time, and time is exactly what Buford is attempting to buy. Pegram unlimbers two three-inch rifled guns of the Fredericksburg Artillery, probably Confederate ten-pounder Parrotts, in the Chambersburg Road about 175 yards west of Marsh Creek on a rise of ground in front of the Samuel Lohr farm house.

One Confederate described the house, which no longer exists, as "a brick building which looked like an old Virginia county courthouse tavern."

The Confederate artillerymen fire a few shells and watch the Yankee skirmish line disappear. Buford has just purchased an hour.

Buford's vedettes fall back to Herr Ridge, and there 550 dismounted horse soldiers fight as infantrymen, except they are using breech-loading single-shot carbines that can be fired twice as fast as muzzle-loading rifle-muskets, and they can be reloaded from a prone position—a real advantage.

At nine o'clock Heth's now deployed 2,900-man Confederate first battle line moves toward Herr Ridge. The Union cavalrymen know it's a good time to fall back across Willoughby Run to the main defensive line on McPherson Ridge. Heth then occupies Herr Ridge and has Pegram place his guns into battery along the crest. Pegram only uses 17 of his 20 guns, deciding to hold back his two 12-pounder howitzers due to their limited range of just over a thousand yards, along with one of his ordnance rifles with a bad wheel.

Willie Pegram is smooth-faced and thickly spectacled—he looks like Dustin Hoffman with glasses—but he is known for his combative nature. Shortly after 9 a.m., while the infantry is moving up, Heth orders Pegram to place 30 minutes of fire onto McPherson Ridge. Then Heth orders Gen. James J. Archer and Gen. Joseph K. Davis to "move forward and occupy the town." Heth has decided to conduct a reconnaissance in force—another move that will lead to a violation of Lee's order to avoid a general engagement.

On McPherson Ridge, Buford's men straddle the Chambersburg Pike. Thomas Devin has extended his brigade to the north. William Gamble's brigade has one battalion north of an unfinished railroad cut, a second battalion between the cut and the Chambersburg Pike, and two regiments south of the pike. The left of his line runs from the McPherson farm and orchard to the left and rear of Herbst Woods.

Dismounted cavalry interspersed with unlimbered and deployed artillery makes Buford's two-brigade front appear longer than it is, and to create this illusion Buford places two guns of Lt. John H. Calef's battery to the right of the Chambersburg Pike and a two-gun section to the left. Six hundred yards south, past Herbst Woods, is the third section. When mounted Confederates appear on Herr Ridge, Calef's section north of the road opens fire, and the first Federal cannon has been fired at Gettysburg. Calef enters in his notebook the serial number, which is 233, of the gun used to fire the first shot. Luckily, when the park is created in 1895, this historic gun is found in Ordnance Department storage and is now one of four three-inch ordinance rifle barrels at the base of the Buford statue. Tube Number 233 faces southwest and is identified with a small oval plaque.

At 4 a.m. John Reynolds receives Meade's orders to march to Gettysburg, but Reynolds sees no reason to hurry, so the head of his column doesn't leave the Marsh Creek campground until around eight o'clock. At 9:30 Reynolds's vanguard, Gen. James S. Wadsworth's division, has come about halfway to Gettysburg on the Emmitsburg Road. Reynolds has ridden ahead of the column, and a courier gallops up and hands Reynolds a note from Buford that he is "fully engaged." Reynolds rides into Gettysburg at a gallop.

Posted in the cupola of the Lutheran Theological Seminary is a Federal signalman, Lt. Aaron B. Jerome, and Buford has him peering southeast through his spyglass—towards Emmitsburg—for any sign of Reynolds's ground-pounders. The pressure from the Confederate advance has already forced Calef to start pulling his artillery back. In a matter of minutes the cavalry will have to fall back. Then, around 10 a.m., Jerome spots the vanguard of Reynolds's column advancing north on the Emmitsburg Road, well south of the John Wentz farm. Buford breathes a sight of relief, and says, "Now we can hold this place."

Reynolds arrives in Gettysburg on a lathered horse and turns west on the Chambersburg Pike. Jerome writes that Buford is with him in the cupola when Reynolds rides up and says, "What's the matter, John?" Buford says, "The devil's to pay." Reynolds says that he will bring his men up as quickly as possible, and asks Buford if he can hold out until the infantry arrives. Buford says, "I reckon I can." With that assurance, Reynolds sends two verbal messages. One goes to Howard's XI Corps. Abner Doubleday recalls the instructions were to "bring his corps forward at once and form them on Cemetery Hill as a reserve." The other message is sent by a courier, Capt. Stephen Weld, to the army commander, Gen. George Meade.

By 11:30 Captain Weld completes the 14-mile ride to Meade's headquarters at Taneytown. He recites Reynolds's message, which sounds like a precursor to Winston Churchill's "we shall fight them on the beaches" speech of 1940. Reynolds promises to fight them inch by inch, and if he is driven into the town, he will barricade the streets and hold them back as long as possible. As a former captain in the artillery, Reynolds knows his ground, and on the way into Gettysburg, he has seen the high ground south of town, and he knows he can't let it fall into Confederate hands. When Meade hears this report, he is disturbed at first and asks to hear the message again.

After listening a second time Meade exclaims, "Good! That is just like Reynolds; he will hold on to the bitter end."

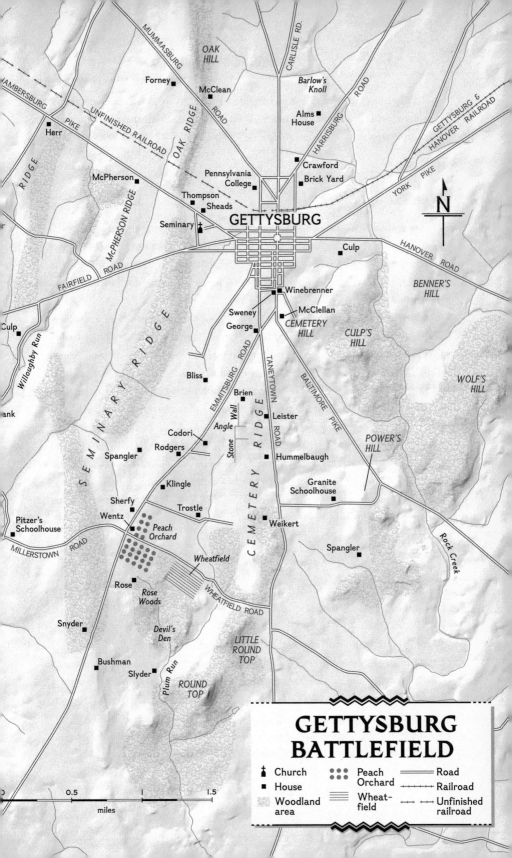

GETTYSBURG BATTLEFIELD

At Gettysburg, Reynolds leaves Buford and returns to the head of his corps, now approaching the brick home of Nicholas Codori. Wadsworth rides up and asks for instructions.

Reynolds replies, "You had better turn off here and form your division as soon as you can."

Wadsworth has the post-and-rail fence torn down on the west side of the road so that his men can travel through the fields directly to McPherson Ridge. Haversacks and blankets are tossed in piles as the men quickstep through the Codori field, across the William Bliss farm, and past the David McMillan house to Seminary Ridge.

Wadsworth, a Yale and Harvard Law School graduate from Geneseo, New York, is one of the wealthiest men in the United States. With him is the famed Iron Brigade of five Western regiments, commanded by Gen. Solomon Meredith, a six-foot-seven-inch North Carolina–born Quaker known as "Long Sol."

The men of the Iron Brigade all wear the black 1858 Hardee hat with a bright brass bugle on the front. In June 1862, their new commander was Gen. John Gibbon, who taught artillery at West Point and who wrote the book that both sides follow for artillery. Gibbon is a martinet—a Regular Army man—not loved by his troops. He trained his men hard, and he gave them a distinctive appearance by equipping them with a black felt hat, long frock coat, and initially, white leggings, that is, until some wise guy put white leggings on Gibbon's horse. At first the men were not happy with Gibbon, their tough training, or their distinctive uniform. But when they first saw battle as a unit at Brawner's Farm during the Battle of Second Manassas on August 28, 1862, they stood up to the famous Stonewall Brigade, and they realized that Gibbon had made soldiers out of them. The next month at Turner's Gap in South Mountain when McClellan saw these Westerners driving the Confederates back, he said to Hooker, "They must be made of iron." When the men went to Antietam on September 17, they were known as the Iron Brigade.

On the morning of July 1 at Gettysburg, Reynolds is not only sending his men into battle, he is going to lead them. He sits astride his big black charger in the Emmitsburg Road just south of the Codori house, and he watches as each regiment obliques left. He wants to be seen by his men as they file by. He then gallops past them across the trampled fields to the front of the column.

By 10:45, Buford's cavalry line is about to collapse. Joe Davis's Confederates are pouring a punishing fire into Devins's men on the right. On the left of the line, the Eighth New York south of Herbst Woods is being pushed hard by Archer's Confederate brigade. Reynolds's men have come just in time, and he deploys a battery of artillery as Wadworth's lead brigade, under Gen. Lysander Cutler, arrives. These men cut an impressive sight. The 14th Brooklyn—officially the 84th New York—with its red breeches and the 95th New York rush to a point south of the Chambersburg Pike near McPherson's farm. Wadsworth sends Cutler's remaining regiments across the pike, with the 147th New York just north of the railroad cut. The men soon come under fire.

Reynolds sees that Archer is working his way toward Herbst Woods, and he turns and sees Wadsworth's other brigade, the Iron Brigade, about one-half mile to the east on Seminary Ridge. He races to the Iron Brigade and turns it left, leading them west into Herbst Woods just as Archer's men emerge from the woods and pour "a murderous volley" into them.

Reynolds yells, "Forward, men, forward, for God's sake, and drive those fellows out of those woods!"

The Second Wisconsin advances another 50 yards to the edge of the woods. Then, as Reynolds looks back to see the progress of the brigade, he is hit in the back of the neck by a ball, which passes through his brain and lodges behind the left eye. He sways in the saddle and falls to the ground. John Reynolds has gone to his great reward. The time is about 11 a.m.

The first portrait statue at Gettysburg is the Reynolds statue in the National Cemetery, sculpted by John Quincy Adams Ward and dedicated in 1872. The statue is made in the European tradition, in that it has been cast using the bronze from cannon. Also, it was partially funded in 1864 by donations from the officers and men of the I Corps, with a maximum donation of $5 per officer and 50 cents per enlisted man—quite a tribute to their leader.

In the meantime, Archer is having a problem commanding his brigade. That's because immediately to the west of Herbst Woods, Willoughby Run flows at an angle southeast. So when Archer's regiments approach the creek through the woods, the ones to the left of the line reach the creek sooner than the ones to the right. The algae-covered stones under the creek water are slippery, and it takes a while for the troops to cross without losing their footing and getting their powder wet. Once across, the men move faster than the ones yet to cross, and a gap opens between the regiments from left to right. The two left regiments move up the ravine and into Herbst Woods while the two right regiments are still crossing the stream.

When the Iron Brigade advances into Herbst Woods, its left is south of the woods in a field of wheat. The Federals find that they have overlapped Archer's men, and the Yanks turn and pour a scathing fire into the right of the outflanked Alabamians and Tennesseans. Caught in a deadly crossfire, Archer's men run back the way they came.

One Confederate who can't run fast is James Archer, a Princeton man. Archer is 45 and has always been frail. The first day of July is a bad one for him, because he is on foot. So he is slow, and when he gets about 30 paces from the stream, he tries to climb over a fence, but he doesn't have much climb in him. Pvt. Patrick Maloney, of the Second Wisconsin, runs out in front of his regiment and grabs Archer by the scruff of the neck. Archer offers his sword to Capt. Charles C. Dow, who politely refuses to take it. Then, as Archer is escorted to the rear, he runs into Lt. D. B. Dailey, on General Meredith's staff, who demands the sword. So Archer is not in a good mood when, reputedly, up rides Abner Doubleday, whom Archer knew in the old army. Doubleday says, "Good morning, Archer! How are you? I am glad to see you!" Archer says, "Well, I am not glad to see you by a damn sight!"

North of the Pike, Cutler's men are attacked by Davis's brigade. Davis is the nephew of Jefferson Davis and has spent the early part of the war on his staff. This is his first command and it will be a disaster. To start, Davis only has three of his four regiments fighting, because the veterans of the 11th Mississippi are on detached duty guarding the division trains. Davis's brigade crosses Willoughby Run about one-third of a mile in front of Cutler's line without any difficulty. The men move forward, and the 55th North Carolina extends past the right flank of the 76th New York. The Tar Heels oblique right and open an enfilading fire on the Empire State regiment. The Union line dissolves, and two regiments turn and race across the extension of Seminary Ridge, called Oak Ridge. But the 147th New York doesn't get the word, because just as Lt. Col. Francis C. Miller is about to give the order to withdraw, a bullet hits him in the head, and his horse bolts and runs to the rear. The 147th is alone and exposed with Confederates coming at them from the west and the north. General Wadsworth sees what is happening and sends a staff officer to order the New Yorkers to retreat. Once alerted, the men turn tail as quickly as they can, but they suffer more than 75 percent casualties.

With Reynolds's death, command of the I Corps passes to Abner Doubleday, and at Gettysburg he experiences his best hours as a fighting general. To counter Davis's threat, Doubleday orders the Iron Brigade's Sixth Wisconsin, commanded by Lt. Col. Rufus Dawes, to advance to the Chambersburg Pike and face north. The Badgers, on reaching the fence, are joined by their comrades of the 95th New York and the 14th Brooklyn. Using the fence rails to steady their rifles, these regiments fire a volley into Davis's right flank. The two Mississippi regiments instinctively dive into the unfinished railroad cut, only 150 yards away from the Yankees' position. The cut is too deep for the Rebs to fire out of, except on the extreme left of the line, so Davis orders his men to leave the cut. But before they can obey, Dawes orders a surge forward over two fences and across a 150-yard-wide field, and all three Federal regiments charge. When they reach the cut, the Mississippians are several feet down in the trench, as helpless as sheep in a pen. Fortunately, level heads prevail on both sides, and the firing ceases. The Mississippians surrender seven officers and 225 men.

Howard arrives in Gettysburg sometime around 10:30, and he climbs to the top of the Fahnestock building in time to see the last stages of the morning fight. He may have seen the retreat of Cutler's three regiments north of the railroad cut. Around 11:30 he learns that Reynolds is dead and that he is the ranking man on the ground. He also learns from Devin that additional Confederate columns are approaching Gettysburg on the Carlisle and Harrisburg Roads. Howard rides to Cemetery Hill, where he meets Gen. Carl Schurz, his senior division commander, on the Taneytown Road. He turns command of the XI Corps over to Schurz, telling him to take two divisions north of town to block the advance of the Confederates there and to leave one division on Cemetery Hill as a reserve.

Schurz then moves down to the junction of the Taneytown and Emmitsburg Road to await the arrival of Gen. Francis C. Barlow's division, which had a slightly shorter route to travel but has been delayed by the I Corps troops and trains moving up the Emmitsburg Road. Barlow doesn't arrive until 1 p.m., and his division is sent with artillery support north through Gettysburg on Washington Street.

At 1 p.m. Howard finally sends messages to the two nearest corps commanders—Sickles and Slocum. Strangely, Howard does not request assistance. A half hour later he sends another message, this time requesting their support. At 2 p.m. he sends a message to Meade, saying only that I and XI Corps are engaged, and that he has ordered the III Corps up. He doesn't mention Reynolds's death, and he doesn't ask for help.

But Buford reports independently to Alfred Pleasonton about 3:20: "A tremendous battle has been raging since 9:30 a.m. . . . General Reynolds was killed early this morning. In my opinion, there seems to be no directing person."

Sickles receives Howard's request for help at 3:15 and sends Meade notice that he is going to march to Gettysburg, but that he will leave two brigades and a battery at Emmitsburg to cover the Federal left. However, it is too late for Sickles to help that day.

On the other hand, Henry Slocum's lead division, commanded by Gen. Alpheus S. Williams, is at Two Taverns, barely five and one-half miles away, and the men can hear the sounds of battle. A Wisconsin soldier recalls that the cannonading "sounded like one continual roll of thunder." They can even see smoke and bursting shells over the distant hills. But Slocum doesn't have orders from Meade, and he plays it by the book. Unlike Wilcox at Salem Church, he is not about to exercise any initiative, thus, justifying the aptness of his nickname, Slow Come.

Slocum does not mention Howard's dispatches in his official report, but he most certainly received the one-o'clock message well before 2 p.m. Eventually, somewhere between 3:00 and 3:30, an aide from Meade delivers a message to Slocum to advise him that Reynolds is dead, that Hancock has been sent to take Reynolds's place, and to urge Slocum to march to Gettysburg as quickly as possible. By then Slocum will also be too late to assist.

George Meade has been in Taneytown discussing the situation and the "Pipe Creek Circular" with Winfield Scott Hancock. Hancock's II Corps has marched from Uniontown and arrived at Taneytown at 11 a.m. At 11:30 a.m. Capt. Stephen M. Weld arrived at Meade's headquarters and delivered Reynolds's "barricade the streets" verbal report. Early that morning, Meade had planned to fall back to Pipe Creek, providing that Reynolds could temporarily hold Lee in check, and then bait Lee into following as he fell back.

But the day's developments have caused Meade to reconsider. Then, at 1 p.m. he hears that Reynolds has been either badly wounded or is dead. At 1:10, Meade sends Hancock to Gettysburg, along with a written order: "The major-general commanding has just been informed that General Reynolds has been killed or badly wounded. He directs that you turn over the command of your corps to General Gibbon; that you proceed to the front, and, by virtue of this order, in case of the truth of General Reynolds's death, you assume command of the corps there assembled, viz, the Eleventh, First, and Third, at Emmitsburg. If you think the ground and position there a better one to fight a battle under existing circumstances, you will so advise the general, and he will order all the troops up. You know the general's views, and General Warren, who is fully aware of them, has gone out to see General Reynolds."

Five minutes later an addendum to Hancock's order is added, ordering Hancock to leave the II Corps in Taneytown: "Reynolds has possession of Gettysburg, and the enemy are reported as falling back from the front of Gettysburg. Hold your column ready to move."

Hancock, escorted by his aides, his chief of staff, and the II Corps signal party, departs for Gettysburg in a map-loaded ambulance so that he can study the ground. He has been given the authority to decide if Gettysburg is a better place to fight than Pipe Creek. Meade knows that Howard, already in Gettysburg, is senior to Hancock, but he knows and trusts Hancock. And Meade has been given the authority by Washington to appoint whom he pleases.

Back in Gettysburg, Gen. Alexander Schimmelfennig moves his XI Corps division out the Mummasburg Road to occupy Oak Hill on Doubleday's right, but as his skirmish line emerges from the edge of town, Confederate artillery opens on it from Oak Hill. Robert Rodes's Confederates have arrived from Middletown, now called Biglerville, and reached Oak Hill first. Schurz, now commanding the XI Corps, decides to halt Schimmelfennig and deploy his men along a line that runs partially along a small stream that originates at the base of Oak Hill and flows eastward into Rock Creek, crossing the Carlisle Road less than one-half mile north of Gettysburg. But there is a problem. Because Schimmelfennig never makes contact with Doubleday's line, a half mile gap is left between I and XI Corps. Barlow's XI Corps division is sent to the right of Schimmelfennig's.

Lee has been unpleasantly surprised. Arriving at the Cashtown Inn about noon, Lee meets A. P. Hill, who has risen out of his sickbed to see what the cannonading is about. All that Hill can tell Lee is that Heth sent an earlier dispatch from outside Gettysburg, saying that he ran into Federal cavalry. Just how Hill explained to his commanding general that he had sent two divisions and two artillery battalions to Gettysburg when his orders were not to bring on a general engagement remains a mystery.

Early that morning Ewell decided to march to Cashtown, but by two different roads. At 8 a.m. Rodes marched on the road to Middletown toward Cashtown, while Early went into Heidlersburg. Early then took the much better Harrisburg Road south to within four miles of Gettysburg with plans to turn west to Mummasburg, on the way to Cashtown. At nine o'clock, Ewell, who was riding with Rodes and was just east of Middletown, received Hill's 5 a.m. message that the III Corps was moving to Gettysburg. Ewell immediately turned Rodes's men south on the Carlisle Road to Gettysburg, and sent a message to Early to continue to Gettysburg on the Harrisburg Road. Early was a short distance past Heidlers-burg when he received the order, so he stayed on the Harrisburg Road.

About eleven o'clock, Rodes's skirmishers on the Carlisle Road run into Devin's mounted vedettes at Keckler's Hill, four miles northwest of Gettysburg, where the road gradually climbs up the east face of Oak Ridge. From here Ewell and Rodes hear the sounds of battle to the south. While the road leads down the ridge to the southeast, they ride straight ahead along the ridge crest, through the woods, for two miles to Oak Hill. From here, they look across the wheat fields of the Forney farm, and they see the troops of A. P. Hill off to their right. To their front they see the right flank of Doubleday's I Corps. Rodes decides not to con-tinue his advance on the Carlisle Road, but to march his men along the crest of Oak Ridge to achieve both surprise and position. Rodes, however, has already been spotted by Devin's cavalry, which alerts Howard of the approaching threat.

Douglas Southall Freeman respects all Confederates, but he loves Virginians most of all. He describes Robert Rodes, a 35-year-old from Lynchburg, as a mar-tial figure, six feet tall, clear-eyed, thin, with a drooping tawny mustache. Free-man says Rodes "stepped from the pages of Beowulf," and is a "Norse god in Confederate gray." Rodes is an 1848 graduate of Virginia Military Institute, but unfortunately for the Confederates, this will not be one of his better days.

With a battle raging in front of him, Rodes peels off his lead brigade, com-manded by Gen. George Doles, and sends it to the level plain east of Oak Hill. Rodes's next two brigades are commanded by two men who are not the best or the brightest. The Alabama Brigade is led by Col. Edward A. O'Neal, who did not perform well at Chancellorsville, so Lee held up his promotion to brigadier general. Rodes orders O'Neal to move forward and deploy his men. The other brigade is Gen. Alfred Iverson's. Iverson is a Georgian, but he commands a bri-gade of North Carolinians. He served in the Mexican War and then became a lawyer and railroad contractor. Rodes has two other brigades, which are not yet up—Gen. Junius Daniel's and Gen. Stephen Dodson Ramseur's.

When Rodes arrives on Oak Hill, perhaps he should have kept his arrival quiet. Instead, he advances eight guns and opens fire on Doubleday's line. If Doubleday's Yankees had been unaware of Rodes's approach, they certainly aren't now. Instantly, three Federal batteries fall back from McPherson Ridge to the swale between that ridge and Seminary Ridge, front north toward Oak Hill, and return fire. The I Corps quickly realigns to meet the threat from the north.

Rodes wants Doles's brigade to keep an eye on the XI Corps units while O'Neal and Iverson attack. Daniel will follow on Iverson's right. Ramseur will remain in reserve. It's about 1:30 when O'Neal deploys his brigade on the crest and the east slope of Oak Ridge. He then makes a fatal mistake. He will neither rest his left on Doles's Georgians down on the plain, nor will he wait for Iverson to come up to his right. He deploys three regiments on the slope of Oak Hill. Unlucky for them, O'Neal's three deployed regiments jump the gun and attack before Iverson's men can get up, and these attacking regiments are masked from Iverson's view by Oak Ridge. As these three regiments advance through the McClean and Forney farms toward the Mummasburg Road, they run head-on into the newly deployed Yankee line of Gen. Henry Baxter's brigade, which is hidden behind a roadside fence and a low stone wall. To make matters worse for the Alabama boys, Schimmelfennig's division is just arriving from Gettysburg and is now on the Alabamians' left flank. In less than 30 minutes the three Alabama regiments are routed. As a result, O'Neal is soon reduced to commanding a regiment, and eventually he will end up in northern Alabama rounding up deserters.

By the time O'Neal has been repulsed, Iverson is ready to advance. He addresses the men with these inspirational words, "Give them hell!" Then he gives the order to advance, but as did O'Neal, he fails to go forward with his men. Even worse, he doesn't send out a skirmish line.

Capt. Vines E. Turner of the 23rd North Carolina, in his history of the regiment, wrote, "Unwarned, unled as a brigade, went forward Iverson's deserted band to its doom."

Iverson's North Carolinians cross the Mummasburg Road and angle to the southeast toward Sheads's Woods, where they think the enemy is located. They haven't seen Baxter's Yanks behind the stone wall along the road, and they haven't seen O'Neal's disaster off to their left front, because that fight has happened down the eastern slope of Oak Ridge.

Since O'Neal has now been repulsed, Baxter is free to turn west and confront Iverson's brigade angling southeast across John Forney's field. He has his men that were facing north shift left from the stone wall on the Mummasburg Road and crowd in with the rest of his men behind a stone wall on the eastern edge of the field. Baxter's men now are facing west, except for the 90th Pennsylvania, which refuses its right flank and extends across the Mummasburg Road, facing northwest. Realizing they haven't been seen, Baxter's men furl their colors and lie down behind the stone wall. It's now an ambush.

Iverson's North Carolinians march down into the swale in the center of For-ney's field, where they cannot see the enemy to their left front. As they move out into the open ground, their alignment is perfect, just like on a parade ground, with flags flying and men in step. The Yanks wait until the left of the gray line is within a hundred yards, and, as the Navy would say, the Confederates "cross the T" in front of the Union line. Baxter yells for his men to stand and fire. They blast a brigade volley, and the Confederates are swept off their feet. Then Cutler's redeployed Yanks appear out of Sheads's Woods to the south and fire another bri-gade volley into the North Carolinians' front as the doomed men are falling face down. One Confederate is found with five bullet holes in the top of his head. Soon the desperate, wounded men are waving anything that's white to stop the shooting. Iverson, watching from the relative safety of Oak Ridge, sees the white flags and hats and screams that his men have mutinied and are going over to the enemy. From behind the stone wall the bluecoat soldiers charge into the belea-guered Carolinians, capturing large numbers of Confederates and battle flags.

"Initiated at Seven Pines, sacrificed at Gettysburg, surrendered at Appomat-tox," Captain Vines chronicled.

Alfred Iverson sent 1,470 men forward and lost 820 of them in just minutes. He will soon be leaving the Army of Northern Virginia and heading for Georgia to command cavalry. When the brigade's pioneers bury the North Carolinians, they find 500 lying dead or terribly wounded, all in a line, just as if they were on dress parade. It's hot, and the pioneers want to get the work done fast, so they dig four shallow pits in the lowest part of the swale behind the main line of the dead. It's usually wet or damp down in the depression of this swale, so the digging is much easier and faster. The bodies lay there under a few inches of earth until 1872, when the good ladies of the South form literary societies, and through these organizations the widows and orphans sell books, sewn articles, firewood, or whatever they can to raise money to have the soldiers' remains brought home. A number of the remains are sent to Raleigh for burial, but most of them are reburied in Hollywood Cemetery in Richmond.

Lt. Walter Montgomery was lucky, because he was in the 12th North Car-olina on the far right, and he survived to come back in 1898 and walk the area with John Forney on his 150-acre farm. Thirty-five years later, Montgomery could still see the long rows of the burial trenches, the height of a man, where the grass grew greener. Forney tells Montgomery that his workers, after the sun sinks behind South Mountain, refuse to stay in the burial area, which by now is called Iverson's Pits. Of course, as happens in low, wet areas, at certain times mists rise from the earth, and these mists are said to be the ghosts of Confederate soldiers.

A short pause in the fighting occurs about 3 p.m. Rodes is not doing well. He has allowed his men to fight piecemeal—a cardinal sin. Arriving are two more of Rodes's brigades, commanded by good men. Gen. Junius Daniel, a West Pointer, class of 1851, is a big man. His North Carolinians are well drilled. Young Gen. Stephen Dodson Ramseur is arguably the best brigade commander in the army. He too, is a West Pointer, class of 1860, and he, too, has a brigade of North Carolinians.

Daniel's orders are to protect Iverson's and the division's right. He splits his command, sending two regiments, the 43rd and 53rd North Carolina, and a battalion to try to help Iverson's men withdraw from Forney's field. Daniel then moves with his other three regiments south to break the Federal line along the Chambersburg Pike. These Federals are the hardy souls of Col. Roy Stone's brigade.

Stone has been an officer in the 13th Pennsylvania Reserves, which is a regiment of skilled hunters. They proudly advertise this with a bucktail adorning their cap, so they are known as the Bucktails. Stone is unsuccessful in organizing a complete Bucktail brigade, and only one new regiment starts wearing the distinctive bucktail on its caps—the 150th Pennsylvania. Of course, the men of the original Bucktails call these newcomers the Bogus Bucktails. Stone commands the Bogus Bucktail regiment, as well as the 143rd and 149th Pennsylvania.

Stone sees Daniel's men approaching, and orders the 149th Pennsylvania into the western edge of the railroad cut—where it is shallow—about a hundred yards to the northwest of the Chambersburg Pike. Stone's men wait until the last second, and then fire into the faces of the North Carolinians and drive them back in confusion. The fire of Stone's men, however, has drawn the attention of Confederate artillery on Herr Ridge, which promptly shifts fire to them. Stone's men are enfiladed by artillery rounds entering the railroad cut from the west, so they fall back to the Chambersburg Pike. Daniel rallies his men and charges again, only to be beaten back a second time. Undaunted, Daniel reorganizes and reforms his men, and he brings his two regiments back from their mission to support Iverson. Daniel is ready to make a third charge. Ramseur is about to charge, but more important, so is Hill's III Corps from Herr Ridge.

Robert E. Lee reached Knoxlyn Ridge about 2:30 and found Dorsey Pender's division already deployed. He soon learned that Archer and Davis had attacked with their brigades and had been beaten back, with Archer captured. Heth, he was told, is resting his men, but is preparing to attack with his entire division, and Hill has told Pender to be prepared to support him. Lee doesn't know what to think as he rides forward to talk to Hill. As he does so, the sounds of firing have died down.

But shortly after three o'clock, Lee is watching from Herr Ridge when the fight renews on Oak Ridge. He sees Rodes's men attacking, and Heth rides up and asks permission to attack. One must wonder where Hill is at this time, and why Heth is reporting directly to Lee, but that is how Heth remembers the day. "No," says Lee, "I am not prepared to bring on a general engagement today—Longstreet is not up." Longstreet, of course, has been delayed behind the 14-mile-long II Corps wagon train. They then watch as Stone's men redeploy along the Chambersburg Pike and as Daniel's brigade is beaten back. But then, they hear the sounds of guns to the east, on the Harrisburg Road, and Lee knows that Early has arrived with his division. Suddenly, the situation has changed. Lee orders Heth to go forward and for Pender to come up.

Heth's Confederates—Brockenbrough's Virginia brigade on the left and Pettigrew's Tar Heels on the right—step off around 3:30 down the eastern slope of Herr Ridge toward Willoughby Run and then up the western slope of McPherson Ridge. The two Federal regiments closest to them at the apex of Herbst Woods are the 19th Indiana and the 24th Michigan. But as Col. Chapman Biddle's brigade is back in the swale between McPherson and Seminary Ridges, the left flank of the 19th Indiana is in the air. When the 26th and the 11th North Carolina cross Willoughby Run, the Yanks open fire, and the bullets zip down the ridge front and into the Carolinians. Still, the Southerners continue up the hill and into Herbst Woods. The 26th North Carolina loses ten color bearers, and the entire color guard is shot down. The commander of the 26th, Col. Henry King Burgwyn, a VMI graduate, is Robert E. Lee's youngest colonel at 21. Burgwyn asks for someone to take the colors, and Pvt. Frank Hunneycutt is given the honor. But before Hunneycutt can pick up the flag, Capt. William McCreery, Pettigrew's ordnance officer, runs up to Burgwyn to deliver a message from Pettigrew: "The 26th has covered itself with glory," Johnston Pettigrew says. McCreery then grabs the flag before Hunneycutt can get to it, and waves it. It will be his last gesture, because a bullet strikes him in the heart, and he "bathes the flag in his life's blood." Lt. George Wilcox picks up the flag and is also shot down. Then Burgwyn is killed as he picks up the flag. Hunneycutt picks the ensign up, but he is no luckier than the officers, and he is promptly shot in the head. Finally, Lt. Col. John R. Lane picks up the colors, and the North Carolinians go forward and drive the 24th Michigan to the eastern edge of Herbst Woods. Lane is shot in the neck, and the bullet exits through his jaws and mouth, but he somehow survives this terrible wound. Fourteen men have borne the flag, and all have been shot down.

The 24th Michigan is blasting away as it falls back. The 19th Indiana is being flanked by the 11th North Carolina and is falling back, and soon the left flank of the 24th is uncovered. The men of the Iron Brigade, after fighting overwhelming odds, have to fall back toward Seminary Ridge. To the right of the 24th Michigan, Col. J. M. Brockenbrough's Virginians hit the two Wisconsin regiments and Stone's 150th Pennsylvania. Brockenbrough is a Virginian and a Virginia Military Institute graduate, but his mediocre leadership in the past has caused General Lee to withhold his promotion to general officer. It looks as though the Virginians will bypass the Badger regiments and go straight for the 150th, but the Confederates have to go around a rock quarry as they climb up out of the bottom of Willoughby Run. The assault of Brockenbrough's men is weak, and the Federal line holds. But suddenly, when the 24th Michigan has to fall back, the 26th North Carolina shows up on the Badgers' flank, and the Second and Seventh Wisconsin regiments have no choice but to withdraw. In the fight, Long Sol Meredith has his horse shot from beneath him, and the dying animal falls on him. Though Meredith suffers internal injuries, he eventually recovers.

Heth is somewhat luckier. As he rides out of Willoughby Run onto the crest of McPherson Ridge, a bullet hits him in the head, about 50 yards south of the 1903 monument to John Burns. Fortunately for Heth, when he arrived in Chambersburg he had lost his hat. One of his staffers purchased a new hat for him, but it was too big. So Heth took a newspaper and inserted folded sheets in the hat band. It is that hat band that the bullet strikes, so instead of shattering Heth's skull, it only gives him a concussion that will keep him off duty for almost two weeks.

On the Federal left, Col. Chapman Biddle finds his brigade being flanked, and after blasting away at the North Carolinians until their musket barrels are too hot to handle, Biddle's Yanks fall back to Seminary Ridge. Now, up comes the 151st Pennsylvania, the School Teachers' Regiment, which is Biddle's reserve. This regiment includes the former principal and nearly a hundred teachers and graduates of the McAlisterville Academy, of which Lt. Col. George F. McFarland, the commander, was the principal. They go into the swale to the right of Biddle, just as everyone else is falling back, and exchange a few volleys with the 11th North Carolina. At 4:20 McFarland is shot through both legs, and his regiment is flanked and falls back.

Although the Federals are driven from McPherson Ridge, they are not through yet. When they fall back to Seminary Ridge, they're fortunate. They find fence rail barricades thrown up earlier by Gen. John C. Robinson's division before it had been ordered up to Oak Ridge. But that luck is short-lived, as they face an attack by Pender's fresh 6,000-man division.

The fighting is desperate and the carnage is terrible as the Confederates charge across the swale toward Seminary Ridge. Three Federal guns south of the railroad are wheeled left, and their fire enfilades the line of Gen. Alfred M. Scales's Tar Heels. The Federal infantry at the Seminary holds its fire until the Confederates are within 200 yards, and then they blast the gray line to pieces. Pender isn't going to break this line with a frontal assault, but a gap in the Union line near the Fairfield Road is exploited by Col. Abner Perrin's South Carolinians, uncovering the Federal left and allowing Perrin to roll up the Yankee position. Soon, the Federals are fleeing through the streets of Gettysburg.

Gen. Gabriel R. Paul's I Corps brigade relieves Baxter's people on Oak Ridge at a bad time, just as the XI Corps line is collapsing and exposing the I Corps flank, and only minutes before Ramseur's Tar Heels attack on Oak Ridge. However, this is the opposite of what Howard soon reports to Meade: that the I Corps precipitated the retreat back from McPherson Ridge to Seminary Ridge.

Gen. Stephen D. Ramseur, whose brigade is Rodes's reserve, has received orders to go to the support of both O'Neal and Iverson as their attacks falter and fail. Two of Ramseur's regiments go to the east slope of Oak Ridge to support O'Neal, and two go to the Forney farm to bolster Iverson. Ramseur attacks with the Second and the Fourth North Carolina regiments to the left and from the north, while his other two regiments, the 14th and the 30th North Carolina, swing around to attack from the west. They have help from the remnants of O'Neal's and Iverson's brigades, and from Daniel's people.

Over on Oak Ridge, General Paul, whose brigade is about to be routed, has been shot in the face, blinding him permanently. Most of his subordinate officers have also been wounded. Col. Charles W. Tilden of the 16th Maine sees Confederates to his right and front, but he has orders from his division commander, Gen. John C. Robinson, to hold "as long as there was a man left." Robinson knows that the XI Corps has fallen back, and he knows that Seminary Ridge is in danger of being lost. If that happens, his men on Oak Ridge are out on a limb. Robinson orders a retreat, and the 16th Maine is to be sacrificed. Undaunted, Tilden posts the 16th Maine's colors at the angle where the stone wall meets the Mummasburg Road. When Ramseur's men attack and close on them like a clam shell, the regiment has to fall back or be crushed. Tilden is captured, but he refuses to give up his sword. Instead he sticks it in the ground and breaks it. His men tear the regimental flag into bits rather than surrender it.

North of Gettysburg, in the open fields, the two XI Corps divisions have met the foe. It is not quite 4 p.m., and a Howard staff officer sees the men of

Ramseur's brigade advancing down Oak Ridge against General Paul's line. Howard's attention is directed to that movement, and he says, "Those are nothing but rail fences, sir!" Howard is focused on attacking the left flank of Doles's Georgia brigade, which is in the air near the Carlisle Road. But Howard is about to have problems of his own, because while Rodes is assailing Paul on Oak Hill, Early is arriving from Heidlersburg on the Harrisburg Road.

When Early sees the Federals to his front and Dole's Georgians out in the fields at the Carlisle Road to his right, he smells blood, and he shouts to his adjutant, "Tell Gordon, Hays, Avery, and Smith to double-quick to the front, and open the lines of infantry for the artillery to pass."

Opposing Early's division is Barlow's division of the two small brigades of Col. Leopold von Gilsa and Gen. Adelbert Ames. Barlow is 28 years old, from Brooklyn, and is the son of a Unitarian minister. He was raised in New England and graduated from Harvard in 1854 at the top of his class. But Barlow is not particularly happy with being in the XI Corps, particularly after the Chancellorsville debacle.

Barlow moves out and deploys his units, anchoring his right on Blocher's Knoll, on the south side of Rock Creek. His men drive Confederate skirmishers off the knoll, replacing them with a four-gun battery. Once von Gilsa moves up, the 153rd Pennsylvania is posted to the front right of the knoll, with skirmishers out front. The 54th New York anchors its right flank on the bridge over Rock Creek and Ames's brigade is brought up to support von Gilsa's left.

This position is a good one to oppose a force approaching on the Carlisle Road, which is what Barlow sees as he looks to the northwest toward Doles's Georgians. But the ground drops off very quickly down the northeast front of the knoll into the woods bordering Rock Creek. Thus Early's troops approaching along the Harrisburg Road from the northeast will have both cover and concealment—that is, they will be protected from fire, and they can't be seen. The man who will ultimately pay for Barlow's limited vision is the unfortunate 19-year-old Capt. Bayard Wilkeson, commanding the artillery on the knoll.

Early takes advantage of the element of surprise and of the favorable terrain to his front. Lt. Col. Hilary P. Jones places 12 guns of his artillery battalion to the left of the Harrisburg Road and opens fire at a range of only 1,200 yards. Early orders the two Georgia brigades of Doles and Gen. John B. Gordon to attack Barlow's men at the knoll. Gordon's men wade across Rock Creek to strike Barlow from the northeast, and Doles's men, who have their left anchored on Gordon's right, attack at an angle from the northwest across the fields west of the creek. Barlow is flanked on both his right and left, and his line collapses.

Von Gilsa's men abandon the defense and set a track record running into Gettysburg. Ames's reserve—the 17th Connecticut and the 75th Ohio—fix bayonets and race north to the knoll in a heroic attempt to halt the rout. The 17th Connecticut goes hand to hand with Gordon's Georgians in a losing fight. Wilkeson has already fallen at his guns, his leg all but severed by an exploding shell. He ties a tourniquet with his handkerchief and, with his pocket knife, amputates his own leg. He dies that night from the shock and loss of blood. His father, Samuel Wilkeson, a newspaper correspondent for the *New York Times,* is at Meade's headquarters and will forever hold Meade responsible for his son's death.

Three days later he writes in the Times, *lamenting "the dead body of an eldest born son, crushed by a shell in a position where a battery should never have been sent."*

General Schurz has discovered that being a corps commander is much different than commanding a division. He sees that Barlow is being overrun, and he sends Col. Wladimir Krzyzanowski's brigade into the fight. Krzyzanowski's men hope to take Doles's brigade in its right flank, but Gordon's Georgians hit them in their right flank instead, and the remainder of the Federal line collapses.

Early turns the pursuit of his vanquished enemy over to Col. Isaac E. Avery's North Carolina brigade and Gen. Harry T. Hays's brigade of Louisiana Tigers. These brigades chase the XI Corps into Gettysburg. Schurz needs help to slow the pursuit, so he sends a request for assistance to his reserve division, Gen. Adolph von Steinwehr's, on Cemetery Hill. Von Steinwehr sends the brigade of Col. Charles R. Coster, accompanied by the four Napoleons of Capt. Lewis Heckman's Ohio Battery, down the slope and into the town. Coster fights his way through the mass of retreating men and leaves his 73rd Pennsylvania at the town square. He then directs the rest of his men up to John Kuhn's brickyard on the north edge of town, where he forms a line on the east side of Stratton Street. While Heckman's artillery can register on the Harrisburg Road, the road is filled with fleeing Federals, so the artillerymen can't fire. Behind the Federals, coming like bats out of hell, are Avery's and Hays's screeching Confederates.

Coster seeks to block the rout with his German immigrant regiment of the 27th Pennsylvania on his left, in a slight depression near today's Stratton Street. He places the 154th New York in the center of the line and the 134th New York on the right. The line, with Heckman's artillery, looks more formidable than it is, and soon the two Confederate brigades overlap both flanks of Coster's line. Again the Federals find that survival is an individual responsibility, and Coster's men retreat in disorder. Heckman, although his battery has fired 113 rounds of canister, cannot stop the gray lines. He limbers up late, and loses two guns as a result. Coster loses 563 out of his 992 soldiers in the brickyard.

Lee has managed, despite A. P. Hill's disobedience of his orders, to all but destroy two Federal corps. The soldiers of the I Corps and XI Corps have been chewed up badly, and they flee through the town. Most do not stop until they reach East Cemetery Hill. Howard is at the cemetery, and with the ghost of Chancellorsville haunting him, he now has the phantom of another disaster to deal with. He first attempts to rid himself of the demon at five o'clock when he sends a very misleading message to Meade.

> Howard reports that "The I Corps fell back, when outflanked on its left, to a stronger position, when the XI Corps was ordered back, also to a stronger position."

Ewell rides from Oak Ridge over to the fields north of Gettysburg behind his victorious troops as they are pursuing the XI Corps into town. He sees Gordon, and Gordon urges Ewell to press forward and capture Cemetery Hill. Then Maj. Henry Kyd Douglas of Johnson's staff rides up to report that Johnson is just a few miles outside of town on the Chambersburg Pike. Gordon is elated, saying his brigade could join with Johnson's division to take the hill. Ewell has no comment, and rides into Gettysburg. Entering the town, Ewell is joined by a staffer, Capt. James Power Smith, who says he was just with Lee on Seminary Ridge. Soon Lee's aide, Maj. Walter H. Taylor, rides up to tell Ewell that Lee wishes for him to attack the hill if he "could do so to advantage."

> Lee recalled in his report: "General Ewell was . . . instructed to carried the hill occupied by the enemy, if he found it practicable, but to avoid a general engagement until the arrival of the other divisions of the army, which were ordered to hasten forward. He decided to wait for Johnson's division, which had marched from Carlisle by the road west of the mountains to guard the trains of his corps, and consequently did not reach Gettysburg until a late hour."

Ewell has been given a discretionary order from Lee, which was Lee's habit of command. Jackson's habit, whom Ewell is accustomed to serving under, was to give specific orders. Ewell, new to corps command, needs specificity, and he is confused. Is he to attack the hill, or is he to avoid a general engagement? As a result, he does nothing. Soon, Isaac Trimble, who is serving as a supernumerary on Ewell's staff, tells Ewell that Culp's Hill needs to be taken. Ewell says nothing. When Trimble repeats his plea, Ewell replies, "When I need advice from a junior officer, I generally ask for it." From one general officer to another, that is the ultimate insult.

Up on Cemetery Hill it is a different story, because decisions are being made. Hancock arrives around 4:30. He rode part of the way in an ambulance with his maps spread out and his horse tied alongside. But that was too slow, and before he arrived at Horner's Mills—modern Barlow—he mounted and rode into Gettysburg.

Accompanied by his staff, Hancock arrives at Cemetery Hill, and he is a dominating presence with his fresh white shirt, his booming voice, and his self-confidence. Howard has been vainly striving to rally the troops, and Hancock tells Howard that he has been instructed by Meade to take command on the field. Howard, although only 32 years old, is a senior major general, and does not graciously acquiesce to the junior Hancock. Not wanting to humiliate Howard and cause a scene between two general officers in front of God and everybody, Hancock says, "I think this is the strongest position by nature upon which to fight a battle that I ever saw. What do you think?" They are both seeking a way out of a difficult situation, and Howard says, "Yes, I agree." The decision is made. They are going to hold at Cemetery Hill.

Ewell's and Hancock's methods of command couldn't be more different. Hancock is not a vacillating old man. Ewell is only seven years older than Hancock, but Ewell is evidently far beyond his physical peak. Hancock then makes probably the most important order of the day. He sees nobody on Culp's Hill, 800 yards to the east, and he says to Doubleday, "General Doubleday, I want you to send Wadsworth and the Iron Brigade over to that hill." Doubleday replies, "But, General, those men are tired and out of ammunition." Hancock says, sharply, and probably with an oral oil painting of obscenity, "General, I want you to understand that I am in command here. Send the Iron Brigade to that hill!" Granted, the Iron Brigade is badly beaten up, but they obediently march over to Culp's Hill. If the Federals are positioned there, that means the Confederates will have to fight for it. That key decision is often overlooked.

Hancock sends a verbal message to Meade, via an aide, apprising Meade of the situation and saying that "he would hold the ground until dark." Then, at

5:25 p.m. Hancock sends a written message to Meade: "When I arrived here an hour since, I found that our troops had given up the front of Gettysburg and the town. We have now taken up a position in the cemetery, and cannot well be taken . . . I think we will be all right until night . . . the ground appears not unfavorable with good troops."

Hancock then adds a bombshell comment: "Howard says that Doubleday's command gave way." Howard decides to rid himself of his phantom at Doubleday's expense. His ambition overrules his honor.

George Meade does not have much use for Doubleday as a combat commander, an opinion that dates back to South Mountain. Based on Howard's report and remarks to Hancock, that night Meade orders John Sedgwick to send Gen. John Newton "to the front with all possible dispatch." Newton, a junior engineer general officer, will take command of Doubleday's infantry corps.

At 6 p.m. Meade sends a message to Hancock and Doubleday, saying, "It seems to me we have so concentrated that a battle at Gettysburg is now forced on us, and that, if we get up all our people, and attack with our whole force tomorrow, we ought to defeat the force the enemy has."

Meade, still in Taneytown, has received the reports from Gettysburg and has decided to concentrate his forces to fight there. He starts sending orders at 6 p.m. He rushes off a messenger to Hancock at Gettysburg to say that the battle will be there. He sends a message to Frederick, Maryland, to be telegraphed to Halleck in Washington that the I and XI Corps have been fighting all day at Gettysburg and that he is shifting the other corps to that town. His orders go out at 7 p.m. to Sykes's V Corps, which is en route from Union Mills to Hanover, to march to Gettysburg as fast as possible. At 7:30 Meade sends orders to move up the two III Corps brigades and the artillery battery at Emmitsburg. At the same time he dashes off a "change-up" message to Sedgwick's VI Corps, which he ordered at 4:30 to move from Manchester to Taneytown. He now wants Sedgwick to take the Baltimore Pike to Gettysburg—a 35-mile march from Manchester which will require some backtracking for Sedgwick's lead elements. The II Corps has been sent from Taneytown toward Gettysburg, but just before sundown Hancock ordered it to halt three miles from Gettysburg on the Taneytown Road, where the men took a position astride the road, just in case they had to forestall a Confederate turning movement in that direction.

Hancock returns to Taneytown, where he meets with Meade just before 10 p.m. and explains the situation. Meade then departs for Gettysburg with two aides, an orderly, and his chief of artillery, Gen. Henry Hunt. In less than an hour, Meade reaches the II Corps, in camp near Big Round Top on the Taney-town Road, and he stops to talk with John Gibbon and tell him to march into Gettysburg at first light. Meade then rides to Cemetery Hill, arriving at the gate-house about midnight.

Meade meets with Slocum, Howard, and Sickles, as well as Chief Engineer Gouverneur K. Warren, and then walks across the road to survey East Ceme-tery Hill. He then rides with Howard, Hunt, an aide, and an engineer captain to sketch the ground and to examine the line of Cemetery Ridge as far south as Little Round Top. Finally, he rides to Culp's Hill and Rock Creek. Meade has quickly familiarized himself with his position in the darkness of the morning hours of July 2.

On the Confederate side, Lee rides ahead from Herr Ridge and arrives at Seminary Ridge around 4:30. He twice sends Major Taylor to find General Ewell, and he awaits the attack on Cemetery Hill. About this time Anderson's division arrives on Knoxlyn Ridge. Why Lee doesn't bring Anderson to the front is unknown. While Lee is waiting for Ewell to resume the attack, Longstreet rides up, and he and Lee discuss the situation. Lee points out the terrain to the front and the activity on Cemetery Hill, and tells Longstreet that he has told Ewell to continue the attack.

Longstreet is already irritated after his two divisions have been held up by Johnson's trains, and he says that attacking Meade on the high ground to the front is not what should be done. Longstreet suggests that they should maneu-ver between the enemy and Washington, and force Meade to attack on ground of Lee's choosing. Lee has seen much on July 1 that Longstreet has not, and he dis-agrees, saying, "If the enemy is there tomorrow, we must attack him." Longstreet replies, "If he is there, it will be because he is anxious that we should attack him; a good reason, in my judgment, for not doing so." At least, that is how Longstreet remembers the conversation years later.

That night Lee talks with Ewell and Early to discuss an attack the next morn-ing by the II Corps on the Union right. Early, speaking first, feels that it would be costly to do so, and Ewell agrees with his subordinate. Then Lee suggests moving the II Corps around to the right, but Ewell and Early don't like that suggestion either. Lee, of course, is disappointed that a corps and division commander are so negative. He decides to go back to Seminary Ridge and again talk with Longstreet.

Longstreet advises Lee that he thinks the army should maneuver around the Federal left, get between Meade and Washington, and force Meade to attack on ground of Lee's choice. This sounds like a great plan, but how is Lee to accomplish this without an adequate cavalry screen? Still, after considering this idea, Lee sends for Ewell. He again says that he wants to move the II Corps around to the Confederate right.

> *Major G. Campbell Brown, Ewell's step-son and II Corps staffer, recalled that he carried a message from Lee to Ewell, saying, "I have not decided to fight here and may probably draw off by my right flank . . . so as to get between the enemy and Washington and Baltimore—and force them to attack us in position."*

Ewell rides to Lee and tells his superior that he has sent Johnson's division to occupy Culp's Hill on the Union right, which will render Cemetery Hill untenable for Meade's men. Finally, thinks Lee, someone is using some initiative. But this information is not exactly true—Johnson has not taken Culp's Hill. He has only been sent to Culp's Hill.

Lee has fought a major engagement and still the eyes of his army—Stuart and his cavalry—are 30 miles north at Carlisle. Stuart has ridden northwest from Dover all day looking for Ewell, and instead has found Pennsylvania militia at Carlisle. When the militia commander at Carlisle defiantly refuses to surrender the town, Stuart is furious, so he burns a lumber yard, a gas works, and the military barracks at Carlisle, which is now the U.S. Army War College. He then begins to shell the town with his horse artillery, doing little damage. By midnight, couriers arrive with Lee's orders to come to Gettysburg immediately, and Stuart heads south from Carlisle for Gettysburg. But he will arrive too late to provide Lee with the information needed to decide on a course of action.

> *The butcher's bill for July 1 is a terrible one. The Federals committed 23,500 men to combat and suffered almost 9,000 casualties. The Confederates sent 28,300 into battle and, at the end of the day, just over 6,000 were casualties.*
>
> *The day ends in what seems to be a Confederate victory. But even though John Reynolds did not live to fulfill his promise, it was nevertheless kept. The Federals fought inch by inch, falling back through the town, and at day's end they hold the high ground.*

Chapter 10
THE BEST
THREE HOURS' FIGHTING

July 2, 1863
After a day of savage fighting on July 1, the ensuing night is a
long one for the soldiers and leaders of both sides at Gettysburg.
A British observer, Lt. Col. James L. Fremantle, wrote in his
diary that Longstreet "spoke of the enemy's position as being 'very
formidable.' " Longstreet said that Meade's men "would doubtless
entrench themselves strongly during the night." Capt. William J.
Seymour wrote, "All night long the Federals were heard chopping
away and working like beavers, and when day dawned, the ridge
was found to be crowned with strongly built fortifications, and
bristling with a most formidable array of cannon."

REPORTER WHITELAW REID OF THE *CINCINNATI GAZETTE* OBSERVES
Meade the morning of July 2, describing him as "the spare and somewhat
stooped form of the commanding general. He is not cheered, indeed, is scarcely
recognized. He is an approved corps general, but he has not yet vindicated his
right to command the Army of the Potomac."

After examining his army's position, Meade establishes his headquarters at
the small white farmhouse of the Widow Lydia Leister on the western side of the
Taneytown Road and on the eastern slope of Cemetery Ridge. While making
his examination, Meade has ordered Capt. W. W. Paine, an engineering officer,
to sketch the ground. Meade tells Paine where to place the various corps on the
map, and he wants copies of this map provided to all the commanders. This takes
time. Meade also tells his chief artillerist, Henry Hunt, to ride the lines again in
daylight. He wants optimal placement of his artillery.

Cemetery Hill is still occupied by the XI Corps and, at 503 feet above sea
level, is 80 feet higher than the town's center. Von Steinwehr's division is stationed

on the left of Cemetery Hill, Schurz's division is in the center, and Barlow's division, now commanded by Adelbert Ames because of Barlow's wounding, is on the right.

On von Steinwehr's left, and extending southward from Ziegler's Grove at the northern end of Cemetery Ridge, are the remnants of Robinson's and Doubleday's beaten-up divisions. Doubleday has been demoted back to division commander because of Howard's criticism, and Meade has placed John Newton in command of the I Corps. On Ames's right and extending over to the crest of Culp's Hill, which is 627 feet above sea level, is Wadsworth's I Corps division. Slocum's XII Corps has been split, with Gen. Alpheus S. Williams's division encamped on the Baltimore Pike, just south of where Rock Creek crosses the road, and Gen. John W. Geary's division on the southern part of Cemetery Ridge, stretched south from the I Corps all the way down to the 650-foot-high Little Round Top, which is perched 150 feet above Plum Run skirting its western base. Sickles's III Corps has encamped on the Abraham Trostle farm and at Sherfy's Peach Orchard.

The men of Meade's other corps are burning up what's left of their shoe leather, or in some cases the bottoms of their bare feet, to get to the battlefield. Often historians forget that Union soldiers were as likely as Confederate ones to be barefooted, as they were sometimes the victims of unscrupulous contractors. Many of their Army-issue shoes were little more than cardboard shadows of shoes, which, of course, wore out very quickly. So there are lots of barefoot Yankees.

Meade knows that he must protect the road network which brought him to Gettysburg, and he immediately looks to build up his right flank. Around 5 a.m. he orders Geary's division back from the Little Round Top area to the right of Wadsworth on Culp's Hill. This extends the Union right flank southeast toward the Baltimore Pike. Williams's division forms on Geary's right, extending southeastward and anchoring its right on Rock Creek.

Meade is near the Widow Leister house when Gibbon reports to him with the II Corps around 6:30 a.m. Meade, possibly because Slocum has mentioned the night before that the right flank will soon be quite strong, considers launching an offensive from his right. When Gibbon arrives, Meade moves the II Corps to a position behind the Union right, near the Granite Schoolhouse Lane. This puts that corps in perfect position to serve as a reserve force for an offensive operation, while leaving room for the arrival of the V Corps and, eventually, the VI Corps.

Now that Meade has strengthened his right, he looks briefly to his left. At seven o'clock he orders Sickles's III Corps to move into Geary's former position.

At 8 a.m., as Meade had hoped, the two lead divisions of Sykes's V Corps arrive on the Union right after a night march from Hanover.

At 9:30, George Meade orders Slocum and Warren to examine the ground fronting the Union right, and to give him "an opinion as to the practicability of attacking the enemy." Meade believes that Slocum's XII Corps, supported by Sykes's V Corps, could attack the Confederate left flank. At 10:30 Slocum advises Meade that he does not think an attack would be successful. So Meade prepares to go on the defensive, but he is still focusing on his right flank.

When Meade abandons his thoughts of an offensive operation, he has the II Corps move from its reserve position to relieve Robinson's and Doubleday's I Corps divisions on the Union left and extend southward on Cemetery Ridge. Hancock has returned to Gettysburg around 7 a.m. to resume command of the II Corps. Being relieved by the II Corps, Robinson and Doubleday move the remnants of their battered I Corps divisions to the rear of Cemetery Hill, in support of the XI Corps. The V Corps, now not needed for an attack, goes into a reserve position at the crossing of Rock Creek and the Baltimore Pike, and will be joined by its third division—commanded by Gen. Samuel W. Crawford—when that division arrives at noon.

From dawn until midmorning on July 2, deployments have changed drastically on the Union side. The Army of the Potomac feels a sense of urgency now that the battle has begun, and the corps commanders are responding as quickly as human, horse, and mule flesh—and the jammed roads—will allow. The II Corps has arrived, two divisions of the V Corps have arrived, and Sickles's two III Corps brigades have arrived. By noon, Meade has six of his seven corps on the field, or 65,000 men. Sedgwick, beginning his march 35 miles away at Manchester, is coming to Gettysburg with just under 14,000 men. Meade has the high ground and has shifted his troops into an organized defensive position.

Lee has established his headquarters on the south side of the Chambersburg Pike, on the western slope of Seminary Ridge. His tents are pitched across the road from a stone house owned by, of all people, Thaddeus Stevens. Renting the house is a widow, Mary Long Sell Thompson. The Widow Thompson is an abolitionist and a friend of Stevens.

In the first minutes of July 2, Ewell asks Johnson for a status report on Culp's Hill. Ewell gets a shock. Johnson has done nothing about Culp's Hill—absolutely nothing. A reconnaissance party is quickly sent up the rocky, wooded slope in the darkness. The party soon comes under fire from I Corps troops, who, per Hancock's orders, occupy the hill and are working away like beavers up there.

On the way back from Culp's Hill, Johnson's reconnaissance party captures a courier with a message from Sykes to Slocum, advising that two V Corps divisions will soon arrive from the direction of Hanover. By the time Lee learns that Culp's Hill is not in his possession and that Meade's right is being reinforced, it is dawn. Lee's options are disappearing, and all of his corps commanders seem to be working against him. Hill disobeyed orders, Ewell failed to use initiative, Longstreet has been uncooperative, and Stuart is nowhere to be found.

Lee has to come up with another plan. Since the Union right is so strong, he decides to have Longstreet strike the Union left flank, while Ewell creates a feint on the right to keep the Federals from shifting troops to the left.

Of course, Lee now needs to know what is on the Union left. Capt. Samuel R. Johnston, an engineer on Lee's staff, and Maj. John J. Clarke, one of Longstreet's engineers, are sent "to reconnoiter the enemy's left and return as soon as possible."

Lee sends Maj. Charles Venable over to see Ewell on the Confederate left to advise him to await the sound of Longstreet's guns on the Confederate right before he has Johnson's division create a feint on the Confederate left. Around 5 a.m. Longstreet arrives at Seminary Ridge, but he is not prepared to take the offensive. McLaws's division was delayed by Johnson's division and Ewell's trains at Greenwood. From there McLaws's division marched 13 miles before bivouacking on the east side of Marsh Creek. Hood followed McLaws and went into camp west of Marsh Creek at 1 a.m. Pickett's division is just now leaving Chambersburg for Gettysburg.

On the morning of July 2, after only two hours of sleep, Hood's people began to march at 3 a.m., and they won't arrive at Herr Ridge until 7:30. McLaws's men leave Marsh Creek at five o'clock and will turn south on Herr Ridge. They will not arrive at the junction of Herr Ridge and Old Mill Road until 8:30. Col. E. Porter Alexander's artillery battalion of 24 guns will not arrive at Herr Ridge until 9 a.m. So Longstreet's I Corps, minus Pickett's division, will not reach the battlefield until midmorning.

There has long been a debate about whether or not Lee issued a sunrise-attack order. That belief is a gross error because Lee did not know the conditions on either enemy flank before sunrise. Whether there was such an order or not, however, Longstreet's divisions were not on the battlefield at sunrise. The duty of a subordinate is to be prepared to respond to the commander's intent, and even though a battle had been fought the day before and would certainly be renewed on this day, Longstreet did not have his men available. Therefore, he limited Lee's options. The lack of urgency on the part of Lee's senior corps commander cannot be excused.

Lee has an army of about 75,000 men in Pennsylvania, but at daybreak, without Longstreet, he has only about 54,000 to face more than 65,000 Federals. Granted, Meade is still building toward that strength until noon, but his tight formation, his interior lines, and his superior defensive position give him an excellent chance to succeed at any point that Lee might try to test him. In contrast to Lee's subordinates, Meade's subordinates have performed very well.

Lee now has to consider his options. He, Longstreet, Hood, Hill, and Heth convene under the trees near the Lutheran Theological Seminary building on the west side of Seminary Ridge. Such a gathering of general officers soon draws the inevitable strap hangers—staff officers, aides, and curious onlookers. This impromptu conference should have adjourned into one of the tents or to the Widow Thompson's house for privacy, because, aside from security considerations, an audience can easily cause the conferees to try to upstage one another. That's just what happens.

The British colonel, Fremantle, unceremoniously climbs a tree on Seminary Ridge to view the conference. He later wrote: "Just below us were seated Generals Lee, Hill, Longstreet, and Hood, in consultation—the two latter assisting their deliberations by the truly American custom of whittling sticks. General Heth was also present; he was wounded in the head yesterday, and although not allowed to command his brigade [division], he insists upon coming to the field."

While Lee waits for his engineer officers to return from their reconnaissance of the Union left, Longstreet continues to advocate a turning movement to search for good defensive ground and force Meade to attack. He, however, has no way of knowing that George Meade has a backup plan—the "Pipe Creek Circular"—that could be used to counter such a move. Lee has already heard Longstreet's plan and has ruled it out. Lee knows that Meade is not Hooker. Meade will not remain static while Lee maneuvers around his flank. Longstreet is posturing, because he, like Lee, has to know that any such move is ridiculous to consider without a cavalry screen.

Sometime after 7:30 a.m. John Bell Hood announces that his division of 7,300 soldiers has reached Herr Ridge, and Lee says, "The enemy is there, and if we do not whip him, he will whip us." Longstreet says nothing, but soon takes Hood aside and says to him, "The general is a little nervous this morning; he wishes me to attack; I do not wish to do so without Pickett. I never like to go into battle with one boot off." Hood notices Lee, and later recalled that Lee "seemed full of hope, yet at times, buried in deep thought."

Finally, at 8 a.m., Captain Johnston and Major Clarke return from their reconnaissance. Johnston wrote in 1892 that they rode south behind Seminary Ridge, crossed Willoughby Run, and turned east and rode toward the Peach Orchard, then turned south on Seminary Ridge, crossed the Emmitsburg Road, and "got up on the slopes of Round Top." On Round Top, Johnston wrote, "I had a commanding view." He recalled he rode farther, "along the base of Round Top," and that they reported to Lee that the only Yankees they saw were three or four cavalrymen on the Emmitsburg Road, who they allowed to pass before recrossing the road.

The strange thing about Captain Johnston's report is that Dan Sickles has two divisions at the Peach Orchard and Trostle farm. True, they could have been hidden on the eastern side of the ridge. Plus, Geary placed two regiments of his XII Corps division on or near Little Round Top, but these regiments could have already departed after getting a 5 a.m. order to go to Culp's Hill. John Buford's cavalry is also patrolling the area, and maybe Johnston and Clarke were just incredibly lucky that they didn't run into more than three or four Federal horse soldiers. In any case, the intelligence provided to Lee is faulty.

McLaws arrives at Lee's headquarters around 8:30 and says his 7,100 men are at Herr Ridge. Lee, bypassing Longstreet, takes McLaws by the arm and points on a map exactly where he wants McLaws to position his division astride the Emmitsburg Road, south of the Peach Orchard, so that his men can roll up the enemy's left flank. From what he can see and has been told by Johnston, Lee believes that Meade's left doesn't extend much farther south on Cemetery Ridge than the area of today's Pennsylvania Monument. He says to McLaws, "I wish you to get there if possible without being seen by the enemy. Can you do it?" McLaws is agreeable, but says he would like to go out with Captain Johnston and see the ground first. Longstreet, upset over Lee's giving orders directly to one of the I Corps division commanders, wades into the discussion and points at the map. He instructs McLaws to place his division parallel to the Emmitsburg Road, not perpendicular to it.

Lee quickly overrules Longstreet, saying to McLaws: "No, I wish you to place your division just so." Longstreet, trying to save face—after all, there is an audience—then tells McLaws that he cannot leave his division to go with Johnston. Lee sees the situation is getting out of hand, so he tells McLaws to stay with his division, but that he can take Johnston along as a guide. The unlucky captain finds himself on the hot seat because he went cross-country on his reconnaissance, and he doesn't know the roads any better than McLaws does.

Lee gives one more command. He tells Hill that he wants Anderson's fresh division to support the attack by hitting the center of the Federal line, to the left of Longstreet's two divisions. Anderson will have to get into position along Seminary Ridge, south of the Lutheran Theological Seminary. Lee has now detached Anderson's division from the III Corps, but he has not attached it to the I Corps. So, to whom does Anderson report—Hill or Longstreet? Lee now turns to Longstreet and says, "I think you had better move on." He does, however, give Longstreet permission to delay the beginning of his march pending the arrival of Law's brigade from New Guilford, seven miles southeast of Chambersburg.

By 9 a.m. Longstreet's artillery has arrived, and he orders Colonel Alexander to take charge of the artillery, replacing Col. James B. Walton. Alexander reports at 10 a.m., and Longstreet gives him instructions in front of Lee. First, Alexander is to conduct a reconnaissance. Second, he is to take the artillery south, being careful to stay out of view of a signal station that can be seen on Little Round Top.

Lee believes everything is now in motion for his attack, and he rides over to talk with Ewell, arriving at Ewell's headquarters somewhere around 10:45. But Ewell is out inspecting his lines.

Lee doesn't want to wait for Ewell to return, so he tells General Trimble at Ewell's headquarters that he would like "to go to some point which would command a view of the country and of the enemy's position." Trimble and Lee ride to the nearby Almshouse and ascend to the cupola to view the area. Lee says, "The enemy have the advantage of us in a shorter and inside line, and we are too much extended. We did not or we could not pursue our advantage of yesterday, and now the enemy are in good position."

Lee and Trimble ride back to Ewell's headquarters, and Ewell is now there. After some discussion, they agree that Ewell will conduct a feint when he hears the sounds of Longstreet's guns and, if the opportunity presents itself, he will capture one of the pieces of high ground in his front. Lee then rides back and finds Longstreet on Herr Ridge sometime before noon, still waiting for Law's five Alabama regiments, which had been left behind at New Guilford to guard the road from Emmitsburg and Waynesboro to Greenwood. Law's Alabamians arrive shortly, and soon afterward, Longstreet begins his march. Lee returns to his headquarters on the Chambersburg Pike.

The errant Jeb Stuart finally reports to Lee. According to Colonel Alexander, Lee remarks, "Well, General, you are here at last." Lee then orders Stuart's cavalry to support Ewell on the Confederate left.

Two and one-quarter miles south of this drama, Union Gen. Dan Sickles at the Trostle farm has orders to assume the former position of Geary's XII Corps division, but Geary has already departed for the Union right at first light, and Sickles is unsure of where he should go. He inspects the ground and is unhappy with it. Cemetery Ridge, south of Hancock's II Corps position, rapidly descends and becomes more of a depression than a ridge until it ascends the northern slope of Little Round Top. Sickles has been assigned almost a three-quarter-mile-long depression, with the valley of Plum Run about 330 yards to his front. Another ridge rises on the western side of Plum Run, about 1,000 yards to Sickles's front, with the Emmitsburg Road running along its crest. This ridge ranges from 8 to 16 feet higher than Sickles's assigned line.

Around 8:30 George Meade sends his son and aide, Capt. George Meade, to see that all is in order on the left flank. Meade rides to Sickles's headquarters and learns from Capt. George E. Randolph, the III Corps chief of artillery, that Sickles is still asleep. Randolph goes into Sickles's tent and returns to tell young Meade that Sickles has not deployed the III Corps because he doesn't know where it should go. Captain Meade beats a hasty path to the Leister house to tell dad. By now the senior Meade is engrossed in considering an attack on the Federal right, and he snaps at his son, repeating to him the same orders to ensure that Sickles is in position.

Captain Meade rides back to Sickles's tent and gives the general the message. Sickles wisely decides it's time to skip the middle man and go talk with the boss. During this time, around 10:30, John Buford's two brigades of cavalry, which are guarding the Federal left flank south of Sickles's position, are ordered to pick up the trains at Taneytown and take them to Westminster. When Buford departs, through confusion in the orders, his men are not replaced. The Union left flank is left unguarded.

Around 11 a.m. Sickles rides to the Leister house to talk to Meade, but Meade is now preoccupied with his right flank. The conversation between Sickles and Meade goes nowhere, as Meade tells Sickles to occupy Geary's former position and Sickles insists that Geary had no position. Then Sickles, a lawyer, manages to get two concessions from his chief. First, he asks if he can post the III Corps as he sees fit, and Meade says, "Certainly, within the general limits I have given you." Second, Sickles asks for Gen. Henry Hunt to come look at the ground, and Meade agrees. Sickles, Hunt, and two captains ride west to the crest of Cemetery Ridge and then south toward the Peach Orchard, which is the high ground to Sickles's front.

Sickles shows Hunt the ridgeline along the Emmitsburg Road, proposing that he anchor his right just south of the Codori farm, in front of the II Corps line. From there, his line will follow the road past the Peach Orchard, and then angle back sharply to follow the high ground west of Plum Run all the way to Devil's Den. Hunt notes several problems. Sickles's right would be 500 yards in front of Hancock's line. Hunt is also concerned about what might be lying in wait in Pitzer's Woods along Seminary Ridge to the front. Sickles agrees to check the woods out. Hunt also notes that, while he likes the high ground at the Peach Orchard, Sickles's proposed line is too long for a single corps.

Suddenly, a skirmish erupts at the Bliss farm and artillery on the northern end of Cemetery Ridge opens fire in support. Hunt feels he is needed at the gun line and starts to leave, prompting Sickles to ask if he can occupy the proposed line. Hunt replies, "Not on my authority. I will report to General Meade for instructions." On his way to his guns, Hunt stops by the Widow Leister's house and advises Meade that Sickles's proposed line, "taken by itself," is a very good line. However, he suggests that Meade go see for himself.

About noon, Sickles has 100 men of Col. Hiram Berdan's First U.S. Sharp-shooter Regiment and the Third Maine probe Pitzer's Woods. Berdan's men are distinctive in their green uniforms, armed with breech-loading Sharp's rifles. They reach Seminary Ridge just south of the Philip Snyder farm and move north, with Berdan riding in front, toward Millerstown Road. Here they make contact with Wilcox's combative Alabamians of Anderson's division as the Southerners extend Hill's III Corps line southward. The ensuing firefight and report from the reconnaissance convinces Sickles that Confederates are about to occupy the ground that he wants. On his own authority, at 2 p.m. Sickles sends two divisions to occupy the new line. This new alignment will not only be a surprise to Meade, it will be a shock to Longstreet.

Alexander's artillery is the vanguard of Longstreet's march to the Federal left flank, and Alexander recalls: "I had gotten my battalion down in the valley of Willoughby Run, in a few hundred yards of the school-house, where

I had to wait on the infantry and Cabell's and Henry's battalions before going further."

Moxley Sorrel, Longstreet's chief of staff, wrote: "As Longstreet was not to be made willing and Lee refused to change or could not change, the former failed to conceal some anger. There was apparent apathy in his movements. They lacked the fire and point of his usual bearing on the battlefield."

McLaws takes the lead on the flanking march, and Longstreet is riding behind with Hood. With Captain Johnston leading the column, 14,500 infantrymen plod southward along the western slope of Herr Ridge. Soon they take a farm lane southwestward to avoid the high ground, where they could have been seen from Little Round Top. They emerge on the Marsh Creek Road about one-third mile west of Black Horse Tavern. They then turn east and cross the Fairfield Road at the tavern, continuing east on the road toward Willoughby Run.

When the Confederate infantry comes to the crest of a small ridge one-quarter mile east of the tavern, the men at the head of the column can see the Federal signal corps flags on Little Round Top. McLaws suggests a countermarch. Longstreet rides to the front, and the decision is made to follow Lee's orders literally, in that McLaws must lead the march. So McLaws's men have to turn around, and the head of the column retraces its steps back to the Fairfield Road, where the soldiers turn right on that road to avoid the congested Marsh Creek Road. Marching toward Gettysburg on the Fairfield Road for one-quarter mile, the column then turns northwest on the Herr Ridge Road. After marching three-quarters of a mile, the column crosses the crest of a hill that also can be seen from Little Round Top.

At 1:30, the signal station at Little Round Top reports: "A heavy column of enemy's infantry, about 10,000 strong, is moving from opposite our extreme left toward our right." At 2:10 a supplemental report is sent, advising that the column was sighted near Dr. Hall's and was moving toward Herr Tavern with an ambulance train in the rear."

The movement of Longstreet's column has been spotted from the Little Round Top signal station, and it leads Meade to believe that Lee is moving to support an onslaught on the Federal right flank anchored on Culp's Hill. Finally, the column advances into the valley of Willoughby Run, where it can turn south following the creek. Then, at Pitzer's Schoolhouse, the column turns east toward Seminary Ridge. Around 2:45, as McLaws posts his division on Seminary Ridge opposite the Peach Orchard, he is astounded to discover Union cannon and troops to his front. This is because Sickles's men have occupied the Emmitsburg Road from the Codori farm down to the Peach Orchard.

Lee's plan is for McLaws's division to roll up the Federal left flank. Hood would follow on McLaws's left, with Anderson's III Corps division following Hood en echelon, from right to left. But now the Union left flank is extended 1,000 yards farther south and is closer by 1,300 yards than it is supposed to be. The Peach Orchard was to be used as Alexander's artillery position against Cemetery Hill, but Yankee guns are already in battery there.

Longstreet, seeing that the entire situation has changed, orders Hood's men to form on McLaws's right by angling south along the southern extension of Seminary Ridge—known as Warfield Ridge—and straddling the Emmitsburg Road. Hood's division is formed in double line of battle, with two brigades in the front and two in support.

When Hood's men get into position, he sends a reconnaissance party toward Round Top. The party returns and advises him that Round Top is unoccupied and that the Federal rear, northeast of Round Top, is undefended. By now, however, it is 3:40, and the only troops that would be available to exploit this perceived weakness are Hood's. Not only that, Longstreet has had enough delays. Despite Hood's repeated protests that he should be allowed to swing around Round Top, Longstreet orders the attack along the Emmitsburg Road.

> *Alexander wrote that Longstreet replied to Hood: "General Lee is already fretting over the delay which had occurred and he was unwilling to add to it by offering further suggestions. Henry's [artillery] battalion moved out with Hood and took positions near the Emmitsburg Pike and became at once hotly engaged and with superior force."*

On the far end of the Confederate crescent, Ewell, when he hears the sounds of Longstreet's guns, obeys his order for a demonstration on the Confederate left. He decides to use the artillery to do his work, and arranges for guns on Seminary Ridge, to the northwest, and on Benner's Hill, to the northeast, to engage Cemetery Hill in crossfire. At 4:10 the Confederate guns open fire. Ewell waits a bit and then has some of his staff climb the ladder into the cupola of the St. Francis Xavier Catholic Church on High Street. There, they can observe Longstreet's progress. As the staffers look south, from the smoke and the sounds, all appears to be going well on Longstreet's front.

On Benner's Hill, Maj. Joseph W. Latimer, a 19-year-old VMI graduate, opens fire as planned for the artillery demonstration. Latimer commands the artillery battalion, and he places 14 guns in a wheat field on the hill, 1,500 yards from Cemetery Hill. This is the best location Latimer can find, but it is 40 feet lower than Cemetery Hill. When Latimer opens fire, Union Col. Charles S. Wainwright responds with 13 three-inch ordnance rifles. Latimer's shells initially fly over the heads of the Union gunners and crash into several tombstones of Evergreen Cemetery, while Wainwright's shells are on target.

Ewell wants his men to be concealed in the shadows of Cemetery and Culp's Hills, and thinks his chances for success will be much better at dusk. He, too, plans an en echelon attack. Johnson will begin the attack at Culp's Hill, followed by Early against East Cemetery Hill, after which Rodes will attack Cemetery Hill from the west. Johnson is supposed to attack at 7:00, and sunset falls at 7:29 p.m.

Over on Cemetery Ridge, shortly after 3:00 p.m., Meade has called a meeting of his officers, because he has been told that thousands of Confederates are moving toward the Chambersburg Pike, which would indicate a move to the Union right. Sickles is late because he's been busy moving his corps. Warren has seen and advised Meade of Sickles's move, and Old Snapping Turtle is angrily waiting for Sickles on the Widow Leister's porch. Sickles cannot even dismount before he gets both barrels from Meade. He tells Sickles to get his damned corps back to where he told him to take it in the first place. Then Meade adds, "I am coming right behind you to see that you do." Meade then wisely turns to Sykes and tells him to get his reserve V Corps over to the left in a hurry, and he sends Warren to Little Round Top to see what force, if any, Sickles has placed there.

After giving orders to Sykes and Warren, Meade adjourns the meeting and rides a few hundred yards to Hancock's left flank on Cemetery Ridge. Spotting Sickles farther south, he rides to him and asks where his men are. Sickles points west to the Emmitsburg Road and says, "Out here, sir."

Meade rides southwest to a position behind Sickles's new Emmitsburg Road line and says, "General Sickles, this is neutral ground, our guns command it, as well as the enemy's. The very reason you cannot hold it applies to them."

Sickles asks if he should withdraw his two divisions. Meade looks across the fields at McLaws's men and thinks for a moment. Then Alexander's artillery opens fire. Meade says, "I wish to God you could, but the enemy won't let you!"

John Bell Hood is now responsible for rolling up the enemy's left. He will be followed en echelon by McLaws and Anderson. Hood's plan to swing around Round Top has been rejected. Nevertheless, he will cheat on his orders and send Law's brigade toward the two Round Tops to swing around and turn the newly found Union left flank. This is in keeping with the commander's intent of turning the Union left flank, but it also incorporates Hood's wants. While this flanking movement is in process, Gen. Jerome Bonaparte "Aunt Polly" Robertson's men will attack the Federal line in front to keep the enemy occupied. Robertson is called Aunt Polly because he's always worried about the health and welfare of his men. He's a doctor, he's been an Indian fighter, and at 48 years old, he's a prohibitionist, which means, of course, he is counter to the morals and habits of most of his Texas and Arkansas soldiers. So he's deemed a do-gooder.

As the Confederates move forward, Hood personally does not get far. Near the Bushman barn he becomes a casualty from possibly the most effective shot that the Federals will fire in the attack, because that shot takes out the key man on the Confederate right wing. A shell explodes overhead and a fragment hits Hood in the left arm, cutting him so deeply that he will never regain full use of it. Hood is carried from the field, and some time will elapse before Law learns that he is the new division commander. Hood's elite division has been rendered leaderless almost at the first shot. Law, when he learns he commands the division, does not appoint his successor as brigade commander; thus the attack on the right breaks down to regimental fighting in Law's brigade.

When Warren arrives at the crest of Little Round Top, he is astounded to find only a signal station on the hill. He sends a courier to ask Meade to rush troops to this position, and he sends Lt. Ranald MacKenzie of his staff to ask Sickles for a brigade. Sickles cannot spare anyone, but Sykes's V Corps is just arriving on the Union left, and as MacKenzie leaves Sickles, he luckily runs into Sykes. The general sends his own courier to Gen. James Barnes to bring his division forward, but the courier fortunately runs into Col. Strong Vincent's brigade near the George Weikert house. Vincent demands to know the orders.

The courier says, "General Sykes told me to direct General Barnes to send one of his brigades to occupy that hill yonder," and points to Little Round Top. Vincent says, "I will take the responsibility of taking my brigade there."

Vincent, a 26-year-old Harvard lawyer, marches his brigade up the east face of Little Round Top on an old logging road and deploys it, left to right—the 20th Maine, 83rd Pennsylvania, 44th New York, and 16th Michigan.

At the same time Col. William Oates's 15th Alabama, with the 47th Alabama on his immediate left, pushes up the western face of Round Top. The Alabamians come under fire from the Second U.S. Sharpshooters, and then, instead of hugging the base of Round Top, Oates pursues the sharpshooters up the steep slope. Oates's men have had a long march to the battlefield and have consumed all their water. While the Alabamians laboriously force their way to the crest of Round Top, the Fourth and Fifth Texas, and the Fourth Alabama cross Plum Run and ascend the much gentler southwest slope of Little Round Top, just as Vincent's soldiers file into line. Before the Confederates can reach the crest, the panting Federals open fire on them from the heights, forcing the Texans and Alabamians to retreat into the woods and boulders bordering Plum Run at the base of the hill. The timing of Vincent's arrival could not have been more critical.

The Confederates attack up the slope of Little Round Top a second time. On the Confederate right, the attacks are made by the 47th and the 15th Alabama, which have now descended from Round Top. The 47th Alabama is commanded by Col. James W. Jackson, but he abandons his command when the bullets begin to zip into his ranks. Lt. Col. Michael J. Bulger, who is 57 years old and Falstaffian in girth, then takes charge. Fortunately for the panting Bulger, the 47th is lower down the slope of Round Top, so the Rebels descend into the saddle between the two Round Tops and then go up the next rocky slope, right into the teeth of the 83rd Pennsylvania. On Bulger's right, Oates's 15th Alabama slams into Col. Joshua Chamberlain's 20th Maine. The fighting is vicious and close range, but the Yankees hold.

The Confederates have meanwhile penetrated to Houck's Ridge, 300 yards west of Little Round Top. The most prominent feature on the ridge is a massive natural formation of igneous rocks which at least one local calls Big Rocks, but is more famously known as Devil's Den. Capt. James E. Smith's Independent Battery, Fourth New York, of six ten-pounder Parrotts has recently arrived from Emmitsburg, and they are ordered to the crest of the ridge at Devil's Den. But there is only room enough in the rocks for four guns, so two of the rifled guns are placed in the right rear, in the valley of Plum Run, to defend against any approach from the southwest. This valley will soon become known as the Valley of Death.

Law's Alabamians attack toward Little Round Top, and Smith's four Parrotts fire canister into the Rebel ranks. Law quickly orders the 44th and 48th Alabama to silence the guns. While the Fourth and Fifth Texas continue to attack Little Round Top, the First Texas and Third Arkansas assail Houck's Ridge. The Texans charge across a triangular-shaped field directly toward Smith's battery. The pressure on the Federals is so great that Gen. Hobart Ward pulls the 99th Pennsylvania from his right flank, near the Wheatfield, over to his left.

Captain Smith's cannoneers have used up their canister, and the battery commander is screaming, "Give them shell! Give them solid shot! Damn them, give them anything!" Col. Augustus van Horne Ellis and Maj. James Cromwell of the 124th New York—the Orange Blossoms from Orange County—lead a counterattack down the slope into a triangular field against the First Texas. Ellis was a New York lawyer before he became a California forty-niner. Always an adventurer, he was led to believe that the king of Hawaii had a naval fleet, and he was offered command of the Hawaiian navy. He went to Hawaii, only to find there was no navy. So he came back to be a lawyer. But at Gettysburg he is a soldier. He and Cromwell are mounted, because, as Ellis says, "The men must see us today." Cromwell has a beautiful horse, and he'll leap the animal over the wall, with the Orange Blossoms following. The downhill attack forces the Texans to break.

Behind Hood's two-brigade front line is a two-brigade second line with Gen. George T. "Tige" Anderson's Georgia brigade on the left and Gen. Henry L. "Rock" Benning's Georgia brigade on the right. Benning's men move forward and into the fight. Benning is a former justice of the Georgia Supreme Court, and like Iverson the day before, he simply says, "Give them hell, boys, give them hell!" But, unlike Iverson, he goes with his men to help deliver some of that fire and brimstone. Benning tells Anderson to come up on his left, and the two brigades of Georgians attack. The 124th New York is overwhelmed, and its bewildered men fall back leaderless with their colonel and major—Ellis and Cromwell—dead in the triangular field.

Smith's Parrott rifles perched on the crest at Devil's Den now have Alabamians on the left, Georgians in front, and Texans on the right. One of Smith's guns is hit by a Confederate shell, and he has to withdraw it. As the 124th New York retreats, Smith yells, "For God's sake, men, don't let them take my guns away from me!" It is too late. The Confederates capture three of his four guns at Devil's Den.

General Ward is in a fix, and he begs for help. The 40th New York from Col. P. Regis de Trobriand's brigade, and the Sixth New Jersey from Gen. Andrew A. Humphrey's division shift over. De Trobriand is a French aristocrat, poet, lawyer, and novelist who came to the States on a dare at age 25. He is an expert swordsman, having fought a number of duels, and he becomes quite the bon vivant in New York City, marrying a wealthy New York socialite.

The 40th New York, called the Mozart Regiment because of its links with the New York City Mozart Hall political machine, attacks down the valley of Plum Run from the north, but runs head-on into the 17th Georgia, the Second Georgia, and the 48th Alabama. The boys from New York City are smashed back. The rocky area of Plum Run at Devil's Den becomes known as the Slaughter Pen, and Hood's men now own Devil's Den overlooking the pen. To exploit their success, the 48th Alabama forms on the left of the Fourth Texas to take Little Round Top.

Warren knows the Rebs are coming again, and he knows that Vincent needs help, so he finds his old V Corps brigade, now led by Gen. Stephen H. Weed. Warren sees the lead regimental commander, Col. Patrick O'Rorke of the 140th New York. Irish-born, O'Rorke was the top man in the West Point class of June 1861—the same class in which George Custer was the goat.

Warren hollers, "Paddy, give me a regiment! Hurry up, and I'll take the responsibility!" O'Rorke instantly responds.

As O'Rorke is coming up the east side of Little Round Top, the Confederates attack up the western slope for a third time, and the 16th Michigan begins to give way. Colonel Vincent is shot down as he steps forward waving his wife's riding crop, hollering, "Don't give an inch!" Suddenly, over the crest comes Paddy O'Rorke and his New Yorkers, and they fire a point-blank volley into the Confederates' faces. O'Rorke is mortally wounded, but the Union line holds.

On the Union left, Chamberlain's 20th Maine has withstood several charges from Oates's Alabamians, but the Yanks are now practically out of ammunition, as are the Alabamians. Chamberlain senses the moment, and gives the command, "Fix bayonets!" He later says the words "ran like fire along the line." The men of the 20th Maine come charging down the slope into the faces of the Alabamians, and Oates later said his exhausted and surprised men "ran like a herd of wild cattle."

Bulger, of the 47th Alabama, on the left of Oates, is hit by a ball, which enters his left breast, passes through his lung, and lodges under the muscle of his left shoulder. He is sitting with his back against a tree with blood running out of his mouth, and a Union soldier comes up and demands his pistol and sword. But the feisty old colonel says he will give his weapons only to an officer as near his rank as possible.

The startled but obedient Union soldier goes and finds Col. James C. "Crazy" Rice of the 44th New York, who, as senior officer, has succeeded Vincent as brigade commander. Rice is from Massachusetts, is a Yale graduate, and has taught school in Natchez, Mississippi. His "crazy" moniker comes from his excited nature in battle. Rice accepts the surrender and makes sure that Bulger is given medical care. Chamberlain later reads this account in a newspaper, and claims that Bulger was found in front of the 20th Maine and that he arranged for Bulger's treatment. Regardless of who helped him, old Bulger is a tough character who ends up living into his 90s.

Oates survives the war, too. In 1880 he is elected to Congress, and he backs the funding of the Gettysburg battlefield as a national memorial. In 1902 Oates decides he wants to erect a small monument to the 15th Alabama. He plans to place it on a large boulder, where he says his flanking maneuver reached when the 15th swung around Chamberlain's left flank, and where his brother, John A. Oates, was killed. There are three battlefield commissioners, and the commission sends Oates's request to Joshua Chamberlain for comment. Chamberlain politely says that Oates's history differs from the facts, at least as Chamberlain recalls them. He says the Rebs never got as far as Oates says they did. So Oates loses the fight a second time and never gets his monument.

When the rest of Weed's brigade arrives at Little Round Top, Weed says that he "would rather die on this spot than see those rascals gain one inch of ground." Maybe Weed should have kept that comment to himself, because he is soon shot as he stands next to Lt. Charles Hazlett's guns. The bullet hits Weed under the right armpit, ranges across his torso, and emerges through the left armpit, severing his spine. He says, "I am cut in two. I want to see Hazlett." Lieutenant Hazlett rushes over, and as he bends down to speak to the wounded general, he is hit in the head by a bullet and killed instantly. As they carry the dying Weed off the hill, someone says to the general that they hope he is not badly hurt. Weed utters the prophetic last words, "I'm as dead a man as Julius Caesar."

All the while, Longstreet has been watching the attack of Hood's division, and it's time to send in McLaws's division, with Gen. Joseph B. Kershaw's South Carolina brigade on the right and Gen. William Barksdale's brigade of Mississippians on the left. They will attack as Hood's people had—en echelon from right to left. Behind Kershaw is Gen. Paul J. Semmes's Georgia Brigade and behind Barksdale is Gen. William T. Wofford's Georgia Brigade. After Hood's division has been committed, Kershaw's South Carolinians step off, and Semmes's Georgians follow Kershaw.

The sector between Ward's Federals on Houck's Ridge and the Federal soldiers at the Peach Orchard along the Emmitsburg Road is held by de Trobriand's brigade. The central features of this line are Rose's wheat field and a hill with stone outcroppings known as Stony Hill. De Trobriand has thrown his infantry forward of these features, with his men along Rose Run, facing southwest. Behind them, on the high ground in what simply becomes known as the Wheatfield, is Capt. George B. Winslow's First New York Artillery Battery.

De Trobriand has been weakened by the deployment of the Mozart Regiment to cover the Plum Run Valley, so a huge gap has opened between the 17th Maine—which has moved up behind a low rock wall—and the Fifth Michigan to its right. This portion of the line has already been hit by Anderson's Georgians, and Sickles has rushed two regiments—the 115th Pennsylvania and the Eighth New Jersey—to fill the gap.

But these two regiments are unsuccessful in holding back the onslaught. They fall back when the Eighth and Ninth Georgia penetrate a gap on the right of the Eighth New Jersey. The 115th Pennsylvania falls back and provides support to Winslow's guns, but the Eighth New Jersey races to the rear. The men of the 17th Maine are on their own so the flank companies redeploy behind a fence fronting Rose Run, and fire into the Georgians, who are charging toward Stony Hill. The Confederate threat is finally beaten back by the timely arrival of two brigades from Sykes V Corps. These brigades take position on the southwest end of the Stony Hill.

Henry Hunt does his part by rushing artillery under Lt. Col. Freeman McGilvery to the Wheatfield Road and amassing 28 guns facing south—a formidable show of firepower. But despite the fire from these guns, the Confederates keep moving forward.

Kershaw's South Carolinians are attacking from the west, directly toward the Stony Hill. But as his men march in front of the Federal batteries, the fire is so heavy that Kershaw has to wheel several regiments and a battalion to the left to focus on the guns. These sweating soldiers march up out of the low ground and are about to overrun the guns when—and no one knows who gave it—the order "right flank" is given. In response, the Palmetto State's infantry obediently wheels to the right and passes in front of the guns. The amazed Union artillerymen, who are attempting to limber up their guns, race back to their pieces and once again open fire into the left flank of the South Carolinians, killing and wounding dozens.

The rest of Kershaw's brigade continues toward Stony Hill. On Kershaw's right, Anderson's Georgians attack again, but the 17th Maine tenaciously holds onto its stone wall. De Trobriand sees Col. William S. Tilton's reinforcing V Corps brigade as it suddenly withdraws, and then he sees that Tilton's men are being followed by Col. Jacob B. Sweitzer's V Corps brigade. De Trobriand tries unsuccessfully to stop them. Realizing that he is unsupported and has to get his men out of that field, de Trobriand orders his soldiers to fall back to the Wheatfield Road. Here he is met by the division commander, Gen. David Birney, who orders de Trobriand back into the Wheatfield. Unfortunately for the Federals, Kershaw's Third and Seventh South Carolina have taken possession of the recently vacated stone wall and are now firing from behind cover, forcing the withdrawal of Winslow's artillery.

A concerned George Meade has told Hancock to keep an eye on Sickles and supply assistance as needed. Hancock assigns the task of supporting Sickles to Gen. John C. Caldwell's II Corps division. When Caldwell shifts southward to the Wheatfield, he finds Barnes's V Corps division already in place, so he returns to his original position. But when Barnes's two brigades retreat, Caldwell is sent back a second time to form along the Wheatfield Road.

Father William Corby, who becomes president of Notre Dame in 1866, stands on a rock over on Cemetery Ridge—a statue of him was placed there in 1910—and the men of Col. Patrick Kelly's under strength Irish Brigade kneel in front of him. He tells them to advance their green flags and he will give them absolution. But he says that the absolution is conditional, because anyone who shows cowardice in the face of the enemy will be denied a Christian burial. The brigades of Col. Edward E. Cross, Gen. Samuel K. Zook, and Colonel Kelly charge piecemeal to the Wheatfield, while Col. John R. Brooke's brigade remains in reserve.

Colonel Cross always wears a red bandanna to shield his bald pate from the sun when he goes into battle, but today he dons a black one. Just before they leave Cemetery Ridge, Hancock rides up to Cross and says, "Colonel Cross, this day will bring you a star." Cross answers, "No, general, this is my last battle."

Down in the Wheatfield, Cross's men move southwest toward the Georgians, still posted behind the stone wall that once sheltered the 17th Maine. Cross's left flank soon enters the Rose Woods while his right marches into the Wheatfield. Zook's men move toward Stony Hill, and Kelly's men follow. Kershaw's bloodied South Carolinians at Stony Hill are caught by surprise, and Kershaw sends a courier back to Semmes asking for help from his brigade. Anderson's Georgians blast Cross's men from behind the stone wall, delivering a devastating fire. Cross walks to the left of his line to order an advance, and he is mortally wounded. Cross's infuriated men charge forward and drive Anderson's men away from the stone wall. On the right, Zook and Kelly press Kershaw's men hard at Stony Hill and continue forward into Rose Woods.

Semmes answers Kershaw's call for help with four good Georgia regiments, and Caldwell quickly sees that it is time to send in Brooke's reserve brigade. As Brooke advances across the Wheatfield Road, his brigade almost spans the width of the field. These men drive Anderson's Georgians back, through Rose Woods, and it looks like Brooke is going to win everything. But he is wounded on the western edge of the woods, and as his men forge ahead, they run into Semmes's fresh reinforcements at the Rose farm. Brooke's and Semmes's men exchange fire, and when Semmes is mortally wounded, his men temporarily fall back.

The en echelon attack continues, and Barksdale's Mississippi Brigade marches toward the Peach Orchard. At age 42, Barksdale is the brother of Confederate congressman Ethelbert Barksdale. William has served Mississippi in the U.S. Congress, and he has served the Confederacy well as a soldier. Gettysburg will be his finest and his last hour.

Immediately confronting Barksdale is a Pennsylvania brigade of the III Corps commanded by Gen. Charles K. Graham. A lawyer and engineer, Graham helped plan New York City's Central Park. Graham has three of his six regiments, the 114th, 57th, and 105th Pennsylvania, and four of the six Napoleons of Lt. John K. Bucklyn's Battery E, First Rhode Island Light Artillery, on the east side of the Emmitsburg Road, extending north from the Wheatfield Road, with the right of this line resting on Trostle Lane. He has the 141st Pennsylvania facing south along the Wheatfield Road at the Peach Orchard. To the left of the 141st and facing south are the four artillery batteries of Patrick Hart, A. Judson Clark, Charles Phillips, and John Bigelow, totaling 22 guns. The 68th Pennsylvania is in reserve behind the 141st, and the Seventh New Jersey of Col. George Burling's brigade is in reserve to the left of the 68th. Poor Burling has had Dan Sickles use his brigade for spare parts, and he has no command. At the salient angle where the Wheatfield and Emmitsburg Roads meet at the Wentz house, Graham has the Second New Hampshire, another of Burling's borrowed regiments. These New Hampshire soldiers are posted at a right angle, with their right anchored on the 114th and their left on the 141st Pennsylvania regiments. West of the Emmitsburg Road and north of the Sherfy house are four more guns—a section of Bucklyn's Napoleons and a section of three-inch ordnance rifles of Capt. James Thompson's Batteries C and F, Pennsylvania Light Artillery. For skirmishers, Graham sends the 63rd Pennsylvania west of the Emmitsburg Road, and he sends out two more attached regiments, the Third Maine of Ward's brigade and the Third Michigan of de Trobriand's brigade, south of the Peach Orchard to protect his left flank.

On Graham's right are the New York regiments of Col. William R. Brewster's New York Excelsior Brigade of Gen. Andrew A. Humphrey's division. The 72nd New York is just north of Trostle Lane, with its left anchored on the right of the 105th Pennsylvania. On the right of the 72nd is the 71st. The 73rd New York, which was recruited from New York City fire departments, and the 120th New York form a reserve line behind these two regiments, with the 70th New York to their rear as a third reserve regiment.

Farther to the right, just south of the Klingle house, is the 11th New Jersey of Gen. Joseph B. Carr's brigade. In front of the Klingle house, the right is anchored by six Napoleons of Lt. Francis W. Seeley's Battery K, Fourth U.S. Artillery. All in all, this line will be a tough nut for Barksdale to crack.

The original Confederate plan was to use the Peach Orchard as an artillery platform for the assault on Cemetery Hill, and to accomplish this, Porter Alexander has placed 24 guns directly west of the Peach Orchard. The resulting artillery duel, at a range of 500 yards, is fierce and deadly. The Yankee artillery is doing well, and their cannon give Barksdale's men a rough time. Particularly troublesome are Bucklyn's four Napoleons just north of the Wentz house.

An aide to McLaws described Barksdale's face as "radiant with joy" as his 1,400 Mississippians scream the Rebel yell and double-time across the Sherfy fields. They crash into the 114th Pennsylvania, known as Collis' Zouaves, who have rushed across the Emmitsburg Road to meet the attack, along with skirmishers of the Seventh New Jersey. The Mississippians go through the Zouaves like a wolf through a flock of sheep. In the melee of hand-to-hand combat, the Sherfy barn catches on fire, and a number of wounded Union soldiers seeking refuge in the barn die of burns and smoke inhalation. Captain Bucklyn, the Rhode Island battery commander, sees the oncoming horde and tries to withdraw his guns.

Bucklyn writes in his diary: "Men and horses fall all around me. The rebel infantry advance to within 40 yards of me and give me a volley. . . . My battery is torn and shattered and my brave boys have gone, never to return. Curse the rebels."

At the Peach Orchard, the 21st and the 17th Mississippi put Graham's Pennsylvanians to flight. Col. Andrew Tippin, trying to stop the hemorrhaging line, loses half of his reserve 68th Pennsylvania in just a few minutes. The

Pennsylvanians form behind the line of cannon on the Wheatfield Road, only to see Kershaw's men coming at them from the south.

Barksdale immediately wheels three regiments of his command to the left, and the Mississippians move up the Emmitsburg Road, crashing into the left flank of the Pennsylvanians, and then into the New Yorkers of the Excelsior Brigade. General Graham is wounded and captured. The 141st Pennsylvania, now posted behind the Wheatfield Road batteries, holds out longest, but Col. Henry Madill, who brings the colors off the field, looks around in a daze, and says, "My God, where are my men?"

At the Wheatfield, McLaws is far from done. By now Zook's and Kelly's brigades have formed a north-south line west of the Wheatfield, with Brooke's brigade south on the Rose farm. Brooke has Anderson's brigade attacking his right flank, with the right of Semmes's brigade attacking his front. Zook and Kelly are occupied with the left of Semmes's brigade and Kershaw's brigade to their front.

Wofford's Georgians follow Barksdale's men and surge forward to exploit the Mississippians' breakthrough. Guiding on the Wheatfield Road, they pass across Stony Hill, and attack the right of Zook's and Kelly's line. Zook, who is mounted, is mortally wounded, and the right of his line begins to fall apart. This collapse puts Kelly and Brooke between a rock and a hard place.

The Union line begins to falter, and Caldwell orders Sweitzer's V Corps brigade back into the Wheatfield. These men race across the field and to the stone wall, but it is too late. The blue lines are crumbling all around Sweitzer's regiments. The Confederates begin to close in from the west and the south. When Col. Harrison H. Jefferds of the Fourth Michigan sees a Confederate reaching for his colors, he races forward, trying to save the flag, and he is bayoneted to death. The Wheatfield is soon in Confederate hands.

But the Regular Army soldiers of Col. Sidney Burbank's and Col. Hannibal Day's V Corps brigades are waiting in the woods to the east of the field. Burbank wheels his brigade to the left, out of the woods, to meet the attackers coming from the direction of the stone wall. This exposes his three right regiments to enfilading fire from Stony Hill, and these regiments suffer 50 percent casualties. Burbank, seeing that his line is being systematically destroyed, orders a retreat. Day's men are luckier, because they occupy the original line in the woods as a supporting position. The regulars are forced to give up the Wheatfield, but they withdraw slowly, in a disciplined manner, turning to fire as they do. Colonel Burbank has lost 447 men—almost a 50 percent casualty rate—and Colonel Day has lost 382.

The sacrifice of Burbank's and Day's men did not go unnoticed, and a volunteer soldier recalled: "For two years the U.S. Regulars taught us how to be soldiers. In the Wheatfield at Gettysburg they taught us how to die like soldiers."

Gen. Dan Sickles and his staff have moved to the Trostle barn as the III Corps line collapses. A solid 12-pounder cannonball comes skipping across the ground like a hailstone and hits Sickles, who is mounted, above his right shin, all but taking the leg off below the knee. Strangely, his horse is not hurt. Sickles dismounts and is taken over to the side of the Trostle barn, where Pvt. William Bullard, a musician from the 70th New York, makes a tourniquet from a saddle strap and stops the bleeding. Sickles pulls a flask out of his pocket, takes a swig, and when he sees Birney ride up, he yells, "General Birney, you will take command, sir!" Sickles and Birney talk for a minute, and Sickles asks for a cigar. As he is carried to an ambulance on a stretcher, he rises up, puffs his cigar, and waves to the troops to let them know he is alive.

Sickles is taken to a field hospital, where Dr. Thomas Sim amputates his right leg, just above the knee. Sim has just read that the new Army Medical Museum needs specimens, so he wraps the leg in a wet blanket and places it in a small box to be shipped to Washington. Sickles's lower leg bones are now on display at the Armed Forces Medical Museum at Walter Reed Army Center, just across the aisle from a display with the bullet that killed Abraham Lincoln.

Falling gradually back from their position on the Wheatfield Road to near the Trostle house and barn, the six 12-pounder Napoleons of Bigelow's Ninth Massachusetts Battery cover the retreat of Sickles's line. Bigelow's horses have been taken to the backyard of the house to save them from enemy fire, and the captain is slowly withdrawing his guns by prolonge, or rope, as the artillery carriages recoil from each round of canister fired at Barksdale's onrushing Mississippians. Bigelow knows he is running out of time, and as his guns finally arrive at the front yard of the house he plans to bring his horses out from behind the farm buildings and withdraw his guns.

McGilvery has ridden from the Trostle farm to Cemetery Ridge and has found a huge gap in the center of the Federal line where Caldwell's division was located before it was sent to the Wheatfield. This is a critical gap, as Barksdale's men are aggressively advancing, and without opposition they will breech the Federal line. McGilvery orders Bigelow to hold his position at all hazards. Bigelow piles ammunition up around his six guns and forms them in a semicircle. When the 21st Mississippi attacks his last line of defense, he opens with solid shot and then with double canister. The cannoneers can't load fast enough, and the Confederates are suddenly on top of them. After hand-to-hand combat, Bigelow's position is overrun. He loses four of his guns, 28 men, and 45 horses. But the gallant captain has bought 30 minutes of time for McGilvery to patch together a new gun line with 23 pieces—the remnants of six batteries.

Barksdale's men are still coming, and behind him to his left is Wilcox's Alabama Brigade of Anderson's division out of Hill's III Corps. To the left of, and behind Wilcox, is Col. David Lang's three-regiment Florida Brigade. It looks like the Confederates will break the Federal main line as the en echelon attack continues.

This is where Hancock is a pillar of strength. He's already used up Caldwell's division in the Wheatfield fight. Now he's going to reach into Gen. Alexander Hays's division. He is going to commit Col. George L. Willard's brigade to the support of McGilvery's guns. Willard's four New York regiments were captured at Harpers Ferry the previous September and have since been paroled and are derided by their comrades as the Harpers Ferry Cowards. Now they want to clear the books, and Hancock personally leads them into position to oppose Barksdale's advancing lines. When Hancock sees Wilcox's Alabamians coming across Plum Run north of Barksdale, he looks around for help. He sees Col. Clinton MacDougall's 111th New York, and he sends these men from their detached position on Willard's left flank to fill the gap on the right. Somehow, Hancock finds people and throws them into the fight, telling them that they have to do it regardless of what they might think of the chance of success. When he sees a regiment in the wrong location, he grabs a private by the arm and leads him out to the front. "Will you stay here?" he yells. The private says, "I'll stay here, General, till hell freezes over." Hancock smiles, and then has the regiment form around this private. Hancock is showing true grit and leadership.

Meanwhile, Willard forms the 39th New York, "The Garabaldi Guards," directly in front of Barksdale's almost-spent soldiers of the 21st Mississippi, who have just overrun and captured the four three-inch ordnance rifles of Lt. Malbone Watson's battery. Barksdale, trying to rally his men in front of the Garibaldi Guards, is first hit in the left leg by a minié ball, then a cannonball almost rips off his left foot, and finally, he is hit in the chest by canister. He falls from his horse near Plum Run, not far from where Willard will be killed.

Barksdale will die in a few hours at a Union field hospital outside the Jacob Hummelbaugh farmhouse, saying, "I die content that my last day's work was well done."

After crossing Plum Run, Willard is killed by a shell fragment that tears away his face and a portion of his head. On Willard's right, Hancock sees a gap in the line, and he sends in Col. William Colvill's First Minnesota. Colvill's men hit Wilcox's Alabamians hard. It's a suicide mission, and the Minnesotans suffer 80 percent casualties. Colvill and all of the field grade officers go down, but Hancock again intercedes, inserting another regiment into the line. Wilcox looks to his left and he sees that Lang's Florida brigade, having captured three of Lt. Gulian V. Weir's six Napoleons, has paused briefly. The Alabamians have had enough, and Wilcox pulls back. Barksdale's Mississippians, now leaderless, also fall back.

Anderson's next brigade, on Lang's left, is Gen. Ambrose "Rans" Wright's Georgians. They charge through the Codori farm and drive back the 82nd New York and the 15th Massachusetts. They cross the Emmitsburg Road and overrun Lt. Frederick Brown's Battery B, First Rhode Island Battery, near the Codori house, capturing two of his six Napoleons. They then smash into Gen. Alexander S. Webb's brigade, only to receive a point-blank volley from the 69th Pennsylvania, as well as canister from the six three-inch rifles of Capt. Alonzo H. Cushing's Battery A, Fourth U.S. Artillery, and the six three-inch rifles of Capt. William A. Arnold's Battery A, First Rhode Island Artillery. The men of the 22nd Georgia and the Third Georgia see a gap in the line to their right, where Caldwell had been. They angle toward the gap and work their way up toward the summit of Cemetery Ridge. But five companies of the 13th Vermont—the nine-month men of George Stannard's brigade who arrived just hours ago—race to oppose them. The Georgians open fire, but the Vermont boys rush into the Georgians with fixed bayonets, and that turns the tide.

The next brigade to the left of Wright's is the Mississippi brigade of Gen. Carnot Posey. Wright looks to his left, and Posey's men, who have occupied the Bliss barn, are content to stay there. Posey is no leader, and his men know it. Wright looks to his right and sees Lang's Floridians, who have seen Wilcox withdraw on their right, pull back. Wright's Georgians are out on a limb by themselves, and they have no choice but to withdraw. Wright is disgusted that he has no support. The Virginia brigade of Gen. William Mahone, the northernmost of Anderson's five brigades, stays put. Mahone refuses to go forward. When Wilcox earlier had asked for help from Richard Anderson, his division commander does not respond, nor does corps commander A. P. Hill.

Back down at the Wheatfield, the action is not quite over. Just as the sun begins to set, Crawford's division of Sykes's V Corps arrives—he has two brigades of Pennsylvania Reserves. One is sent to the Wheatfield, and the other to support Little Round Top. Also arriving on the battlefield are two brigades of Sedgwick's VI Corps, after their 35-mile march from Manchester.

Hood's and McLaws's Rebels cross the southern portion of the Wheatfield for one final assault on Little Round Top. Attacking are the brigades of Kershaw, Semmes, and Anderson. Across the northern portion of the field is Wofford's brigade. By now all the Confederate brigades are disorganized and fought out.

Crawford, riding a handsome blood bay, sees the Rebs coming and grabs the flag of the First Pennsylvania Reserves and leads it into the Valley of Death of Plum Run. Crawford is a short distance in front of his brigade with the Stars and Stripes waving for all to see. Then he gives it back to a fretful color sergeant. But after a shot or two, the event is over. At the sight of more fresh Yankees, the exhausted Confederates withdraw, and Longstreet's attack ends.

Longstreet called this attack "the best three hours' fighting ever done by any troops on any battlefield," and he was right. In any battle, the offensive force can be expected to suffer greater casualties. On July 2 at Gettysburg, however, Longstreet's Confederates inflicted greater casualties on their defending opponent. But what Longstreet forgot to consider is the value of leadership. Time and again on the afternoon of July 2 it was the individual initiative of a handful of Union leaders, inspired by Hancock the Superb, that won the day.

When Longstreet assaulted the Union left, George Meade ordered Henry Slocum, his XII Corps commander, to send reinforcements to that part of the battlefield. But that caused a problem in the command structure of the Army of the Potomac. The "Pipe Creek Circular" of July 1 placed Slocum in command of the XII and V Corps to form the center of the proposed line east and west of Union Mills, and Slocum assumed that he was still in command of these divisions on the Federal right at Gettysburg. Thus, he was now the "right-wing commander" of the army. The confusion led to a dangerous drawdown of troops on the Union right on the evening of July 2.

Slocum, believing he is in command of both the XII and V Corps as a wing commander, has placed his First Division commander, General Williams, in command of the XII Corps, and Williams has passed his divisional command to Gen. Thomas H. Ruger, one of his brigade commanders. However, because Sykes's V Corps was sent to the Union left during Longstreet's attack, this makes Slocum's "right wing" a phantom command.

At 6 p.m. on July 2, Slocum orders Williams to send Ruger's division and Lockwood's brigade—a brigade that has recently arrived on the field—to the Union left. Williams's other division, under Gen. John Geary, remains on the right. Williams personally escorts Ruger and Lockwood to the left. At dark Lockwood is sent to support McGilvery's artillery on the Plum Run line.

For reasons unexplained, shortly after Williams departs, Slocum orders Geary to rush two of his three brigades to the Union left. Ewell's demonstration has done nothing to prevent Meade from shifting troops toward Longstreet's attack.

Geary promptly marches off into the night with two of his brigades, commanded by men whose names complement each other—Col. Charles Candy and Gen. Thomas L. Kane. Geary is a large, boisterous, and overbearing man. He's six feet six inches tall and well over 250 pounds. He was the first and youngest mayor of San Francisco, and Geary Street there is named for him. In the late 1850s, he was territorial governor of Bleeding Kansas, where he clamped down on both Border Ruffians and Jayhawkers. But he isn't in San Francisco or Kansas on the night of July 2, and he gets lost in the dark and marches his men down the Baltimore Pike, finally stopping on the south side of Rock Creek. Instead of countermarching, in typical male fashion he refuses to ask for directions. He just stays where he is.

After Slocum orders Candy and Kane to the Union left, this leaves only the brigade of Gen. George Sears Greene on Culp's Hill—1,400 men—to hold a front previously held by six brigades totaling 9,000 Yankees. Greene thins his men and sends them from the upper slope of Culp's Hill downhill to his right to form a single line—not the normal double line.

At 62 years of age, George "Pop" Greene is the oldest Union general on the field. He's a West Point graduate, second in his class of 1823, and he will become one of the true heroes of Gettysburg. It's too bad he isn't as articulate as Joshua Chamberlain. By the time he dies at age 98, he's already arranged for a two-ton boulder to be moved from Culp's Hill to Warwick, Rhode Island, to be placed on his grave.

Greene was a professor of engineering at West Point. Therefore, all day on July 2, he has his men entrenching. Early in the war, in '61 and '62, no self-respecting soldier entrenched. Entrenchments for field engagements were looked upon by West Pointers as inhibiting the fighting spirit of the soldier. In fact, Geary makes patronizing remarks that afternoon about Pop Greene and his entrenchments.

Greene's men are lucky that he has them construct the fortified line, because they will need them. His men can't dig deep because there is very little soil on

Culp's Hill, so they build breastworks of logs, earth, and rocks. He also has his men construct a traverse down the hill, near the Culp's Hill saddle.

Greene studies the ground and knows that humans and animals move across it the same way that water does—they take the path of least resistance. Greene knows the enemy will move upward into a saddle, where the water flows downward, because that's the easiest way. Greene blocks that route, at a right angle to his line, near his right flank.

On Benner's Hill, Major Latimer's men have been firing for two and one-half hours. After firing more than a thousand rounds, Latimer advises Allegheny Johnson that his position is untenable. The Confederates evacuate all but four guns, which remain to support the infantry attack that will begin at 7 p.m.

When Major Latimer's four guns open fire at 7 p.m., at least 36 Federal guns concentrate on them, and Latimer is mortally wounded when a piece of a shell shatters his right arm and his horse falls on him.

Hearing the sounds of Latimer's fire, Johnson's brigades step off, and the soldiers soon have to traverse Rock Creek, the waters of which are backed up behind MacAllister's Mill and are about waist high because of a freshet. As the soldiers cross the creek, they come under fire from the skirmish line of the 78th New York. Once across, the Confederates quickly drive the Federal skirmishers back into Greene's line. There, the 78th New York reforms between and behind the 102nd and 149th New York regiments.

Gen. John M. "Rum" Jones's Virginia Brigade climbs up the slope of Culp's Hill, which they find quickly becomes very steep and rocky, destroying any sense of a formation. It is dark in the shadowy woods, and the bullets coming from above make the climbing slow, difficult, and dangerous.

Col. Jesse M. Williams's Louisiana Brigade to the left has better terrain to its front, even though it is rough and steep, and the Cajuns soon outdistance the Virginians. The Confederates dart from rock to rock and from tree to tree, with no real formation. Finally, about a hundred yards in front of Greene's line, they drop to the ground and fire at the Yankee muzzle flashes licking out of the breastworks.

When the shooting starts, Greene sends for help from Culp's and Cemetery Hills. Wadsworth of the I Corps sends the Sixth Wisconsin of the Iron Brigade, as well as the 14th Brooklyn and the 147th New York from Cutler's brigade. Howard rushes four XI Corps regiments from Schimmelfennig's brigade toward the right of Greene's line.

Confederate Gen. George H. "Maryland" Steuart, on the far left, commands three Virginia regiments, two North Carolina regiments, and a Maryland battalion that is the size of a regiment. As he presses up the rocky hill and through the dense woods of Culp's Hill's lower crest, the Virginia regiments on his left find Candy's and Kane's slight entrenchments only lightly defended, and farther to the left, they find the works unmanned. The men of the 23rd Virginia are first to see the weak spot, and assisted by three companies of the First Maryland Battalion, these Confederates quickly occupy the abandoned breastworks.

Again in a crisis, Hancock is seemingly everywhere. He hears the firing from Culp's Hill and instinctively sends the 71st Pennsylvania over from Cemetery Ridge. But Col. Richard Penn Smith of the 71st is not up to the task, and one volley from the Virginians and Marylanders convinces him to withdraw his Philadelphians and return to Cemetery Ridge. He rationalizes his withdrawal by saying, "I am not going to see my men murdered."

The men of the 23rd Virginia and their Maryland friends pivot to their right and form a perpendicular line to the Yankee main line. They are joined by the First and Third North Carolina and they pour fire into the flank of the 137th New York, forcing that regiment to fall back into Greene's right-angle traverse. Situated on the extreme right flank at the traverse is Col. David Ireland, a rival for Joshua Lawrence Chamberlain. Ireland commands the 137th New York. Few people today recognize the name of David Ireland. Born in Scotland, he was 31 years old at Gettysburg, and he will die of disease in Atlanta on September 10, 1864. Fewer people know of the 137th New York, because no one writes that regiment's history as do historians of other regiments after the war. But on this day the 137th holds off six regiments while Chamberlain fought only two. Chamberlain, however, lives to be 85 and before he dies in 1914 he writes prolifically about his war experiences. In 1974, Michael Shaara has his book *The Killer Angels* published. The next year the book wins the Pulitzer Prize for fiction, and then in 1993, there is *Gettysburg,* a movie based on Shaara's book. Poor David Ireland is not mentioned in either the book or the movie, so he, much like George Sears Greene, now takes a back seat in the public's memory.

Despite being badly outnumbered, the 137th New York will not break. Finally, Wadsworth's and Howard's reinforcements arrive, and the Federal line manages to hold off the attackers. Sometime between 10 and 11 p.m., Steuart gives up and pulls his men back to the captured breastworks.

On Cemetery Hill, Howard has been hearing the firing on Culp's Hill, and he knows the en echelon attack is rolling his way. Facing to the northwest, he has

25 guns, backed up by two divisions of infantry, and facing to the northeast, he has 22 guns, backed by Barlow's division, now commanded by Adelbert Ames. Col. Andrew Harris has Ames's old brigade, and von Gilsa has the other. Harris posts his men 120 yards downhill, near the base of the hill, behind a low stone wall along Brickyard Lane. On the left of the line, at a salient angle, facing to the north, is the 107th Ohio. Five regiments extend this arm of the angle off to the Ohioans' right. The men nervously wait in the gathering darkness for the attack they know is coming.

Ewell plans for two brigades of Early's division on Johnson's right to seize East Cemetery Hill. Avery's North Carolina Tar Heels are to strike from the northeast and Hays's hell-raising Louisiana Tigers are to strike from the north. Both brigades will attack out of Winebrenner's Run, where they have been lying in the hot sun all afternoon.

After the Confederate attack crests against Culp's Hill, first Hays, then Avery, begin their en echelon assault. When they advance, two Union skirmish regiments in Culp's Meadow fall back to von Gilsa's right flank, with the Rebels closing fast.

Avery's North Carolinians sweep across Culp's Meadow, aiming directly at von Gilsa's men. The Tar Heels are soon greeted by the roar of the six Napoleons of Battery E, Fifth Maine Light Artillery, up on the western face of Culp's Hill. As the North Carolinians advance, Avery is knocked from his horse by a bullet to the neck. He knows it's a mortal wound, and he knows that no one has seen him go down in the dark. He manages to pull a pencil stub and a scrap of paper out of his pocket, and he scrawls a final note to his friend, Maj. Samuel Tate of the Sixth North Carolina: "Major: Tell my father I died with my face to the enemy." Tate saves the note, covered in Avery's blood, which today is in the North Carolina Archives.

The North Carolinians' night attack terrifies von Gilsa's men, and the 54th New York, the 68th New York, and the 153rd Pennsylvania cut and run just as they did at Chancellorsville on May 2, and at Barlow's Knoll on July 1. The Yanks flee up East Cemetery Hill, with the North Carolinians hot on their heels, and the pursued men run so recklessly that some of them go uphill into the deadly canister of the six ordnance rifles of Capt. Robert Bruce Ricketts's Batteries F and G, First Pennsylvania Light Artillery.

On the Union left, Hays's men see a weak spot in Harris's line between the 25th and 75th Ohio, and the Rebs move in for the kill. One Confederate sergeant recalled that they went over the stone wall like deer. They rout the 25th and 107th Ohio, but the 75th Ohio and 17th Connecticut won't budge from the wall, and the fighting is hand to hand in the dark at Brickyard Lane on East Cemetery Hill. The Louisiana Tigers continue up the steep face of East Cemetery Hill, into the face of the four ordnance rifles of Capt. Michael Wiedrich's Company I, First New York Light Artillery. A Louisianan stands at the muzzle of a cannon and yells, "I take command of this gun." The German cannoneer replies, "*Du sollst sie haben!—*Thou shalt have it!" The artilleryman poleaxes the Louisianan with a handspike and has the last say in the matter.

The attack looks good for the Confederates. They are pouring through two gaps in the Yankee line. Soon they have two of Ricketts's six guns and are threatening Lt. James Stewart's Battery B, Fourth U.S. Artillery, just to the right and rear of Ricketts's guns. Hays and his men are ecstatic—they've done the impossible and have overrun Wiedrich's cannon. They've taken East Cemetery Hill!

Rodes's division is to move through the streets of Gettysburg and strike from the northwest as part of the en echelon attack. If these men don't come, Hays won't be able to stay. Inexplicably, Gordon's brigade does not pick up the attack behind Hays. Early and Gordon do nothing to reinforce the temporary success scored by their comrades. Rodes's division halts west of town. Rodes blames the confusion of the streets of Gettysburg for his failure to attack. The matter becomes more obscured following Lee's death on October 12, 1870, when Early will focus on Longstreet's perceived July 2 miscues and the finger-pointing will begin.

On the other hand the Yanks are coming, once again sent by Hancock. Three regiments of Col. Samuel Sprigg Carroll's brigade charge in a column to the southeast of the Evergreen Cemetery gatehouse. Carroll is a West Pointer, class of '56, and he is balding, but what hair is left is red, so he's known as Brick Top. Like any good redhead, he has one hell of a temper. Charles Carroll's grandfather was the only Catholic signer of the Declaration of Independence, and was the last signer to die. The elder is mentioned in the third stanza of the state song "Maryland, My Maryland," and is depicted in the beginning of the film *National Treasure*. Behind Colonel Carroll is the 106th Pennsylvania from Alexander Webb's Philadelphia Brigade. Krzyzanowski's and Coster's brigades also come charging up the west slope to get into the fight. So the same thing that happened to Wright's Georgians that afternoon on Cemetery Ridge happens to Hays's Louisianans and Avery's North Carolinians on Cemetery Hill. They are unsupported, and they face fresh Union regiments coming from all directions. They have to leave in a hurry.

Not content to watch the Rebels run, Carroll's brigade charges through Ricketts's battery, down the hill, over the stone wall, and out into the fields to the town below. When Carroll suddenly realizes he may be out too far, he sends word back to the XI Corps to move up to his support. Word comes back that Ames doesn't have confidence in his men to hold a line that far forward. Carroll's temper flares, and he rightfully says, "Damn a man who has no confidence in his troops!"

At 8 p.m., George Meade sends a message to Henry Halleck: "The enemy attacked me at about 4:00 p.m. today, and, after one of the severest contests of the war, was repulsed at all points." He goes on to say: "I shall remain in my present position tomorrow, but am not prepared to say, until better advised of the condition of the army, whether my operations will be of an offensive or defensive character."

Around nine o'clock, Meade meets with Hancock, Slocum, and Colonel Sharpe, of the Bureau of Military Information, in the Widow Leister's house. Sharpe tells Meade that they have interviewed prisoners and learned that Lee has thrown everything he has at Meade, with the sole exception of Pickett's division. Meade says, "Are you sure about that?" Sharpe responds, "Let me verify that," and goes off to get more information. He comes back and says he is sure. Hancock is elated, and says, "General, we've got them nicked!"

One general after another shows up in the cramped Leister house, and soon there are a dozen. There is Meade, Newton, Hancock, Gibbon, Birney, Sykes, Sedgwick, Howard, Williams, Slocum, Warren, and Butterfield. There is a discussion on the condition of the army, and Meade listens. But then, he decides he wants written minutes of the meeting. Butterfield takes the minutes, and then just as did Hooker at Chancellorsville, Butterfield suggests they vote on the matter. The key questions are: Should the army stay at Gettysburg, and if so, should it attack or defend? Following some discussion, all in attendance vote to stay, and all vote to wait for Lee to attack. If Lee doesn't attack, they will convene tomorrow night to again discuss their options. However, this council of war, which ends about midnight, creates the image of Meade as an irresolute leader.

Alpheus Williams receives orders from Slocum after dark to send Ruger's and Geary's divisions back to Culp's Hill. Around 10 p.m., Geary's wayward division returns to Culp's Hill from Rock Creek on the Baltimore Pike, and the Yanks plan to reoccupy their old works on the upper crest of the hill. The 29th Pennsylvania of Kane's brigade shows up initially, and these men don't know that Steuart's Confederates are now in the lower position—from Greene's traverse all the way down to the Rock Creek. So, Kane's men give a good Yankee huzzah in the darkness to let Greene know they are back, and the Confederates, hearing this uniquely Yankee yell, present the Pennsylvanians with a volley fired from behind a low stone wall, killing and wounding 14. Col. William Rickards of the 29th Pennsylvania thinks the volley is friendly fire from Greene's men. Regardless, he has his men withdraw back to the Baltimore Pike, because any solider knows that "friendly fire ain't." Kane then moves his brigade farther up the western slope and comes in on Greene's rear, where Pop's men have held the line behind their breastworks and along their right-angle traverse. Kane forms a line behind a stone wall that runs perpendicular to Greene's breastworks, basically extending Greene's traverse toward the Baltimore Pike. Candy's brigade follows Kane and forms behind Greene's main line at the breastworks. Geary, now with all three of his brigades ensconced behind Greene's defenses, has no more smart remarks about Pop Greene having his people dig in.

Ruger's division soon arrives, and his men discover that Confederates occupy their former position on the lower crest of Culp's Hill extending down to Rock Creek. Ruger forms an east-west line south of Spangler's Spring, with the left of his line anchored on the Baltimore Pike and his right on Rock Creek.

Williams, the acting XII Corps commander, has been attending the meeting at Meade's headquarters and doesn't return to Culp's Hill until after midnight. When he learns that the Confederates have occupied much of his position, he asks for and receives permission to "attack with infantry and artillery at daylight" and recover the lost ground.

Robert E. Lee doesn't hold a council of war that night. He doesn't even meet with his corps commanders. He decides that "the general plan is unchanged." Around 10 p.m. he sends orders to Longstreet and Ewell, probably verbal orders, because no copies have been found. Lee knows that Steuart's brigade has a toehold on the lower crest of Culp's Hill. So he orders Ewell "to assail the enemy's right" at daylight, while Longstreet is to attack the Union left again. So Lee's plan for the third day calls for a converging attack at dawn.

But there is a problem. Earlier, George Pickett rode ahead of his men to Gettysburg in time to see Longstreet during the afternoon attack. While they talked, one of Pickett's aides, Maj. Walter Harrison, delivered a message to Pickett from Lee: "Tell General Pickett I shall not want him this evening; to let his men rest; and I will send him word when I want him." For the second time on July 2, Lee deals directly with one of Longstreet's division commanders. This irks an already peeved Longstreet.

That night, Porter Alexander visits Longstreet's headquarters and learns that they will "renew the attack early in the morning." He hears that Pickett's division is to conduct the principal assault, and Alexander believes that the attack will be to the left of the Peach Orchard. So, if Alexander remembers correctly, Longstreet was aware of Lee's orders. But Longstreet is unhappy and he does not pass these orders on to Pickett, assuming that Lee is dealing directly with him. Of course, every army officer, from day one of their training, has been taught to never assume.

Unlike the previous day, Ewell doesn't argue with Lee's orders. He takes Daniel's and O'Neal's brigades from Rodes's division and Extra Billy Smith's brigade from Early's division and gives them to Johnson for the early morning attack. Johnson will now have seven brigades to assail Culp's Hill at daylight.

Jeb Stuart's cavalry is to operate on Ewell's left and rear, and Lee's chief of artillery, Gen. William N. Pendleton, will bombard the Union lines as early as possible on July 3. Pendleton has 250 guns available to him, not including the 31 guns in Jeb Stuart's cavalry division. The Federals have 372 guns, which includes the 52 guns in Pleasonton's cavalry corps.

As July 2 comes to an end, it has been another rough day. The Federals suffer an additional 10,000 casualties, compared to 6,800 Confederate. But the Army of the Potomac still holds the high ground.

Chapter 11
GIVE THEM THE COLD STEEL

July 3–4, 1863
At Vicksburg on July 3, Grant has not been overly secretive about his plans for an all-out assault in three days. Pemberton and his officers know that time is running out. Under a flag of truce, Grant and Pemberton meet between the lines near the Jackson Road at 3 p.m. to discuss the surrender.

GRANT LATER WROTE: "NEARBY STOOD A STUNTED OAK-TREE, *which was made historical by the event. It was but a short time before the last vestige of its body, root, and limb had disappeared, the fragments taken as trophies. Since then the same tree has furnished as many cords of wood, in the shape of trophies, as 'The True Cross.' "*

Pemberton, a native of Philadelphia, the Cradle of Liberty, fully appreciates the symbolism of a Fourth of July surrender, and he uses that knowledge as leverage to negotiate better terms than Grant's trademark "unconditional surrender." By day's end, the two sides reach agreement—Vicksburg is to be surrendered at 10 a.m. on July 4.

At Gettysburg, Robert E. Lee's plan of attack for July 3 is a simultaneous sunrise assault on Meade's right and left. He orders Ewell "to assail the enemy's right" at daylight, while Longstreet is to attack the Union left. Ewell will attack Culp's Hill with Johnson's reinforced division of seven brigades. Longstreet will use Pickett's division—reinforced with the four brigades of Heth's division, now commanded by Gen. Johnston Pettigrew because of Heth's head wound, and two brigades of a new division commanded by Gen. Isaac Trimble. Longstreet's attack will include the divisions of Pickett, Pettigrew, and Trimble—nine brigades—with six of them from Hill's III Corps.

Lee has made his plan, and at 4:30 a.m., thinking once again he has matters taken care of, he rides to Longstreet's headquarters on Seminary Ridge, west of the Peach Orchard, to watch the morning attack. Yet at dawn Pickett's division is still three miles away. It appears that Longstreet, after hearing Lee say that he would send word to Pickett when he wanted him, thought Lee was sending orders directly to Pickett, and Longstreet never informed Pickett of the attack plan. The end result of the mix-up is that Pickett's men are not in position for a dawn attack.

When Lee arrives, Longstreet once again argues for a flanking movement, protesting a frontal assault. He probably over dramatically remembers the event when he writes: "General, I've been a soldier all my life. I have been with soldiers engaged in fights by couples, by squads, companies, regiments, divisions, and armies, and should know, as well as any one, what soldiers can do. It is my opinion that no 15,000 men ever arrayed for battle can take that position." In actuality, Longstreet has 12,600 men.

Longstreet argues against the attack, but Lee is not listening. He's had enough of foul-ups and recalcitrant subordinates. Then he hears the sounds of guns from the north, and he assumes they are fired by Johnson's reinforced division of Ewell's II Corps. But the opening guns are fired by Alpheus Williams's Yankees, not by Allegheny Johnson's Confederates.

Williams, per his agreement with Slocum, is attempting to reclaim his position on Culp's Hill, and his artillery fires on Johnson first. Williams's plan is to open with an artillery bombardment, then attack with Geary's division in a division line that runs south from the crest of the hill and gradually curves to the southwest toward Baltimore Pike. Greene's brigade is on the left of this line, Kane's is in the center, and Candy's is on the right. The plan is to sweep downhill and drive the Confederates from their lodgment on the lower slope.

At 4:30 a.m., 26 cannon open fire on Steuart's men in the former Union breastworks on the lower slope of Culp's Hill. Geary intends to charge when the cannon cease firing, but Steuart's Rebels beat the Yanks to the punch and attack first. On upper Culp's Hill, the Virginians on the Confederate right face steep, rocky slopes and are quickly repulsed. Lower down the hill, the Louisianans in the center of the Confederate line also fail to penetrate Greene's formidable breastworks.

On the lower slopes, where the Rebels have occupied the Union breastworks, Johnson has three brigades: Steuart's, Daniel's, and Walker's. This is the position that Alpheus Williams wants to reclaim, so here the Federals concentrate heavy artillery and small-arms fire. Despite this hailstorm of lead and iron, Steuart's men advance westward from the meager breastworks to the south edge of Pardee Field, as it will later be named, in honor of Lt. Col. Ario Pardee of the 147th Pennsylvania. Steuart's 900 men then wheel right and face north, or uphill. Across the field they see Candy's Fifth Ohio and 147th Pennsylvania extending the line of the Federal traverse toward the Baltimore Pike. As Steuart's line advances across the 250-yard-wide field, the men are hit by small-arms fire from the front.

Daniel's brigade is to advance on Steuart's right, but the attack is not coordinated, and Steuart's men fall back before Daniel's Tar Heels move forward. The Confederates suffer terribly and, after several charges, fall back behind a stone wall on the northeast side of the field. Even the unnamed mongrel dog mascot of the First Maryland Battalion is shot down at the head of the charge. Afterward, as Kane recalled, "He licked someone's hand after he was perfectly riddled." All that Steuart can say is: "My poor boys!"

The Federals now counterattack across the field. The First Maryland Potomac Home Brigade crosses the field and gets to within 20 yards of the Confederates at the stone wall before the Federals have to fall back. However, Pardee's 147th Pennsylvania charges again, and the Confederates abandon the wall and fall back to the breastworks.

Ruger's Federal division is south of Steuart, and at 10 a.m. Col. Silas Colgrove is told to attack two of Extra Billy Smith's regiments, which are guarding Steuart's left flank. The attack will have to cross the low ground of Spangler's Meadow against two Virginia regiments firing from behind a stone wall. Colgrove sends the Second Massachusetts and the 27th Indiana from his right. These two regiments are caught in a deadly cross fire in the middle of the field and are slaughtered. Then Smith makes the mistake of sending his two regiments out into the field in a counterattack, and they suffer the same fate. By now it is obvious this is a killing ground, and the Confederates fall back.

The much-ignored final fight for Culp's Hill that begins at dawn's early light lasts about seven hours. It involves seven Rebel brigades in a desperate struggle against the bluecoats of the XII Corps, reinforced by two VI Corps brigades. It ends with the Confederates abandoning the fight and withdrawing across Rock Creek. The Union line is intact on the right.

By about 11 a.m. Jeb Stuart has ridden two and one-half miles east on the York Pike, and he is turning south toward the Hanover Road to get behind the Federal line. He has reached Cress Ridge, three miles east of Gettysburg, and for reasons unknown, he has Capt. W. H. Griffin fire four rounds, in various directions, from one of his three-inch rifles. Stuart has with him around 430 men of Jenkins's brigade, led today by Lt. Col. Vincent A. Witcher, and he also has the brigades of Chambliss, Wade Hampton, and Fitz Lee, so he has about 4,000 men. Stuart also has 12 pieces of artillery.

His troopers are soon confronted by two Union brigades of 3,200 hell-for-leather horsemen that have ten three-inch ordnance rifles with them. One of the brigades is commanded by George Custer, who was posted at the intersection of the Hanover and Low Dutch Roads, two and one-half miles north of Two Taverns. Custer has received orders to ride south and rejoin Farnsworth's division and operate against the Rebel right in the Round Top sector, but Gen. David M. Gregg has with him only one of his two mounted brigades, Col. John McIntosh's, which is guarding Meade's right when Stuart's men are sighted. Gregg knows he will need Custer, so he decides to keep him.

Longstreet's assault is preceded by a cannonade, with the opening gun firing at 1:07 p.m., and Jeb Stuart uses the report of this gun as the signal to move his mounted troops forward. Meanwhile, the horse artillerymen of both sides exchange rounds at 2,500 yards. But the superior Yankee ammunition at this range makes a huge difference, and the Rebel gunners begin to suffer. Stuart's First Virginia leads a cavalry charge, galloping southeastward across the farms of John Rummel and Jacob Lott, causing the Yankee skirmishers to run for their horses. Gregg sends Custer out in a countercharge, and Custer places himself at the head of the Seventh Michigan, yelling, "Come on, you Wolverines!" The two lines of horsemen crash together at a fence, and the weight of the animals soon breaks the fence rails. Custer skewers a Reb trooper with his saber, and the Virginians break. Stuart sends in more troopers, and this time the Yanks fall back. Both sides now eye one another at a distance.

Stuart brings up Wade Hampton's brigade and charges. The Union gunners fire shell, then canister, as the Confederate horsemen gallop across the Rummel farm. Custer now leads the First Michigan directly at Hampton's men, and when the two lines of animals crash together, horses tumble and men and flashing sabers fly into the air. Saber and pistol and carbine combine in a wild struggle, with men on the ground, horses struggling to regain their feet, men still on horseback, all in a shroud of smoke and dust. McIntosh sends forward every man he can find, and the troopers charge into the Confederate right, while the Third Pennsylvania hammers the Rebel left. Hampton suffers a serious saber wound and receives shrapnel in the hip as the Pennsylvania troopers ride down the Confederate line, slashing and stabbing. Finally Stuart withdraws his men, but the Yanks are too bruised and tired to pursue. In Stuart's strange foray, the Federals lose 254 men, 219 of them from Custer's brigade. Stuart suffers 181 casualties.

Back at Gettysburg, the artillery that Jeb Stuart heard at 1:07 is the greatest artillery bombardment yet heard in the Western Hemisphere. About 150 Confederate guns are involved. General Pendleton, West Point, class of 1830, is Lee's chief of artillery. Pendleton is not a career officer, having left the Army to become an Episcopal priest, so he has the training, but not the experience or instinct, to be a good artilleryman. He has been given this job because of his friendship with Jefferson Davis and Robert E. Lee. Known as Old Mother and Granny behind his back, he is jokingly compared to an elephant—that is, he is fun to look at, but he is too expensive to maintain.

Another Confederate artilleryman, Edward Porter Alexander, is the one that is most remembered. He wrote a frequently quoted memoir, *Fighting for the Confederacy,* and he gets good coverage in the movie *Gettysburg.* But he only commands the 87 guns of the Longstreet's I Corps artillery. He doesn't command the 79 guns of the II Corps, which are under the command of Col. J. Thompson Brown, and he doesn't command the 84 guns of the III Corps artillery, which are under the command of Col. R. Lindsey Walker. Even so, Alexander wonders why the guns of the II Corps artillery, which could have been used to place cross fire on Cemetery Hill and Ridge, remain silent.

The best and the most knowledgeable artillerist in America fights for the North. That man is Henry Hunt. He and Hancock are going to have a dispute that's going to carry on for years until Hancock joins the great majority in 1886. Hunt doesn't want the guns to rapid fire. Instead he orders one shot every two minutes. Hunt has also told all of his battery commanders that any infantry assault will be preceded by a bombardment from massed artillery. Hunt says the primary mission of the artillery battery commanders is to fire on advancing infantry. The secondary mission is counterbattery fire. When the artillery barrage begins, they are instructed to wait 15 to 20 minutes before returning fire. Then they should fire slowly, and only at targets that are a threat. He wants aimed, accurate fire, and he wants it to be deliberate.

But Hancock is an infantryman, and he doesn't give a damn about being deliberate—he wants noise. He wants his men to know that the Yankee artillery is responding in kind to the Rebel guns. This puts Capt. John G. Hazard, Hancock's artillery commander, between a the devil and the deep blue sea.

Meade meets with Hunt that morning to make sure everything is in order. Of the 372 Federal guns, Hunt has 139 between Little Round Top and Cemetery Hill in three groupings: the right group is at Cemetery Hill, the center is at II Corps artillery, and the left is Colonel McGilvery's guns and those on Little Round Top. Hunt also has 95 guns in reserve, parked behind the center of the line near Meade's headquarters, for easy deployment as the situation demands.

Meanwhile, in the borough of Gettysburg late that morning, 20-year-old Mary Virginia "Ginny," or as the press will call her, Jenny, Wade is kneading biscuit dough in the McClellan house, the home of her sister on Baltimore Street at the foot of Cemetery Hill. A shot rings out, and Jenny is killed instantly when a bullet rips through two wooden doors and strikes her in the heart, making her the only civilian killed in the battle. From the location of the holes in the two doors, the marksman could have been a Confederate sharpshooter in the garret of the Harvey A. Sweney house, today's Farnsworth House. This soldier may have used the doorknob on the outer door to adjust his windage.

Professor Michael Jacobs of Pennsylvania College, now Gettysburg College, is keeping hourly records of temperature, wind conditions, and other factors. He records the early afternoon of July 3 as clear, humid, and still, with a temperature of 87 degrees. At 1:07, according to Jacobs's watch, a signal is fired by two Napoleons of Capt. Merritt B. Miller's Third Company of the Washington Artillery in Longstreet's artillery. Then, after the signal, in comes a screaming barrage of iron.

Initially, the Confederate guns fire too high. Plus, the black powder produces lots of gray smoke, restricting line of sight. One of the first shells rips into a man in the II Corps line in a swale south of a small cluster of trees on Cemetery Ridge. After the battle this patch of woods will forever be known as the Copse of Trees. This man is Lt. Sherman Robinson of Company A, 19th Massachusetts, who stands up after eating his lunch, and the round cuts him in half.

At first the most dangerous place to be in the Union line seems to be the Widow Leister's house, Meade's headquarters. One shell hits the front step. Another knocks down the porch foundation on the south side of the house. A third smashes through the door of the west side. A fourth goes through the loft, and a fifth shell whizzes past Meade as he stands in the doorway. He calmly leaves the house and paces back and forth in the small backyard on the east side, while his staff races to the shelter of the Leister barn. A shell bursts in the distance and a fragment about half the size of a hand bounces along the ground near the barn and hits Dan Butterfield in the side. Butterfield "gracefully" keels over and is taken away in an ambulance, but none of the staff is concerned that the wound is serious. The incoming shells do kill a lot of horses in the nearby trains and artillery teams on the Taneytown Road, and they force the reserve artillery to move back about one-half mile. Meade has to temporarily relocate his headquarters to Power's Hill.

Uphill from the Leister house, on Seminary Ridge, Gibbon is commanding the II Corps, because Hancock again commands the left wing of the army. Gibbon's headquarters is in a small draw on the east side of Cemetery Ridge, less than one-quarter mile southwest of Meade's headquarters. Earlier, one of Gibbon's staffers has caught a rather large hen, and the chicken was reduced to chicken and dumplings. Gibbon and Meade had brunched there. Now, the brunch is over; Meade has gone back to the Leister house; and Gibbon is lounging in the draw, congratulating himself on hosting the "old man."

Then the bombardment starts. Gibbon's orderly brings the general's horse up. A shell cuts the orderly in half, and Gibbon's horse runs off. Gibbon walks up to the crest of the ridge and is joined by an aide, Lt. Frank Haskell. Gibbon is an old artilleryman, and he notices how some of the rifled shells tumble in their flight. He sees that when they descend to earth they plow furrows in the ground.

Besides shooting too high, the Confederates don't have enough artillery ammunition for a long fight. So they know the bombardment has to be short, savage, and decisive. The key batteries for the Confederates to knock out are along the section of the line from the Plum Run line north to beyond the Brien barn. They have to silence the 28 guns in the five batteries of the II Corps.

Alexander is handed a note from Longstreet around noon. "Colonel: If the artillery fire does not have the effect to drive off the enemy or greatly demoralize him, so as to make our effort pretty certain, I would prefer that you should not advise Pickett to make the charge." Longstreet is attempting to delegate his responsibility for ordering the attack, and Alexander is shocked. Alexander shows Longstreet's note to Rans Wright, and Wright says, "He has put the responsibility back upon you."

Alexander asks Wright about the chances of success, and Wright says, "Well, Alexander, it is mostly a question of supports. It is not as hard to get there as it looks. I was there yesterday with my brigade. The real difficulty is to stay there after you get there—for the whole infernal Yankee army is up there in a bunch!"

The Confederate attack line has Pickett's all-Virginia division, with 15 regiments, on the right in Spangler's Woods. The rightmost brigade on Pickett's front line belongs to Gen. James L. Kemper. To Kemper's left is Gen. Richard B. Garnett's brigade. Gen. Lewis A. "Lo" Armistead's brigade is in the rear of Garnett. They will advance in line of battle.

The left of their line is held by four brigades of Pettigrew's division of the III Corps. On the front's left is Brockenbrough's numerically small brigade. To Brockenbrough's right is Joe Davis's brigade; on Davis's right is Col. James Marshall's brigade; and finally, on the far right is Col. Birkett Fry's brigade. They will advance by battalion front.

Fifty yards behind the right of Pettigrew's division is Trimble's division. Col. William Lowrance's brigade is on the right and on the left is Lane's brigade. Their formation is in regimental battle line. In all, the front for the Pickett-Pettigrew-Trimble charge will stretch more than a mile.

Also, two other brigades will be advancing, but they won't go forward as planned, and they will not move until after the repulse of Pickett, Pettigrew, and Trimble. They are far off on Pickett's right, and they fought there the day before. They are Wilcox's Alabama Brigade and Lang's Florida Brigade.

When the Yankee artillery returns fire, almost 600 Confederates will not come out of Spangler's Woods, because they are dead or wounded. The ground beneath trees is not a good place to be during an artillery bombardment, because the shells hit the branches and explode overhead, raining razor-sharp metal and huge tree limbs and jagged splinters.

Out in front of Pettigrew's division, one-third of the way to Cemetery Ridge, is the William Bliss farm. This farm is in a no-man's-land, littered with the dead and wounded. At noon the Bliss house and barn are ordered burned by Alexander Hays when he grows tired of struggling to hold that location. That leaves a pall of smoke filling the swales between the lines, and the eastern slope of Seminary Ridge is quickly enveloped with smoke from the cannon. So visibility is almost zero.

Longstreet's heart is not in this attack, and he sits on a rail fence back on Seminary Ridge near Spangler's Woods. The tree line of Spangler's Woods juts out eastward for about 300 yards, and this serves as the separation line for Pickett's and Pettigrew's divisions. Pettigrew forms his men back in the woods along the ridge, while Pickett has his men in the woods that jut out on Pettigrew's right. Pettigrew has his men in line of battle, shoulder touching shoulder. Two steps behind the first rank, the second rank is also shoulder to shoulder. Behind the second rank are the S.O.B.s—the sergeants and the second lieutenants—who are the file closers to exercise control. So because those woods jut out, when Pickett advances, he will travel several hundred yards before Pettigrew moves out, because Pettigrew cannot see beyond Pickett's men due to the 300-yard tongue of trees. But that will not really bother Trimble and Pettigrew, since they have the shortest distance to go. They will go straight, while Pickett's men will have to oblique to the left and go much farther.

Despite the folklore, Garnett is not the only officer going forward on horseback. At least 21 other officers, including Kemper, are mounted. However, Garnett will be one of the few that's wearing a heavy coat in 87-degree weather, because he has a fever.

Fifty yards behind Garnett's brigade is Armistead's brigade. In the old Army, Lo Armistead and Hancock were close friends at Fort Tejon, California. When Armistead resigned from the Army, they had a drinking contest in Hancock's home in Los Angeles. While Hancock's wife played the piano, Hancock, Garnett, Albert Sidney Johnston, and Armistead sang nostalgic songs.

As the cannon boom, Wilcox, an old West Point classmate of Pickett, says to Pickett, "George let's have a drink." To understand Pickett's reply, it's necessary to know that he and 20-year-old La Salle "Sallie" Corbell are desperately in love. Pickett is a widower once, losing his wife in childbirth in Texas in 1851. He's widowed twice if one considers a common law marriage. Pickett undoubtedly hasn't told Sallie about the Indian princess, Morning Mist, who died after giving him a son out in Washington Territory. When Wilcox offers the drink, Pickett says, "I promised Sallie I wouldn't have a drink on the campaign." Wilcox replies, "George, it doesn't matter, in 30 minutes you and I are going to be in hell or in glory."

A few Union guns return fire, and soon Alexander's rounds home in on Lt. T. Frederick Brown's First Rhode Island Battery. Brown is firing away against Hunt's orders, because Hancock wants flash and bang. But the boom, fire, and smoke of Brown's guns attract attention to his position. The Confederate shells soon screech in, and one of Brown's guns is hit in the muzzle by a shell just as Pvt. Alfred Gardner is loading it. Gardner's arm is ripped off, and the cannon is dented, permanently wedging the loaded round in the muzzle. As Gardner bleeds to death, he waves his stub, saying, "Glory to God! I am happy! Hallelujah!"

Today that dented gun, known as the Gettysburg Gun, is in the statehouse in Providence. In 1962, during the Civil War Centennial, more than two pounds of black powder had to be removed from the gun barrel, because someone finally realized that a shell stuck in a gun barrel had to have powder behind it.

In an angle formed by the stone wall along Cemetery Ridge just south of Cemetery Hill, Lt. Alonzo Cushing's Company A, Fourth U.S. Artillery, is also taking a pounding. Shell fragments are flying, and Cushing is first hit in the shoulder and then in the groin. Still, he stays with his guns, saying to one of his sergeants, "I stay right here and fight it out or die in the attempt."

At 1:35, Alexander sends a message to Pickett: "If you are coming at all, you must come at once, or I cannot give you proper support, but the enemy's fire has not slackened at all. At least 18 guns are still firing from the cemetery itself."

Up on Cemetery Hill, Maj. Thomas Osborn of the XI Corps suggests to Hunt that his 29 guns cease fire to lure the Confederates into thinking the artillery bombardment has been successful. Hunt likes the idea, despite what Hancock thinks, and the word is passed to "Cease fire!" This happens about the time that Alexander writes his first note to Pickett, and Osborn's guns are the first to cease firing.

The ruse works. Alexander immediately sends a second message to Pickett: "For God's sake come quick. The 18 guns are gone. Come quick or I can't support you."

Pickett rides back to Longstreet and hands him Alexander's note. As Longstreet reads it, Pickett asks, "General, shall I advance?" Longstreet can't bring himself to say anything. He sits on the fence, and he just looks away. He knows the charge has to be made, but he can't give the order. After a few seconds, Pickett says, "I am going to move forward, sir!"

With his staff, Pickett takes position on the right of Garnett and on the left of Kemper. Pickett faces the ranks and tells his officers to get across that field as fast as they can, because it's one hell of an ugly place. But to his men, he says something different. He says, "Up, men, and to your posts! Don't forget today, that you are from Old Virginia!" With that, out of the woods they come at quick time—80 steps a minute. It is a magnificent sight.

As Pickett moves forward, his men are several hundred yards in front of Pettigrew and Trimble. The Virginians march across fields that had been planted in wheat, corn, and clover, but have been trampled for two days by the feet of thousands of soldiers. Pickett's line moves straight toward Cemetery Ridge. But after 500 yards, he halts, dresses his lines, and then obliques to his left, because when they reach the Emmitsburg Road, Pickett wants his left to touch Pettigrew's right. When that happens, they will go forward toward the low stone wall along Cemetery Ridge.

About a hundred yards west of the Emmitsburg Road, Pickett's left wing is in a low swale, so they're in defilade, and are briefly protected from fire. Here, Pickett dresses his lines again. Then they continue to a slight rise, just west of the Emmitsburg Road and to the front of the Codori house, and here they link up with Fry's right-hand brigade of Pettigrew's division for the final surge across the road and up the western face of Cemetery Ridge. But, on this rise, they're exposed to the Yankee guns to the left on Cemetery Hill, they're exposed to the artillery in their front, and they're exposed to the cannon on Little Round Top to the right. There are lots of Yankee cannon up there, and they are going into the jaws of hell.

In front of Pettigrew's men on the Confederate left, Alexander Hays of the II Corps has posted the Eighth Ohio out on the Emmitsburg Road to his right to guard his flank, and Lt. Col. Franklin Sawyer has raced these Ohioans into the cornfield to his front. He sees the mass of Confederates passing to his left, and they are paying him no attention. He wheels his men to the left and pours fire into the left flank of Brockenbrough's Virginians, who break and run for the rear, exposing Davis's Mississippians and North Carolinians to the deadly enfilading fire.

To the front of Pettigrew, in a blue line extending south from the Brien barn is Col. Thomas Smyth's brigade, and on his right and north of the barn is Col. Eliakim Sherrill's brigade, which the day before had been Willard's. Their division commander is Alexander Hays, West Point class of '44, a good friend of Hancock and Grant. Grant will be devastated when Hays is killed in the Wilderness. Hays is one in a million because he savors combat, but he's smart enough to know that other men don't. So whether his men like it or not, he's had them standing at attention, putting them through the manual of arms all the while the Rebels are advancing, up until the time the Confederates cross the Emmitsburg Road. He figures it will take his men's minds off those gray lines coming forward with that forest of red flags flapping in the breeze. He races them southward from Ziegler's Grove, and they form a line behind a low stone wall just south of the Brien barn and house.

Bordering the Emmitsburg Road are two stout, bullproof, post-and-rail fences that the Confederates have to cross. Yes, Reynolds's people tore the fence sections down on the west side of the road early on July 1, but that was south of the Codori farm. Yes, some sections were broken down in the July 2 fighting. But a lot of the fence remains. Most of the Confederates have to cross the fences on both sides of the road under heavy fire, and the only way to cross is to clamber over them as fast as possible.

The small-arms fire from the front is now ripping into the Confederates, because Hays has finally given his men permission to fire. Hays has packed two brigades behind 260 yards of stone wall. The men and their rifle-muskets are three and four deep, and his soldiers are firing at will. Soldiers in the 69th Pennsylvania have five or six loaded rifles each, because they have policed these weapons from the battlefield of the day before.

Just south of the Brien barn, the 12th New Jersey is firing obsolete .69-caliber buck-and-ball smoothbores, which at long range are virtually useless, but at short range are murderous. Two companies of the 14th Connecticut have Sharps breechloaders, so their rate of fire is rapid. The volume of Federal fire is so heavy that many Confederates seek to use the bed of the road for cover, because at the fence it is two feet deep.

After the Confederates scramble over the two fences bordering the Emmitsburg Road, a 200-yard-stretch of open ground must be crossed to reach the low stone wall, behind which is a line of blue uniforms, cannon, muskets, and bayonets. By now Pettigrew has been hit in the hand by shrapnel and has been unhorsed, but he still leads on the ground. Fry has been shot in the thigh and is out of action. Jimmy Marshall goes down with two bullets in his brain, and all four of his North Carolina regimental commanders are gunned down. Brockenbrough and his men have taken to their heels, so Joe Davis is the only brigade commander left standing in Pettigrew's division. Many of Pettigrew's men stop at the road and lay down fire, but the 11th Mississippi and the 55th North Carolina on the left flank boldly cross the road—despite the flanking fire from the Ohioans on their left, despite the artillery fire from Cemetery Hill, and despite the canister from the six Napoleons of Lt. George A. Woodruff's First U.S. Battery near Ziegler's Grove. The Mississippians and the Tar Heels race across the field and get into the Brien barn and yard, and there the few survivors take whatever cover they can find.

Some of Fry's and Marshall's men, now leaderless, use the fence rails along the road to steady their rifles, and both of Hays's brigade commanders—Smyth and Sherrill—are shot down. Other Confederates scale the fences and charge the stone wall. The 26th North Carolina, which lost 13 color bearers and its colonel on July 1, loses four more flag bearers in this charge on July 3. The 47th North Carolina, led by Lt. Col. John Graves, has 150 men almost to the stone wall. Isaac Trimble's two brigades, Lane's and Lowrance's, make it to the road, but many of the men will not go farther. Trimble, riding his mare, Jinnie, is badly wounded in the lower left leg as he crosses the road. The leg will have to be amputated, and he will be captured and spend the rest of the war in a Union prison, where he will make himself a real pain in the butt to his captors, the same as the legless Royal Air Force hero Douglas Bader did to the Germans in World War II.

Pickett's men are now nearing the road, trying to get over those fences. Garnett's men hit the fence at an angle, and a lieutenant gets his head stuck between two rails as he tries to crawl through. As the bullets slap into the rail, he is terrified he will be killed and found in this embarrassing predicament, but he manages to pull free with a neck full of splinters. Later, after the battle is over, a 16-foot-long fence rail is found to have 836 musket balls embedded in it.

Kemper rides back to Armistead and says, "General, I am going to storm those works, and I want you to support me." Armistead says, "Of course." Then Armistead points to his brigade. He beams and says, "Did you ever see anything better on parade?" Kemper says, "I never did," and salutes. These men are soldiers of the finest order.

Armistead's men reach the fence, and it's a matter of who can climb the fastest, scamper across the road, and scale the second fence. A scene in the movie *Gettysburg* shows a terrified teenage boy crouching behind the fence, and Armistead says, "Get up, boy! What will you think of yourself tomorrow?" These men all know each other; they are from the same town or the same county, and they are often related. If they run now, they can never go home again.

The stone wall juts west from Hays's left for more than 250 feet before it turns back south, and after the battle, this section of wall will forever be called "the Angle." Where it again turns south, Alexander Webb's Philadelphia Brigade is defending, supported by two of Cushing's three-inch rifles, which the badly wounded Cushing has moved up to the wall. On Webb's left are the brigades of Col. Norman J. Hall, Gen. William Harrow, and Gen. George J. Stannard's nine-month Vermont Brigade, which has executed a rugged seven-day forced march and has reached Gettysburg on the evening of July 1, reporting to the I Corps. Stannard only has three of his five regiments on the line, because the 12th and 15th Vermont are guarding trains. Stannard's Vermonters have earlier been out skirmishing with Pickett's advancing troops but have now fallen back. Then, as Pickett's men oblique to the left, Stannard sees a chance to hit them on their right flank.

In Stannard's 13th Vermont is Lt. Stephen F. Brown, who was placed under arrest for disobeying orders by falling out of the march to Gettysburg to fill the canteens of his thirsty men. His sword has been taken away from him while he was under arrest. But on July 3, every man is needed, and Brown races into battle with a camp hatchet as his symbol of authority. Brown, using his hatchet, captures a Confederate officer during the flanking movement and takes his sword. When the 13th Vermont Monument is dedicated in 1899, Brown is honored as the figure on the pedestal. The original design depicted him going into battle with the hatchet, but the War Department disapproved this design, because it would be a tribute to disobedience. Instead, Brown is shown holding the captured Confederate sword in one hand, and as a compromise, the hatchet is lying at his feet.

Hancock has been up and down the line all day, and when the attack starts, one of his subordinates says, "General, the corps commander ought not to risk his life that way." Hancock looks out at the approaching Confederates and says, "There are times when a corps commander's life does not count." Then, just as Stannard has gotten the 13th and 16th Vermont regiments into position, Hancock rides up and shouts, "You have gone to hell." Hancock doesn't understand what Stannard is doing. At this moment a bullet hits the pommel of Hancock's saddle and goes into his right thigh, under the groin, taking with it wood fragments and a large nail. He's helped from his horse by aides, and he's bleeding badly, but it's a tough place to try to tie a tourniquet. Alexander Dougherty later removes the nail, which they then assume the Confederates are shooting.

Hancock is evacuated to an army hospital in Philadelphia to recuperate, but he loses a lot of weight. He goes from 220 pounds down to about 160. They send him to his father's home in Norristown to help get him out of the city heat. In August, Dr. Louis Read, who lives in Norristown, visits Hancock. Dr. Read says, "General, what position were you in when you were shot?" Hancock says, "I was in the saddle." So, the physician gets a chair and has Hancock sit in it. Then Dr. Read takes a probe with a porcelain cap, because if the porcelain touches lead, it will carry a stain. Read breaks the scab, and sticks the probe in while Hancock grimaces. Read works the probe in six inches, and the porcelain cap comes out with lead on it. The next day, August 21, the doctor lays Hancock on a gurney and removes the bullet. Still, pieces of shattered bone remain in the wound, and it won't heal, resulting in a severe case of osteomyelitis. Hancock has to ride in an ambulance when he returns to duty. The wound discharges pieces of bone throughout the summer of 1864, and eventually, in October, Hancock goes on sick leave. When he returns to duty, he is assigned to the invalid corps.

Leading his Virginians, Kemper is shot almost the same way as Hancock, and just several hundred yards away from where Hancock is wounded. Kemper is mounted, and he rises up in the saddle, looks at the Yankee line, and says, "There are the guns, boys, go for them!" A bullet penetrates his left thigh near the groin, just missing the femoral artery. It hits his thigh bone, glances up into his body cavity, and lodges near his spine. He is temporarily paralyzed from the waist down. This bullet can't be removed, and Kemper spends the rest of his life in pain and on crutches.

Gibbon, too, is shot while riding among the troops. He is with the 19th Maine when a bullet hits his left arm and slices along his left shoulder blade. Command of the II Corps passes to General Harrow, and Gibbon is taken to the rear.

Pickett is watching from just north of the Codori barn, and he sees his three brigades begin to merge into one tangled mass of humanity seeking to get to the stone wall. The Confederates must reach that wall to stop the hailstorm of lead and iron flying at them in unimaginable quantities.

Pickett's men, after climbing the two fences, have to cross the open ground and the low stone wall, the top of which now appears to be on fire from the Federal muzzle flashes. Kemper's men are taking fire from Stannard's Vermonters on their right, so the 24th Virginia and part of the 11th Virginia wheel to face that threat. Kemper's left flank units pass through the field south of the Copse of Trees in the center of the Union line and open fire. Then they charge the wall. Garnett's brigade is to Kemper's left, and Armistead's people are behind Garnett, but soon their men are intermingled.

Cushing has now loaded his guns with triple canister. He orders, "Fire!" At that split second a bullet whizzes into his open mouth, and that's the end of the valiant Alonzo Cushing. But the blasts of his canister mow the Confederates down.

Garnett's men move up in front of the 69th Pennsylvania and close on Cushing's two guns. The 69th is an all-Irish regiment commanded by Col. Dennis O'Kane, a bartender and hotel operator. He will mix no more drinks after this day. Garnett is still in his uniform coat, waving a black felt hat with silver cord.

There's smoke and fire and noise, and point-blank cannon blasts, and all of a sudden Garnett's black charger, Redeye, comes running back out of the smoke with a huge gash in the right shoulder, and Garnett's body is never found. His sword will show up in a Baltimore pawn shop long after the war and will be bought by George Steuart.

Somewhere near where Garnett is killed, Col. Waller Tazewell "Tad" Patton, commander of the Seventh Virginia, and the great-uncle of the famous Gen. George S. Patton of World War II fame, receives a mortal wound. Tad graduated from VMI in 1855, and he appears briefly in the movie *Gettysburg,* portrayed by Ted Turner. In the movie, Tad Patton takes a clean torso wound; in reality, the wound that he suffers is more terrible, taking away the lower jaw and severing his tongue. He is taken prisoner and, with no jaw, starves to death in agony on July 21.

Capt. Andrew Cowan's six three-inch rifles of the First Battery, New York Light Artillery, race up to replace Brown's and Cushing's batteries. Cowan places one rifle north of the Copse of Trees, behind Cushing's battery, and the other five rifles go south of the trees. Then they blast canister into Garnett's and Armistead's men at near point-blank range.

Less than a hundred yards to Garnett's left, Armistead leads his men to the stone wall. Cushing is dead, and his guns are out of ammunition. The 71st Pennsylvania, which Col. Richard Penn Smith pulled away from the fighting at Culp's Hill the night before, has eight companies crammed into the space between the Angle and Cushing's guns. Smith is in the rear with the two other companies of the regiment. When Cushing's guns fall silent, one of Smith's companies breaks and runs. The other front line companies engage in hand-to-hand combat as the Confederates surge into the gap. Then the remaining seven companies of the 71st cut and run. Gen. Alexander Webb is mortified, writing that he "almost wished to get killed."

Seeing his chance, Armistead yells, "Come forward, Virginians! Come on, boys, we must give them the cold steel. Who will follow me?"

Armistead goes over the stone wall, followed by Lt. Col. Rawley W. Martin of the 53rd Virginia, and about a hundred men. With them is the flag of the 53rd. Armistead angles toward Cushing's two abandoned guns, to the right of the 69th Pennsylvania, causing that regiment's Companies A and I to open fire so close that the muzzle flashes burn their opponents. Company F remains facing forward, so a gap appears in the Pennsylvania line, and Armistead and his Virginians rush into the gap, killing Capt. George Thompson and taking a number of the company prisoner.

The remainder of the 69th Pennsylvania is south of the point of penetration, and these soldiers pull back their right battalion, rally, and swarm the Confederates. Armistead reaches Cushing's still hot guns, puts a hand on one of them, and yells: "The day is ours, men, come turn this artillery upon them." Maj. Samuel B. Roberts of the 72nd Pennsylvania orders several soldiers to "shoot that man," and three bullets slap into Armistead's shoulder and leg. He falls and is captured and taken to the XI Corps hospital at the George Spangler house, where he dies on July 5.

The Yankees keep coming. Up races the 19th Massachusetts and the 42nd New York, accompanied by the 19th Maine, the 15th Massachusetts, and what's left of the First Minnesota. There's nothing left for the outnumbered Confederates to do but get back to Seminary Ridge the best way they can, and as they break, the Yankees taunt them by shouting, "Fredericksburg! Fredericksburg!"

After Stannard's Vermonters have done their duty on the left flank, they suddenly see Wilcox's and Lang's brigades coming across the field to the south. These two brigades, however, are far too late to be of any benefit to Pickett's men. They didn't step off in time to protect the left flank of the Virginians from Stannard's flanking fire. In fact, they didn't start forward until Pickett's men were fighting at the wall, and now as they march east across the fields between the Codori and Klingle houses, 59 Federal guns open up on them. When they reach Plum Run, Stannard's 16th Vermont simply faces about and, joined by the 14th Vermont, double-times southward and fires into the Confederate flank. The bewildered Southerners go tumbling back. The attack is over.

That morning, Alfred Pleasonton, the Union chief of cavalry, ordered Kilpatrick's division, which had bivouacked the previous night at Two Taverns, to strike the Confederate right flank and rear and prevent the Union left from being turned. Kilpatrick is to be assisted by Merritt's cavalry brigade of Buford's division. Merritt's troopers are in Emmitsburg, only seven miles south of the Confederate right.

Kilpatrick has two brigades in his division—Farnsworth's and Custer's—but Custer's brigade is north of Two Taverns on the Hanover Road. Kilpatrick sends orders for Custer's brigade to return. However, without Kilpatrick's knowledge, Custer is retained by General Gregg for the fight with Jeb Stuart, and Kilpatrick rides west toward the Emmitsburg Road with only Farnsworth's brigade.

On the Confederate right between the Emmitsburg Road and Round Top are John Bell Hood's four brigades of infantry, now commanded by General Law, because of Hood's wounding. During the cannonade preceding the Pickett-Pettigrew-Trimble attack, Law spies a cavalry brigade approaching up the Emmitsburg Road from the south. He orders two artillery batteries on Warfield Ridge to face southward and shell the Yankees.

General Merritt departed Emmitsburg around noon and arrives on the Emmitsburg Road, one and one-half miles southwest of Round Top, about the same time Farnsworth's troopers arrive and go into position just over one-half mile west of Round Top to the west of Bushman Hill. The sounds of the massive cannonade preceding what is now known as Pickett's Charge rumble down the Emmitsburg Road from the north, and Merritt, hoping to turn the Confederate right flank, dismounts his troopers and attacks parallel to and west of the road for about one-half mile. Law shifts three infantry regiments of Anderson's Georgia Brigade to face Merritt's troopers and sends 250 South Carolina cavalrymen, commanded by Col. John L. Black, to protect his right flank.

When Black sends word that Merritt is shifting farther to the west to stretch the thin Confederate line and turn their right flank, Law personally leads the remaining two regiments of Anderson's brigade to the right. Black's cavalry gives way to Merritt's troopers, but the Confederate infantry counterattacks and quickly drives the Federals back. By 3 p.m. Merritt's attack is over. The young general has unwisely dismounted his cavalrymen in relatively open ground and lost the advantage of mobility. And although the Yankee breech-loading carbines could fire rapidly, they did not have the range or accuracy of the Rebel muzzle-loading rifles. Lastly, the cavalrymen did not have the training or experience to compete with veteran infantrymen.

General Law later recalled that his success against Merritt's brigade "reduced my front to manageable dimensions and left some force at my disposal to meet any concentrated attack that the enemy might make."

When Longstreet's attack is repulsed, Pleasonton is with George Meade, and as Meade ponders a counterattack, Pleasonton sends orders to Kilpatrick to make a diversion on the Confederate right flank. At 5 p.m. Kilpatrick receives Pleasonton's instructions and orders a charge. Kilpatrick explains to Farnsworth that he plans to conduct both a direct attack and a flanking maneuver on the Confederate batteries on Warfield Ridge. Farnsworth sees that a cavalry charge over such ground against defending infantry and artillery will be suicidal. The attack will have to be over rough terrain, stone walls, fences, and through woodlots directly into the muzzles of rifles and cannon. But orders are orders.

The First West Virginia Cavalry will make the direct attack on the guns, and the 18th Pennsylvania Cavalry will form on the West Virginians' left and charge in support. The First Vermont Cavalry will be divided into three battalions, two battalions to charge and one to remain in place as skirmishers and a reserve.

The assault will have artillery support from the six three-inch ordnance rifles of Capt. William M. Graham's Battery K, First U.S. Artillery, posted east of the Emmitsburg Road, one-half mile south of the Ridge Road, and the four ordnance rifles of Lt. Samuel S. Elder's Battery E, Fourth U.S. Artillery, which have been hauled to the crest of Bushman Hill.

Farnsworth is ordered forward, and his West Virginians and Pennsylvanians charge headlong into the First Texas, which is hunkered down behind stone walls. The Mountaineers and men from the Keystone State don't fare well, but the two charging battalions of the First Vermont slash through the Confederate line and race into the fields south of the John Slyder and George Bushman farms.

On Law's order, the Fourth Alabama races downhill from the slope of Round Top to Plum Run, and moves into position to the east of Maj. William Wells's Vermonters. West of Wells's column, the Ninth Georgia moves to form the opposite side of the box. The four Napoleons of Capt. William Bachman's South Carolina Artillery are perched on Warfield Ridge and are ordered to face left across Plum Run Valley. The First Texas forms the bottom of the box on the south. The Federal cavalry has to run a gauntlet of Confederate lead and iron as it tries to escape Law's trap. Farnsworth, after losing one horse and mounting another, falls dead with five bullet wounds, but Wells finally leads the rest of the troopers southward to safety. He will be awarded the Medal of Honor in 1891 for his actions.

Shortly before Farnsworth's charge, Meade abandons his temporary Power's Hill command post and returns to the area adjacent to his Leister house headquarters. As soon as Pickett's men fall back, he rides with his son to the crest of Cemetery Ridge to Hays's position. The smoke is too thick to see, so they turn right, toward Ziegler's Grove, and north of the Brien barn, they see the cannoneers of Woodruff's battery blasting canister down the Brien farm lane at the retreating Confederates. Meade looks down toward the Emmitsburg Road and observes Alexander Hays riding back and forth in the fields, dragging a number of Confederate flags in the dirt behind him. He asks Lt. John Egan, commanding the section of guns, if the enemy has been turned. Egan says, "Yes. See, Hays has one of their flags." Meade snaps, "I don't care for their flag. Have they turned?" Egan realizes his error and replies, "Yes, sir! They are just turning."

The two Meades then ride south down the line, through Hays's position to Webb's, and they see Gibbon's aide, Lieutenant Haskell, who confirms that the enemy has withdrawn. Meade then rides to see General Howard on Cemetery Hill to check on the situation there. Meade soon returns to Ziegler's Grove, and the troops begin to cheer. He then rides down the line, accompanied by a gathering entourage of officers, all the way to Little Round Top, being saluted by the cheers of his men.

Meade receives the report of the Federal cavalry charge on his left flank and decides that the Confederates still have a lot of fight in them. His units are disorganized and intermingled; it has been a rugged, rough day; and it will soon be dark. He decides not to counterattack. He returns to the Widow Leister's house to find that it is being used as a field hospital. At 8:35 he sends a message to Halleck that he has repelled the assault and that the enemy appears to be withdrawing. Meade, exhausted, then moves one-quarter mile down the Taneytown Road and sleeps among the rocks.

Lee is expecting a counterattack, and when he spies Pickett, he says, "General Pickett, place your division in rear of this hill, and be ready to repel the advance of the enemy should they follow up their advantage." Pickett replies, "General Lee, I have no division now. Armistead is down, Garnett is down, and Kemper is mortally wounded." Lee calmly says, "Come, General Pickett, this has been my fight and upon my shoulders rests the blame. The men and officers of your command have written the name of Virginia as high today as it has ever been written before."

Wilcox attempts to report to Lee, but his emotions overwhelm him, and Lee says, "Never mind, General, all this has been my fault—it is I that have lost this fight, and you must help me out of it the best way you can."

At 6 p.m. a long and continuous Yankee cheer is heard, and it is misread as the beginning of a Federal counterattack. But the cheering turns out to be for George Meade as he rides along the Union line. Thus Lee has time to reorganize. He knows that he must retreat. His army has suffered such terrible losses that it cannot possibly continue on the offensive. His artillery is virtually out of ammunition. Subsistence will be hard to find, now that the Federals can restrict his movements, and he has thousands of wounded to evacuate. Lee decides it is time to meet with his generals.

A staff officer recalled, "The generals had a council at Gen. A. P. Hill's headquarters on the Cashtown Road, about sundown, and decided to fall back."

Lee spends much time the night of July 3 with Hill, discussing the withdrawal of the III Corps. Hill will finally do something—he will lead the retreat column, followed by Longstreet, then Ewell.

The next day, July 4, was a memorable one at Vicksburg. Grant described it in his memoirs: "I rode into Vicksburg with the troops and went to the river to exchange congratulations with the navy upon our joint victory. . . . This news, with the victory at Gettysburg . . . lifted a great load of anxiety from the minds of the President, his Cabinet, and the loyal people all over the North."

Meanwhile, in Middle Tennessee, Rosecrans plans to make a full frontal assault against Bragg at Tullahoma. But before Rosecrans moves, once again, disagreement between Bragg and his subordinate generals results in his issuing a retreat order from Tullahoma. Bragg's army withdraws to Chattanooga unmolested and crosses the Tennessee River on July 4. Rosecrans is elated over the relatively bloodless success of his Tullahoma Campaign and is content.

An exhausted Lee returns to his Seminary Ridge headquarters at 1 a.m. on July 4. Gen. John D. Imboden arrived with his cavalry brigade earlier in the day, and as ordered, he is waiting for Lee.

Imboden describes Lee that night: "The moon was high in the clear sky and the silent scene was unusually vivid. As he approached and saw us lying on the grass under a tree, he . . . reined in his jaded horse. . . . The moon shone full upon his massive features and revealed an expression of sadness that I had never seen before upon his face."

Imboden speaks first: "General, this has been a hard day on you." Lee replies, "Yes, it has been a sad, sad day to us." Then, after a minute or two, Lee, who has been leaning against Traveller, suddenly stands straight and turns to Imboden, "I never saw troops behave more magnificently than Pickett's division of Virginians did today in that grand charge upon the enemy." Lee pauses, and adds, "We must now return to Virginia."

Lee wants to shorten his battle line on July 4, so he orders Ewell to fall back through Gettysburg and dig in along Oak and Seminary Ridges. Soon, breastworks and rifle pits extend for two and one-half miles from the Mummasburg Road to the Emmitsburg Road on the western slope of the ridgeline, hidden by the trees. If Meade attacks on July 4, it will be across open ground against well-defended positions. Lee need not have worried about an attack, because Meade advises his commanders that July 4 would be a day to rest and refit.

At 1 p.m. it begins to rain heavily at Gettysburg. General Imboden recalled: "The very windows of heaven seemed to have opened. The rain fell in blinding sheets; the meadows were soon overflowed, and fences gave way before the raging streams. During the storm, wagons, ambulances, and artillery carriages by hundreds—nay, by thousands—were assembling in the fields along the road from Gettysburg to Cashtown. . . . About 4:00 p.m. the head of the column was put in motion."

At 4:15, Meade issues General Orders Number 68, saying: "Our task is not yet accomplished, and the commanding general looks to the army for greater efforts to drive from our soil every vestige of the presence of the intruder."

EPILOGUE

WHEN LEE SAID ON JULY 3, "THE FAULT IS ENTIRELY MY OWN," HIS *declaration is commonly interpreted to refer only to the Battle of Gettysburg. Yet Lee knew that his failure meant much more. He had marched his Army of Northern Virginia into Maryland and Pennsylvania, full of hope that he could strike the blow that would lead to a political end to the war. He believed this, and he had convinced his civilian leadership to choose the northern invasion over the Mississippi River defense. Lee knew that he was responsible for much, much more than the failure of a single charge, or for the loss of a single battle.*

After Lee failed at Gettysburg, he offered to resign on August 8, 1863. He wrote to Jefferson Davis: "The general remedy for the want of success in a military commander is removal. . . . I cannot even accomplish what I myself desire. How can I fulfill the expectations of others?" On August 12, he received a response from Davis: "To ask me to substitute you by some one in my judgment more fit to command, or who would possess more of the confidence of the army, or of the reflecting men of the country, is to demand an impossibility." But, despite the rhetoric, both men had to know that the opportunity was gone.

In Washington, at 7 p.m. on July 6, Abraham Lincoln telegraphed George Meade: "I left the telegraph office a good deal dissatisfied. . . . I did not like the phrase, in Orders No. 68. . . . 'Drive the invaders from our soil.' " It was Lincoln's position that all of the United States was "our soil," and he said that he felt such statements were not "connected with a purpose to prevent [Lee's] crossing [the Potomac River] and to destroy him." When Lincoln learned on July 14 that the Army of Northern Virginia had escaped across the Potomac on the night of the 13th, he moaned to his secretary, John Hay: "We had them within our grasp. We had only to stretch forth our hands and they were ours." Lincoln knew that the opportunity was gone.

In Middle Tennessee, on July 7, Rosecrans received a telegram from Secretary of War Stanton advising that Lee was beaten and that Vicksburg had surrendered. Stanton then added: "You and your noble army now have a chance to give a finishing blow to the rebellion. Will you neglect the chance?" Rosecrans replied to Stanton: "Just received your cheering telegram announcing the fall of Vicksburg and confirming the defeat of Lee. You do not appear to observe the fact that this noble army has driven the rebels from Middle Tennessee." Rosecrans remained immobile until August 16, not understanding that the opportunity was gone.

At Vicksburg, Ulysses Grant recalled: "The fate of the Confederacy was sealed when Vicksburg fell. Much hard fighting was to be done afterwards and many precious lives were to be sacrificed; but the morale *was with the supporters of the Union ever after." Grant knew that both the military and political pendulums had finally swung to the Union side.*

On July 13, 1863, Abraham Lincoln wrote to Ulysses Grant: "My Dear General: I do not remember that you and I ever met personally. I write this now as a grateful acknowledgment for the almost inestimable service that you have done the country. I wish to say a word further. When you first reached the vicinity of Vicksburg, I thought you should do, what you finally did—march the troops across the neck, run the batteries with the transports, and thus go below; and I never had any faith, except a general hope that you knew better than I, that the Yazoo Pass Expedition, and the like, could succeed. When you got below, and took Port Gibson, Grand Gulf, and vicinity, I thought you should go down the river and join Gen. Banks; and when you turned northward east of the Big Black, I feared it was a mistake. I now wish to make the personal acknowledgment that you were right and I was wrong."

Abraham Lincoln knew that in Grant he finally had a general who understood what he had been trying to teach his other generals; that it was not the seizure of real estate, but the destruction of the army on that real estate that mattered. More important, Lincoln knew that the war was now militarily and politically beyond winning for the South. The Confederate high tide had receded.

REFLECTIONS

IT WAS LATE NOVEMBER AND THE AUDIENCE WAS SPECIAL—SOLDIERS FROM Walter Reed Army Medical Center and their families. They were on a Thanksgiving weekend tour of Gettysburg sponsored by the Blue and Gray Education Society. The temperature was mild, but the wind had a bite and so this would be primarily a bus tour. Yet when it came time to go to Little Round Top, they all got off the bus, and some struggled, supported on both arms, to our point of lecture a hundred yards away. They could have stayed on the bus, but these soldiers came.

Battlefields are special places, where ordinary people become extraordinary. They don't ask for the attention, and most are motivated to serve by the most basic of instincts—patriotic love and respect for their country. I know that feeling because it inspired me to join the United States Marine Corps. It binds me to them this day.

Standing atop Little Round Top, I can see the legions of Longstreet's corps coming from as far as the eye can see. The monument of Warren warms to near human form as he calls reinforcements to this unoccupied point. Noteworthy features like the Devil's Den, Houck's Ridge, Round Top, the Valley of Death, and the Slaughter Pen all come into focus—there is the site where John Bell Hood was wounded, knocking the steam out of the attack; to my left are the monuments to Strong Vincent and Paddy O'Rorke, whose men responded to Warren's call and paid with their lives. Out of sight is the Union left, where Joshua Lawrence Chamberlain and his men repulsed Oates's 15th Alabama at the point of a bayonet. My mind shifts momentarily to the opposite side of the battlefield, where troops under "Pop" Greene and David Ireland did equally great things. I won't have time today to take these young warriors to Culp's Hill. Darkness will come quickly, and those soldiers' heroic deeds will be denied recognition yet again.

Millions of people have and will visit Gettysburg, and yet so few will ever understand what this battlefield means to America and Americans. Chamberlain predicted that countless unknown and faceless visitors would come to visit these fields and ponder what these soldiers did for them. So too on this day would modern heroes return to pay tribute to the long gray line. People walked past us, not knowing that these were Iraq and Afghanistan veterans, or that I was bloodied in WWII. Perhaps some who walked past us were also veterans.

Soldiers serve and move on, their contributions often remembered by nothing more than a certificate or a mass-produced medal. They move on to other things, some physically scarred and others mentally scarred. None know but them and their families. All we have to remind us of their often nameless sacrifice is the battlefield and the interpretation of it. At Gettysburg, 180,000 men struggled for the future of the nation, and when they left three days later, 51,000 had left all or a part of their youth. All would be marked for life. Many died unknown and in obscure corners of the battlefield; the lucky died instantly. Others lingered for days, and the truly unfortunate may have survived the bullets only to fall months later to disease or a weakened constitution.

Lincoln had it right on November 19, 1863, when he spoke about the men who had consecrated the ground. He challenged the living to rededicate themselves to the task at hand, which meant winning the war and reuniting the country, to ensure the honored dead of Gettysburg and other battles would not have died in vain. Battlefields mean something; they tell us something. And our visit was part of a ritual that started long ago, when those veterans came back here for reunions. Some of those elderly men died soon after they returned home from the final 75th reunion, where President Franklin Roosevelt dedicated the Peace Light Memorial on Oak Hill. Soon a whole new generation of Mighty Men would come forth to contest World War II.

Farther away, another of my special places sits much as it was nearly 150 years ago. The Vicksburg Campaign was a great event in U.S. military history. It marked its victor, Ulysses S. Grant, for the most profound challenges this country would face. As a military man he succeeded; however, as a politician he fumbled—reminding us how elusive true greatness is. It helps you appreciate the magnitude of Dwight Eisenhower's and George Catlett Marshall's achievements during and after World War II.

Not surprisingly, Americans often turn to their military heroes for leadership in uncertain times. After the gulf war of 1991, both Norman Schwarzkopf and Colin Powell were touted as presidential timber. Missed in the story is that both declined to run—that too is typical for soldiers. Service to country is unique to each person who performs it. Soldiers like Washington, Jackson, Taylor, Harrison, Garfield, McKinley, Theodore Roosevelt, Kennedy, and George Bush, Sr., joined Ike as war-hero leaders. Others served but had lower profiles.

When I take people on my standard three-day tour of Vicksburg, I know that few will grasp the enormity of what Grant envisioned and accomplished. William Tecumseh Sherman didn't grasp it until they reached the fortifications of

Vicksburg—he then understood. Abraham Lincoln thought Grant was wrong and later confessed his doubts. Grant understood the calculus of war at Vicksburg and later in Virginia. That so few people understand the yearlong process of getting at and capturing Vicksburg is a shame, because as the military art goes, it is a classic.

Today I give people what they most want to see, a courtesy look at the remains of Grant's Canal and then the naval action and four of the five land battles that defined the final acts at Vicksburg: Grand Gulf, Port Gibson, Raymond, Champion Hill, and Big Black Bridge. Unfortunately, Jackson doesn't have much to see. At Vicksburg, I take them to the display of the ironclad U.S.S. *Cairo,* and yet I know that they cannot fathom the full import of the relic in front of them: an iron-plated wooden boat that found a torpedo in the Yazoo River and sank rapidly. The hole in the bow is softened by the deterioration of the wood surrounding it, and yet I can remember all the drama and difficulty in finding and raising it nearly 50 years ago. I've told the story in a book and in countless lectures, but it still humbles me to think what happened on that 12th day of December 1862.

When we wind around the paved roads in the military park, I stop at the Shirley house and recount the story of the mining operations and the fierce assault there. I think of the tenacity of the sappers and the desperate countermining of the Confederates, all of them knowing that at any moment they could be blown to atoms. Time usually doesn't allow me to walk them up the Great Redoubt attack route, and yet it is a scene of extraordinary courage and demanding physical strength. The Stockade Redan and the 27th Louisiana Lunette saw some of the fiercest fighting through a gorge that was practically impenetrable and across an open field under the Confederates' very guns—an approach so deadly that some of the attackers were called the forlorn hope. Many made it into the ditch only to find themselves bombarded with hand grenades and shells rolled over the earthworks and into their midst.

Vicksburg has so many other stories that a day is easily filled moving over to the Railroad Redoubt, the Second Texas Lunette, and the Square Fort. The zigzag approaches in front of the fort resemble a mere scar in the earth today, and yet the engineering was designed to protect soldiers planning to breech and assail that defiant fortification.

As rewarding as this tour is, people don't see it as a campaign, nor do they understand why so many Union resources were expended against it as early as the late spring of 1862. I devoted a good portion of my professional life studying the campaign and wrote a three-volume study of it that remains the most comprehensive work on the subject to date. The Blue and Gray Education Society and my co-author, Parker Hills, devote eight tours and 30 days to my three volumes. Yet another nine days and three other tours—Fort Henry and Fort Donelson, Streight's raid into Alabama, and the campaign against New Orleans—are also properly associated with this major effort.

It is all about the Mississippi River, a line of communications and commerce so powerful as to dominate the western frontier. There are more interesting topics, and the eastern battles generally dominate most studies of the war, but it is the control of that artery that ultimately determines the outcome of the war. Once the Union controls it, a major portion of the Confederacy is severed and the western United States again has access to it for its commerce. While the Confederates control the Lower Mississippi River Valley they are whole, and they create extraordinary political pressure on the Lincoln Administration. This simple reality drove both Union and Confederate strategies. Grant's operations in Mississippi and Louisiana in 1863 had repercussions in Richmond and for Robert E. Lee. The Vicksburg Campaign didn't cause Gettysburg, but Gettysburg was Lee's and the Confederate government's response to the Vicksburg dilemma. It was a response that failed.

The Civil War took place in the 19th century, and we are now in the 21st century. As educational curriculums change, less attention is paid to history and its lessons. There seems to be more attention paid to telling a "balanced" story, and that leaves little room for detail. The Civil War is falling victim to the shear volume of contemporary history that documents our republic. That is why battlefields are important. They are reminders of the very high cost of our democracy and, as Lincoln said at Gettysburg, our "new birth of freedom." I have visited these two sites literally thousands of times. Vicksburg was a daily experience for me for years. I still appreciate them and hope that others will do so too.

ACKNOWLEDGMENTS

WHEN I PUT LISA THOMAS OF THE NATIONAL GEOGRAPHIC SOCIETY AND Len Riedel of the Blue and Gray Education Society together to discuss a book on the Civil War, I had no way of knowing that nearly four years later that book, *Fields of Honor,* would still be in print and selling steadily. It is a tribute to both Lisa and Len that this new effort, *Receding Tide,* is now in your hands.

Len prepared an interesting and challenging proposal for a second book and after a July 2007 meeting with NGS, we agreed to bring Parker Hills into the project as an editor. Parker, a retired brigadier general, has led many tours of both the Vicksburg and Gettysburg campaigns and was well suited for the task.

Parker moved with alacrity and completed his first draft on schedule in January 2009. Following the standard period of revisions and edits the resulting quality of the text was extraordinary. Parker had created an overarching, smooth flowing narrative that seamed my words into a wonderfully readable text that I enjoyed reviewing and which needed little editing.

As Parker progressed, he relied upon some invaluable friends and experts. Pat Strange, Terry Winschel, Sam Price, Sgt. Maj. Ron Graves, and Mike Ballard have each contributed to Parker's mastery of the Vicksburg campaign. Al Scheller and Warren Grabau mentored him before they passed. But no contribution was more significant than that of his wife of more than 40 years. Carol Hills provided encouragement, companionship, and a critical eye.

I counted on Len as an extra pair of eyes; but as the book reached a critical phase, Len needed open heart surgery. Thanks to his wife, Pamela; daughter, Katherine; and able deputy, Beth Cromwell, he fulfilled his obligations.

This manuscript was a true collaborative effort. John Paine's line edits gave us much to think about as we tightened the text. Parker, Carl Mehler, and Tracy Morrill did an outstanding job with the maps. Bridget English and others on the NGS staff shepherded this to completion when Lisa went on maternity leave. Any errors that now remain are my responsibility.

I must thank my invaluable friends, Kathleen Colburn, Cecil Jones, and Jack Dawson. They continue to volunteer their time converting tour video tapes into typed manuscripts. Without them these books would never have happened.

Battlefield preservation is an important by-product of all my work. Many are now carrying the torch. Central Virginia Battlefields Trust and the Friends of the Wilderness Battlefield are actively saving additional land and resisting further encroachment around Fredericksburg. Art Taylor is single-handedly working to increase the protected land at the North Anna Battlefields. Many people share credit for the change in attitude toward preservation of the Franklin battlefield, and State Representative Steve McDaniel has led impressive interpretative efforts at Parkers Crossroads and elsewhere in Tennessee.

Kudos go to the Friends of Raymond, Mayor Isla Tullos and Dick Kilby. Thanks are also due to Ted Kendall of The Gaddis Farms for his generous support. Parker Hills has played a leading role in turning Raymond into a first-rate battlefield experience. I appreciate Becky and Jim Drake, who prepared a tribute to my wife, Margie, at Champion Hill. Sid Champion also played a role in the personal recognition. The Champion Heritage Foundation is working hard to advance the understanding of that important battle. Preservation efforts now extend to Fort Pemberton in Greenwood, Mississippi, a key point in the Yazoo Pass expedition detailed in this book.

I also salute my old friend and colleague, the late Warren Grabau. Warren and Parker recently prepared and published the definitive Vicksburg Campaign Driving Guide. The spiral bound book and weatherproof maps, funded by the American Battlefield Protection Program and sponsored by the Friends of the Vicksburg Campaign and Historic Trail, are a godsend for people wanting to get into a detailed study. At Vicksburg National Military Park, John Nau, Bill Nichols, and Terry Winschel's various tree-cutting projects were some of the most important restoration efforts ever undertaken there and I applaud them.

Since my last survey in late 2005, states have taken an aggressive position in interpretation. Now trails and sites are presented across the Old South, in border states, and Pennsylvania. Such work will help regular folks engage in self-paced studies at most of the key sites and many secondary ones. Some veterans of the National Park Service are moving on—Chris Calkins has been hired to manage Sailor's Creek Battlefield Park. It is in good hands. Will Greene continues to steer Pamplin Historical Park through the turbulent waters, albeit without their kind benefactor—Robert Pamplin, who has also sadly left us.

Wayne Motts and Tim Smith are doing wonderful things at the Adams Country Historical Society by creating a Battle of Gettysburg Study Center. It will be a superb resource for students of the battle. The Licensed Battlefield Guides keep Gettysburg alive for the hundreds of thousands of visitors to the park. Dr. John Latschar provided firm leadership at Gettysburg and pursued an aggressive

ACKNOWLEDGMENTS

tree-cutting project that has the battlefield looking very much as it did in 1863—well done! My friend Dan Beattie has made a significant contribution with his recent book on Brandy Station. Waite Rawls at the Museum of the Confederacy has reversed adverse trends and they are operating profitably again. I am pleased to learn that Glen Hopkins and John Neff are establishing a much needed Center for Civil War Research at the University of Mississippi.

Preservation groups and Civil War Round Tables are at the heart of the national interest in the Civil War. The Civil War Preservation Trust remains the leading land trust organization devoted to preservation on a national level. Under the steady leadership of Jim Lighthizer, the trust has now saved over 28,000 acres of battlefield land in more than 20 states. With motivated and capable subordinates like Jim Campi, the message of preservation is effective and constantly trumpeted. The American Civil War Round Table UK is actively involved in preserving and developing a Civil War Heritage Trail in Liverpool, London, and Paris. Leaders like Greg Bayne, Peter Lockwood, Jerry Williams, Len Ellison, Charles Priestley, and Bob Jones are preserving sites there and have donated to preservation projects at Cedar Creek and Raymond.

The BGES continues to produce results far beyond its resources: The efforts on this book have been herculean. It has also partnered to place an operating reproduction artillery piece at Pamplin Historical Park and restored the flags that adorn the President's box at Ford's Theater. Its ongoing program with Walter Reed Army Medical Center and the Yellow Ribbon Fund provides wounded soldiers, like Master Sergeant Joel Samuelson, and their families much needed relief from the monotony of rehabilitation. BGES always seems to finds a way to get things done, and under Len's leadership it recently celebrated its 16th anniversary by opening a national headquarters in Chatham, Virginia. I still turn to Len for help in adding to my personal archives at Marine Corps Base Quantico. In 2010, Quantico will open most of my archives to the public—Len, Mike Miller, and Jim Ginther are all working that project.

Still, there is a caution—the meetings seem to be a little smaller, tours are too often conducted in vans instead of buses, and governmental support appears to be waning. Important sites like Confederate Memorial Hall in New Orleans suffer from a lack of funding or recognition within their communities. No national Civil War sesquicentennial commission exists, and Congress has been unmotivated to act on any such bills. State commemorations are muted and many planning committees seem to lack the well-known historians who have played such a role in both interpreting the war and in preserving sites. Overt enthusiasm is lacking and some fear that it is not in their professional interest to spend much time on the study of the war. This is not a time for such timidity. The Civil War teaches us that we still have much to learn.

The impact of one person can be dramatic. Karen Needles, without any public or private funding, has established a website, www.lincolnarchives.us, and is scanning the archives of the departments of the Lincoln Administration. BGES is funding the site, but more resources are needed. This project is in a line of magnitude with the amply funded Centennial projects presenting the papers of Jefferson Davis and Ulysses S. Grant. Incidentally, Grant's papers have now been moved to Mississippi State University where my friend, John Marszalek has taken over as editor.

I want to congratulate my old friend and colleague Gabor Boritt. Gabor recently retired after an unprecedented and important run as the head of the Civil War Institute at Gettysburg College. Along with Ted Alexander at Chambersburg, he provided a popular vehicle for people studying in and around Gettysburg.

I am pleased to see that this book will also be printed in a special leather bound edition to help the BGES in its work. My personal thanks go to Jeanette and Carl Christman, Jan and Bill Riedel, Trish and David Dubose and Jim Davis for their extra generous leadership in this effort.

I have been a student of the Civil War for more than 70 years and have given thousands of tours and lectures. While the nature of the study of the Civil War has changed, it remains a rich and common ground for Americans and other nationalities to grasp history and understand it in context. The books, tapes, tours, and discussion groups across the world prove its resilience. Over the years we have lost many lions of this discipline like Jerry Russell, Alan Nolan, Brian Pohanka, John Simon, Bob Younger, Robin Roth, Bob Pamplin, Pete Jorgenson, Al Scheller, Dr. Guy Vise, Carrington Williams, and Warren Grabau, to name but a few; but none is more regretted and missed than my wife, Margie. She was my partner. To her and all my other friends this book is dedicated.

Edwin C. Bearss
Arlington, Virginia
January 22, 2010

THE BLUE AND GRAY EDUCATION SOCIETY IS A NONPROFIT, TAX-EXEMPT educational organization based in Chatham, Virginia. Founded and incorporated in Virginia in 1994, the organization has built an excellent reputation for its reliability and integrity in educational projects. It remains committed to revealing our nation's past for our nation's future.

The BGES is a multifaceted membership organization undertaking battlefield educational programs that include historically accurate and intellectually challenging tours and studies of battlefields. Over the past 16 years, we have taken people to over 400 different battlefields. We present thematic studies of the American Revolution, the War of 1812, the Texas War of Independence, the Mexican War, the Civil War, the Indian Wars, World War I, and World War II. Current programming through 2015 can be found at www.blueandgrayeducation.org. This matrix includes a systematic Civil War sesquicentennial program and a bicentennial study of the War of 1812. Plans are underway for a 75th anniversary study of World War II.

BGES has developed and placed interpretive markers and influenced preservation efforts at South Mountain, Cedar Creek, McDowell, Port Republic, North Anna, Vicksburg, Price's Raid, Mobile, Holly Springs, and Island Mound. BGES has also published 19 scholarly monographs, as well as two books with the National Geographic Society.

Members are active in leadership roles in other preservation-minded organizations, such as the Civil War Preservation Trust, Friends of Manassas, Central Virginia Battlegrounds Trust, Save Historic Antietam Foundation, Cedar Creek Battlefield Foundation, the Museum of the Confederacy, Confederate Memorial Hall, Save the Franklin Battlefield, and many others. BGES has also been a tireless advocate and supporter of restorative and public education programs such as the Ford's Theater Flags restoration, Pamplin Historical Park Adventure Camp, the digitization of the archives of the Lincoln Administration, and the Medford Historical Society's phenomenal photographic collection.

BGES members are enthusiastic supporters of an ongoing partnership with the nonprofit Yellow Ribbon Fund in Washington, D.C. Since 2007, BGES members have funded and staffed approximately eight tours annually for disabled war veterans undergoing longterm rehabilitative care and their family members at Walter Reed Army Medical Center.

BGES is supported by tax-deductible donations from donors and friends and from educational program revenues. Royalties from this book and our previous book, *Fields of Honor,* will produce a significant source of revenue for our programs. All members of the public are welcome to participate in the BGES and can obtain further information by visiting our Web site at www.blueandgrayeducation.org or calling 434-250-9921 or e-mailing bgesexecutivedirector@yahoo.com.

INDEX